Externship Pedagogy and Practice

Externship Pedagogy and Practice

Gillian Dutton
Director of the Externship Program
Associate Professor of Lawyering Skills
Seattle University School of Law

Kendall Kerew
Associate Clinical Professor of Law
Director of the Externship Program
Georgia State University College of Law

Kelly Terry
Ben J. Altheimer Professor of Law
Associate Dean for Experiential Learning
and Clinical Programs
University of Arkansas at Little Rock
William H. Bowen School of Law

Cynthia Wilson
Clinical Professor of Law
Director of the Center for Externships
Bluhm Legal Clinic
Northwestern University Pritzker School of Law

Carolina Academic Press
Durham, North Carolina

Library of Congress Cataloging-in-Publication Data

Names: Dutton, Gillian (Law teacher), author. | Kerew, Kendall, author. | Terry, Kelly (Kelly S.), author. | Wilson, Cynthia (Law teacher), author.
Title: Externship pedagogy and practice / by Gillian Dutton, Kendall Kerew, Kelly Terry, Cynthia Wilson.
Description: Durham, North Carolina : Carolina Academic Press, LLC, [2022] | Includes index.
Identifiers: LCCN 2022033619 (print) | LCCN 2022033620 (ebook) | ISBN 9781531011819 (paperback) | ISBN 9781531011826 (ebook)
Subjects: LCSH: Law—Study and teaching (Internship)—United States.
Classification: LCC KF282.7 .D88 2022 (print) | LCC KF282.7 (ebook) | DDC 340.071/55—dc23/eng/20220919
LC record available at https://lccn.loc.gov/2022033619
LC ebook record available at https://lccn.loc.gov/2022033620

Carolina Academic Press
700 Kent Street
Durham, NC 27701
(919) 489-7486
www.cap-press.com

Printed in the United States of America

Contents

Section III • Teaching the Externship Course

Acknowledgments

The authors would like to thank D'lorah Hughes for identifying the need for this book, prompting us to write it, and providing invaluable insight and suggestions regarding its content. Without her vision, this book would not have happened. The authors would also like to thank Cynthia Batt for sharing her years of knowledge and expertise in the formative stages of this project.

Preface

Alexander Scherr

This book gives you all that you will need to design and teach an externship course. But even a brief exposure to externships will highlight the importance of reflection, both as an assigned task in a course and as a requirement of American Bar Association regulations on externships.[1] In that spirit, this Preface contains my reflections after teaching externships for more than two decades and after supporting and advocating for externships nationally. During this time, I have taught in other formats too: podium courses; in-house clinics; practicums; and simulations. Inevitably, this reflection compares teaching formats, with a stress on the uniquely valuable features of the externship approach. At some points, I speak directly from my own experience; at others, I make assertions without personalizing them and will cite to discussions I have found especially persuasive. Please accept both forms of discourse as expressions of my convictions based on those years spent on externships.

Externship teaching differs from other kinds of law teaching in at least three ways.[2] First, externship teachers play distinctive roles in relationship to the other participants in the course. Second, externship teachers work with a different context than other kinds of teachers. Third, externship courses offer unique learning outcomes and a unique set of possible missions for the teacher. Role, context, and mission help to frame the satisfactions and challenges of externship teaching.

Role and Relationship

Relationships in an externship course form a triangle. As an externship teacher, I work with a student who works directly with a supervisor who I have recruited

1. I use the term "externships" to describe what the American Bar Association refers to as "field placement" programs. ABA STANDARDS AND RULES OF PROCEDURE FOR APPROVAL OF LAW SCHOOLS, 2022–2023, STANDARD 304. The requirement of "faculty-guided reflection" appears in ABA Standard 304(a)(5).

2. For convenience, in this Preface, I will refer to the faculty member in an externship course as an "externship teacher" and to the faculty member in an in-house clinic as a "clinic teacher." I mean to dodge the long-standing debate over whether externship teachers are "clinicians." It is more productive to look at what teachers do in each setting, as this Preface and indeed this book mean to do for externship courses.

and with whom I maintain a separate relationship. This division of labor varies substantially between different kinds of externship courses.[3] In the arrangement with which I am most familiar, the supervisor assigns and reviews work in the law practice, the externship teacher teaches a seminar and prompts student learning and reflection, and the student learns from both of us. As the externship teacher, I handle the closing evaluation, whether graded or ungraded, with input from both supervisor and student.[4]

This network of relationships differs from other courses in a law school. A podium course looks much more like an exchange between teacher and student, where the teacher delivers content and prompts analytical discussion with the students. A writing seminar intensifies that exchange into something that involves bespoke feedback on a student's work product. A simulation course offers a similar exchange between teacher and student, often with students working in teams and learning from each other. Finally, in an in-house clinic, the teacher and student have a similarly two-way relationship, with the teacher and student serving the needs of the client or cause on which the clinic focuses its work.[5] As with seminars and simulations, in a clinic, the teacher can provide tailored feedback based on first-hand knowledge of a student's work in the clinic practice.

This description highlights one role an externship teacher does *not* play. As an externship teacher, I typically do not have daily exposure to an extern's legal work. An externship teacher may have prior experience with the practice area, especially in practice-specific externships such as criminal defense or corporate counsel. But the externship teacher usually cannot give students the same detailed feedback on specific work that is available to a teacher in a writing seminar, simulation, or clinic or, for that matter, to a supervisor at the student's placement.

The lack of this particular first-hand knowledge forms the central challenge of externship teaching. As a teacher in this format, I can mitigate this lack of knowledge in several ways: regular reflective journals from students; case rounds in class; one-to-one meetings with students; site visits and other check-ins with supervisors; even regularly reviewed time sheets. But oversight of multiple students and multiple

---

3. This division of roles forms part of the "written understanding" between teacher, supervisor, and student that the American Bar Association requires of externship courses. ABA Standards and Rules of Procedure for Approval of Law Schools 2022–2023, Standard 304(d)(i).

4. As this book will discuss, many variations exist, even within this traditional arrangement of roles. "Hybrid" courses further press this particular envelope, in some cases moving the externship teacher into the supervisor's law practice, in others bringing the supervisor to the task of teaching the seminar or assessing the student's overall performance.

5. It would be fair to reframe an in-house clinic as having its own triangular structure: a teacher works with a student (or team of students), who in turn works with a client or cause to whom both the teacher and the student bear ethical responsibilities. The relationship between the clinic teacher and the client or cause further differentiates this model from externships. The externship teacher typically lacks that direct relationship with client or cause, even in specialized externship courses where students work in the same kinds of law practices.

placements, coupled with the obligation to preserve confidences imposed by the rules of ethics, places a firm cap on what I can know about the legal work that any one of my students has done.

This looks like a fatal weakness of the externship method; but it is one of its strengths. These limitations allow me to assume other roles as an externship teacher that are difficult, if not impossible, to replicate in any other teaching format. To be sure, separating the externship teacher from the law practice eliminates any realistic chance for direct feedback on legal work. But it opens me and my students to a different relationship, one focused on critical reflection of the experience: a mentoring role, in which I can frame opportunities for learning and self-development and prompt a student to make the most of what they see and do at their placement.

The externship teacher has other relationships, ones not present in any other form of teaching. Specifically, I have a relationship with the supervisor at each placement. Some programs consist primarily of one-time, student-initiated placements. In my programs, I chose a different approach: my relationships with placements persisted over time, often for many years. This fact allowed and even required me to exert influence over the learning environment at that placement. Through recruitment, training, site visits, conversations, and end-of-semester feedback, I found that, in many cases, I could improve the capacity of the supervisor to provide feedback and guidance similar to what a student receives in an in-house clinic.

Similar, but not identical. A key difference exists between the supervision provided by an in-house teacher in a clinic and the supervision given by a supervisor. To over-simplify, as a clinic teacher, I set out to create a law practice intentionally designed to teach. An externship site supervisor does not start with that intention; the shape of the outside practice reflects other goals and purposes. While a supervisor may have a calling as a teacher or mentor, the goals of their practice predominate. This is a key reality of the real world of externships, addressed in the next part of this Preface.

An externship teacher relates not only to the student and supervisor, but also to the relationship between them.[6] The externship teacher has a direct concern with the quality of that relationship. If it is working, the externship teacher can help the student make the most of the learning it provides. If it does not work, the externship teacher can and should help the student take corrective steps. In the worst case, I would help a student to "learn from the negative," helping the student extract insights from the current challenge that might lead them to find and eventually create better practices in the future.

One last point: I have often held an internal debate about how "present" I should be as an externship teacher in my relationship with a student. On the one hand, I

6. In visual terms, imagine a line drawn from one vertex of a triangle to the center point of the line connecting the other two vertices.

have a natural desire to do and be seen as doing something that has impact and value. This performative desire characterizes classroom teaching and in-house clinic teaching alike; it reflects the reality that I am being paid to teach and that I am identified as a teacher by the students who take the course.

On the other hand, I can advance an argument that the best externship teacher should be invisible in the student's learning process. Yes, I have put the work into creating the course, matching the student with the supervisor, developing a seminar, and prompting reflective analysis. But once started, the learning experience becomes about what the student gains and achieves in the world of their placement. Having suggested some frameworks for understanding and set some assumptions about reflection, I should then disappear and let the student learn how to learn on their own.

Or at least, so goes that side of my inner debate. Two realities make perfect invisibility impossible: the need to be active when things go wrong for the student, and the power that inheres in end-of-semester evaluations. Both pull a teacher out of the role of unseen influencer. Personality and temperament also make complete disappearance unlikely; I confess to enjoying the performative aspects of teaching. But there is a useful humility and discipline that comes from recognizing the secondary, supportive, complementary role that externship teachers play in their students' encounters with the real-world context of their placement.

Context

Externship courses show students the world of practice as it is, including its pressures, limitations, and challenges. Among law school courses, only in-house clinics come close to this reality. A well-designed, well-taught in-house clinic asks students to work for clients' causes, problems, or concerns with the benefit of close supervision and supportive feedback. As a clinical teacher, I have the chance to model both good law practice habits and good legal judgment within my own style of practice and supervision. Well-designed clinics demonstrate reflective lawyering both in the relationship between the teacher and student about clinic work and in the cross-resonance between the clinic seminar and the clinic practice. In short, students in an in-house clinic benefit from an intentionally designed learning environment that maximizes what they can learn from that practice. This intentional design brings them into contact with the real world while remaining within a well-framed, reflective structure.

Exposure to exemplary practice, with a focus on student learning, can occur in an externship placement. But the realities of a non-clinical law practice change the kind and quality of learning available to students. In my work as an externship teacher, I worked with a range of supervisors. Some took their role as teachers and mentors seriously and invested the time and resources to provide students with the best possible learning experience. Far more often, supervisors had to balance their role as teachers with the other demands of their practice. In some, and I believe very few, student learning was at best incidental and at worst irrelevant to the main goals of the practice. Rather than reduce the number of placements only to those with dedicated teachers/supervisors, I chose a broader range of opportunities, knowing that students in different placements would have different experiences and would need different things from me as an externship teacher.

This diversity in learning environments matches other kinds of diversity inherent in the externship method of experiential education. Generalist externship courses offer an obvious example. Students in these courses may work in judicial chambers, public interest practices, governmental agencies, or private firms, a reality that poses a special challenge to the externship teacher both in the seminar and in that teacher's one-to-one relationship with a student trying to understand the special features of that practice. Specialized externships, those focused on specific practice areas, ease these challenges, especially for a teacher with experience in that area. But even there, the diversity in offices' cultures, personalities, and cases creates a more diverse context for learning about lawyering than a single in-house clinic can deliver.

Externships also bring students in touch with certain practical dimensions of law practice they will encounter in the years after they graduate. To help frame this context, I created and regularly used a "lawyering audit" exercise designed to help students come to terms with these realities.[7] The audit focuses on pressures common to all law practices: the differences between billing and non-billing practice; the opportunity costs of decisions during case acceptance; differences in practice structure, hierarchical, collaborative, or otherwise; the size of caseloads; and the pressure to specialize. Externs can observe how different lawyers relate to clients or causes; how practices divide the work of lawyering between practice roles, including investigators, paralegals, and administrative staff; who controls decision-making about cases and by what standards; how negotiation styles affect outcomes; and how each practice evaluates the performance of lawyers in decisions about job advancement and compensation.

Many of these pressures exist in an in-house clinic; a well-designed clinic makes them as transparent as possible, a topic for discussion. But a fundamental difference exists in how law office culture functions in a clinic as compared to an outside practice. Externship courses can help students see how practice works *after* they are finished with law school, creating unique opportunities for learning, reflection, and career planning.

Two other aspects of the externship context deserve mention: maintaining well-being and sustaining a high quality of practice. As to the former, in my experience with externships, students learn as much about well-being and what it takes to have a full and satisfying life as a lawyer as they do about anything else. Students

7. Alexander Scherr, *Learning About Lawyering, in* LEARNING FROM PRACTICE: A TEXT FOR EXPERIENTIAL LEGAL EDUCATION 385–93 (Leah Wortham et al. eds., 2016).

observe and evaluate the lawyers at their placements as models for how to live. Students can take reassurance from those lawyers who have found satisfaction in their work... and a warning from those who have not. In an in-house clinic, students imprint on what their clinic teacher shows them. By contrast, an externship teacher's approach to well-being matters little, if at all. Instead, the externship teacher can frame quiet questions about how lawyers at the placement shape and structure their lives as lawyers.

As to quality of practice, in my experience with externship teaching, students are often surprised to see the difference between the standards they have learned in law school and those they encounter in practice. Law school, including in-house clinic courses, can and should create models for exemplary practice, whether in writing, in investigation, in relating to clients, or even in routine record keeping. By contrast, what students observe in externships often varies from these models. For example, when asked about the kind of written assignments they receive from busy supervisors, many students note with surprise that they are *not* asked to write in traditional "IRAC" format or even to do more than summarize a list of cases. More generally, experience in the real world of a placement can and should expose students to wide disparities, not just in the quality of lawyering, but in the definitions of quality. These can result from too much work, too little time, inadequate resources, and the lack of perfect knowledge. This encounter with imperfection in the real world places a special demand on the externship teacher: to help a student appreciate how the analytical and practice habits developed in law school relate to long-term success and professional satisfaction with the craft of lawyering.

Mission

Faced with the structured chaos of practice outside law school and with a wide diversity in ways to practice law, one can forgive an externship teacher for lacking a clear sense of mission. This uncertainty appears repeatedly at externship conferences: what should I do with the seminar? What should I ask students to discuss in their reflective essays? What frameworks can I offer students as they grapple with what they encounter at their placements? These questions are both professional and personal: professional, in the sense of defining and integrating learning outcomes in a specific externship course; and personal, in the sense of centering the complexity of the externship experience around the teacher's own sense of what most needs teaching. I have come to see them as variations of one overriding question: what am I trying to do with this course? What is my mission?

This Preface cannot address all the different missions an externship course might serve. To some extent, the range of available missions is as broad as the number of externship teachers or even of externship courses. This book gives you a start on determining how to implement your own sense of mission through externship course design, management, and delivery. I have become convinced that externships offer just as many opportunities for intentional, mission-driven teaching as any other form of law school teaching. The remainder of this Preface suggests how the distinctive features of the externship method may influence the selection of externship mission.

First, a note of caution about externship design. In nearly 25 years of externship teaching, I have yet to find an externship course that has the same goals as any other. This includes courses at my own school and courses I have taught. My own school offers several generalist externship courses alongside specialized externships in prosecution, criminal defense, capital defense, and corporate counsel practices. The generalist courses themselves have quite different goals. A part-time externship in my local small city looks and teaches differently than a full-time course in our state's capital city; and full-time externships themselves differ among in-state, Washington D.C., or remote placements in other regions. This perspective prompts an initial suggestion: what you might try to achieve with an externship course should take advantage of the specific externship experiences your students will have.

Second, I discussed above some of the limits on what an externship course can do. The mission you choose for your externship should respect those limits. For example, if you intend to deliver specific formative feedback about your students' legal work at their placements, make sure to consider carefully whether your course design and your relationship with the attorneys/supervisors at your placements will make that possible. The creation of hybrid clinical courses, those in which the externship teacher directly supervises case work at the placement, can fairly be described as driven by the goal to provide close, high-quality feedback on student work in a manner similar to an in-house clinic.

Third, I have already noted how the center of learning in an externship does not lie in the clinic seminar or in the relationship between externship teacher and student. It may also be true that what happens at the placement is also not at the center of learning, although it comes closer. As with an in-house clinic, the real focus of learning in an externship rests in the mind, heart, and spirit of the student, in whatever lessons and long-term guidance the student takes away from the experience into their future practice. The separation in an externship between what happens at the placement and what happens at the law school reinforces the notion that students learn in the transitions between the two, more perhaps than in any other law school course.

To me, this explains some of the powerful attraction of professional self-development as an appropriate goal of an externship course: an intentional focus on the formation of a law student's professional identity. Initially identified as one of the three "apprenticeships" of legal education by the Carnegie Report,[8] the mission of

8. William M. Sullivan et al., Educating Lawyers: Preparation for the Profession of Law (2007).

"professional identity formation" has become so widespread and so well-articulated[9] that it has become a required part of legal education.[10] This mission seems especially well-suited to the externship method. Externship students must negotiate the separation in contexts between law school and placement and the division in role between externship teacher and supervisor. In doing so, the locus of learning falls squarely on students' sense of themselves and on their newly emerging identity as lawyers. An externship course that focuses on professional identity formation has found a good match between method and mission.

The power of the externship method, however, offers goals that go well beyond a focus on professional identity. As already described, externship courses bring students into contact with the world of lawyering as it is, with its many sub-cultures, economic pressures, and organizational structures, not to mention its inequities, uncertainties, and barriers. For many students, the whole point of an externship is to become a part of that world, not least to join the networks and learn the language used by those who may help them find future work. This encounter with the hard-edged pressures and realities of practice deserves recognition. I find a point made recently by Spring Miller especially persuasive:

> For all the recent discussion of helping students cultivate a professional identity and an ethic of professionalism in law school, the reality is that the institutions into which students go on to work will heavily shape (and often limit) the professional, ethical, and career-related choices available to them. Students need information and tools to understand the particular constraints and opportunities associated with practice in widely diverse institutions of the profession so that they can forge careers that align with their professional, ethical, and personal values, as well as their material and financial needs.[11]

A mission that focuses on the "constraints and opportunities" of law practice and legal institutions is also well-suited to a course that gives students experience outside the law school's walls.

This exposure to the institutions of law practice leads me to identify another congruence between externship method and mission: the role of an externship course in prompting critique of the law itself and of the legal profession. The separation between externship teacher and practice context creates an opportunity for

---

9. *See* Kelly S. Terry, *Externships: A Signature Pedagogy for the Apprenticeship of Professional Identity and Purpose*, 59 J. Legal Educ. 240 (2009); Timothy Floyd and Kendall Kerew, *Marking the Path from Law Student to Lawyer: Using Field Placement Courses to Facilitate the Deliberate Exploration of Professional Identity and Purpose*, 68 Mercer L. Rev. 767 (2017).

10. ABA Standards and Rules of Procedure for Approval of Law Schools, 2022–2023, Standard 303(b).

11. Spring Miller, *The Generalist Externship Seminar: A Unique Curricular Opportunity to Teach About the Legal Profession*, 27 Clinical L. Rev. 301, 311 (2021).

the teacher to inquire critically about how laws and legal institutions accomplish justice and advance broader social concerns. As Robert F. Seibel and Linda H. Morton have noted,

> Externship programs also provide an ideal structure for helping students to gain perspective on the legal system—to examine legal doctrine in the context of societal problems, apply jurisprudential and other philosophical considerations to the practice of law, and compare and critique legal systems.[12]

I know that interrogation of how law and legal process serve societal goals has long been at the center of law school teaching and scholarship. The last half-century and more has seen that interrogation carried in new directions by the increased use of experiential methods. Externship courses place students in a position to interrogate these realities both from within a given law practice and from without.

The distinctive combination of role, context, and mission that frames this reflective Preface leads me to one final, speculative point. I have often heard externships described as a good way for law students to get their first job. Given the opportunities for networking and immersion in a community of practice, I see that point. But I have come to believe that I should focus my externship teaching not on finding or starting the first job, but on a later transition. Most starting practitioners face three to five years of immersion in a new apprenticeship, a fuller and more long-lasting version of the transient practice they first encounter in a clinic or externship. At the end of that apprenticeship, many begin to feel a sense of mastery in their work as lawyers.[13]

12. Robert F. Seibel & Linda H. Morton, *Field Placement Programs: Practices, Problems and Possibilities*, 2 Clinical L. Rev. 413, 420 (1996).

13. If we assume a 40-hour week and two weeks a year of vacation, five years of practice comes to 10,000 hours: similar to Malcolm Gladwell's much criticized version of the time it takes to achieve mastery in a complex field. *See generally* Malcolm Gladwell, Outliers: The Story of Success 41 (2008). More hours per week (and less vacation) would accelerate that process. Gladwell bases his theory in large part on psychological research, specifically on the amount of practice required to master a musical instrument. K.A. Ericsson, R.T. Krampe, & C. Tesch-Römer, *The Role of Deliberate Practice in the Acquisition of Expert Performance*, 100 Psychological Rev. 363–406 (1993). One of the authors of that study, Anders Ericsson, has challenged Gladwell's reading of the study, asserting, at least in part, that it fails to account for the role of "deliberate practice," that is, work under the guidance of a teacher. Jeffrey Young, *Researcher Behind '10,000-Hour Rule' Says Good Teaching Matters, Not Just Practice* (May 5, 2020), https://www.edsurge.com/news/2020-05-05-researcher-behind-10-000-hour-rule-says-good-teaching-matters-not-just-practice.

I believe, without any empirical proof, that it is at that point that a lawyer asks not "Can I do this job?" but rather "Is this what I want to do? Is this what brought me to the law in the first place?" The young lawyer may stay or may move to something else. But a young lawyer who has experienced a well-designed externship course will have acquired a habit of reflection, a confident identity, and a clear-eyed, critical appraisal of the world as it is. With these, I believe, that lawyer will make decisions more likely to lead to longer-term satisfaction, fuller engagement with all life's commitments, and the pursuit of a more just and compassionate world.

Introduction

The Purpose and Vocabulary of This Book

"Legal education is a powerfully transformative experience."[1] During their course of study, law students must learn the law, the legal profession's way of thinking and problem-solving, the practice skills required of lawyers, and the ethical obligations that govern lawyers. They must learn how to manage time, communicate with clients and others, work with supervisors, and take on the responsibilities and problems of those they represent. Students also must learn the norms and values of their chosen profession and integrate those norms and values with their own personal attitudes, values, and beliefs.[2] Thus, legal education shapes students in profound and lasting ways that affect them for the course of their careers.

Law school externship courses can be a crucial component of this transformative process. Externships are for-credit courses that place students in law offices, judicial chambers, and other settings to engage in authentic lawyering tasks under the direction of a qualified supervisor there, who works in partnership with a faculty member at the law school to provide a rigorous educational experience. By immersing students in the real world of practice, externships provide students the opportunity to see the law in action, work with real clients and cases, practice their developing legal skills, experience the pressures and time demands of practice, and begin to form their own sense of who they are and will be as members of the legal profession. Students begin to realize the nuance and complexity of real legal issues, which cannot be replicated in a casebook hypothetical or a simulation exercise. They see firsthand the effects that bias, poverty, discrimination, and lack of resources have on the justice system, in both civil and criminal matters. They learn about the impact that legal issues can have on an individual, a family, or a business. Most importantly,

---

1. Timothy W. Floyd & Kendall L. Kerew, *Marking the Path From Law Student to Lawyer: Using Field Placement Courses to Facilitate the Deliberate Exploration of Professional Identity and Purpose*, 68 Mercer L. Rev. 767, 767 (2017).

2. *See, e.g.*, William M. Sullivan, Anne Colby, Judith Welch Wegner, Lloyd Bond & Lee Shulman, Educating Lawyers: Preparation for the Profession of Law (2007).

they experience these issues through a structured educational program that is focused on their learning and professional development.

With the increasing demands for law graduates to be more "practice ready," as well as the decreasing opportunities for employer-provided training and mentorship, externship courses have increased in number over the years and become an essential component of legal education. They now are an established part of the curriculum at the vast majority of law schools in the United States. Along with law clinics and simulation courses, externship courses are one of the three forms of experiential education recognized by the American Bar Association's law school accreditation standards.[3] Many externship courses now fall within the purview of an associate dean for experiential education, a position created by many schools to oversee their experiential offerings[4] in light of the requirement that all students must complete six hours of experiential education prior to graduation.[5]

Like all courses in the law school curriculum, externships are expected to adhere to best practices in instructional design, teaching methods, and assessment of student learning. However, externships differ from other experiential courses because they require the participation of persons outside of the law school—the supervising attorneys at the externship sites—in the education of students. The externship faculty member and the site supervisor must work in tandem with one another, and with the externship student, to ensure that the desired student learning is achieved. For example, externship faculty must vet prospective externship sites to ensure that supervising attorneys understand the teaching and supervision expectations and that they have the capacity to meet them. Faculty also must vet students to determine their eligibility to take an externship course, and some faculty screen students to match them with externship sites. Faculty also are responsible for training site supervisors, communicating with them as they manage students, ensuring that they provide a rich learning experience, and evaluating their performance as a supervisor. In addition, faculty must help students resolve any difficulties they encounter at their externship sites. Students often work in different types of practices, engage in different lawyering tasks, and confront different challenges. Some students may be working in the same geographic area as the law school, while others may be working in a different state or abroad in other countries. Thus, externship courses involve

---

3. ABA Standards and Rules of Procedure for Approval of Law Schools 2022–2023, Standard 304(a). The complete ABA Standards are available at www.americanbar.org/content/dam/aba/ administrative/legal_education_and_admissions_to_the_bar/standards/2022-2023/2022-2023-aba-standards-and-rules-of-procedure.pdf.

4. *See* Margaret Martin Barry, Robert Dinerstein, Phyllis Goldfarb, Peggy Maisel & Linda H. Morton, *Exploring the Meaning of Experiential Deaning*, 67 J. Legal Educ. 660 (2018).

5. ABA Standards and Rules of Procedure for Approval of Law Schools 2022–2023, Standard 303(a)(3).

many moving parts that must work together seamlessly to provide the optimal learning experience for students.

Our purpose in writing this book is to create a resource that allows all of the various constituents with a stake in externships to easily access information about the design, teaching, and educational benefits of these courses. Faculty new to externship teaching often are overwhelmed by the volume of decisions and tasks that confront them. Experienced externship teachers regularly need to refresh their understanding of the ABA accreditation requirements or look for inspiration when they want to retool their course or need to create a new one. Deans and associate deans for experiential education, who may not be familiar with externship pedagogy, will benefit from information that explains the unique nature of externship teaching and supervision, and the resources that it requires. Site supervisors will be better mentors and teachers if they understand the educational rationale for placing students in their offices and how they can further the law school's mission of creating competent and well-prepared lawyers.

Thus, this book is designed to provide the foundational knowledge that is necessary for every person involved in the design and implementation of externship courses, including externship faculty, directors of externship programs, site supervisors, deans, associate deans, and other law school administrators. Our goal is to provide a shared body of common knowledge so that each school can implement its externship programs and courses in the most educationally beneficial manner. To that end, we have made certain choices regarding the vocabulary we use to ensure consistent usage throughout. Below is a list of the common pedagogical terms that we use, and our definitions for each of those terms.

> ***Experiential Education***: "is an active method of teaching that 'integrates theory and practice by combining academic inquiry with actual experience.' It encompasses 'many methodologies in which educators purposefully engage with learners in direct experience and focused reflection in order to increase knowledge, develop skills, clarify values, and develop people's capacity to contribute to their communities.'"[6] We distinguish experiential education, which requires facilitation and guidance by an instructor, from experiential learning, which is simply learning from one's own experiences.[7]
>
> ***Externship Site***: A practice setting outside of the law school, such as a law firm, government agency, corporation, nonprofit organization, or judge's chambers, in which a student enrolled in an externship course engages in lawyering tasks under the supervision of a licensed attorney or an individual qualified to

6. Susan L. Brooks, Cynthia Adcock, Stephen Ellmann, Robert L. Jones, Jr., Christine Cimini & Margaret Berry, *Experience the Future: Papers from the Second National Symposium on Experiential Education in Law: Alliance for Experiential Learning in Law*, 7 Elon L. Rev. 1, 15 (2015) (internal citations omitted).

7. *Id.*

supervise. We use the term "externship site" in lieu of the term "field placement," which is used in the ABA Standards, because the academic literature more commonly uses the term "externship."

Site Supervisor: An employee of the externship site who has the requisite qualifications to supervise an externship student's work there and who directly manages the student's day-to-day work at the externship site.

Externship Program: "The collection of courses within a school's clinical legal education program that provides students with the opportunity to integrate academic inquiry with work experiences in the law for academic credit. Students are immersed in legal practice settings external to the law school, and supervision of students is shared by faculty and [site] supervisors."[8]

Externship Course: "A course in which a significant part of the learning relies on students either representing clients or performing other lawyering roles under the supervision of practicing lawyers or other qualified legal professionals, such as judges, mediators, and legislators. These field supervisors share supervision of students with faculty."[9] Externship courses satisfy the requirements of ABA Standard 304(d).[10]

General Externship Course: An externship course that enrolls students working in different types of practice settings.[11]

Subject-Specific Externship Course: An externship course that enrolls "students who are working only in a particular type of practice setting (criminal, judicial, corporate, etc.)."[12]

Externship Faculty: A member of the law school faculty who teaches one or more externship courses; supervises the students in the course; guides the students in ongoing, contemporaneous reflection on their externship experiences; ensures that externship sites in the course provide students with substantial lawyering experience and opportunities for performance, feedback, and self-evaluation; and evaluates the educational achievement of the students in the course.[13]

---

8. *Id.* at 18.

9. *Id.* at 20 (quoting Roy Stuckey & Others, Best Practices for Legal Education: A Vision and a Roadmap 198 (2007)).

10. ABA Standards and Rules of Procedure for Approval of Law Schools 2022–2023, Standard 304(d).

11. *See* Spring Miller, *The Generalist Externship Seminar: A Unique Curricular Opportunity to Teach About the Legal Profession*, 27 Clinical L. Rev. 279, 281 (2021) ("generalist externship" refers to "an externship course that includes students working in diverse practice settings").

12. *Id.*

13. *See* ABA Standards and Rules of Procedure for Approval of Law Schools 2022–2023, Standard 304(a) and (d).

Externship Program Director: A member of the law school faculty or administration who oversees the operations of an externship program.

Externship Seminar: A class that students take concurrently with their externship work that provides a means for them to engage in "ongoing, contemporaneous, faculty-guided reflection."[14]

A Roadmap for Using This Book

While we hope all sections of this book will be useful to many readers, we expect that some readers will find certain sections more beneficial based on their specific roles and responsibilities. To that end, we provide this roadmap to help readers quickly find the information that is most useful to their particular needs:

Section One: Externship Foundations and Context

This Section consists of two chapters that provide foundational information about the development of externships and the regulatory landscape in which they operate. Chapter 1, *Externships Overview*, provides a brief history of the development of externships, explains the role of externships in the broader context of experiential education, and introduces the core components of externship pedagogy. Chapter 2, *ABA Standards and Other Regulatory Requirements*, explains the ABA accreditation requirements that govern externship design and implementation, as well as the requirements of regional accrediting agencies that impact externship teaching.

Section Two: Designing and Implementing Externship Programs and Courses

This Section consists of five chapters, all of which focus on discrete aspects of the design, implementation, and teaching of externships. Chapter 3, *Designing and Executing Externship Programs*, provides a guide for designing an externship program comprised of multiple courses and addresses issues such as the different types of program models, student eligibility and application processes for externships, the selection of externship sites, and the credit hours awarded for student work. Chapter 4, *Selecting, Training, and Evaluating Site Supervisors*, explains how externship faculty should work in conjunction with site supervisors to ensure an educationally beneficial experience for students. While the issues explored in these chapters often are classified as merely "administrative," each decision in these areas is an important component of externship pedagogy.

Chapter 5, *Establishing and Assessing Student Learning Outcomes for Externship Programs*, discusses how to establish student learning outcomes for an externship program comprised of multiple courses and how to gather and evaluate data to deter-

---

14. ABA Standards and Rules of Procedure for Approval of Law Schools 2022–2023, Standard 304(a)(5).

mine whether students are achieving the outcomes. Chapter 6, *Special Considerations Regarding Remote Work Environments and Site Locations Away From the Geographic Area of the Law School*, explores program design considerations in the specific context of externships taught remotely or located outside of the law school's immediate geographic area. Chapter 7, *Designing Individual Externship Courses*, explains how to apply best practices for instructional design in creating externship courses, including student learning outcomes, selection of instructional materials, and assessment methods, while also satisfying the ABA requirements for externships.

Section Three: Teaching the Externship Course

This Section consists of four chapters, all of which focus on methods for providing externship students a means for engaging in ongoing, contemporaneous, faculty-guided reflection. Chapter 8 explores essential elements that should be part of any externship course, including student goal-setting, meaningful learning experiences, and the ability to engage in the skill of reflection. Chapter 9, *Topic Ideas for the General Seminar*, suggests topics that externship teachers can address in a seminar that includes students working at different types of placements. Conversely, Chapter 10, *Topics for Subject-Specific Seminars*, offers suggestions for topics that teachers might include in a seminar in which all of the students are working in the same type of practice setting. Chapter 11, *Teaching Techniques and Resources for Externship Teachers*, explores adult learning theory and provides guidance on different types of teaching techniques that can be used to maximize student learning, including rounds discussions, simulation exercises, quick-writes, and small-group work, among others. Chapter 12, *Using Online Technology in Teaching Externships*, recognizes the increasing role of online instruction in legal education and discusses methods for teaching externship courses online in synchronous, asynchronous, and hybrid formats.

Section Four: Guidance for Site Supervisors

Section Four consists of a single chapter—Chapter 13, *Guidance for Site Supervisors*. This chapter is intended primarily to be a stand-alone chapter to serve as a resource for the attorneys, judges, or other supervisors who oversee students in their work at externship sites. It also may be useful to those working with site supervisors, since it provides a general overview of design and implementation considerations for externship courses.

Appendix

The final section of the book is an Appendix, which compiles samples of resources for externship teaching and administration, including rubrics, supervisor and student evaluation forms, student learning agendas, mid-semester evaluations, and other relevant materials.

A Final Introductory Thought

Externship courses are a vibrant and enriching component of the law school curriculum. The pedagogy of externship teaching is dynamic and rigorous, and teachers in the externship community are collegial and generous. Ideas and resources are shared freely and frequently via the externship listserv,[15] the LexternWeb website,[16] and at externship and clinical conferences.[17] LexternWeb in particular is a treasure trove of resources, with examples of course syllabi, manuals for site supervisors, teaching materials, learning outcomes, rubrics, and links to externship scholarship. We find our work teaching externship courses deeply meaningful and gratifying, as we help students in their journey to become a lawyer. We hope you do as well, and we hope this book proves to be a helpful resource for you, whether you are a veteran teacher or are completely new to externship teaching.

15. To subscribe to the externship listserv (LEXTERN@listserv.gsu.edu), please send an email to Professor Kendall Kerew at kkerew@gsu.edu.

16. *See* www.lexternweb.org (last visited March 21, 2022).

17. *See* www.lexternweb.org/clinical-conferences (last visited March 21, 2022) (information about biennial conferences for externship faculty and annual national and regional conferences for clinical faculty).

Section I

Externship Foundations and Context

Chapter 1

Externships Overview

1. A Brief History of Externships in the Law School Curriculum

Today's externship courses have their roots in the earliest form of lawyer training in the United States: apprenticeships with practicing lawyers. Until the end of the 19th century, most people became lawyers through an apprenticeship with an experienced lawyer, often combined with individual intensive study of available law books.[1] While this approach was experiential in nature, the results were inconsistent at best. Some lawyers had the ability, time, and resources to provide supervision, mentoring, and exposure to a diverse practice, but most were sole practitioners with limited time to devote to apprentices.[2] Some lawyers began to hire permanent clerks instead of taking on apprentices.[3] There were a number of proprietary law schools that provided training, but universities did not initially provide comprehensive legal education.[4]

Universities increasingly began to offer academic legal studies in the 1870s, with the goal of improving the quality of legal education.[5] By the 1890s, law schools were adopting the casebook method, which focuses on the analysis of appellate cases, as the preferred way to prepare students for the legal profession.[6] Legal education

---

1. *See* Peter A. Joy, *The Uneasy History of Experiential Education in U.S. Law Schools*, 122 Dick. L. Rev. 551, 552 (2018).
2. *Id.*
3. Peter A. Joy & Robert R. Kuehn, *The Evolution of ABA Standards for Clinical Faculty*, 75 Tenn. L. Rev. 183, 185 n.5 (2008).
4. *See* Joy, *supra* note 1, at 552 n.2 and n.5; Marc Stickgold, *Exploring the Invisible Curriculum: Clinical Fieldwork in American Law Schools*, 19 N.M. L. Rev. 287, 292 (1989).
5. Joy, *supra* note 1, at 552; Joy et al., *supra* note 3, at 186.
6. Joy, *supra* note 1, at 552; Joy et al., *supra* note 3, at 184; Spring Miller, *The Generalist Externship Seminar: A Unique Curricular Opportunity to Teach About the Legal Profession*, 27 Clinical L. Rev. 279, 281 (2021).

shifted from an apprenticeship model to an academic model. Accompanying this shift was a devaluation of experiential education.[7]

Members of the bar also played a role in the rise of the university-based law schools. The American Bar Association ("ABA") was founded in 1878, at the same time when universities began offering more legal academic training.[8] Some lawyers objected to the low standards used by the states to allow someone to practice law, feeling that they decreased professionalism and threatened the economic and social standing of lawyers.[9] The ABA pushed to impose educational requirements that made it more time-consuming and costly to become a lawyer, which in turn restricted entrance to the profession and raised its status.[10] In 1881, shortly after it was founded, the ABA passed a resolution recommending a three-year course of study and passage of a bar examination to qualify an applicant as an attorney.[11]

The ABA continued to play a major role in legal education. The ABA first began approving law schools in 1921 and became the federally-recognized accrediting agency in 1952.[12] The ABA regulated law schools through its Council of the Section of Legal Education and Admissions to the Bar ("Council"). For many years, the ABA had only basic standards and did not try to impact law school decisions on curricular offerings.[13] Even when it started to push for higher standards between 1920 and 1940, it did not advocate for any clinical experiences.[14]

Although the ABA did not require or even encourage experiential education in law schools for many years, some schools offered experiential opportunities. Law students and at least one law school dean established legal aid bureaus in the late 1890s and early 1900s.[15] During the 1930s and 1940s, some of the most respected members of the legal academy, including Judge Jerome Frank and Karl Llewellyn, criticized law schools' exclusive reliance on doctrinal teaching.[16] In 1933, Judge Frank asked if "the law schools should once more get in intimate contact with what clients need and what courts and lawyers actually do?"[17] In spite of this advocacy, a survey in 1951 found that only 28 law schools had some kind of legal aid clinic

7. Joy, *supra* note 1, at 553–54; Joy et al., *supra* note 3, at 186.

8. Joy, *supra* note 1, at 556.

9. *Id.* at 558.

10. *Id.*

11. Joy et al., *supra* note 3, at 185.

12. United States Government Accountability Office, *Report to Congressional Requesters: Higher Education Issues Related to Law School Accreditation* (2007), *at* https://www.gao.gov/assets/gao-07-314.pdf at 11 (last visited March 7, 2022).

13. Joy, *supra* note 1, at 563.

14. Joy et al., *supra* note 3, at 186–87.

15. Joy, *supra* note 1, at 562; Thomas Geraghty, *Legal Clinics and the Better Trained Lawyer, Part II: A Case Study of Accomplishments, Challenges and the Future of Clinical Legal Education*, 16 Nw. J. L. & Soc. Pol'y 47, 48 (2020); Robert MacCrate, *Educating a Changing Profession: From Clinic to Continuum*, 64 Tenn. L. Rev. 1099, 1102–03 (1997).

16. Joy et al., *supra* note 3, at 187.

17. Jerome Frank, *Why Not a Clinical-Lawyer School?*, 81 U. Pa. L. Rev. 907, 913 (1933).

program.[18] Some of these early clinical programs used an externship design; they included "an independent legal aid society or public defender's office which assigns cases to students, usually provides some student supervision, and usually supplies office space."[19]

The growth of modern clinical education, including externships, was spurred by the continuing demand that law students learn more practice skills,[20] as well as a push for more law school involvement in social justice work. As Elliot Milstein, one of the giants of clinical legal education, described it, "[m]odern clinical education grew out of the progressive reform movement of the 1960s and 1970s and responded to students' desire to learn how to use the law as an instrument of social change and to be involved in the legal representation of poor people."[21] Although clinical legal education included simulation courses, in-house clinics, and externships, much of the financial focus was on development and funding of in-house clinics. The Ford Foundation jump-started the growth of in-house clinics in law schools with grants totaling over $13 million between 1959 and 1978.[22] The Department of Education awarded over $87 million to support clinical legal education between 1978 and 1997.[23]

While externship programs generally did not benefit from these grants, externships for credit existed at most law schools. Reports from the Council on Legal Education for Professional Responsibility indicate that in the 1970s, about 30% of the reported clinical programs were based on an externship model, and these programs existed at two-thirds of the reporting schools.[24] A survey of 105 law schools in 1982 revealed that 76% of responding schools had in-house clinics, and 75% had "field placements."[25]

Despite their presence in the curriculum of the majority of law schools, some academics and others did not appreciate the educational value of externships.[26] They worried, sometimes with good reason, that there was insufficient faculty oversight and guidance of externship education.[27] Although many externship teachers were

18. Quintin Johnstone, *Law School Clinics*, 3 J. LEGAL EDUC. 535, 535 (1951).

19. *Id.*

20. *See, e.g.*, Warren E. Burger, *The Special Skills of Advocacy: Are Specialized Training and Certification of Advocates Essential to Our System of Justice?*, 42 FORDHAM L. REV. 227 (1973) (the U.S. Supreme Court Justice argued that many lawyers are not prepared for serious cases and urged law schools to expand their curricula to provide more lawyering skills training).

21. Elliott S. Milstein, *Clinical Education in the United States: In-House Clinics, Externships, and Simulations*, 51 J. LEGAL EDUC. 375, 375 (2001).

22. Margaret Martin Barry, Jon C. Dubin & Peter A. Joy, *Clinical Education for the Millennium: The Third Wave*, 7 CLINICAL L. REV. 1, 18–19 (2001).

23. *Id.* at 19–20.

24. Stickgold, *supra* note 4, at 297.

25. *Id.* at 298.

26. *See* Stickgold, *supra* note 4, at 297; Robert F. Seibel & Linda H. Morton, *Field Placement Programs: Practices, Problems, Possibilities*, 2 CLINICAL L. REV. 413, 417 (1996).

27. Henry Rose, *Legal Externships: Can They Be Valuable Clinical Experiences for Law Students*, 12 NOVA L. REV. 95, 102 (1987–88); Stickgold, *supra* note 4, at 297.

developing sound pedagogies for their courses, there was limited scholarly exploration of that pedagogy until the 1990s.[28]

Gradually the situation began to change, and externship pedagogy became more understood and respected. In 1986, externship faculty formed an Externship Committee at the annual AALS Clinical Conference.[29] Early articles by externship faculty defended externship teaching and described its advantages, including offering students a wide variety of practice settings and specialized areas of practice, exposing students to the complexity of law practice, and encouraging self-directed learning.[30] In 1998, The Catholic University of America's Columbus School of Law sponsored a conference devoted entirely to legal externships.[31] Over 170 people from more than 100 law schools participated. One of the conference organizers noted an increase in interest in legal externships in the law school curriculum.[32] The conference "was conceived as a step toward bringing together law teachers engaged in designing, managing, and evaluating externships to share current knowledge, to build on that knowledge and ultimately, to create better models for legal externship programs."[33] The *Clinical Law Review* published seven articles based on papers presented at the conference.[34]

Continued external pressure on law schools to expand opportunities for law students to learn professional skills and values also influenced the growth in and respect for externship pedagogy. One source of the external pressure was a report issued in 1992 by the Task Force on Law Schools and the Profession: Narrowing the Gap, a group established by the Council of the ABA Section of Legal Education and Admissions to the Bar. The *MacCrate Report*, as it was known, recommended that law schools expand course offerings teaching lawyering skills and stress the importance of examining the fundamental values of the profession.[35] The Report also suggested changes to the ABA Standards, including requiring law schools to not only prepare "'graduates for admission to the bar,'" but also "'prepare them to participate effectively in the legal profession.'"[36] Fifteen years later, two other influential publications, the Carnegie Foundation's *Educating Lawyers: Preparation for the Practice*

---

28. *See* Stickgold, *supra* note 4, at 297; Harriet Katz, *The Past and Future of Externship Scholarship*, 23 Clinical. L. Rev. 397, 397 (2016).

29. Katz, *supra* note 28, at 400.

30. *Id.* at 399–401.

31. J.P. "Sandy" Ogilvy, *Introduction to the Symposium on Developments in Legal Externship Pedagogy*, 5 Clinical L. Rev. 337, 337 (1999).

32. *Id.*

33. *Id.* at 338.

34. *Id.* at 337.

35. *See* ABA Section of Legal Education and Admissions to the Bar, Legal Education and Professional Development—An Educational Continuum (Report of the Task Force on Law Schools and the Profession: Narrowing the Gap) 330–31 (1992) (hereinafter "MacCrate Report").

36. *Id.* at 330.

of Law ("*Educating Lawyers*")[37] and *Best Practices for Legal Education : A Vision and a Road Map* ("*Best Practices for Legal Education*"),[38] urged legal educators to focus more attention on preparing students to do what lawyers do in practice.[39] *Educating Lawyers* noted the "potential of clinical-legal education for bringing together the multiple aspects of legal knowledge, skill, and purpose," and acknowledged that many of the same principles and practices developed in clinical education applied to externships.[40] The authors of *Best Practices for Legal Education* noted that "it is only in the in-house clinics and some externships where students' decisions and actions can have real consequences and where students' values and practical wisdom can be tested and shaped before they begin their practice."[41] The book highlighted other benefits of experiential courses, including externships, and set forth a set of best practices for externship teaching.[42]

While externship pedagogy and respect for and understanding of that teaching continue to evolve, it is vastly improved from even a decade ago.[43] Externship faculty are respected members and leaders of both the Section on Clinical Legal Education of the Association of American Law Schools[44] and the Clinical Legal Education Association.[45] The bibliography of scholarship relating to the design, critique, and pedagogy of legal externships hosted on the LexternWeb site contains over 500 entries.[46] Externship courses are a key component of the curriculum at nearly every law school in the country.[47]

37. William M. Sullivan et al., Educating Lawyers: Preparation for the Profession of Law (2007) (hereinafter "Educating Lawyers").

38. Roy Stuckey et al., Best Practices for Legal Education: A Vision and a Road Map 55 (2007) (hereinafter "Best Practices for Legal Education").

39. Cynthia Batt, *A Practice Continuum: Integrating Experiential Education into the Curriculum*, 7 Elon L. Rev. 119, 120 (2015).

40. Educating Lawyers, *supra* note 37, at 120.

41. Best Practices for Legal Education, *supra* note 38, at 114.

42. *Id.* at 198–205.

43. While much progress has been made, it is important to recognize that some schools still do not give externship teachers the titles, respect, and resources that they merit.

44. *See* https://www.aals.org/sections/list/clinical-legal-education/ (last visited March 7, 2022). The Clinical Section supports and provides programming and resources for externship and in-house clinic faculty, including the annual Conference on Clinical Legal Education.

45. *See* https://www.cleaweb.org/ (last visited March 7, 2022). CLEA advocates for clinical legal education as fundamental to the education of lawyers.

46. LexternWeb, *Lextern Web Externship Bibliography*, https://www.dropbox.com/s/ rik82mtsz-0joag3/Externship%20BibliographyAlpha%20by%20Last%20Name_Organization.docx.pdf?dl=0 (last visited March 7, 2022).

47. Robert R. Kuehn, Margaret Reuter & David A. Santacroce, Center for the Study of Applied Legal Education, 2019–20 Survey of Applied Legal Education 9 (2020), www.csale.org/#results (last viewed *March* 7, 2022) (hereinafter "2019–20 CSALE Report").

2. Experiential Education in Law Schools

Experiential courses are those where "experience is a significant or primary method of instruction."[48] The ABA currently requires that each law student complete one or more experiential courses totaling at least six credit hours.[49] While many different courses may include experiential elements, only simulation courses, in-house clinic courses, and externship courses qualify as experiential courses under the Standards.[50]

As noted in the Introduction, it is important to distinguish between "experiential education" and "experiential learning." Experiential learning happens when people learn on their own through experience. Experiential education "involves active and purposeful design and teaching."[51] Faculty teaching experiential courses must guide and structure the student experience to achieve predetermined learning goals.

Experiential courses are necessary for law schools to satisfy the mandate that they prepare students for admission to the bar and "for effective, ethical, and responsible participation as members of the legal profession."[52] Practice-based experiential courses, such as externships and clinics, further this mission in at least three general ways. First, they involve active learning, which helps motivate students to be learners and is particularly useful in fostering critical thinking and legal analysis.[53] Second, they give students context for the work of lawyers, which helps students transfer their law school learning to the practice of law.[54] As *Educating Lawyers* noted, "Taking the role of the lawyer in real cases makes visible the ways in which the lawyer's decisions and actions contribute to the larger functioning of the legal order."[55] Finally, when students are put in the role of the lawyer, they are able to build a variety of lawyering and professional skills.[56]

Externships are an important part of any law school's experiential course offerings, and they provide many of the same learning opportunities as in-house clinics.

---

48. Best Practices for Legal Education, *supra* note 38, at 165.

49. ABA Standards and Rules of Procedure for Approval of Law Schools 2021–2022, Standard 303(a)(3).

50. *Id.*

51. Building on Best Practices: Transforming Legal Education in a Changing World 163 (Deborah Maranville, Lisa Radtke Bliss, Carolyn Wilkes Kaas & Antoinette Sedillo Lopez eds., 2015) (hereinafter "Building on Best Practices").

52. ABA Standards and Rules of Procedure for Approval of Law Schools 2022–2023, Standard 301(a). The complete ABA Standards are available at https://www.americanbar.org/content/dam/aba/administrative/legal_education_and_admissions_to_the_bar/standards/2022-2023/2022-2023-standards-and-rules-of-procedure.pdf.

53. *See* Building on Best Practices, *supra* note 51, at 163–64; Michael Hunter Schwartz, Sophie M. Sparrow & Gerald F. Hess, Teaching Law by Design: Engaging Students from the Syllabus to the Final Exam 18–19 (2d ed. 2017) (hereinafter "Teaching Law By Design").

54. Building on Best Practices, *supra* note 51, at 164.

55. Educating Lawyers, *supra* note 37, at 121.

56. *See id.*

As one veteran clinical faculty member who taught both in-house clinics and externship courses noted, "A field placement program can meet any of the goals which clinical legal education addresses: skills instruction, professionalism, understanding the law in a practice context, learning to learn from experience, exploring lawyering roles, and institutional critique."[57] However, externships and in-house clinics are not fungible; they offer two different educational models for engaging in the world of practice.[58]

Externship courses offer some opportunities and practice settings not readily available in in-house clinical courses, including work in judicial chambers, government agencies, law firms, and corporate counsel offices. Many students will end up practicing in workplaces like these after graduation, so getting an educational experience in such a setting during law school is advantageous. Some of these externship sites do not offer many entry-level opportunities, so students have a unique chance to find out more about these work settings. Externships can also cover a wider range of legal subject matters than most in-house clinics and can involve training in highly specialized areas of law, such as corporate finance, securities regulation, or antitrust. While in-house clinic courses provide students with faculty supervision of legal work on cases that are often selected in part for their value as a learning opportunity, externships expose students to the realities of practice outside an educational setting. "Students are exposed to the time pressures, working relationships, cost limitations, fee considerations, and ethical concerns that they will confront in their future legal practices."[59] Finally, externship courses offer rich opportunities for students and faculty to engage in critique of the legal system and the legal profession.[60] Externship faculty are not engaged in the legal practice with the students, which gives them more time and latitude to facilitate honest and critical reflections on lawyer behavior, supervisory styles, the effectiveness of the law as a tool of social change, and many other topics.

3. Characteristics of Externship Courses

Today's externship courses are very different from the early legal apprenticeships described earlier in this Chapter. Modern externship courses include both immersion in practice settings outside the law school and a partnership between law school faculty members and experienced practitioners to ensure good educational outcomes for students. Externship courses can vary significantly from school to school, and sometimes within a single institution. Variable factors include class size, available placement sites, subjects taught in the course, and the number of credits award-

57. Linda F. Smith, *Designing an Extern Clinical Program: Or as You Sow, So Shall You Reap*, 5 Clinical L. Rev. 527, 535 (1999).

58. Seibel & Morton, *supra* note 26, at 421.

59. Rose, *supra* note 27, at 103.

60. *See* Smith, *supra* note 57, at 536; Seibel & Morton, *supra* note 26, at 420.

ed. It is not surprising that those outside of the externship community sometimes find it difficult to discern common pedagogical principles or design features. While creativity and flexibility in course design are important to externship teaching, there are certain characteristics that all externship courses should share. As explained below, they include (a) externship sites outside the law school, (b) teaching by both a faculty member and a site supervisor, (c) transfer of learning from law school to a law office, (d) guided reflection, (e) inclusion of professional responsibility and professionalism concepts, and (f) focus on professional identity formation.

a. Practice Settings Outside the Law School

Of the three types of experiential courses recognized by the ABA, only externships involve the performance of legal work in a setting outside the law school. ABA Standard 304(d) requires that externships provide a "substantial lawyering experience that is reasonably similar to the experience of a lawyer advising or representing a client or engaging in other lawyering tasks outside a law clinic...."[61] Externship placements are in settings that exist primarily to serve clients and the administration of justice, rather than primarily to educate law students. Students engage in and experience the realities of actual practice, encounter real clients, collaborate with lawyers and judges, and contend with the challenges, pressures, and joys of professional work.

Immersion in practice settings outside the law school encourages students to assume the role of a lawyer. As students engage in the tasks that lawyers perform, they also assume a level of responsibility for the outcomes and quality of the representation. As *Educating Lawyers* highlighted, "it is through this experience of lived responsibility that the student comes to grasp that legal work is meaningful in the ethical, as well as cognitive, sense."[62]

Externship students should perform work that is authentic and part of the on-going mission of the externship site. Assignments should be significant enough to make the student feel accountable to the client or the end product.[63] Providing students with context for their work helps build accountability. Context includes understanding how their contribution affects the representation of the client and how the legal matter itself affects the client. As students engage with practicing lawyers, perform work that is authentic, and assume responsibility for the clients they serve and the outcomes that result, they are learning the knowledge, skills, and professional values needed for the practice of law. They are also experiencing first-hand the realities of modern law practice by interacting with lawyers and judges.

61. ABA Standards and Rules of Procedure for Approval of Law Schools 2022–2023, Standard 304(d).

62. Educating Lawyers, *supra* note 37, at 121.

63. *See* Batt, *supra* note 39, at 145.

b. Teaching by Both Externship Faculty and Site Supervisors

Externship courses combine immersion in practice with a dual teaching and supervision model that allows students to learn both from the law faculty member and from the site supervisor. The dual supervision model includes supervision by an attorney at the externship site who is responsible for the student's experience.[64] The site supervisor's work includes determining assignments, providing feedback, and assessing legal and professional skills.[65] Supervisors should also include students in meetings and court appearances and help students understand the context for the work they are doing, the placement's mission, and its impact in society. Chapter 13 of this book contains detailed guidelines for supervisors.

The law school faculty member plays several important roles, including supporting the site supervisor. The faculty member is responsible for oversight and ensuring that both the placement and the law school fulfill the agreed-upon responsibilities.[66] As described in Chapter 4, the faculty member can support the supervisor in the teaching partnership in a variety of ways, including CLE training, a written supervisor manual, site visits, and email or phone communication. Faculty may also want to collaborate with site supervisors in other ways, including sharing externship course syllabi, inviting them to speak at a class session, and consulting with them on student evaluation tools. Supervisors often have useful perspectives about students' understanding and application of the law, their work with others, and their general well-being.

Faculty also support supervisors by helping students learn how to ensure they receive good supervision and learn from it.[67] Knowing how to receive good supervision and how to learn from feedback are important skills for lawyers in busy law practices, where careful assessment of and feedback on work are often not high priorities. The externship provides a bridge to that practice, with the faculty member teaching the student how to understand an assignment, when to seek guidance from a supervisor, how to solicit meaningful feedback, and how to make changes in response to the feedback. The faculty member also provides the academic structure

---

64. ABA Standards and Rules of Procedure for Approval of Law Schools 2022–2023, Standard 304(d).

65. *See* J.P. Ogilvy, *Guidelines for the Self Evaluation of Legal Education Clinics and Clinical Programs*, 15 T.M. Cooley J. Prac. & Clinical L. 1, 155–57 (2014) (discussion of recommended guidelines for externship supervisors).

66. Building on Best Practices, *supra* note 51, at 221 (the externship teacher is in charge of approving supervisors and sites and "monitoring and at times helping to improve the quality of the lawyering and the supervision").

67. See Laurie Barron, *Learning How to Learn: Carnegie's Third Apprenticeship*, 18 Clinical L. Rev. 101, 104 (2011) ("Externships... offer an optimal opportunity for students to learn the skill of being effectively supervised by another lawyer not trained in the art of supervision.").

for the externship course, including integrating doctrine, theory, and legal ethics supporting the legal skills being developed at the externship.[68] In turn, students learn to reflect on their personal experiences and growth as a legal professional. There are many ways of providing that academic structure, as will be discussed in detail in Chapters 3 and 7. Externship teachers also are often charged with designing and implementing the academic and administrative scaffolding that provides structure for the course and positions it within the curriculum. This may include the determination of credit, the method by which students choose externship sites, assessment tools, and scheduling of seminar and externship hours. That work will be discussed in more detail in Chapter 3.

As noted in the Preface and explained above, relationships in an externship among the faculty member, site supervisor, and the student are triangular. Each participant is dependent on and in communication with the other. Student education is the ultimate goal of these relationships.

c. Transfer of Learning from Law School to Professional Work

Law students learn about doctrine, legal analysis, effective writing, and many other topics in their classes. Effective legal education includes helping students learn how to transfer the theory, skills, and values they learned in law school into their professional post-graduation work, which is known as transfer of learning.[69] Embedded in the workplace, externship students observe the methods and strategies of working lawyers, and do the work that lawyers do. Simultaneously, they increase their understanding of the knowledge, practical skills, and professional values needed to competently serve a client. Buttressed by supervision at their externship site and instructional components from law school faculty, students engage in a process that encourages continuous learning from experience.

Students in externships develop a wide variety of legal and professional skills, including legal analysis, research, and writing. Students have started to develop those skills in the law school classroom, but using them in real externship cases helps them transfer their classroom learning to practice and to deepen their skill level and understanding. Externships also allow students to combine those skills in new ways by engaging in problem solving on behalf of a client.

Problem solving is fundamental to the lawyer's role. "The core function of practicing lawyers is to help people and institutions resolve legal problems."[70] Externship assignments help students understand that problem identification and resolution

---

68. *See* ABA Standards and Rules of Procedure for Approval of Law Schools 2022–2023, Standard 304; Building on Best Practices, *supra* note 51, at 221 (the teacher is "in charge of the overall educational quality of the course").

69. Building on Best Practices, *supra* note 51, at 90.

70. *Id.* at 62.

are an intrinsic part of a lawyer's work. Externships allow students to discover that legal doctrine is not a subject to be memorized but rather is one of the tools that can be used to solve legal problems. As students work to resolve legal problems and struggle with the fluidity of facts in the real world, they are developing the practical judgment they will need to be effective professionals.

d. Guided Reflection

"Reflective lawyering is the process by which lawyers evaluate their work in order to develop professional expertise. It is a skill that helps identify successful actions, avoid prior mistakes, adjust current conduct based on past learning, and apply current learning to future practice."[71] Reflection is such an important part of externship education that the ABA Standards require some form of faculty-guided reflection for all externship courses.[72] Externship teachers provide students with multiple opportunities to reflect, using a variety of pedagogical tools including class discussions, written journals, papers, online comments, and individual meetings. Chapter 8 will discuss in detail methods for teaching the skill of reflection.

In addition to faculty-guided reflection, externship courses provide opportunities for site supervisors to assist students with reflection. Setting goals, obtaining quality feedback, and using evaluations are all areas where the supervisor can work with students to reflect and maximize their learning. Teaching students the skill of reflection gives them the tools to continue to engage in reflection throughout their professional careers.

e. Incorporation of Professional Responsibility and Professionalism

Most professional responsibility teachers would agree that there is considerable distance between students being able to articulate an ethical standard and being able to recognize compliance or noncompliance in action. Externships provide an ideal venue for students to learn about professional responsibility in real cases and professionalism in real practice settings. Grounded in the legal workplace, externships afford students the opportunity to see lawyers confront ethical issues as they actually unfold. More significantly, since externship students are performing legal work on

71. Alexander Scherr & Margaret Martin Berry, *Reflection and Writing Journals, in* LEARNING FROM PRACTICE: A TEXT FOR EXPERIENTIAL EDUCATION 203 (Leah Wortham, Alexander Scherr, Nancy Mauer, Susan L. Brooks eds., 3d ed. 2016).

72. ABA STANDARDS AND RULES OF PROCEDURE FOR APPROVAL OF LAW SCHOOLS 2022–2023, STANDARD 304(a)(5).

behalf of real clients, they learn to recognize the factual contexts that trigger the ethical rules and ensure that their own professional behavior complies with those rules.

Rules governing confidentiality, competence, diligence, reporting duties, the unauthorized practice of law, and supervisory responsibility are all relevant to externship students. Site supervisors and teachers should work together to help students understand the relevant rules and develop standards for their own performance. Site supervisors should carefully explain their expectations regarding workplace performance and how they relate to the rules. They should also highlight areas of practice where ethical violations often happen. Externship faculty teach students the pertinent rules and build hypotheticals and reflective exercises that provide students with practice in identifying and solving ethical dilemmas. Chapter 9 offers ideas for teaching ethics in the externship seminar.

Externships also offer rich opportunities for students to explore the meaning and implications of professionalism, under the guidance of both a practitioner and a faculty member. While there is no one definition of professionalism, it includes "good judgment, effective problem solving, and leadership" and "being part of a learned profession that serves the public and contributes to societal good."[73] Depending on their placements, students can observe how judges and lawyers perform their duties and interact with clients and the public. The site supervisor is well-placed to share perspectives about the practical implications of professional standards in the legal system as well as breaches of those standards. Externship faculty can guide students to articulate characteristics associated with professionalism and to develop personal standards for professionalism.

f. Focus on Professional Identity Formation

Externship courses are an excellent place to help students start to develop their professional identity. Teaching about professional identity formation engages students at a deeper level by asking them to internalize core values of the profession so that their actions are tied to these values.[74] To accomplish this, students must identify and examine their own personal core values and integrate them with those of the profession. A focus on professional formation also encourages externs to change their mindset from that of a student to that of a practitioner who accepts responsibility for clients and for achieving excellence in the competencies of the profession.[75] Externship courses require student self-determination and self-reliance, which helps

---

73. Nancy Maurer, *Professionalism, in* Learning From Practice, *supra* note 71, at 239.

74. Building on Best Practices, *supra* note 51, at 253, 256. *See also* Lawrence S. Kreiger, *The Inseparability of Professionalism and Personal Satisfaction: Perspectives on Values, Integrity, and Happiness*, 11 Clinical L. Rev. 425 (2005).

75. Timothy W. Floyd & Kendall L. Kerew, *Marking the Path from Law Student to Lawyer: Using Field Placement Courses to Facilitate the Deliberate Exploration of Professional Identity and Purpose*, 68 Mercer L. Rev. 767, 775 (2017).

them form their professional identity. "Student mastery of self-directed learning is a significant aspiration of legal education which is greatly enhanced through externship programs."[76]

While most law school courses offer assignments and content created by a teacher in a familiar environment, externships put students in unfamiliar territory where they must set their own learning goals, seek out assignments, complete their work in a competent and diligent manner, and learn from feedback. While externship faculty and site supervisors are both available to assist, students may need to solicit that assistance. Students' motivation to be an active participant in their learning enhances their externship experience. By building self-reliance and self-direction, externships intentionally foster the growth of professional identity. Chapter 9 will offer specific techniques for teaching professional identity formation.

4. Externship Partners in the Law School

While externship faculty must of course maintain partnerships with external sites, they should also develop partnerships with people inside the law school. Members of the administration, faculty, and staff can affect many aspects of an externship program, including budget, credits awarded, faculty to teach externship courses, sites available for externships, and many other factors. Building internal partnerships can help externship faculty build stronger programs and courses.

a. Experiential Faculty and Experiential Dean

Experiential faculty, using the definition in ABA Standard 304, include those who teach in-house clinics, externship courses, and simulation classes. These courses share many of the same pedagogies and educational benefits to students. Faculty who teach other experiential courses can be natural allies to externship faculty, and it is often helpful to seek out opportunities to discuss teaching methods, challenges, and other topics with people in this group.

Many schools are hiring Deans of Experiential Education, who oversee all experiential courses.[77] This dean may control or have an influence on important parts of an externship program, including budget, credits awarded, faculty status, and other factors. Some of these deans have a good understanding of and appreciation for externship programs and pedagogy, while others need to be provided this information by externship faculty.

Experiential deans who understand how successful externship programs operate will be more likely to include an appropriate budget for the program or to advocate for such a budget with the law school dean and others. Funding impacts many as-

76. Seibel & Morton, *supra* note 26, at 419.

77. *See* 2019–20 CSALE Report, *supra* note 47, at 5.

pects of externship design and execution, including but not limited to compensation for faculty and staff, administrative support, and class size. According to the Center for the Study of Applied Legal Education ("CSALE") Report of 2019–20, of the nine major challenges facing externship programs, three were directly related to financial support: insufficient administrative/secretarial support, insufficient number of clinical faculty, and insufficient hard money.[78]

Having an insufficient number of faculty can have a detrimental effect on externship courses. While the standard faculty to student ratio for in-house clinics is generally set at 1:8, the ratio for externship courses is generally much higher,[79] and there is no agreed-upon upper limit. Chapter 3 explains why a ratio of 1:16 for externship courses is consistent with best practices in externship teaching. Externship faculty have a wide range of duties beyond designing and teaching the externship seminar. They are involved before the course starts in helping students find externship placements that meet their educational goals and ensuring that those placements will provide appropriate assignments and supervision. During the semester, they need to be in regular contact with site supervisors, provide supervisors with guidance and training, and perhaps visit each externship site.[80] Most externship faculty meet individually with students one or more times each semester and spend substantial time reviewing and assessing the often lengthy reflection journals or papers and other assignments.

Experiential deans and faculty can also be partners with and advocates for externship teachers on the issue of faculty status. The current ABA Standards require faculty to teach externships and assign specific responsibilities to them.[81] However, the Standards do not require any particular type of faculty status for externship faculty or program directors. Some externship faculty are considered part of a school's clinical faculty, and full-time clinical faculty generally must have "a form of security of position reasonably similar to tenure...."[82] Some schools have a unitary tenure track system for both doctrinal and clinical faculty. But other externship faculty are slotted into categories like adjunct, visiting, and lecturer.[83] Law faculty hierarchies and categories significantly impact the compensation, working conditions, power, and job security of the faculty member.

Currently more than half of the externship directors are recognized as full-time faculty, and slightly over one quarter are tenured or on a tenure track. The most recent CSALE Report details the status of the externship directors as follows: tenure or

---

78. *Id.* at 11.

79. *See id.* at 39 (median number of students that externship faculty teach or oversee is 25 students; some oversee more than 100 students).

80. ABA Standards and Rules of Procedure for Approval of Law Schools 2022–2023, Standard 304(d)(5).

81. *Id.*

82. *Id.* Standard 405(c).

83. *See* 2019–20 CSALE Report, *supra* note 47, at 41.

tenure track (24%), long-term presumptively renewable contract (27%), short-term contracts (15%), and administrative with or without faculty title (32%).[84]

While there is much variation from school to school, it is clear the status of the externship program director and the externship faculty impacts an externship program. Lack of or limited faculty status may mean less access to law school leadership, an inability to vote on important educational issues at faculty meetings, and no opportunity to serve on faculty committees. Status may also affect access to funds for research assistance and conferences. Teachers without faculty status may not have time for research and scholarship. Program directors who lack the job security of full-time faculty can find it hard to push back against efforts to erode academic quality and standards that are key to strong program design.[85] They may also have less credibility with site supervisors,[86] which can make it more difficult to implement supervisor training, negotiate with placements, and manage compliance with the requirements of the ABA Standards. Finally, externship program directors who are also part of the career development office may be faced with competing missions. As a career development specialist, their primary goal is to generate jobs and post-graduate hiring. They may face pressure to design a program that pleases potential employers rather than one focused on the educational goals of students.[87]

b. Podium Faculty

Support from and partnership with faculty who do not teach experiential courses is also important. This group of faculty may not have a strong understanding of externship pedagogy and educational benefits for students. Externship faculty may want to enhance understanding and appreciation by sharing information about the externship program in the form of newsletters, periodic reports at faculty meetings, and email communication on the faculty listserv. Co-teaching classes, serving together on law school committees, and collaborating on service projects can also enhance this understanding and appreciation.

Having good relationships with members of the doctrinal faculty can help the externship faculty in crucial ways. Podium faculty may have connections to possible externship placements that relate to their areas of expertise. They may also have relationships with alumni and local lawyers who might make good externship supervisors. Some of these faculty members may encourage students with an interest in a specific area of doctrinal law to consider an externship in that area. They may be appropriate guest speakers for externship courses focused on particular areas of the law. They can keep the externship faculty aware of law school developments

84. *Id.*

85. Nancy M. Maurer & Liz Ryan Cole, Design, *Teach and Manage: Ensuring Educational Integrity in Field Placement Courses*, 19 Clinical L. Rev. 115, 139 (2012).

86. *See id.* at 140.

87. *Id. See also* Building on Best Practices, *supra* note 51, at 223–24.

and proposed curricular changes. They can also help generate support for the issues described above, including budget and staffing increases and improved faculty status for externship teachers.

c. Law School Dean

A strong working relationship between the externship program director and the law school dean can be a valuable asset for the program. An increasing number of deans today are aware of the importance of experiential education. Some have participated in clinics and externships while in law school. Some have taught experiential courses during their teaching careers. Other deans have not had that exposure. Regardless of the dean's prior experience with externship courses, it is important for the program director to make sure the dean understands how the externship program works at their school.

In order to work most effectively with the dean, externship faculty should have a clear understanding of leadership's priorities and goals and be ready to advocate as to how the externship program can further those goals. Scheduling regular meetings and providing written semester and year-end reports allow the program director to detail the successes and challenges of the program and the progress in furthering the priorities of the law school leadership. Fostering a collaborative dialogue that increases the dean's understanding of the externship program can create greater receptivity and support for the kind of funding, staffing, and faculty status issues described above.

d. Administrative Offices

All faculty in the law school owe a huge debt to the work of the Offices of Admissions, Alumni, Development, and Career Services. Together they recruit students, raise money to support students and pay faculty, and help students find post-graduate jobs. Each of these offices provides partnership opportunities for externship programs.

The mission of the Admissions Office is to attract talented prospective students to the law school by emphasizing those aspects of the school that may be most attractive. The breadth and depth of experiential education is often one of those features. Externship faculty and admissions staff should work closely to ensure that information about externships is accurate, and that prospective students' expectations are appropriate.

Collaboration between the Career Services office and externship faculty can be productive for both offices. For example, Career Services staff are often most current on the professional qualities sought by major and local employers. This information can be helpful to prospective externship students in choosing externships and can be the stimulus for reflection and growth during externship classes. Career Services staff may also be good guest speakers if the externship course includes a session on career development and planning.

Sometimes challenges arise in this relationship because of the differing focus of the work. Career Services offices are focused on assisting students in obtaining employment, especially post-graduate employment. Externship faculty focus on providing high quality educational experiences for students. Career Services staff may inadvertently convey a message to students that an externship is an extended try-out or audition for a post-graduate position, rather than an educational experience for the primary benefit of the student. Career Services staff may also ask externship faculty to establish placements at offices where they hope to increase post-graduation hiring. As with similar requests from anywhere in the law school, externship faculty should ensure that everyone understands the educational mission of externships, the benefits that accrue to students, and the standards and expectations of placement supervisors. Finally, as explained above, externship program directors who are also part of the Career Services office may face pressure to design a program that pleases potential employers rather than one focused on the educational goals of students.[88]

Development and Alumni offices solicit financial and other support for the law school. Sometimes alumni and donors ask for an externship student to work at their place of business, which can create good new externship sites for students. Some alumni might also be interested in funding a certain type of externship placement. It is important for externship faculty to educate these offices as to the process and requirements necessary to establish an externship placement. Some opportunities may be better suited to a paid position not for class credit or a pro bono project.

88. For a discussion of the challenges of placing an externship program within the Career Services Office, *see* Building on Best Practices, *supra* note 51, at 223–24.

Chapter 2

ABA Standards and Other Regulatory Requirements

The Council of the ABA Section of Legal Education and Admissions to the Bar is recognized by the United States Department of Education as the accrediting body of J.D. programs in the United States and its territories.[1] As the national accrediting body, the Council handles all matters related to ABA approval of law schools,[2] sets the Standards for Approval of Law Schools, and determines the Rules of Procedure that govern the law school accreditation process.[3]

Chapter 3 of the ABA Standards governs the program of legal education at all ABA-approved law schools. While externship faculty should be familiar with all of the Standards and any Interpretations of the Standards[4] set forth in Chapter 3, this discussion will focus on the handful of Standards and Interpretations that directly implicate the design, pedagogy, and administration of externship programs and courses. In addition, this discussion will incorporate Guidance Memoranda written

---

1. https://www.americanbar.org/groups/legal_education/about_us/.

2. As the ABA explains,

> USDE recognition criteria require an accrediting agency within a professional association to operate separately and independently of the association of which it is a part. Therefore, it is the Council, and not the American Bar Association that is the formally recognized accreditor. Nonetheless, for ease of reference, law schools accredited by the Council are referred to as "ABA-approved." While the ABA supports the Council and its work in a variety of ways, including financially, "separate and independent" means, at a minimum, that the ABA is not involved in any way in the approval of a law school or the enforcement of the ABA Standards for Approval of Law Schools against law schools, including findings of non-compliance, imposition of sanctions, or withdrawal of approval.

Preface, ABA Standards and Rules of Procedure for Approval of Law Schools 2022–2023.

3. The complete ABA Standards are available at https://www.americanbar.org/content/dam/aba/administrative/legal_education_and_admissions_to_the_bar/standards/2022-2023/2022-2023-standards-and-rules-of-procedure.pdf (last visited Sept. 30, 2022).

4. "In their current form, the Standards often include Interpretations that provide additional guidance concerning the implementation of a particular Standard.... The Rules also contain provisions related to the operation of the Office of the Managing Director." Preface, ABA Standards and Rules of Procedure for Approval of Law Schools 2022–2023, Standard 303(a)(3).

by the Section's Office of the Managing Director in an effort to clarify or provide direction regarding the implementation of a particular Standard or Interpretation.[5]

1. Standard 303

Standard 303 sets forth the minimum requirements of a law school curriculum as follows:

> Standard 303. CURRICULUM
>
> (a) A law school shall offer a curriculum that requires each student to satisfactorily complete at least the following:
>
> (1) one course of at least two credit hours in professional responsibility that includes substantial instruction in rules of professional conduct, and the values and responsibilities of the legal profession and its members;
>
> (2) one writing experience in the first year and at least one additional writing experience after the first year, both of which are faculty supervised; and
>
> (3) one or more experiential course(s) totaling at least six credit hours. An experiential course must be a simulation course, a law clinic, or a field placement, as defined in Standard 304.
>
> (b) A law school shall provide substantial opportunities to students for:
>
> (1) law clinics or field placement(s);
>
> (2) student participation in pro bono legal services, including law-related public service activities; and
>
> (3) the development of a professional identity.
>
> (c) A law school shall provide education to law students on bias, cross cultural competency, and racism:
>
> (1) at the start of the program of legal education, and
>
> (2) at least once again before graduation.

For students engaged in law clinics or field placements, the second educational occasion will take place before, concurrently with, or as part of their enrollment in clinical or field placement courses.[6]

---

5. https://www.americanbar.org/groups/legal_education/accreditation/consultants_memos/.

6. https://www.americanbar.org/content/dam/aba/administrative/legal_education_and_admissions_to_the_bar/standards/2022-2023/2022-2023-standards-and-rules-of-procedure.pdf (last visited Sept. 30, 2022). Standards 303(b)(3) and 303(c) are new law school curriculum requirements adopted in February 2022. Schools will be required to "have a plan [for implementation of new Standards 303(b)(3) and 303(c)] in place by fall of 2022 as to how the school plans to comply with the Standard 303 amendments with full implementation of the plan by fall of 2023." Posting of William

a. Experiential Courses

One of the minimum requirements of the law school curriculum is that law students must complete at least six credit hours of experiential coursework,[7] which is limited to simulations,[8] law clinics,[9] and field placements,[10] as defined by the Standards. The Standards use the term "field placement" rather than "externship," but these terms are used interchangeably in legal education. In addition to requiring six experiential course credits, therefore, Standard 303(b)(1) requires law schools to provide substantial opportunities for students to participate in law clinics or field placements. The March 2015 Managing Director's Guidance Memo attempts to clarify this requirement by explaining that it:

> Does not mean the school must guarantee each student both a field placement and a clinic opportunity, or even guarantee each student can enroll in one or the other. Instead, a school must offer sufficient opportunities so that a student desiring at least one of those experiences has a realistic chance of enrolling in such a course prior to graduation.[11]

Despite not being a requirement, an increasing number of law schools now guarantee a law clinic or field placement to every student.[12]

The Interpretations to Standard 303 provide important guidance regarding the application of the Standard. Interpretation 303-1 prohibits a law school from allowing a student "to use a course to satisfy more than one requirement" of Standard 303:

> For example, a course that includes a writing experience used to satisfy the upper-class writing requirement [see 303(a)(2)] cannot be counted as one

---

Adams, William.Adams@americanbar.org, to LEAP-DEANS@mail.americanbar.org (February 24, 2022) (on file with authors).

7. As Professor Peter Joy explains,

> Law schools did not typically require any experiential education, such as simulation courses, in-house clinical courses, or externships until 2010 when the American Bar Association (ABA) began requiring law schools to provide each law student with minimal experiential education of at least one credit. Even with the current experiential education requirement of one or more courses totaling at least six credit hours, which was adopted in 2014, legal education is distinct from other types of professional education that typically requires one-quarter to one-half of required credits through experiential education.

Peter A. Joy, *The Uneasy History of Experiential Education in U.S. Law Schools*, 122 Dick. L. Rev. 551, 555 (2018).

8. A simulation is defined in Standard 304(b).

9. A law clinic is defined in Standard 304(c).

10. A field placement is defined in Standard 304(d) and will be discussed in detail below.

11. ABA Section of Legal Education and Admissions to the Bar, Managing Director's Guidance Memo on Standards 303(a)(3), 303(b), and 304 (March 2015), https://www.americanbar.org/content/dam/aba/administrative/legal_education_and_admissions_to_the_bar/governancedocuments/2015_standards_303_304_experiential_course_requirement_.pdf (last visited Sept. 30, 2022).

12. Robert R. Kuehn, *Universal Clinical Legal Education: Necessary and Feasible*, 53 Wash. U. J. L. & Pol'y 89 (2017).

> of the experiential courses required in Standard 303(a)(3). This does not preclude a law school from offering a course that may count either as an upper-class writing requirement [see 303(a)(2)] or as a simulation course [see 304(a) and 304(b)] provided the course meets all of the requirements of both types of courses and the law school permits a student to use the course to satisfy only one requirement under this Standard.[13]

b. Professional Identity Formation

Standard 303(b)(3) requires law schools to provide substantial opportunities for the development of professional identity.[14] Interpretation 303-5 defines professional identity for law schools as follows:

> Professional identity focuses on what it means to be a lawyer and the special obligations lawyers have to their clients and society. The development of professional identity should involve an intentional exploration of the values, guiding principles, and well-being practices considered foundational to successful legal practice. Because developing a professional identity requires reflection and growth over time, students should have frequent opportunities for such development during each year of law school and in a variety of courses and co-curricular and professional development activities.[15]

Because externship courses orient students in real-world practice settings, they are a natural place to explore each student's emerging professional identity as a lawyer. Thus, while professional identity formation should be addressed in classes across the curriculum, externships are a "signature pedagogy"[16] for exploring professional identity. Chapter 9 discusses how to incorporate professional identity formation, values, and well-being into the externship seminar.

c. Bias, Cross Cultural Competency, and Racism

Standard 303(c) requires law schools to educate law students on bias, cross cultural competency, and racism twice during the course of law school.[17] Importantly,

---

13. ABA Standards and Rules of Procedure for Approval of Law Schools 2022–2023, Interpretation 303-1.

14. ABA Standard 303(b)(3), *supra* note 6.

15. Interpretation 303-5, *supra* note 6.

16. Kelly S. Terry, *Externships: A Signature Pedagogy for the Apprenticeship of Professional Identity and Purpose*, 59 J. Legal Educ. 240 (2010). "Signature pedagogies are the 'typical practices of teaching and learning by which schools induct new members into the field' .... Through signature pedagogies, 'the novices are instructed on the fundamental dimensions of professional work—*to think, to perform, and to act with integrity*.' Such teaching methods are 'signature' because they are 'readily identifiable and unique to the field.'" *Id.* at 247.

17. ABA Standard 303(c), *supra* note 6.

if a student enrolls in a law clinic or field placement, the student must receive the second educational experience before, at the same time, or as part of the law clinic or field placement course.[18] A law school can satisfy this requirement through a number of ways, a course being one of them.[19] Regardless of the method of satisfying the requirement, "law schools must demonstrate that all law students are required to participate in a substantial activity designed to reinforce the skill of cultural competency and their obligation as future lawyers to work to eliminate racism in the legal profession."[20] Chapter 9 discusses the rationale for including instruction about bias, racism, and cross-cultural humility in the externship seminar, a means of assessing the existing curriculum and developing learning outcomes, and principles of pedagogy in teaching about these topics.

2. Standard 304

Standard 304, specifically sections (a), (d), and (f), sets forth the general requirements for experiential courses. Standard 304(a) states the requirements that simulations, law clinics, and field placements must meet to qualify as "experiential," while Standard 304(d) defines a field placement course and articulates four components specifically required of field placements: written agreements; site selection, training, evaluation, and communication; evaluation of student educational achievement by a faculty member; and sufficient control of the student experience, including documentation. Standard 304 provides:

> Standard 304. EXPERIENTIAL COURSES: SIMULATION COURSES, LAW CLINICS, AND FIELD PLACEMENTS
>
> (a) Experiential courses satisfying Standard 303(a) are simulation courses, law clinics, and field placements that must be primarily experiential in nature and must:
>
> (1) integrate doctrine, theory, skills, and legal ethics, and engage students in performance of one or more of the professional skills identified in Standard 302;
>
> (2) develop the concepts underlying the professional skills being taught;
>
> (3) provide multiple opportunities for performance;

18. *Id.*

19. "Standard 303(c)'s requirement that law schools provide education on bias, cross-cultural competency, and racism may be satisfied by, among other things, the following: (1) Orientation sessions for incoming students; (2) Lectures on these topics; (3) Courses incorporating these topics; or (4) Other educational experiences incorporating these topics." Interpretation 303-7, *supra* note 6. In addition, Interpretation 303-8 provides, "Standard 303 does not prescribe the form or content of the education on bias, cross-cultural competency, and racism required by Standard 303(c)." *Id.*

20. Interpretation 303-7, *supra* note 6.

(4) provide opportunities for student performance, self-evaluation, and feedback from a faculty member, or, for a field placement, a site supervisor;

(5) provide a classroom instructional component; or, for a field placement, a classroom instructional component, regularly scheduled tutorials, or other means of ongoing, contemporaneous, faculty-guided reflection; and

(6) provide direct supervision of the student's performance by the faculty member; or, for a field placement, provide direct supervision of the student's performance by a faculty member or a site supervisor.

(b) A simulation course provides substantial experience not involving an actual client, that is reasonably similar to the experience of a lawyer advising or representing a client or engaging in other lawyering tasks in a set of facts and circumstances devised or adopted by a faculty member.

(c) A law clinic provides substantial lawyering experience that involves advising or representing one or more actual clients or serving as a third-party neutral.

(d) A field placement course provides substantial lawyering experience that (1) is reasonably similar to the experience of a lawyer advising or representing a client or engaging in other lawyering tasks in a setting outside a law clinic under the supervision of a licensed attorney or an individual otherwise qualified to supervise, and (2) includes the following:

(i) a written understanding among the student, faculty member, and a person in authority at the field placement that describes both (A) the substantial lawyering experience and opportunities for performance, feedback and self-evaluation; and (B) the respective roles of faculty and any site supervisor in supervising the student and in assuring the educational quality of the experience for the student, including a clearly articulated method of evaluating the student's academic performance;

(ii) a method for selecting, training, evaluating and communicating with site supervisors, including regular contact between the faculty and site supervisors through in-person visits or other methods of communication that will assure the quality of the student educational experience. When appropriate, a school may use faculty members from other law schools to supervise or assist in the supervision or review of a field placement program;

(iii) evaluation of each student's educational achievement by a faculty member; and

(iv) sufficient control of the student experience to ensure that the requirements of the Standard are met. The law school must maintain records to document the steps taken to ensure compliance with the Standard, which shall include, but is not necessarily limited to, the written understandings described in Standard 304(d)(i).

(e) Credit granted for such a simulation, law clinic, or field placement course shall be commensurate with the time and effort required and the anticipated quality of the educational experience of the student.

(f) Each student in such a simulation, law clinic, or field placement course shall have successfully completed sufficient prerequisites or shall receive sufficient contemporaneous training to assure the quality of the student educational experience.[21]

a. The Threshold Requirement

As a preliminary matter, Standard 304(a) provides that all experiential courses must be "primarily experiential in nature." The March 2015 Managing Director's Guidance Memo addresses this requirement by explaining the meaning of the word "primarily" as follows:

> "Primarily" means essentially, mostly, chiefly. It suggests more than simply inserting an experiential component into an existing class, without regard to whether that component makes up a majority (51%) of the class minutes. "Primarily" is used to indicate the main purpose of something. The experiential nature of the course should, in this sense, be the organizing principle of the course, and the substantive law or doctrinal material that is part of the course should be incidental to it, not the other way around. Taken as a whole, the language used in the Standard suggests that to qualify as an experiential or simulation course, the course must be easily identifiable as such. It seems likely the Council and the Accreditation Committee will expect the character of courses that the school holds out as meeting the requirement to be clearly experiential and will not engage in "minute counting" in order to qualify a particular course. By meeting the requirement that a course be primarily experiential in nature, the requirement that the course provide "substantial experience" likely is also met, as long as the course also includes "direct supervision of the student's performance by the faculty member" and "opportunities for performance, feedback from a faculty member, and self-evaluation" as further required by the Standard.[22]

21. ABA Standards and Rules of Procedure for Approval of Law Schools 2022–2023, Standard 304.

22. Guidance Memo on Standards 303(a)(3), 303(b), and 304, *supra* note 11. Although the March 2015 Guidance Memo addressed a previous version of the Standards, which had the "primarily experiential in nature" language in Standard 303, this language is now contained in Standard 304.

In other words, merely "inserting some skills instruction or skills exercises in a substantive course" will not meet this requirement.[23]

b. The Other Requirements for Experiential Courses Under Standard 304

1) Standard 304(a)(1)-(6)

In addition to being primarily experiential in nature, all experiential courses must satisfy several other requirements set forth in Standard 304(a)(1)-(6). Because students must complete at least six credits of experiential courses as part of the program of study, ABA-accredited law schools will want to ensure that their externship courses qualify as experiential.

First, experiential courses must "integrate doctrine, theory, skills, and legal ethics, and *engage students in performance of one or more* of the professional skills identified in Standard 302."[24] Standard 302 enumerates the following professional skills:

> (a) Knowledge and understanding of substantive and procedural law;
>
> (b) Legal analysis and reasoning, legal research, problem-solving, and written and oral communication in the legal context;
>
> (c) Exercise of proper professional and ethical responsibilities to clients and the legal system; and
>
> (d) Other professional skills needed for competent and ethical participation as a member of the legal profession.[25]

Interpretation 302-1 defines "other professional skills" as those "determined by the law school and may include skills such as, interviewing, counseling, negotiation, fact development and analysis, trial practice, document drafting, conflict resolution, organization and management of legal work, collaboration, cultural competency, and self-evaluation."[26] Because externship courses place students in actual practice settings, they integrate doctrine, theory, skills, and legal ethics by their very nature. Specifically, externs both observe and complete assignments that require knowledge, application of that knowledge, exercise of professional and ethical judgment, and a variety of other professional skills. The design of the placement course, the type of legal practice setting, and the student's identified learning goals likely will determine the particular professional skills he or she performs. Design ideas, considerations

---

23. Guidance Memo on Standards 303(a)(3), 303(b), and 304, *supra* note 11, at 4.

24. ABA Standards and Rules of Procedure for Approval of Law Schools 2022–2023, Standard 304(a)(1) (emphasis added).

25. ABA Standards and Rules of Procedure for Approval of Law Schools 2022–2023, Standard 302.

26. ABA Standards and Rules of Procedure for Approval of Law Schools 2022–2023, Interpretation 302-1.

regarding different types of placements, and student goal-setting are discussed in Chapters 3, 7, and 8.

Second, experiential courses must "develop the concepts underlying the professional skills being taught."[27] In a placement, this teaching can be done both by the site supervisor and the externship teacher. Chapters 9 and 10 offer ideas for how externship teachers can develop these underlying concepts, and Chapter 13 offers ideas for site supervisors.

Third, the courses must "provide multiple opportunities for performance."[28] Accordingly, an extern in a placement must be given the opportunity to perform a particular professional skill more than once. For example, an extern in a judicial externship ideally would be given the opportunity to write more than one bench brief to allow the extern to write and receive feedback on the first bench brief and then apply that feedback when writing the second bench brief.

The fourth, fifth and sixth requirements for experiential courses are different for externship courses than for in-house clinics and simulation courses. The fourth requirement states that experiential courses must "provide opportunities for student performance, self-evaluation, and feedback."[29] This part of the Standard states that the feedback should come "from a faculty member, or, for a field placement, a site supervisor."[30] This language leaves some room for ambiguity regarding the source of feedback for externship students. It is a best practice, however, for an externship course to provide opportunities for performance and self-evaluation (through a formal evaluation or reflective assignments); for faculty members to provide feedback on the course work they directly assign and observe; and for site supervisors to provide feedback on the fieldwork they directly assign and observe. Chapters 8 and 13 focus on different self-evaluation and feedback methods that can be employed by both externship teachers and site supervisors.

The fifth requirement allows multiple options for externship teachers to design the course. Specifically, the course can employ "a classroom instructional component, regularly scheduled tutorials, or other means of ongoing, contemporaneous, faculty-guided reflection."[31] In other words, a classroom component, while considered a best practice, is not required if the externship teacher has regular contact with

27. ABA Standards and Rules of Procedure for Approval of Law Schools 2022–2023, Standard 304(a)(2).

28. ABA Standards and Rules of Procedure for Approval of Law Schools 2022–2023, Standard 304(a)(3).

29. ABA Standards and Rules of Procedure for Approval of Law Schools 2022–2023, Standard 304(a)(4).

30. *Id.*

31. ABA Standards and Rules of Procedure for Approval of Law Schools 2022–2023, Standard 304(a)(5).

the student and guides the student's reflective process. These different approaches to teaching an externship course are discussed in Chapters 7 and 8.

The sixth requirement specifies that a field placement course must "provide direct supervision of the student's performance by a faculty member or a site supervisor."[32] Presumably, this requirement contemplates that students may be learning and performing certain professional skills from either the externship teacher, site supervisor, or both. Considerations regarding student supervision are discussed in Chapters 7 and 13.

2) Standard 304(e)

As set forth in 304(e), another requirement of all experiential courses, including externships, is that the credit granted is commensurate with the time and effort required and the anticipated quality of the educational experience of the student.[33] Standard 310 is instructive here. Standard 310 governs the amount of work that is required for each credit hour and "reflects the definition of credit hour established by the Department of Education, which includes both time spent in class and time spent on out-of-class work."[34] Standard 310 provides:

> Standard 310. DETERMINATION OF CREDIT HOURS FOR COURSEWORK
>
> (a) A law school shall adopt, publish, and adhere to written policies and procedures for determining the credit hours that it awards for coursework.
>
> (b) A "credit hour" is an amount of work that reasonably approximates:
>
> (1) not less than one hour of classroom or direct faculty instruction and two hours of out-of-class student work per week for fifteen weeks, or the equivalent amount of work over a different amount of time; or
>
> (2) at least an equivalent amount of work as required in subparagraph (1) of this definition for other academic activities as established by the institution, including simulation, field placement, clinical, co-curricular, and other academic work leading to the award of credit hours.[35]

---

32. ABA Standards and Rules of Procedure for Approval of Law Schools 2022–2023, Standard 304(a)(6).

33. ABA Standards and Rules of Procedure for Approval of Law Schools 2022–2023, Standard 304(e).

34. ABA Section of Legal Education and Admissions to the Bar, *Managing Director's Guidance Memo on Standard* 310 (May 2016), https://www.americanbar.org/content/dam/aba/administrative/legal_education_and_admissions_to_the_bar/governancedocuments/2016_standard_310_guidance_memorandum.pdf (last visited Sept. 30, 2022) at 2 (citing 34 C.F.R. § 600.2 (2010)).

35. ABA Standards and Rules of Procedure for Approval of Law Schools 2022–2023, Standard 310.

The May 2016 Managing Director's Memo is helpful in interpreting this Standard as applied to field placements. Specifically, the memo provides that "there is no minimum amount of in-class instruction required" for field placements.[36] Instead, the Standard requires "at least an equivalent amount of work as required in subparagraph (1).... This 'equivalent amount of work' requirement must also be met to comply with the requirement in Standard [304(e)],"[37] which provides that "[c[redit granted for such a simulation, law clinic, or field placement shall be commensurate with the time and effort required and the anticipated quality of the educational experience of the student."[38] The Memo specifies that, "In terms of total time, 42.5 hours per credit is required: 15 'hours' in class (50 minute 'hours') and twice that—30 hours—out of class (60 minute hours)" and provides the following example:

> **Field placement or clinic:** 42.5 hours per credit of time spent in class, performing field placement or clinic work, preparing for class or completing class assignments (e.g., reflective writing assignments), and preparing for and taking an exam, if applicable.[39]

In addition, the memo suggests, "The school should design the clinic or field placement to insure that the required number of logged hours plus the time spent in any classroom sessions and preparing for those sessions equals or exceeds the 'not less than one hour of classroom or direct faculty instruction and two hours of out-of-class student work per week for fifteen weeks' specified in Standard 310(b)(1)."[40]

3) Standard 304(f)

As set forth in 304(f), another requirement of all experiential courses, including field placements, is the requirement that students "have successfully completed sufficient prerequisites or shall receive sufficient contemporaneous training to assure the quality of the student educational experience."[41] Therefore, externship teachers should ensure that students have taken the courses and have the skills necessary to maximize student learning from externship site supervisors while working at the externship site. The establishment of prerequisites and the provision of contemporaneous training is addressed in Chapters 4, 7, and 13.[42]

---

36. *Guidance Memo on Standard 310, supra* note 34, at 3.

37. *Id.*

38. ABA Standards and Rules of Procedure for Approval of Law Schools 2022–2023, Standard 304(e).

39. *Guidance Memo on Standard 310, supra* note 34, at 3–4.

40. *Id.* at 5.

41. ABA Standards and Rules of Procedure for Approval of Law Schools 2022–2023, Standard 304(f).

42. *See* Seattle University School of Law Student Clinic/Externship Planning Guide in the Appendix materials for Chapter 3.

c. Field Placement Courses and Standard 304(d)

While Standards 304(a) and (f) set forth requirements for all experiential courses, including field placements, Standard 304(d) articulates those requirements specific only to field placements.[43] As an initial matter, Standard 304(d) defines a field placement as a course that "provides a substantial lawyering experience...."[44] In addition, the substantial lawyering experience must include four specific components.

First, an externship course must have a written understanding among the extern, externship teacher, and a supervisor at the placement.[45] In other words, it needs to be a written three-way agreement signed not only by the student and the externship teacher, but also by a supervisor at the placement who has primary responsibility for supervising the extern. In addition, the written agreement must describe two things: "the substantial lawyering experience and opportunities for performance, feedback and self-evaluation"; and "the respective roles of externship teachers and any supervisor in supervising the extern and in assuring the educational quality of the experience for the student, including a clearly articulated method of evaluating the student's academic performance."[46] A detailed discussion of written understandings can be found in Chapter 4.

Second, the externship course must include "a method for selecting, training, evaluating and communicating with site supervisors, including regular contact between the externship teachers and supervisors through in-person visits or other methods of communication that will assure the quality of the student educational experience."[47] The methods externship teachers use to approve and place students with placements vary widely, as do the methods they choose to use to train, evaluate, and communicate with supervisors. For example, in some cities with several law schools, externship program directors have developed consortiums to collaborate on supervisor trainings and to streamline supervisor materials, while areas with only one law school have employed other methods to ensure that this part of the Standard is met.[48]

In addition, both the Standard and Interpretation 304-1 provide that "[w]hen appropriate, a school may use faculty members from other law schools to supervise

---

43. ABA Standards and Rules of Procedure for Approval of Law Schools 2022–2023, Standard 304(d).

44. *Id.* Externship programs have interpreted this language to include "J.D. Advantage" placements such as, for example, compliance offices, the legislature, and lobbying groups.

45. ABA Standards and Rules of Procedure for Approval of Law Schools 2022–2023, Standard 304(d)(i).

46. *Id.*

47. ABA Standards and Rules of Procedure for Approval of Law Schools 2022–2023, Standard 304(d)(ii).

48. To date, there are seven externship consortia. These include the Bay Area Consortium on Externships (BACE), the Capitol Area Consortium on Externships (CACE), the Georgia Association of Legal Externships (GALE), the Mid-Atlantic Area Consortium of Law School Externship

or assist in the supervision or review of a field placement program."[49] Not only does this provision contemplate the consortium model described above, but it also applies to full-time placements where students are located away from the law school and within a closer proximity to another law school. The methods of selecting, training, evaluating, and communicating with supervisors are discussed in detail in Chapter 4.

Third, the externship course must include "evaluation of each student's educational achievement by a faculty member."[50] The explicit requirement that the person doing so be a faculty member is a relatively new and important one. Student evaluation by a faculty member is discussed in more detail in Chapter 7.

Fourth, the externship course must have "sufficient control of the student experience to ensure that the requirements of the Standard are met. The law school must maintain records to document the steps taken to ensure compliance with the Standard, which shall include, but is not necessarily limited to, the written understandings described in Standard 304(d)(i)."[51] These records can include supervisor manuals, student manuals, written understandings, and other documents, which are discussed along with suggested document retention methods in Chapters 3, 4, 7, and 13.

3. Standard 307

In addition to Standard 304, externship programs with international placements must satisfy Standard 307, which governs placements outside of the United States. Standard 307 provides:

> Standard 307. STUDIES, ACTIVITIES, AND FIELD PLACEMENTS OUTSIDE THE UNITED STATES
>
> (a) A law school may grant credit for study outside the United States that meets the requirements of the Criteria adopted by the Council.
>
> (b) A law school may grant credit for field placements outside the United States that meet the requirements of Standard 304.
>
> (c) A law school may grant up to two-thirds of the credits required for the J.D. degree for study outside the United States provided the credits are obtained in a program sponsored by an ABA-approved law school.

Programs (MACE), the New England Externships (NExt), the New York Area Consortium of Externship Directors, Faculty, and Administrators (NYACE), the Ohio Legal Externships Alliance (OLEA), and the Southern California Externships (SoCalEx).

49. This language is identical in both Standard 304(d)(2)(ii) and Interpretation 304-1.

50. ABA Standards and Rules of Procedure for Approval of Law Schools 2022–2023, Standard 304(d)(iii). Chapter 4 of the ABA Standards governs requirements related to law school faculty. *Id.* at Chapter 4.

51. ABA Standards and Rules of Procedure for Approval of Law Schools 2022–2023, Standard 304(d)(iv).

Programs sponsored by an ABA-approved law school include programs held in accordance with the *Criteria for Approval of Foreign Summer and Intersession Programs Established by ABA-Approved Law Schools*; programs held in accordance with the *Criteria for Approval of Foreign Semester and Year-Long Study Abroad Programs Established by ABA-Approved Law Schools*; and field placements outside the United States.

(d) A law school may grant up to a maximum of one-third of the credits required for the J.D. degree for any combination of 1) student participation in study outside the United States under the *Criteria for Accepting Credit for Student Study at a Foreign Institution* and 2) credit for courses completed at a law school outside the United States in accordance with Standard 505(c).[52]

(e) Credit hours granted pursuant to subsections (b), (c) and (d) shall not in combination exceed two-thirds of the total credits required for the J.D. degree.

(f) A student participating in study outside the United States must have successfully completed sufficient prerequisites or must contemporaneously receive sufficient training to assure the quality of the student educational experience.

Standard 307 specifically includes international placements as courses for which a law school may grant credit provided the placement does not alone or in combination exceed two-thirds of the credits required for the J.D. degree and that the placement meets the requirements of Standard 304 discussed previously. As is required in Standard 304(f), Standard 307(f) explicitly requires the law school to ensure that the participating student has "successfully completed sufficient prerequisites or must contemporaneously receive sufficient training to assure the quality of the student educational experience."[53] In addition, international placements should comply with Standard 306 to the extent they meet the definition of a distance education course as discussed below. Chapter 6 provides a comprehensive discussion of international placements.

4. Distance Education and Standard 306

Historically, Standard 306 alone governed law school distance education courses. In August 2020, the Council reserved and deleted Standard 306 and instead defined "distance education course" in the "Definitions" section of the Standards. The 2021–22 Standards defined a "distance education course" as "one in which students are separated from the faculty member or each other for more than one-third of the

52. ABA Standards and Rules of Procedure for Approval of Law Schools 2022–2023, Standard 307 (emphasis in original).

53. *Id.*

instruction and the instruction involves the use of technology to support regular and substantive interaction among students and between the students and the faculty member, either synchronously or asynchronously."[54]

In August 2022, several changes to the definition of "distance education course" and Standard 311 were approved, and a new version of Standard 306 became effective.[55] The definition of distance education course now states "that a course will be a distance education course only if students are separated from *all faculty members* teaching the course" and no longer includes "the phrase 'or each other' so that the presence of one remote student in an otherwise in-person course will not 'convert' the course to a distance education course for all students enrolled in that course (including those students taking the course in-person)."[56]

In addition, Standard 306 has been reinstated and reflects the United States Department of Education's explanations of what "regular interaction" and "substantive interaction" must include in terms of distance education courses.[57] Standard 306 reads as follows:

> **Standard 306. DISTANCE EDUCATION**
>
> Distance Education law school courses for which credit is given towards the J.D. degree must provide regular and substantive interaction among students and between the students and faculty teaching the course. Distance education credits may not be counted towards the J.D. degree if they exceed the credit hour limitations in Standard 311(e).
>
> (a) Regular interaction between a student and a faculty member in a distance education course shall include:
>
> (1) providing the opportunity for substantive interactions with the student on a predictable and scheduled basis commensurate with the length of time and the amount of content in the course as defined by Standard 310(b);

---

54. ABA Standards, Definitions, https://www.americanbar.org/content/dam/aba/administrative/legal_education_and_admissions_to_the_bar/standards/2021-2022/2021-2022-aba-standards-and-rules-of-procedure.pdf (last visited September 30, 2022).

55. Standards and Rule Amendments Approved by the Council at its February 2022 Meeting, https://www.americanbar.org/content/dam/aba/administrative/legal_education_and_admissions_to_the_bar/council_reports_and_resolutions/feb22/22-feb-standards-rules-amendments.pdf. After these changes were adopted, the Managing Director of the ABA Section of Legal Education and Admissions to the Bar issued a Guidance Memo in November 2022 to answer questions about the circumstances in which an externship course might constitute a distance education course for purposes of the ABA Standards. ABA Section of Legal Education and Admissions to the Bar, Managing Director's Guidance Memo on Definition (7), Standards 304(a)(5), 304(d), and 310 (Nov. 2022), www.americanbar.org/content/dam/aba/administrative/22-nov-guidance-memo-field-placements.pdf (last visited Nov. 12, 2022).

56. *Id.* ABA Standards, Definitions, https://www.americanbar.org/content/dam/aba/administrative/legal_education_and_admissions_to_the_bar/standards/2022-2023/2022-2023-standards-and-rules-of-procedure.pdf (last visited September 30, 2022).

57. *Id.*

(2) monitoring the student's academic engagement and success; and

(3) ensuring that the faculty member is responsible for promptly and proactively engaging in substantive interaction with the student when needed on the basis of such monitoring, or upon request by the student.

(b) Substantive interaction in a distance education course requires engaging students in teaching, learning, and assessment, consistent with the content under discussion, and includes at least two of the following:

(1) providing direct instruction;

(2) assessing or providing feedback on a student's coursework;

(3) providing information or responding to questions about the content of a course; or

(4) facilitating a group discussion regarding the content of a course.

(c) Remote participation in a non-distance education course by a student as an accommodation provided under law (such as the Americans with Disabilities Act) or under exceptional circumstances shall not cause the course to count towards the distance education credit limits in Standard 311(e) for that student. The law school shall document all instances in which it permits a student's remote participation in a non-distance education course for which the credits will not be counted towards the credit hour limits in Standard 311(e).[58]

In addition to the new language of Standard 306, the Council added language to Standard 311(e) to ensure that schools know that there is a limit on the number of distance education credits a student may earn.[59] The new language of Standard 311(e) is as follows:

Standard 311. ACADEMIC PROGRAM AND ACADEMIC CALENDAR

(e) A law school that does not offer a J.D. degree via distance education under Standard 105(a)(12)(ii) may grant a student up to one-third of the credit hours required for the J.D. degree for distance education courses; up to 10 credit hours required for the J.D. degree for distance education courses of those credit hours may be granted during the first one-third of a student's program of legal education.[60]

58. *Id.*
59. *Id.*
60. *Id.*

Finally, law schools are prohibited from counting externship fieldwork toward the 64 credits of "regularly scheduled classroom sessions or direct faculty instruction" required under Standard 311(a) "as a condition for graduation."[61]

The November 2022 Managing Director's Memo provides guidance regarding when an externship course qualifies as a distance education course. Whether an externship course meets the "distance education course" definition, must comply with Standard 306, or can count toward the 64 credit hours of "regularly scheduled classroom sessions or direct faculty instruction" under Standard 311(a) depends on the structure of the externship course. A structure that combines faculty instruction delivered through a seminar or guided reflection and the student's fieldwork into a single course will qualify as a distance education course only if more than one-third of the faculty instruction involves the use of technology to support regular and substantive interaction among students. To calculate whether the one-third threshold has been met, the faculty member should look to see how many minutes of the course are attributed to the seminar or guided reflection and how many minutes are attributed to the student's fieldwork. If the faculty member delivers more than one-third of the total minutes of instruction away from all students using technology, then the course would qualify as a distance education course under the Standards.

If the externship program credits the externship seminar and the fieldwork hours separately, the result may be different. A separately-credited externship seminar could qualify as a distance education course if more than one-third of the externship seminar is delivered using technology to support the regular and substantive interaction among students. Likewise, the seminar could qualify as "regularly scheduled classroom sessions or direct faculty instruction" under Standard 311(a).[62] The separately credited fieldwork course, on the other hand, would not qualify as a distance education course or "regularly scheduled classroom sessions or direct faculty instruction" even if the student is remote from the site supervisor because the instruction is out-of-class student work and has been specifically excluded from Standard 311(a).

Fully remote externship courses such as a semester-in-practice, which places students away from the law school and the faculty member, and in which the faculty member uses technology to support the regular and substantive interaction among students, may qualify as distance education courses depending on the structure of the course as described above. If so, those courses will need to comply with Standard

61. ABA Standards and Rules of Procedure for Approval of Law Schools 2022–2023, Standard 311(a). Section 311(a) provides, "A law school shall require, as a condition for graduation, successful completion of a course of study of not fewer than 83 credit hours. At least 64 of these credit hours shall be in courses that require attendance in regularly scheduled classroom sessions or direct faculty instruction." *Id.* Interpretation 311-1(b)(1) provides that, "In calculating the 64 credit hours of regularly scheduled classroom sessions or direct faculty instruction for the purpose of Standard 311(a), the credit hours shall not include any other coursework, including, but not limited to: (1) Credit hours earned through field placements in compliance with Standard 304 and other study outside of the classroom in compliance with Standard 305." *Id.*

62. *Id.*

306. In addition, they must comply with Standard 304 as discussed previously. See Chapter 6 for a comprehensive discussion of the design and teaching methods used in distance externships.

5. The Accreditation Process and Site Visits

As part of the law school accreditation process, the Council requires a site evaluation visit and self-study at regular intervals:

> Site evaluations are held in accordance with Rule 4 of the ABA Rules of Procedure for Approval of Law Schools. Generally, site evaluations occur when a law school applies for provisional approval, in years two and four following provisional approval, when a law school applies for full approval, in the third year following full approval, and every tenth year thereafter.[63]

A site team appointed by the Managing Director's Office conducts the site evaluation visit.[64] The Procedures for 2022–2023 Site Evaluation Visits provide:

> In addition to the chair, the team will normally include a lawyer, judge or public member, a university administrator, and several persons who are members of the faculty or staff at other law schools. This composition is not required, and some teams may therefore not consist of this exact line-up of professionals.[65]

A law school must submit a completed self-study to each member of the site team at least eight weeks in advance of the site visit. Standard 204 governs the self-study process and specifically provides:

> Standard 204. SELF STUDY
>
> Before each site evaluation visit the law school shall prepare a self study comprising:
>
> (a) a completed site evaluation questionnaire, and
>
> (b) a law school assessment that includes
>
> (1) a statement of the law school's mission and of its educational objectives in support of that mission,
>
> (2) an evaluation of the educational quality of the law school's program of

63. Procedures for 2022–2023 Site Evaluation Visits, https://www.americanbar.org/content/dam/aba/administrative/legal_education_and_admissions_to_the_bar/Questionnaires/2022/22-23-procedures-for-site-visits.pdf (last visited Sept. 30, 2022).

64. *Id.*

65. *Id.* The Association of American Law Schools (AALS) conducts its site visit in tandem with the AALS reporter functioning as a member of the site team.

legal education, including a description of the program's strengths and weaknesses, and

(3) a description of the school's continuing efforts to improve the educational quality of its program.[66]

If a law school is scheduled for a site visit and self-study in the near future,[67] it is essential to review the applicable Site Evaluation Questionnaire—Site Report Template (referred to as the "SEQ-SRT Form") as soon as possible. A school's responses to the narrative portion of the Site Evaluation Questionnaire are now merged with the Site Report Template, which will become the final Site Report. A review of the SEQ-SRT Form applicable to the year before the scheduled site visit can give law schools and externship faculty a sense of the questions that will be asked and the information that will need to be provided. The Form routinely includes a series of questions about externship courses. A regular review of the current SEQ-SRT Form can also give externship teachers a sense of how the Council is applying the Standards in accreditation decisions.[68] In addition, if an externship course falls under Standard 307, there is an additional questionnaire that must be completed.[69]

While externship teachers need not submit additional materials along with their narrative answers to the SEQ-SRT Form, additional materials will need to be provided for on-site inspection. For 2022–2023, the required documents include:

> 32: Standard 304(a) and (d) [Field Placement Programs]. For any field placement program, provide a syllabus or other documents (including sample or form written understandings) demonstrating compliance with Standard 304. Any manuals or instructions developed for the training of site supervisors involved with field placement programs. A list of all current academic year field placement site supervisors with addresses, emails, and phone numbers.[70]

66. ABA Standards and Rules of Procedure for Approval of Law Schools 2022–2023, Chapter 2.

67. The schedule for site visits can be found here: https://www.americanbar.org/groups/ legal_education/accreditation/law_school_site_visits/future_site_visits/ (last visited March 20, 2022).

68. The current SEQ-SRT can be found here: https://www.americanbar.org/groups/legal_education/resources/site_evaluation_resources/ (last visited Sept. 30, 2022).

69. *Id.*

70. 2022–2023 Self Study Site Evaluation Questionnaire—Required Supplementary Materials, https://www.americanbar.org/content/dam/aba/administrative/legal_education_and_admissions_to_the_bar/Questionnaires/2022/22 23 seq onsitematerials.pdf (last visited Sept. 30, 2022).

Therefore, it is important to determine a method of maintaining records to demonstrate compliance with Standard 304, to facilitate administration, and to greatly simplify the process of responding to the SEQ-SRT Form.

6. Regional Accreditation

As stated previously in this Chapter, the ABA Council of the Section of Legal Education and Admissions to the Bar is recognized by the United States Department of Education as the national accrediting body of law schools. However, the "United States does not have a centralized authority exercising singular national control over postsecondary educational institutions."[71] Keep in mind that the purpose of accreditation is to:

1. assess the quality of academic programs at institutions of higher education;
2. create a culture of continuous improvement of academic quality at colleges and universities and stimulate a general raising of standards among educational institutions;
3. involve the faculty and staff comprehensively in institutional evaluation and planning; and
4. establish criteria for professional certification and licensure and for upgrading courses offering such preparation.[72]

To determine an institution of higher education's eligibility for "participation in a variety of federal programs, including HEA Title IV federal student aid programs, the federal government has come to rely on accrediting agencies to help ensure a level of acceptable quality across eligible educational programs and institutions of higher education."[73]

In addition to the ABA Standards, externship teachers should be aware of the standards and requirements of the applicable regional accreditor for their school and be prepared to participate in periodic accreditation visits and reviews similar to the ABA Site Visit process described above. There are seven regional accreditors.[74] These accreditors include the Higher Learning Commission (HLC),[75] the Middle States

---

71. Congressional Research Service, An Overview of Accreditation of Higher Education in the United States (October 16, 2020), https://crsreports.congress.gov/product/pdf/R/R43826 (last visited March 20, 2022).

72. *Id.*

73. *Id.*

74. https://wcetfrontiers.org/2019/11/22/regulatory-odyssey-final-accreditation-regulations/ (last visited March 20, 2022).

75. Historically, the HLC has focused on institutions in Arizona, Arkansas, Colorado, Illinois, Indiana, Iowa, Kansas, Michigan, Minnesota, Missouri, Nebraska, New Mexico, North Dakota, Ohio, Oklahoma, South Dakota, West Virginia, Wisconsin, and Wyoming.

Commission on Higher Education (MSCHE),[76] the New England Commission of Higher Education (NECHE),[77] the Northwest Commission on Colleges and Universities (NWCCU),[78] the Southern Association of Colleges and Schools Commission on Colleges (SACSCOC),[79] and the Western Association of Schools and Colleges Senior College and University Commission (WSCUC).[80] Several of these accreditors, while once limited to a regional scope, are now dropping their regional boundaries,[81] so it is important to confirm the "regional" accreditor responsible for one's institution. California has its own law school accreditation process and mandates standards that California-approved law schools must follow.[82] While California law schools approved by the ABA are deemed accredited by the State Bar's Committee of Bar Examiners, there are some California law schools that are accredited by the State Bar's Committee of Bar Examiners only and not the ABA.[83]

The regional accreditation process typically includes an academic program review similar to the ABA's SRQ-SRT and self-study process, which requires responses and supporting materials, and a formal site visit. As with the ABA process, externship teachers should be ready to contribute to the academic program review of the law school's program of study including experiential learning courses. This may mean coordinating with both the law school administrators, faculty, or staff preparing the academic program review and, to the extent applicable, those involved in preparing similar reports in other units of the university.

76. Historically, the MSCHE has focused on Delaware, the District of Columbia, Maryland, New Jersey, New York, Pennsylvania, Puerto Rico, and the Virgin Islands.

77. Historically, the NECHE has focused on Connecticut, Maine, Massachusetts, New Hampshire, Rhode Island, and Vermont.

78. Historically, the NWCCU has focused on Alaska, Idaho, Montana, Nevada, Oregon, Utah, and Washington.

79. Historically, the SACSCOC has focused on Alabama, Florida, Georgia, Kentucky, Louisiana, Mississippi, North Carolina, South Carolina, Tennessee, Texas, Virginia, and Latin America.

80. Historically, the WSCUC has focused on the Western United States.

81. https://www.highereddive.com/news/western-us-accreditor-to-break-rank-on-regional-boundaries/573052/; https://www.highereddive.com/news/another-regional-accreditor-drops-geographic-limits/581610/; https://www.careereducationreview.net/2021/03/higher-learning-commission-may-be-the-next-regional-accreditor-to-expand-service-area-higher-ed-dive/. Information about regional accreditors usually can be obtained from an institution's Provost office.

82. https://board.calbar.ca.gov/docs/agendaItem/Public/agendaitem1000027445.pdf; Karen Sloan, California Overhauls Its Law School Accreditation Rules, Emphasizing Diversity and Student Learning (May 19, 2021); https://www.calbar.ca.gov/About-Us/News/state-bar-board-of-trustees-approve-revamped-law-school-accreditation-rules; https://www.law.com/therecorder/2021/05/19/california-overhauls-its-law-school-accreditation-rules-emphasizing-diversity-and-student-learning/.

83. Rules of the State Bar, Title 4 Div. 2, https://www.calbar.ca.gov/Portals/0/documents/rules/Prior-Rules-Title4-Div2.pdf (last visited March 6, 2022); Cal. Rules of Ct., Rule 9.30, https://www.courts.ca.gov/cms/rules/index.cfm?title=nine&linkid=rule9_30 (last visited March 6, 2022).

Section II

Designing and Implementing Externship Programs and Courses

Chapter 3

Designing and Executing Externship Programs

This Chapter provides a guide for designing an externship program to meet the law school's array of pedagogical goals. In addition to such goals, program design should consider the law school's resources, student demographics, and geographic constraints. This Chapter focuses on externship design at the program level,[1] not the individual course level.[2] It offers guidelines for determining adequate externship resources (including class size, and the role of faculty, adjunct faculty, and administrators); program design choices (eligible students, site development, and credits); and program implementation choices (student counseling and externship applications). Program design also includes supervisor selection, training, and evaluation, which are covered in Chapter 4, and establishing and assessing program and course-level student learning outcomes, which are covered in Chapters 5 and 7. Special program design considerations for remote and international placements are addressed in Chapter 6.

Externship faculty need to be involved in all aspects of the program design process. While some parts of program design can be left to a non-faculty administrator, the critical function of externships in experiential education requires that a person with knowledge of pedagogical goals should be involved in most decisions. Design of the overall program, the seminar or guided reflection, and learning outcomes is a task for faculty who are knowledgeable about course design and can collaborate with other doctrinal and clinical faculty at their schools. Faculty involvement with student advising and site selection is also helpful if students are to grasp the ways in which each externship will develop their professional knowledge, skills, and values. Finally, faculty interaction with site supervisors helps clarify the learning outcomes

1. An externship program is defined in this book's Introduction as "the collection of courses within a school's clinical legal education program that provides students with the opportunity to integrate academic inquiry with work experiences in the law for academic credit." (citations omitted.)

2. An externship course, also defined in the Introduction, includes both the seminar or guided reflection and the work at the externship site.

that are to be achieved at the placement. This communication also helps supervisors understand the process of reflective learning that is the hallmark of clinical education.[3]

Most faculty will inherit a program that has evolved over time in response to resource availability, faculty input, the ABA Standards, and student demands. A few will be designing a program from the ground up. All faculty can improve their programs by familiarizing themselves with design components; this Chapter presents a comprehensive review that will be helpful to program design regardless of how long a program has existed.[4] It begins with a section that establishes guidelines for program capacity.

1. Guidelines for Externship Resources

Externship faculty have been slow to develop guidelines for externship resources, in part because of the variation in externship programs, the relative newness of experiential education in the law school curriculum, and the pressure to accommodate growing student demand. However, as this Chapter explains, establishing adequate resources is the first step in good program design.

Awareness of optimal numbers for seminar size, faculty positions per student served, adjunct faculty needed, and administrative staff required is necessary for the establishment and functioning of a quality program that meets the ABA Standards and is sustainable.[5] Budget pressures in a law school may lead to proposals to decrease funding for experiential education. Without guidelines or standards, it is difficult to determine how to reduce costs without affecting educational quality or to balance the costs of externships with other programs at the law school. Budget cuts that include reducing externship faculty and staff may diminish program quality, leading to student dissatisfaction, a negative ABA audit, or in worst cases, harm to students in the form of discrimination or harassment.[6]

Creating standards or guidelines with data to support them is critical given the unique resource needs of externship programs. Doctrinal faculty without experi-

---

3. *See* Nancy M. Maurer & Liz Ryan Cole, *Design, Teach and Manage: Ensuring Educational Integrity in Field Placement Programs*, 19 Clinical L. Rev. 115 (2012), for a thorough review of the multiple roles of faculty in externship programs; *see generally* Linda F. Smith, *Designing an Extern Program: Or As You Sow, So Shall You Reap*, 5 Clinical L. Rev. 527 (1999), for more on design; *see also* Mary Jo Eyster, *Designing and Teaching the Large Externship Clinic*, 5 Clinical L. Rev. 347 (1999).

4. The need to critically assess programs in an area of expansion and restricted budgets is discussed in Allison Korn & Laila L. Hlass, *Assessing the Experiential (R)Evolution*, 65 Vill. L. Rev. 713 (2020).

5. Other considerations such as resources for faculty travel to sites, financial assistance for student costs, or numbers of site supervisors, affect an externship program budget but are not discussed here.

6. Externship programs must have adequate resources to perform this monitoring function. *See* Philip C. Rothschild & Connor L. Rothschild, *The Unpaid Internship: Benefits, Drawbacks, and Legal*

ence in experiential education may underestimate the impact of externships on a student's selection of law school, identification of relevant doctrinal classes, development of career path, and success in obtaining post-graduation employment.[7] Clinical faculty have first-hand knowledge of the time needed to help students reflect on what they are learning, practice skills, gain knowledge, develop professional values, and deal with emergencies they encounter in their personal lives.

However, neither doctrinal nor in-house clinical faculty usually have direct experience of the faculty and staff resources necessary to evaluate and approve new externship sites and supervisors, provide ongoing guidance to site supervisors, select and mentor adjunct externship faculty, and help students find and obtain externships. Lacking knowledge of how the pedagogical goals and structure of externship programs differ from internships and employment, law school administrators may erroneously conclude that externship programs are similar to law school career offices.[8] Administrators and non-externship faculty may also be unaware of the extent to which externship programs ensure that students will get legal experience early in their law school careers, regardless of whether they are able to find paid employment in a competitive job market.[9]

Although externship programs vary in how they provide experiential education, sufficient data and experience exist that can provide guidelines to serve as a roadmap when setting up a program and a target when evaluating an existing one.[10] The tuition from externship courses is a significant part of the revenue of many law schools

---

Issues, 10 ADMINISTRATIVE ISSUES JOURNAL: EDUCATION, PRACTICE & RESEARCH 1–17, 6–7 (2020) (discussing unpaid internships at the undergraduate and graduate level and pointing out that universities should be proactive in protecting students from potentially dangerous situations, taking steps such as monitoring the intern's experience and ending partnerships with potentially dangerous or disreputable organizations, or risk liability if the student is harmed).

7. Externship faculty regularly hear from judges and supervisors who have either hired former externs or recommended to other employers that they hire the student, yet most externship programs lack the resources to accurately measure this impact, particularly in comparison to other law professor recommendations and the work of the career office.

8. In their survey of law schools following the 2008 recession, Cynthia Baker and Robert Lancaster found that externships played a larger role as paid employment opportunities declined. While both offices worked closely in most schools, there were tensions between helping students gain legal experience and worries that if externships were allowed in private firms, it would undermine the paid legal market. On the other hand, externship faculty worried about their increased workloads and the fact that they were being seen as career advisors rather than classroom professors. Cynthia Baker & Robert Lancaster, *Under Pressure: Rethinking Externships in a Bleak Economy*, 17 CLINICAL L. REV. 71, 77–83 (2010).

9. One example is Seattle University Law school, where just under half of the first-year class was enrolled in an externship during the Summer 2021 semester. The increase in externship enrollment during an economic downturn is a phenomenon that has been documented previously. *See id.* at 83–86.

10. *See id.* at 88–91 for a good review of the evolution of standards for externships that were codified in classroom texts and the ABA Standards, as well as the risk that under-resourced programs will not meet those standards.

and further underscores the need to ensure that externships are of high quality. The following discussion on seminar size and resources for faculty, adjunct faculty, and administrators provides guidelines for optimal program design.

a. Seminar Size

Law school class sizes typically range from a high of 90 students in first-year doctrinal classes, down to 16 to 18 students in second- and third-year seminars, eight students in clinics,[11] and as low as one individual student in independent study courses. Externship classes, like many other seminars, require a small class size for interactive discussion. Although externship seminars do not allow students to discuss confidential case information as they do in clinics, where students are members of the same law firm, externship seminars require students to discuss and reflect on the learning experiences at their sites. Other similarities to the in-house clinic include that students work on individual learning goals and gain practical legal experience in real-life settings.[12] Externship seminars also require students to evaluate themselves as future members of the profession and discuss the practical challenges that lawyers and judges face as a group.[13] This type of discussion requires a class small enough that students can feel comfortable in disclosing vulnerabilities to assess themselves and learn.

Finally, unlike most doctrinal classes that have a single exam at the end of the semester, externship seminars typically require faculty to review student timesheets, assessments, and goal setting documents; to meet with students and supervisors at the middle of the semester; and to read and respond to student reflections and papers on an ongoing basis. This continuous interaction is not only necessary for student learning; it is also critical to the externship faculty member's role in monitoring the student's experience at a site external to the law school. Externship faculty are also an important resource for students as they navigate the realities of law practice. Faculty may serve as the only link to the law school for those students doing full-time externships, especially those located in another state or country.

An externship seminar limit of 16 students is consistent with the requirements of individual student interaction and reflection in an experiential setting and is

---

11. *See* Robert Dinerstein, *Report of the Committee on the Future of the In-House Clinic*, 42 J. Legal Educ. 508, 552 (1992) (setting out the recommended student-teacher ratio for clinics).

12. An example of the theory and practical application behind this goal setting and assessment process is discussed in Elizabeth G. Ford, *Toward a Clinical Pedagogy of Externships*, 22 Clinical L. Rev. 113 (2015).

13. *See* Spring Miller, *The Generalist Externship Seminar: A Unique Curricular Opportunity to Teach About the Legal Profession*, 5 Clinical L. Rev. 279, 281 (2021) (discussing how externship seminars bridge the gap in legal education by educating students about the diverse institutions of the profession and its commitment to equal justice to further the students' own personal and professional development).

described by many educators as a necessity.[14] Mary Jo Eyster discusses the limits of a large class size, describing a Civil Practice Internship Seminar of 60 students in which she "could do little more than lecture" until she broke students into groups of 15 in order to teach skills and make the class more interactive.[15] Peter Jaszi mentions that externship seminars are typically taught with 18 students.[16] James H. Backman also suggests that the class limit for externship seminars should be between 12 and 18 students.[17] Setting a limit of 16 students in the externship seminar size is particularly important given that the challenges of over-large classes are both well-documented and supported by empirical evidence.[18]

With limits imposed on class size, many externship programs will include more than one seminar. While externship faculty often teach two seminars in one semester, and thus would teach and monitor 30 to 35 students at a time, faculty responsible for larger numbers face substantial challenges in responding to student reflections, conducting mid-semester site visits, and communicating with supervisors. Those faculty who provide faculty-guided reflection in lieu of a seminar also struggle if they are responsible for large numbers of students. In such circumstances, they must reduce the oversight of their students' experiences. Establishing a limit on the number of students one externship faculty member should teach or guide addresses the negative consequences of inadequate oversight on student learning. It also allows faculty to meet the additional duties under the ABA Standards to ensure that students are safe and not at risk, as well as to report discrimination and abuse.[19] Given all these reasons, those designing externship programs should resist designing or continuing programs with faculty-student ratios that are too high.

---

14. The CSALE 2019–20 survey showed that the majority (59%) of externship seminars fall in a range of 1 to 15 students, with an additional 12% with a class size of 16–20 students. Only 16% of classes are above 30 students, but 7% of those include classes with over 51 students. Robert R. Kuehn, Margaret Reuter & David A. Santacroce, Center for the Study of Applied Legal Education, 2019–20 Survey of Applied Legal Education 44 (2020) (hereinafter "CSALE Survey"), www.csale.org/#results (last visited March 6, 2022).

15. Eyster, *supra* note 3, at 269–70.

16. Peter Jaszi et al., *Experience as Text: The History of Externship Pedagogy at the Washington College of Law, American University*, 5 Clinical L. Rev. 403, 420–25 (1999).

17. James H. Backman, *Practical Examples for Establishing an Externship Program Available to Every Student*, 14 Clinical L. Rev. 1, 21 (2007).

18. Budget cuts brought on by the 2008 recession led to an increase in seminar size with challenges in monitoring student experience and participation. In their article, Cynthia Baker and Robert Lancaster warn of the danger of economic pressures leading to the diminution of a high-quality externship program and discuss the need to match growth with resources. Baker & Lancaster, *supra*, note 8, at 93.

19. Requirements under the ABA Standards are discussed in Chapter 2.

b. Resources for Faculty

Externship programs are usually directed by one faculty member[20] who teaches one or more of the seminars.[21] According to data from the Center for the Study of Applied Legal Education, slightly more than half of externship faculty are either on tenure tracks or presumptively renewable contracts,[22] and most of these positions come with the responsibilities of scholarship, teaching, and service. Producing scholarship is challenging for externship faculty who are on 12-month contracts and have significant administrative duties related to running the externship program, because they do not have summers off to research and write. However, providing externship faculty with research assistants, publication incentives, and support in the form of workshops and peer review provides many benefits. Scholarship gives an opportunity for the faculty member to develop their externship pedagogical approach, expand their expertise in a particular area of law, or connect externships with social justice and other professional objectives. Whatever the area of scholarship, faculty can use their research to assess and improve the educational experience of their externs. The process of researching also identifies new resources on law and lawyering that can be shared with students, site supervisors, and the externship community as a whole.[23]

While not all externship program directors teach the seminars, teaching at least one class helps connect them more directly to their students' externship experiences. Changes such as a shift to remote work, challenges to the rule of law, and increased focus on diversity, equity, and inclusion necessitate new teaching techniques and topics. Ensuring that externship faculty are not overwhelmed by administrative duties allows them to devote adequate resources to teaching the externship seminar and guiding reflection. They in turn share this teaching with the site supervisors through continuing legal education, site approval meetings, mid-semester assessments, and often, continuing legal education provided to the broader legal community on emerging issues.[24]

---

20. At two-thirds of law schools, one individual has oversight responsibility for all externship courses, an increase from 59% in 2016–17, 55% in 2013–14, and 54% in 2010–11. However, 89% of the directors responsible for externship courses have other responsibilities in addition to their externship teaching. CSALE SURVEY, *supra* note 14, at 39–40.

21. The 2019–20 CSALE data show 85% of those who teach an externship course either head up the school's overall externship program or direct a distinct externship course, and 72% of externship instructors teach both the classroom and fieldwork/casework components. *Id.* at 39.

22. Fifty-one percent of directors in the 2019–20 survey were either tenured, tenure track, clinical tenured, clinical tenure track, or on long-term presumptively renewable contracts. The rest were on a short-term contract or administrative position with or without a faculty title. *Id.* at 41.

23. *See* Harriet N. Katz, *The Past and Future of Externship Scholarship*, 23 CLINICAL L. REV. 397–428 (2016), for a discussion of the evolution of externship scholarship. A bibliography of selected externship resources is included after the Appendix.

24. The CSALE 2019–20 survey shows that 75% of externship programs conduct site visits at their externship sites, and 85% of programs have individual discussions with the supervisor. CSALE SURVEY, *supra* note 14, at 29.

Externship faculty who engage in service to the individual law school and the greater community of legal educators contribute greatly to both. Externship faculty possess knowledge about what students experience in the legal community that is of value to all their colleagues—doctrinal, clinical, and legal writing included. Their knowledge of current practice conditions is relevant to law school curriculum design and assessment, as well as professional development and social justice programming. Because externship programs often have one or only a small number of faculty, those faculty may spend a greater percentage of their time in this law school and community service than their colleagues.

The professional development of externship faculty requires the same resources for conferences, travel, bar dues, professional association memberships, and supplies as other faculty. Ensuring resources for this kind of professional development is important, since most law schools have a small number of externship program faculty responsible for the design and implementation of the whole program. Communicating and collaborating with peers through national organizations like the Association of American Law Schools (AALS) Clinical Section, the Clinical Legal Education Association (CLEA), and the Society of American Law Teachers (SALT) provides resources and avoids the need for externship faculty to reinvent the wheel.[25] International clinical education organizations such as the Global Alliance for Justice Education (GAJE) are also important sources of innovation and a comparative perspective.[26] Many programs function with the help of adjunct faculty, but they will likely have limited time to engage in these activities because of their other responsibilities.

In addition to teaching, externship faculty perform administrative duties in policy development, student counseling, site selection, site approval, site supervisor training, and the selection and mentoring of adjunct faculty if used in the program. While these duties may vary in volume and scope, they are governed specifically by the ABA Standards that set guidelines to ensure that students receive a quality legal education.[27] Assuming that one person is responsible for adequately monitoring the student's offsite educational experience, a program that has over 40 students doing externships in any one semester will need to plan for a second person to share those responsibilities.[28] Each program will vary in its design, and not all faculty will have

25. *See* Top Ten Resources for New Externship Clinicians on LEXTERNWEB, at https://www.dropbox.com/s/ho0o32n57l8cyju/Top%20Ten%20Resources%20for%20New%20Externship%20Clinician%20%2811-20-19%29.pdf?dl=0.

26. *Id.*

27. The ABA Standards, which provide guidance on the seminar, the site placement, the site supervisors, and the need for reflection and multiple opportunities for performance, are discussed in Chapter 2.

28. The median number of students that externship instructors teach or oversee in all their externship courses during the academic year (excluding any summer term) is 25 students, but 14% percent of instructors teach or oversee 100 or more students. CSALE SURVEY, *supra* note 14, at 39–40.

scholarship and service obligations, but all externship faculty members are responsible for ensuring the educational experience of each of their students.

c. Adjunct Faculty

The number of programs employing adjunct faculty is large and growing, and adjuncts serve an important role in the expansion of experiential education.[29] Since all externship programs provide a seminar or guided reflection that accompanies a student's field experience, one design question that arises is who should teach the seminar or provide feedback on student reflections. For some programs, the externship director fulfills the role of faculty in one or more seminars, and in others, the director may or may not teach but provides guidance to faculty or adjunct faculty who teach the seminar.[30]

Advantages of hiring adjunct faculty are that they allow the program to offer more specialized instruction in courses focused on specific practice areas and that they reduce the teaching burden on the externship program director. Adjunct faculty usually teach in addition to continuing their practice, and they can bring in perspectives as diverse practitioners (*e.g.*, as women, LGBTQ, persons of color) or as lawyers working in diverse areas of practice (*e.g.*, cybersecurity, criminal justice reform, legislation). Hiring adjuncts can help keep the seminar size limited and can help expand or contract a program depending on student demand.

At the same time, hiring, evaluating, guiding, and training adjunct faculty will require resources to ensure that they understand and use clinical teaching methods such as reflection and that they provide educational programming consistent with the law school and externship program learning outcomes.[31] Unlike full-time faculty who regularly attend workshops and conferences as part of their employment, adjunct faculty may not have the time to do more than absorb an orientation to externship pedagogy.[32] They do not usually take on the responsibilities of site visits,

29. *See* Karen A. Jordan, *Enhancing Externships to Meet Expectations for Experiential Education*, 23 Clinical L. Rev. 339 (2016), for a discussion on the use of adjunct faculty in hybrid externship programs; *see also* James H. Backman, *Practical Examples for Establishing an Externship Program Available to Every Student*, 14 Clinical L. Rev. 1, 23 (2007).

30. Eighty-five percent of those who teach in a field placement course either head up the school's overall field placement program or direct a distinct field placement course(s). CSALE Survey, *supra* note 14, at 39.

31. *See* Karen Tokarz, *A Manual for Law Schools on Adjunct Faculty*, 76 Wash. Univ. L. Rev. 293 (1998), for a good example of written guidance for adjuncts and teaching in law schools.

32. *See* Wallace J. Mlyniec, *Where to Begin? Training New Teachers in the Art of Clinical Pedagogy*, 18 Clinical L. Rev. 505 (2012), for an overview of the training and conferences for clinical teachers; *see also* Colleen F. Shanahan & Emily A. Benfer, *Adaptive Clinical Teaching*, 19 Clinical L. Rev. 517, 530–37 (2013), for a description of "adaptive clinical teaching," a structured method of guided analysis and reflection that applies to any clinical teaching situation, allowing a clinician to make her teaching choices based on as much knowledge and with as much intentionality as possible.

student placement, and counseling.[33] Many will stay for the enjoyment of working with students, but if low pay[34] leads to adjunct faculty turnover, full-time externship faculty may need to expend significant resources to find them, hire them, and develop their skills.[35]

d. Administrators

Most programs will need an administrator in addition to a faculty member. Administrators will engage in a variety of tasks depending on the program. They can help act as a liaison with site supervisors, schedule meetings, organize travel for site visits, find out which sites are accepting students, send and keep track of applications, register students, assist with technology for online classes, and gather data for program assessment and ABA compliance.[36] Administrators can also assist in administering an externship budget for site visits and providing support for students who need help with transportation, parking, and other expenses connected to their externships. Gathering data on the impact of strong externship programs, from admissions before law school, to student engagement in law school,[37] and job placement after graduation[38] is critical to both program design and implementation. Externship faculty can work with administrators to ensure that data is gathered and analyzed in a process of regular assessment and implementation of program improvements.

33. The CSALE 2019–20 report shows only 5 to 6 % of schools involve adjuncts in these tasks. CSALE Survey, *supra* note 14, at 42.

34. Adjunct salaries tend to be low because the bulk of law school tuition is for the externship site credits, and most externship seminars are from 1 to 2 credits. According to the 2019–20 CSALE report, 57% of courses are 1 credit, 35% of courses are 2 credits, and only 11% are 3 or more credits. *Id.* at 44.

35. James Backman describes the training needed for adjuncts to be used successfully in an externship program. James H. Backman, *Practical Examples for Establishing an Externship Program Available to Every Student*, 14 Clinical L. Rev. 1, 23 (2007).

36. The CSALE 2019–20 report shows that administrative assistants handle placement of students and host office and site supervisor relations but not reflection, grading, or assessment. These roles are also handled by career service or pro bono staff, adjuncts, or others within the law school. CSALE Survey, *supra* note 14, at 42.

37. According to the CSALE 2019–20 survey, 37% of schools reported an increased demand for externships, and 46% reported that the demand remained constant; only 7% reported a decrease. "The most common reasons given for the increase were: students believe field placement courses improve marketability (at 80% of the schools); students believe field placements improve skills (70%); new ABA 6-credit experiential requirement (50%); increased interest in substantive areas of practice within field placements offered (44%); and increased support and promotion by law school (43%)." *Id.* at 17.

38. Robert R. Kuehn, *Measuring Clinical Legal Education's Employment Outcomes*, 2015 Wis. L. Rev. 645 (2015); *see also* Maxwell D. Rosenthal, *The Bridge: How to Launch Your Career Through a Legal Internship* (LexisNexis2015).

2. Program Design Choices

This section describes how to design a program considering the following factors: students served; site development; and number of hours and credits at the field placement.

a. Students Served

With the requirement of six credits of experiential education for all graduates[39] and the growing appreciation of the value of externships,[40] designers of a program should aim to provide these opportunities to as many students as possible.[41] Some law schools guarantee externships for all students.[42] Most law schools offer externships to full-time law students, who typically complete their degrees in two to three years, as well as to part-time students, who usually need four years or more to finish. Students who are completing either a post-JD degree such as a Master of Laws (LLM) or a non-JD degree such as a Master of Legal Studies (MLS) also benefit from externships tailored to their specific needs. Each school will design its program differently; choices that should be considered for each group are covered here. As program design also requires consideration of future possibilities, this section anticipates a gradual expansion in externships based on the recent legal education history of increasing experiential learning.

Many externship programs have evolved over time, often changing in response to resources available or faculty and administrator experience. When considering design, directors should keep in mind that a flexible program helps accommodate all students and minimizes the need for administrative processes to overcome barriers that come with more rules. In determining which rules to adopt, directors should examine the reason for the rule and check for supporting data. For instance, many schools limit externships to students above a particular class rank or Grade Point Average (GPA)[43] based on a belief that students need to enroll in doctrinal classes

---

39. ABA Standards are discussed in Chapter 2.

40. The ABA recommends experiential education as the only effective way to really apply knowledge gained in law school. Max Rosenthal, *The Importance of Gaining Practical Legal Skills*, STUDENT LAWYER (Apr. 1, 2016), https://abaforlawstudents.com/2016/04/01/the-importance-of-gaining-practical-legal-skills/.

41. The 2019–20 CSALE survey data show the median student participation in externships to be 50%, similar to the 2016–17 and 2013–14 surveys. CSALE SURVEY, *supra* note 14, at 14.

42. According to the CSALE 2019–20 report, 38% of schools have a written guarantee promising any J.D. student enrollment in a clinic or field placement course. Among these schools, 18% guarantee participation in a clinic, 4% in a field placement course, and 78% in a law clinic or field placement course. This is a large increase from the 2016–17 survey, when only 13% of schools guaranteed a law clinic or field placement course. *Id.* at 12.

43. *See* Lewis & Clark Law School Externship Program Guide, LEWIS & CLARK L. SCH. (Feb. 2017), for one example of a school with a comprehensive externship guide and specific GPA requirements.

rather than experiential opportunities in order to pass the bar.[44] However, the data do not demonstrate that time spent in externships or clinics has any negative effect on bar passage rates.[45] Such decisions are often made at the decanal or general faculty level, but externship faculty involved in design should inquire into the reasons and history behind the limits.

On the other hand, student knowledge of the practice of law, understanding of the application of doctrinal courses, and development of connections and skill level critical to future employment are enhanced through experiential learning.[46] Preventing students with lower GPAs from accessing these benefits may be counterproductive. Students are aware of the advantages of externships and often select schools based on the quality of their experiential education programs and the breadth of opportunities.[47] A good program design will define who can participate as broadly as possible.[48]

1) Full-Time JD[49]

Full-time JD students generally can enroll in externships starting the summer after their first year.[50] Most schools also allow students to do part-time or full-time (defined by the Center for the Study of Applied Legal Education as 10 academic credits or more per semester)[51] externships in the fall and spring of both the second and third year of law school. For the reasons described above, most law schools encourage or even require their full-time students to participate in at least one externship before they graduate.

---

44. Scott Johns, *A Statistical Exploration: Analyzing the Relationship (If Any) between Externship Participation and Bar Exam Scores*, 42 Okla. City U. L. Rev. 281 (2018).

45. Johns, *supra* note 44; Robert R. Kuehn & David R. Moss, A *Study of the Relationship Between Law School Coursework and Bar Exam Outcomes,* 68 J. Legal Educ. 624 (2019).

46. Kuehn, *supra* note 38; *see also* Rosenthal, *supra* note 38.

47. If faculty are seeking to remove GPA or class rank limits as part of program design, working with student academic support and career placement offices can address perceptions that time away from the classroom may negatively impact student learning outcomes.

48. *See* CSALE Survey, *supra* note 14, at 11 (for the results of a survey on which students are permitted to enroll in externships, specifically question 5j).

49. A full-time law student is one who will generally complete a full course of study, defined by the ABA Standard 311(a) and (b) as not fewer than 83 credit hours, in a period of time ranging between 24 and 36 months. Standard 311(c) sets the upper limit per semester for full-time students as no more than 20% of the total credits required to graduate. ABA Standards and Rules of Procedure for Approval of Law Schools 2022–2023, Standard 311. The complete ABA Standards are available at https://www.americanbar.org/content/dam/aba/administrative/legal_education_and_admissions_to_the_bar/standards/2022-2023/2022-2023-standards-and-rules-of-procedure.pdf.

50. *See* CSALE Survey, *supra* note 14, at 49 (reporting that 57% of externship courses are offered during the summer term).

51. *Id.* at 10.

2) *Part-Time JD*[52]

Many part-time or evening students forgo externship opportunities out of a belief that their schedules do not permit them to participate. The majority of schools allow part-time students to enroll, even though the numbers remain small compared to full-time students.[53] Given the benefits of externships in professional formation and in knowledge, skills, and values development, permitting and encouraging participation in experiential learning for part-time students is a recommended feature of program design.[54] As discussed above, program designers will need to determine whether externships should be available for all students regardless of class rank.[55] Ways to increase part-time student enrollment in externships are through student counseling, allowance of reduced credits, flexible hours, remote work, site cultivation, and supervisor preparation.

Part-time students can often make time for externships and clinics through advanced planning. Part-time students take fewer courses than full-time students and need to be aware of the law school's policy as to when they can first participate in the externship program. Some law schools do not allow part-time students to take externships until after the students have completed their second part-time year, because students may be at a disadvantage without having completed all courses required of full-time first-year students, especially if site supervisors expect students to have that foundational knowledge. Other law schools that allow part-time students to take externships after their first part-time year do so because externships may improve their ability to incorporate practical experience into their doctrinal classes, help them identify future career paths, and increase their motivation to move from their current employment into the practice of law. The ABA Standards leave the decision to the discretion of the school, stating only that each student in an externship course "shall have successfully completed sufficient prerequisites or shall receive sufficient contemporaneous training to assure the quality of the student educational experience."[56]

Part-time students typically have busy schedules and decreased time on campus, so outreach is crucial for those programs wishing to encourage them to participate.

---

52. A part-time student, often referred to as an evening student, is one who will complete a full course of study in no later than 84 months except in extraordinary circumstances. *See* ABA STANDARDS AND RULES OF PROCEDURE FOR APPROVAL OF LAW SCHOOLS 2022–2023, STANDARD 311(b).

53. *See* CSALE SURVEY, *supra* note 14, at 44 (showing that 89%, up from 78% in the 2016–17 survey, of the schools that have part-time students allowed them to enroll in externships).

54. *See* David Chavkin, *Clinic Under the Stars: Giving Part-Time Students Their Due*, 13 CLINICAL L. REV. 719 (2007), for more on ways to design experiential learning opportunities that are accessible to part-time students.

55. This recommendation does not include students on probation; those whose low GPA puts them at risk of being dropped from law school should not plan to do an externship in an upcoming semester given the possibility they may not be enrolled as students.

56. ABA STANDARDS AND RULES OF PROCEDURE FOR APPROVAL OF LAW SCHOOLS 2022–2023, STANDARD 304(f).

Many students who are working full-time may be able to work a flexible schedule or use vacation leave to pursue externships during regular work hours. Others will have fewer options and will wish to do their externships outside the regular workday at night and on weekends.

One lasting impact of the 2020 coronavirus pandemic is the increased availability of remote externships and flexible work schedules. The experience of working remotely for a year or more resulted in both law firms and law schools adopting a range of options that allowed some staff and students to continue working remotely. It also increased the familiarity of most lawyers and judges with the technology of video conferences and other remote communication, expanding choices for all students and for part-time students in particular. See Chapter 6 for more on remote externships; the techniques in that chapter can be employed as a means of increasing opportunities for full and part-time students.

Externship faculty should be cautious and consider a number of factors when determining which sites and which students might gain substantial experience in a remote environment.[57] For example, some sites, such as courts, may always require some in-person participation. For those part-time students who do not have flexibility in their schedule when they begin law school and who may plan to eventually reduce their current employment or quit altogether to complete their final semester or two of law school, externships may be a way to gain an important law school in-person experience. Placements such as a judicial externship can form an important part of this final training.

Faculty should also encourage externship site supervisors to be flexible wherever possible, so that part-time students can be offered the same kind of experiential learning opportunities as their full-time colleagues. While most students benefit from spending more time at the site, routinely asking all sites whether they will accommodate part-time students can ensure that the opportunities are there when needed. Other ways to accommodate student schedules are to develop sites that operate during the evening and on weekends. When discussing part-time student participation with site supervisors, it can be helpful to point out that many sites greatly appreciate the prior career experience, excellent planning skills, and efficient work habits that most part-time students have already developed.

3) Post-JD Degrees: Master of Laws (LLM)

Many law schools have expanded LLM programs to increase revenue and provide specialization for those who have already earned a JD. Such programs attract a variety of students from within and outside of the United States. The ABA Standards

57. For a checklist of factors to consider when evaluating a remote placement, *see* the recording and materials of the March 15, 2021, call of the International and Semester Away Subcommittee available on LexternWeb at https://www.dropbox.com/sh/rahpws227zylu4w/ AACqaQY2dTODrFy3RqkbNU-AQa?dl=0.

state that a law school may not offer a degree program other than its JD degree program unless: "the degree program will not interfere with the ability of the law school to operate in compliance with the Standards and to carry out its program of legal education."[58]

LLM student needs in externships will vary.[59] When designing such programs, directors should keep in mind that LLM program externships are not covered by the ABA Standards and may be run by another department within the law school. Nonetheless, where resources permit, considering the needs of LLM students in program design can avoid confusion within the legal community and unnecessary duplication of effort within the academic institution. This may be true for many aspects of program design discussed in this section, including student counseling, creation of the seminar or other structured tutorials, and site development.

Externships for LLM students can be fundamental in exposing them to specialized practice.[60] LLM students also benefit from the goal setting and reflective process present in the externship seminar or accompanying tutorial even if, as practicing lawyers, they do not need the more basic law practice information. Using a similar process for LLM site development and site visits ensures smooth communication to site supervisors. Of course, such expansion takes additional resources in order to be successful.[61]

Foreign-trained LLM students may have language challenges[62] and need different cross-cultural orientation from their U.S.-educated counterparts. When considering placements, faculty should keep in mind the degree to which high levels of written English are required. Some sites also require U.S. citizenship or legal permanent residence.[63] Even if the externships are not paid, foreign-trained students will need to be aware of any restrictions on their own immigration status and may have to get Curricular Practical Training (CPT) authorization.[64] In designing or collaborating with others to create LLM externships, coordination with the LLM program director and legal writing faculty is key. Law schools can provide resources to improve

---

58. ABA Standards and Rules of Procedure for Approval of Law Schools 2022–2023, Standard 313(c).

59. *See Programs by School*, A.B.A. https://www.americanbar.org/groups/legal_education/resources/llm-degrees_post_j_d_non_j_d/programs_by_school/ (last visited Aug. 17, 2021), for a list of LLM and Post JD programs by school.

60. Some sites, such as in-house counsel where the generalized practice can be challenging for JD students, may actually prefer LLM students, particularly those who have a specialization relevant to the company, such as finance, technology, labor law, or immigration law.

61. For example, UCLA, USC, NYU, Loyola LA and Seattle University all offer externship opportunities for LLM Students.

62. *See About the TOEFL iBT Test*, ETS TOEFL https://www.ets.org/toefl/ibt/about/ (last visited Aug. 17, 2021), for more on the Test of English as a Foreign Language (TOEFL).

63. Most federal agencies require lawful permanent residence status, and many require externs to be U.S. citizens.

64. *See Curricular Practical Training (CPT) for F-1 Students*, Mich. Int'l Center https://www.internationalcenter.umich.edu/students/f1-students/cpt, for an example of the resources needed.

students' written and oral English and also help students capitalize on their fluency in non-English languages.[65]

4) Master of Legal Studies (MLS) and Other Non-JD Programs[66]

These are programs offered to students who are looking for legal training for jobs that do not require a law degree but do require some legal knowledge. They often involve regulatory compliance.[67] Non-JD students often participate in a set curriculum of regular law school courses and benefit from gaining practical experience as part of their academic training.[68] Faculty designing externships for these students should be aware that differences in learning goals and legal knowledge will mean some placements are not appropriate.[69] While these programs are still developing, a best practices approach suggests that a pedagogical framework, adequate resources, and ongoing assessment are all important.

b. Site Development

Like most aspects of program design, the development of externship sites depends on a number of variables and the resources available.[70] Many schools have several rationales for the continuous development of new sites: providing opportunities in emerging areas of law, responding to requests for assistance from the legal community,[71] and encouraging students to generate opportunities tailored to their

65. The Director of the LLM Externship Program at Georgetown Law School reports that, in many cases, sites in Washington D.C. *prefer* foreign-trained externs.

66. Academic master's degrees for nonlawyers include the following programs: J.M. Juris Master; M.J. Master of Jurisprudence; M.S. Master of Science or Master of Studies; M.P.S. Master of Professional Studies; and M.L.S. Master of Legal Studies. Research and academic-based doctorate level degrees, such as J.S.D. (Doctor of Jurisprudence), S.J.D. (Doctor of Judicial Science), and D.C.L. (Doctor of Comparative Law) are less likely to include experiential education such as externships but are not precluded from doing so as long as they comply with ABA Standard 313(c) discussed above. *See Post-J.D. and Non-J.D.*, A.B.A., https://www.americanbar.org/groups/legal_education/resources/llm-degrees_ post_ j_d _non _j_d/ programs_by_school/.

67. *See Post-J.D. and Non-J.D.*, A.B.A., https://www.americanbar.org/groups/legal_education/resources/llm-degrees_post_j_d_non_j_d/ (last visited Aug. 17, 2021), for more on the types of programs that can be offered.

68. MLS programs are also prohibited from interfering with the ability of the law school to comply with the Standards and carry out its JD programs. ABA STANDARDS AND RULES OF PROCEDURE FOR APPROVAL OF LAW SCHOOLS 2022–2023, STANDARD 313(c).

69. For instance, sites requiring the student to operate independently in court will generally not accept non-JD students due to the courts' student practice rules.

70. As described above, externship directors are often short of resources. The CSALE data on the major challenges they face lists the following top four: other demands on faculty's time, insufficient administrative/secretarial support, insufficient faculty, number of clinical faculty, and insufficient faculty status. CSALE SURVEY, *supra* note 14, at 11.

71. According to the CSALE 2019–20 Report, "(t)wo hundred thirty field placement courses estimated their students provided a total of over 1,600,000 hours of free legal services during the 2018–19 academic year to nonprofit organizations, governmental offices, and judicial chambers, or almost 7,000 hours per field placement course." *Id.* at 51.

own unique career interests. Other schools have a limited number of sites to ensure quality and consistency from year to year. This section provides an overview of the options, including type, number, and location. It also gives suggestions for how to decide among them when designing a program.

Whether creating a program from the ground up, or modifying an existing one, externship program directors should consider working with the law school's career center, pro bono coordinator, and other doctrinal and clinical faculty to gather information on student employment and to benefit from faculty connections in the legal community. Collaboration with all these individuals at the law school can also provide information when deciding which sites to approve or develop.[72] Development and career offices will have contacts with law school alumni; faculty will know lawyers working in their fields of research. Designing externship opportunities to expand into areas of practice not offered by the law school's clinics can also be a useful strategy. Consideration of a school's ranking and location may help determine whether to focus on a small or large number of placements,[73] and on local or remote geographic areas. For instance, students at a school with high rankings may have little difficulty being selected as externs in comparison to their lower-ranked peers; diversity and quantity of sites may help address this problem. Similarly, schools that are not near large metropolitan areas may want to expand their placements to give students a broader range of legal practice options.

1) Types and Number of Placements

One of the first considerations in selecting externship sites may be what type of placements to approve. The selection of sites, whether done by a faculty member as part of a deliberate plan, or done by students pursuing their individual career trajectories, must be consistent with both the law school's and the student's learning goals.[74]

Externship programs have developed placements at a range of sites including the following: courts and administrative tribunals; legal services organizations and other nonprofits; prosecuting attorneys and public defenders; private law firms; corporations; and federal, state, and local government agencies, including legislative bodies.[75] All law schools offer litigation or dispute resolution focused externships, and most also offer transactional, regulatory, and legislative or policy

---

72. *See* Sarah E. Ricks & Susan C. Wawrose, *Comment: Survey of Cooperation Among Clinical, ProBono, Externship, and Legal Writing Faculty*, 4 J. Ass'n. L. Writing Directors 56 (2007), for a brief summary of the benefits and potential obstacles to collaboration.

73. The CSALE 2019–20 survey found that 68% of programs have under 30 sites (with 23% having five or fewer during terms other than summer), 24% of programs place students in over 30 separate offices, and only 8% utilize over 60 placement offices. CSALE Survey, *supra* note 14, at 48.

74. For more on learning outcomes, *see* Chapter 5.

75. CSALE Survey, *supra* note 14, at 10.

options.[76] Externship placements are often broken down by practice area so that students can gain more focused experience.[77] The ideal design will have sites that can accommodate the skill and experience level of students ranging from those who have just finished their first year all the way to those who are able to appear in court to represent clients under the supervision of a licensed attorney.[78]

In determining how many placements to include in a program, faculty must weigh the advantages and disadvantages of a constant group of placements versus a continually growing number. Where the group of placements is stable, faculty can become familiar with the organization and law practice, cultivate relationships with supervisors, and provide training through regular Continuing Legal Education (CLE) programming. A stable group of sites can also reduce staff and faculty time needed for additional site approval and mid-semester site visits. On the other hand, a set group of placements may narrowly restrict student skill acquisition and career development. Smaller numbers of sites may miss new and developing areas of law and may mean that externships rarely lead to jobs at the placements due to the limited capacity of a smaller group of placements to hire regularly.

A constantly growing group of placements is generally only possible as a design option when resources are adequate. Advantages and disadvantages are the opposite of those described above. While there are greater opportunities for adding sites in emerging areas of law and for tailoring externship experiences to specific student career goals, the time needed to acquire and maintain a large database of sites can be considerable.[79] Keeping track of whether all sites are actively taking student applications can also require staff time. If not done, students may waste effort on cover letters and applications, missing out on available opportunities in the meantime.[80] One other disadvantage of a large number of sites is the pressure to constantly fill them even when student demand may fluctuate. Informing sites up front of factors like shrinking student enrollment, trends in semesters with smaller class sizes, the

76. *Id.*

77. One example is the externship database from Seattle University that has over 700 sites divided into 28 different folders: Administrative Law Judges; Courts of Appeals; Federal District Court; Federal Court of Appeals; Superior Court; Supreme Court; Bankruptcy Law; Civil Rights/Human Rights; Elder Law/Estate Planning; Family Law/Child Advocacy; Criminal Defense; Criminal Prosecution; Education; Environmental Law/Land Use; Housing/Real Estate; Employment and Labor Law; Consumer/Financial Regulation; In-House Counsel; Intellectual Property; Health Law; Immigration Law; Indian Law; Mediation/Dispute Resolution; Military; Municipal Law; Policy: Administrative and Legislative; Poverty Law; and Tax Law.

78. *See Georgetown Law Library Clinical Research Guide*, Geo. L. Libr., http://guides.ll.georgetown.edu/c.php?g=271042&p=2020140 (last visited Aug. 17, 2021), for a good list of articles on student practice rules.

79. The technology for designing databases changes quickly and serves specific needs in each law school. For current options, it is best to reach out through the Lextern listserv or check LexternWeb for resources at https://www.lexternweb.org.

80. One option is to regularly expunge sites from a program if they have not accepted students in a number of years.

availability of other experiential opportunities, and a greater diversification of student interests can be done when the site is approved. It will help ensure that sites do not take the lack of applications as a sign of low student interest, prior negative experience of a particular student, or failure of the externship program to inform students of available opportunities.

In deciding which approach best fits a school, directors should keep in mind that some schools use a hybrid approach of some set placements and some new, and others allow students to apply on their own. The schools then use a set list of criteria and require that faculty approve the placement before the extern can start. No matter which design is adopted, applying the principles of establishing good supervisor communication and setting formal goals can ensure that the student learning outcomes will be met at each approved site. Whether designing a large and expanding list or a small and restricted set of sites, directors should be aware that supervisor turnover can be high and remember to plan for orientation and regular education of new supervisors in all sites.

Another consideration when developing sites is whether to prioritize social justice[81] and access to justice needs within the public interest community. Some externship programs do not allow for-profit sites, believing that positions at for-profit sites do not align with the school's public service mission.[82] Other schools permit some positions at for-profit sites so that students can develop a unique skill set or experience.[83] One example of this is in-house counsel positions, which rarely hire new

---

81. A presentation from the Externships 9 Conference at the University of Georgia Law School on March 9, 2018 describes social justice motivations for choosing sites that allow students to work with real clients and develop an understanding of the implications of law practice. *Social Responsibility and Justice: Fostering the Ethos in All Students*, Univ. Ga. Sch. of L., https://digitalcommons.law.uga.edu/xconf/2018/Schedule/15/ (last visited Aug. 17, 2021); *see also* Alexi Freeman, *Teaching for Change: How the Legal Academy Can Prepare the Next Generation of Social Justice Movement Lawyers*, 59 How. L.J. 99 (2015). *See Social Responsibility and Justice: Fostering the Ethos in All Students*, Univ. Ga. Sch. of L., https://www.dropbox.com/s/rik82mtsz0joag3/Externship%20Bibliography-Alpha%20by%20Last%20Name_Organization.docx.pdf?dl=0 (last visited Aug. 17, 2021), for a growing list of articles on the importance of social justice values in externships and clinics in the LexternWeb bibliography.

82. For guidelines on when students can extern without pay at for-profit firms without violating the Fair Labor Standards Act, see Niki Kuckes, *Designing Law School Externships That Comply with the FLSA*, 21 Clinical L. Rev. 79 (2014–2015). *See also* Stephen A. Mazurak, *The Unpaid Intern Liability for the Uninformed Employer*, ABA J. Labor & Employment Law, Fall 2013, at 101, https://www.americanbar.org/content/dam/aba/events/labor_law/2013/03/employment_rightsresponsibilities-committeemidwintermeeting/30_mazurak.authcheckdam.pdf.

83. *See* Emma Lloyd Best, *Satisfying Experiential Education Requirements Through Expanding Externships in For-Profit Placements*, 21 Clinical L. Rev. 1 (2014).

graduates and thus do not typically have summer associate programs. A number of schools allow students to get experience at private law firms.[84]

An additional consideration is whether to grant credit for students who are also being paid.[85] Initial concerns that allowing paid externships would adversely affect the educational experience have not been borne out in the data gathered to date, but schools permitting paid externships are still in the minority.[86] Student pressure for schools to allow credit and compensation has received renewed consideration due to concern that students who are black, indigenous, and people of color (BIPOC) or from marginalized communities may be unable to forgo paid employment to enroll in externships. To combat this concern and recognizing that many placements may not have adequate funds to pay externs, some schools are working with advancement offices and other externship sites to raise funds for student assistance. The latest CSALE report shows that the number of schools allowing compensation, many with conditions or limits, has increased from 10% to 18%.[87] Of those schools, 74% allow compensation such as a fellowship or stipend, provided it is from a source other than the externship site, and 37% limit compensation to certain types of placement offices such as government or nonprofit.[88]

2) Location of Placements

The location of placements can generally be described as divided into four groups: local, regional, national, and international. Resource availability will influence choice of locations to some degree. It will be helpful to use the answers to the

---

84. *See* Bernadette Feeley, *Examining the Use of For-Profit Placements in Law School Externship Programs,* 14 Clinical L. Rev. 37 (2007); Bernadette T. Feeley, *Guiding Law Students Through For-Profit Field Placements,* 19 Clinical L. Rev. 57 (2012); Carolyn Young Larmore, *Just Compensation: An Empirical Examination of the Success of Legal Externships for Pay and Credit* , 70 Drake L. Rev. 145 (2022), for more on arguments in favor of private firms.

85. In August 2016, the ABA revised Standards 304 and 306 to allow law schools to offer credit for paid externships. *See* Survey of Schools on Payment of Students for For-Credit Externships (CLEA Externship Comm. 2020) for the most recent data on which law schools are allowing payment and showing a gradual increase in schools allowing payment, available at https://www.dropbox.com/s/fggbjfl3rhg4arf/CLEA%20Paid%20Externships%20Survey%20Report.10-20-20.FINAL.pdf?dl=0 (last visited March 6, 2022). Many in the externship community opposed the change for reasons described in this letter from CLE to the ABA. Comment on Interpretation 305 3 (Apr. 18, 2014), https://www.dropbox.com/sh/lzxeus4rf2zjty3/AAB5QzlQaYGMvCvk69n7ighga/CLEA%20Comment%20on%20Interpretation%20305-3%20%28April%2018%202014%29.pdf?dl=0. *See* Clinical Legal Educ. Ass'n, *CLEA Externship Committee Webinar,* Dropbox, for a webinar on the issue that gives a good overview of the debate, https://www.dropbox.com/s/m1xo3638iyhobqr/CLEA%20Externship%20Committee%20Webinar%20-%20Paid%20Externships%20-%20September%202018.mp4?dl=0 (last visited Aug. 18, 2021).

86. The 2019–20 CSALE Survey reported that 18% of schools allowed students to receive compensation in addition to academic credit, up from 10% in the 2016–17 Survey. CSALE Survey, *supra* note 14, at 10.

87. *Id.*

88. *Id.*

design questions discussed above, especially regarding number of placements and students served, to guide the decision on where placements should be located.

An obvious choice is to have externship sites at the local and state level. The number of graduates who plan to practice locally is one reason to do this, although it can be very useful for those students to extern in both national and international sites even if they are bringing those experiences back to their state. Other factors determining location of placements are whether the law school has satellite campuses or a sister school. Externship sites outside the area of the law school may require either remote work by the student or remote instruction by the teacher. The latter topic is covered in Chapter 12. An in-depth review of the logistics and benefits of international and other remote placements, and the increase of virtual opportunities and working from home, are discussed in Chapter 6.[89]

c. Number of Hours and Credits at the Externship Placement

As described in Chapter 2, the rules on how many hours are required in both the field placement and the seminar give faculty many options for structuring their programs. Schools offer a variety of options ranging from a minimum of 2 credits up to 15 credits. Programs fall into two categories: one group offers variable credits, and the other offers fixed credits.[90] Variable credits allow students and sites the maximum flexibility but require more work on the part of faculty and program administrators. Fixed credits may be favored when faculty want to ensure that students stay within a set overall credit limit or that students in a particular externship get a similar amount of work from semester to semester.

Design questions regarding externship credits include whether to cap them, whether to offer courses year round or only in certain semesters, and whether and when to allow full-time placements.[91] Schools range from requiring externships or clinics as a condition of graduation[92] to placing a cap on the number of externship credits students may earn.[93] A majority of schools offer externship placements in

---

89. *See* LexternWeb, *International Organizations*, https://www.lexternweb.org/international-organizations (last visited Aug. 18, 2021), for a list of international organizations to help in the development of international field placement sites.

90. The CSALE survey shows the variable option is used by 53% of schools in the 2019–20 data, down from 58% in the 2016–17 Survey. CSALE Survey, *supra* note 14, at 45.

91. *Id.* at 10 (showing that fifty-four percent of schools allow students to extern full-time).

92. CSALE survey data from the 2019–20 survey show 23% of schools requiring a clinic or field placement course, with 2% requiring that it be a field placement course. *Id.* at 12.

93. Sixty-two percent of schools limit the number of field placement credits a student may apply toward graduation requirements (in addition to the school-wide restriction on non-classroom credits under ABA Standard 311), a decrease from 71% in 2016–17 and 80% in 2013–14. The most common limit is 12 credits. *Id.* at 15.

the summer, but only 2% do not also offer placements during the school year.[94] Two advantages of allowing students to do part-time or full-time[95] externships during the academic year are that students can do a larger variety of externships over six to eight semesters instead of just two summers and that the longer fall and spring semesters give opportunities for deeper engagement with the legal work. While full-time externships are viewed by some law schools as presenting a risk that students will not participate in enough doctrinal classes to pass the bar or that faculty may not have the resources to provide the appropriate level of supervision required, growing evidence suggests that full-time externships boost student confidence, allow them to take on more substantive work, and lead to post-graduate employment.[96]

Other questions about credits, such as whether to divide the credits between the seminar and placement, whether to give a letter grade to one or both, and whether to allow credit for repeat enrollment in similar kinds of placements, are discussed in Chapter 7. As described above, flexibility is often most useful for meeting student goals, but may require additional administrative time and resources.

3. Program Implementation Choices

The following section describes two processes, student counseling and assistance with externship applications, for which there are a range of options. Each provides a description of the various design choices to be made along with the corresponding advantages and disadvantages. The processes will be determined by the degree to which each program has resources, including administrative support, within the externship program, as well as by the existence of support outside the program elsewhere in the law school.

a. Student Counseling[97]

The decision to provide student counseling regarding externship applications depends on several factors: resources; number of placements to choose from; and existence of counseling resources elsewhere in the law school.[98] The goals of counseling are generally to help students plan their courses, use credits wisely, and acquire a range of skills in a progressive manner throughout their time at law school.[99]

94. *Id.* at 49.

95. *Id.* at 10.

96. Kuehn, *supra* note 38.

97. This section covers counseling students regarding which externships and other experiential learning such as clinics will help them develop their knowledge, skills, and values to prepare for practice. For more on counseling to help students set goals and assess their development, *see* Chapter 8.

98. *See* Harriet N. Katz, *Counseling Externship Students*, 15 CLINICAL L. REV. 239 (2009).

99. *See* the Student Externship Clinic Planning Guide in the Appendix for this chapter, for one example of this from the Seattle University School of Law Externship Program.

Counseling can also include where an externship might fit in a student's course progression and which sites might best fit the student's interests and desired kind of work. Counseling can be particularly helpful for non-traditional students or those who might need additional preparation for a competitive placement. In some schools that screen students to match them directly with externships sites, counseling may be a part of the application process. Done well, counseling can provide students with concrete steps and a plan to achieve their goals.

While most schools agree on the importance of student counseling, many do not necessarily see this as connected to externship program design.[100] One option is to have the career office provide counseling and information about externships along with other not-for-credit opportunities. Proponents of this approach point to the efficiency of all advising being handled by one office in the law school. Another advantage is reduced confusion from law offices and courts outside the law school who are likely unaware of the distinction between externships and other opportunities. Disadvantages can be that the career counselors do not know the site supervisors or student legal work as well as the externship faculty, who have conducted a site visit, regularly communicate with supervisors, and gather additional site information from students through their reflections, class participation, and end-of-semester feedback. Another more critical concern is that placing part of the externship process in the career office may undercut the pedagogical goals of what is designed to be a program of clinical experiential education.[101]

Another option is to have student counseling as a shared responsibility of all faculty. This can be done in a variety of ways: by assigning students in their first year to faculty on a random basis, by assigning students based on faculty legal specialty and student interest, or by simply encouraging students to reach out to their faculty individually on their own. Advantages of this approach are a reduced workload for externship faculty and increased connection between students and other doctrinal and clinical faculty. Those connections may lead to additional student engagement in law school classes and valuable connections to post-graduate employment. Disadvantages can be that not all faculty are willing to spend time counseling students, and some faculty do not have a broad knowledge of experiential options, especially if they themselves have limited practice experience.

When externship programs do have the resources, including administrators and faculty, to provide student counseling, several options exist. Scheduling appointments can be handled by administrators or through online options. Some programs ask students to meet with faculty and discuss current résumés, classes taken, and both short and long-term goals. Such a process can allow faculty to

---

100. In addition, many students are used to finding such information online rather than in a meeting. *See* Bill Chamberlain, *What To Know About Your First Summer Internship*, STUDENT LAWYER (Dec. 1, 2016) https://abaforlawstudents.com/2016/12/01/what-to-know-about-your-first-summer-internship, for one example of such written advice.

101. *See* Baker & Lancaster, *supra* note 8, at 77–83.

explain that a number of externships and other experiential education opportunities will be needed to gain the variety of skills needed for practice. Combining externship counseling with advising regarding experiential opportunities can also highlight the ways in which experiential education is a deliberate process to gain certain knowledge, skills, and values through these experiences. This is different from simply applying for a position that may be neither related to a student's goals nor designed to give the student a meaningful increase in knowledge, skills, and values. This approach can be especially supportive for students from marginalized communities and first-generation law students who may lack both the confidence and background to compete as easily for positions. Disadvantages can be the lack of externship program faculty knowledge about the whole spectrum of student opportunities. It can also take time for one externship faculty member to acquire knowledge of the many different legal fields and externship options needed to effectively advise students.

Having a formal student counseling process as part of program design also encourages the development of specialized counseling for particular groups of students. For example, some evening students need to be encouraged to consider the same range of experiential options as regular JD students. Applying their knowledge in a practical setting can be critical as they are moving from one professional framework to another. Design of student counseling can counteract a tendency for evening students to have less information about career planning and the experiences needed to be practice ready. Helping students avoid postponing these experiences until they are almost ready to graduate will generally enable them to be more successful in using their JD for employment purposes after graduation. Similarly, LLM and other non-JD students may benefit from the added expertise of externship faculty who provide counseling with a deeper knowledge of both sites and supervisors.

b. Externship Applications

There are a variety of design options for processing student externship applications. As described above, some schools leave it to the students to reach out to the site, send necessary materials, go to the interview, and accept the position pending faculty approval, all before involving the externship program office. Others maintain a database of approved sites, actively soliciting and publicizing information about which sites are looking for students. When students are interested, the externship faculty review student materials, give suggested edits, and then send out the application from the school itself. These programs still review and keep track of student applications even when the applications must be submitted by the students directly online. Some programs only allow the student to apply through the externship office, while many allow students to also find placements themselves. Still other programs screen and interview all students who apply, match students with a particular placement, and then recommend the student to the placement site, which then conducts its own interview. Many programs use a mixture of these approaches, and often vary the degree to which they can provide assistance based on their staffing levels and available time and resources.

One advantage of the non-assisted model is that it teaches students the skills they will later need for their job searches. It is also less resource intensive and relies more on student initiative. Disadvantages are that if students feel intimidated or overwhelmed and fail to secure an externship the first time they try, they will be at an increased disadvantage for future job and externship searches. The disadvantages of such a process should be carefully considered in schools that serve a large number of BIPOC students, first-generation students, or students from marginalized communities. Taking an active role to assist these students may be necessary to counteract the negative effects of institutionalized racism that fall disproportionately on students who lack the privilege of other students. The process itself can expose students to discrimination and microaggressions[102] with the resulting risk of additional discouragement for students trying to break into a profession that is lacking in diversity.[103] Some students may be additionally stressed by a competitive process and become further alienated during the law school experience, which is already recognized as conducive to substance abuse and mental illness.[104]

Advantages of the assisted model are that it helps most students apply and provides a guarantee of experiential learning for students who are qualified. Students also learn how to improve their cover letters and receive feedback about specific approaches such as using a deferential tone when addressing a cover letter to a judge. This may be particularly helpful for students disadvantaged by biases due to race, class, gender, or lower grades. Disadvantages of the assisted model are that it is more resource intensive, may unintentionally mask student deficits, and may deprive them of building the resilience and skills necessary to secure post-graduate employment.

No matter which approach a program director chooses, it is important to collaborate, share information, and learn about resources from a range of sources in the law school. Each law school's academic resource center, pro bono and access to justice institutes, career offices, and faculty are all important sources of information and should be included in the design process even if they do not play a formal role in either counseling students or sending applications.

---

102. *See* Alexi Freeman, *Don't Hire Me as a Token: Best Practices for Recruiting and Supporting Externs From Historically Marginalized Backgrounds*, 72 S. Car. L. Rev. 357 (2020), for more on how to help these students have a positive experience.

103. For an examination of the causes of the underrepresentation of African American lawyers in the legal profession and some solutions to address it, see Martina Cartwright & Thelma Harmon, *#blacklawyersmatter: The Importance of Pro Bono Initiatives and Experiential Opportunities at Historically Black College and University Law Schools in Preparing a New Generation of Social Engineers*, 18 Fla. Coastal L. Rev. 315 (2017).

104. *See ABA Law Student Mental Health Resource*, https://abaforlawstudents.com/events/initiatives-and-awards/mental-health-resources/ (last visited Aug. 18, 2021).

Chapter 4

Selecting, Training, and Evaluating Site Supervisors

Site supervisors are a crucial component of meaningful and educationally enriching externship experiences. As discussed previously in Chapter 1, the externship student, the externship faculty member, and the site supervisor all work in conjunction to promote the student's learning and achievement of educational outcomes.[1] This dual supervision by both externship faculty and site supervisors is at the heart of externship design, and effective supervision at the placement site is the linchpin of the student's externship experience.[2]

Empirical research demonstrates the importance of site supervisors to externship students' success. Professors Anahid Gharakhanian and Carolyn Young Larmore conducted a study to evaluate student performance in externships and identify the factors that contribute to their success. Based on the results of surveys completed by both extern students and site supervisors, Gharakhanian and Larmore concluded that "a hands-on supervisor, who provides feedback on externs' work—in effect embracing the teacher role that's the ideal for effective externships—results in the extern performing better and closer to a first-year attorney level."[3] In addition, students overwhelmingly attributed their externship success to their relationship with the site

1. *See, e.g.*, Cynthia Adams, Cynthia Baker, Shawn Boyne, Max Huffman, Andrew Klein, Margaret Ryznar, Mark Shope & Frank Sullivan, *Upward—Higher: How a Law Faculty Stays Ahead of the Curve*, 51 IND. L. REV. 413, 430–31 (2018) (explaining externship triangle and types of communications it represents in externship pedagogy).

2. BUILDING ON BEST PRACTICES: TRANSFORMING LEGAL EDUCATION IN A CHANGING WORLD 230 (Deborah Maranville et al. eds., 2015) (hereinafter "BUILDING ON BEST PRACTICES"); *see also* Barbara A. Blanco & Sande L. Buhai, *Externship Field Supervision: Effective Techniques for Training Supervisors and Students*, 10 CLINICAL L. REV. 611, 612 (2004) ("Effective supervision is acknowledged as the most essential element of law student training in an off-campus setting or externship.").

3. Anahid Gharakhanian, Carolyn Young Larmore & Chelsea Parlett-Pelleriti, *Achieving Externship Success: An Empirical Study of the All-Important Law School Externship Experience*, 45 S. ILL. U. L.J. 165, 200 (2021).

supervisor, "with 82% choosing that as one of their top three factors contributing to their externship success."[4]

1. ABA Standards Regarding Site Supervisors

Recognizing the important role of site supervisors, ABA Standard 304 imposes specific requirements regarding their participation in externship courses. According to Standard 304(d), a site supervisor must be "a licensed attorney or an individual otherwise qualified to supervise"[5] externship students. Additionally, the externship course must have "a method for selecting, training, evaluating and communicating with site supervisors, including regular contact between the faculty and site supervisors through in-person visits or other methods of communication that will assure the quality of the student educational experience."[6] Each of these requirements is explored in turn below.

2. Selecting Site Supervisors

Although ABA Standard 304 states that externship courses must have a method for selecting site supervisors, it does not prescribe any particular process or selection criteria, other than that a supervisor must be a licensed attorney or "an individual otherwise qualified to supervise." Moreover, it does not define the term "otherwise qualified to supervise." Thus, externship faculty have wide discretion in choosing the site supervisors who participate in their courses.

In exercising that discretion, externship faculty should develop written criteria that they follow in selecting site supervisors.[7] An initial question to decide is whether the faculty member will pre-screen and recruit site supervisors to participate in the course, will accept applications from attorneys who are interested in hosting and supervising an extern but have not been recruited by the faculty member, will accept supervisors who have been identified by students at an externship site, or use some variation or combination of these approaches. Another threshold question for externship faculty is whether prospective placements and supervisors must submit a written application to participate in the course. Some faculty, for example, require

---

4. *Id.* at 202.

5. ABA Standards and Rules of Procedure for Approval of Law Schools 2022–2023, Standard 304(d). The complete ABA Standards are available at www.americanbar.org/content/dam/aba/administrative/legal_education_and_admissions_to_the_bar/standards/2022-2023/2022-2023-aba-standards-and-rules-of-procedure.pdf.

6. ABA Standards and Rules of Procedure for Approval of Law Schools 2022–2023, Standard 304(d)(ii).

7. *See, e.g.*, Roy Stuckey and Others, Best Practices for Legal Education: A Vision and a Roadmap 201 (2007) (hereinafter "Best Practices for Legal Education") (law schools should have criteria for approval of externship sites and supervisors).

prospective supervisors to complete a written application, including a questionnaire in which the supervisor provides information about her qualifications, the mission and work of the proposed placement site, the learning opportunities that would be available to externs there, and the supervision that would be provided to them.[8] Other faculty do not require a formal application, but they require prospective supervisors to complete a profile, provide their résumé, and answer questions about their supervisory style. Faculty also may take a less formal approach and simply communicate with prospective supervisors via telephone, videoconference, or email to address these topics and obtain this information. In light of increased attention to sexual harassment and bias in the workplace, faculty also may want to ask potential supervisors about the training they have received on these topics and their offices' policies on them. Once an externship faculty member decides on her method for selecting site supervisors, she should put it in writing and apply it consistently to all prospective placements and supervisors.

In addition to these process questions, the externship faculty member must determine the substantive qualifications that site supervisors must meet. Some threshold requirements might include having a J.D. degree, having passed a bar exam, having a certain number of years of practice experience, and being recognized as an expert in one's field of practice.[9] Legal expertise, for example, is an essential characteristic for site supervisors in Vermont Law School's Semester-in-Practice program. According to the program's founding director, Professor of Law Emerita Liz Ryan Cole, a site supervisor "must be someone who is acknowledged by the legal community, within which he or she practices, to be expert in his or her area(s) of concentration. They know their substantive areas(s) very well and, just as significantly, they know how to get things done."[10] The ABA does not mandate such qualifications, however, so externship faculty must decide for themselves the qualifications that are most important for accomplishing the learning outcomes in their course.[11]

In selecting site supervisors, a primary consideration should be whether they "have a demonstrated commitment to mentoring law students, consistent with the

8. An example of a site-supervisor questionnaire is included in the Appendix.

9. For example, the externship program at the University of Arkansas at Little Rock William H. Bowen School of Law requires all site supervisors to have at least five years of post bar exam work experience. Seattle University School of Law requires at least three years of practice experience to serve as a supervisor.

10. Liz Ryan Cole, *Training the Mentor: Improving the Ability of Legal Experts to Teach Students and New Lawyers*, 19 N.M. L. Rev. 163, 164–65 (1989); *see also* Best Practices for Legal Education, *supra* note 7, at 179 (externship supervisors "must have adequate and appropriate experience, skills, knowledge, and values to represent clients and perform any other professional roles required by the job").

11. Some schools, for example, such as Georgia State University College of Law, have established placements in university athletic departments that handle NCAA compliance issues, and they have found the non-attorney compliance officers to be effective extern supervisors. Other schools, such as Seattle University School of Law, allow non-attorney legislators to serve as supervisors.

school's goals for the students."[12] During the course of the externship experience, a student necessarily will spend more time in the presence of the site supervisor than the faculty supervisor, since the student must complete a required number of work hours at the placement site.[13] Accordingly, site supervisors are co-teachers in the externship endeavor, and they should be encouraged and expected to embrace this role. Externship faculty should advocate "an approach that proactively fosters an experiential learning partnership between the law school and each participating legal department."[14]

In selecting site supervisors, faculty also should consider the prospective supervisors' motivations for participating in the externship course. Supervisors should seek to participate because they want to teach law students and provide a valuable, real-life practice experience to them, understanding that it often takes more time to supervise an extern's completion of a task than it would take for supervisors to complete the task themselves.[15] Other laudable motives include a commitment to the law school or to legal education itself, based on each lawyer's professional responsibility to improve the legal system "by impacting the early development of young law students."[16] Potential supervisors who simply want to benefit from free or low-paid student labor, or have students complete menial, non-lawyer work, should be rejected. Site supervisors should be selected "for their excellence, their experience, their love of their work, and their passion to convey what they know to others."[17]

Site supervisors also must be willing to provide effective supervision and have the time to do so. Effective supervision includes providing the students with an appropriate range and depth of meaningful lawyering tasks and quality guidance, critique, and feedback throughout the externship experience.[18] Indeed, the best site supervisors take the time "to develop assignments for the student geared to the student's past experience, interests, and abilities based on the quality of the student's

---

12. Best Practices for Legal Education, *supra* note 7, at 201. *See also* Mary Jo Eyster, *Designing and Teaching the Large Externship Clinic*, 5 Clinical L. Rev. 347, 387–88 (1999).

13. Externship courses typically require a minimum of 85 hours of fieldwork for a two-credit course and 170 hours of fieldwork for a four-credit course. Robert R. Kuehn, Margaret Reuter, and David A. Santacroce, Center for the Study of Applied Legal Educ., 2019–2020 Survey of Applied Legal Education 45 (2020), https://www.csale.org/#results (last visited February 24, 2022).

14. Carl J. Circo, *An Educational Partnership Model for Establishing, Structuring, and Implementing a Successful Corporate Counsel Externship*, 17 Clinical L. Rev. 99, 116 (2010).

15. Cole, *supra* note 10, at 165 (two extremely important variables in whether a site supervisor is a good teacher "are time and desire: mentors must have the desire to teach and the time to do it").

16. James Backman, *Externships and New Lawyer Mentoring: The Practicing Lawyer's Role in Educating New Lawyers*, 24 BYU J. Pub. L. 65, 86 (2009); *see also* Circo, *supra* note 14, at 122 (supervisors should be motivated by "a commitment to legal education in general or to the specific law school, or both").

17. Cole, *supra* note 10, at 164.

18. J.P. "Sandy" *Ogilvy, Guidelines for the Self Evaluation of Legal Education Clinics and Clinical Programs*, 15 T.M. Cooley J. Prac. & Clinical L. 1, 139 (2013).

initial work product and initiative."[19] Good supervisors also explain assignments well, clarify expectations and deadlines, and provide students with the larger context and background of the assignment they are being asked to complete.[20] Once students submit assignments, supervisors must provide feedback on the work—either oral, written, or both—so students can learn how to improve. "Opportunities to receive critical evaluations of work performed in a timely manner are among the best teaching moments arising in the externship."[21] Through their accomplishment of these critical responsibilities, supervisors also model good lawyering behavior, which is another important component of effective supervision.[22]

Best Practices for Legal Education: A Vision and a Roadmap provides a comprehensive set of standards for effective externship supervision, which could form the basis for an application for prospective site supervisors. Alternatively, faculty might simply discuss these standards with prospective supervisors and ask if they are willing to meet them. According to *Best Practices for Legal Education*, site supervisors should be expected to:

- Understand the educational objectives of the externship course or program,
- Provide an orientation to the resources and mission of the placement site,
- Assist students in developing appropriate individualized educational objectives that are appropriate to the work of the field placement and that take advantage of all the experiences the placement has to offer to students,
- Assign work consistent with the principles stated in *Best Practices for Legal Education*,
- Encourage students to evaluate their field experience critically and regularly engage the student in constructive critical evaluation of the students' field experience,
- Observe or review student performances at regular intervals, and provide constructive feedback on student performance designed to improve student skills and understanding,
- Provide constructive evaluation to students about their general professional development,

19. Backman, *supra* note 16, at 85.
20. *Id.* at 85.
21. *Id.* at 86.
22. Building on Best Practices, *supra* note 2, at 230; Cynthia Baker & Robert Lancaster, *Under Pressure: Rethinking Externships in a Bleak Economy*, 17 Clinical L. Rev. 71, 88 (2010).

- Regularly communicate with the externship faculty about student progress, and
- Model the reflective and conscientious practitioner and welcome questioning of aspects and techniques of practice.[23]

Externship faculty at law schools that are in close proximity to other law schools may want to explore adopting a collective approach to selecting and working with site supervisors. In the mid-1990s, for example, externship faculty at six law schools in the Los Angeles area formed the Greater Los Angeles Consortium on Externships, which was known as "GLACE."[24] Working together, these faculty members established joint standards for the site supervisors who participated in their externship courses.[25] Joint standards are beneficial because they provide consistent expectations for all site supervisors who work with students from a consortium's schools, so the supervisors do not have to learn and satisfy multiple sets of standards, depending on the individual school that a student attends.[26] GLACE subsequently expanded to include additional law schools and changed its name to "SoCalEx."[27]

3. Training Site Supervisors

"Simply because people are knowledgeable, it does not automatically follow that they will be able to teach."[28] Most practicing attorneys have no formal training as educators, so externship faculty must train site supervisors to ensure that they are well-prepared to structure and provide a meaningful learning experience to the students who work in their offices. Training also is important because, under the rules of professional conduct, supervising attorneys are responsible for ensuring that law students who work with them comply with the governing ethical rules.[29] In designing training opportunities, externship faculty should consider both the content of the training and the methods for delivering it.

---

23. Best Practices for Legal Education, *supra* note 7, at 202.

24. Blanco & Buhai, *supra* note 2, at 625–27.

25. *Id.* at 626–27.

26. *Id.* at 627.

27. Other externship consortia include the Bay Area Consortium on Externships (BACE), the Capitol Area Consortium on Externships (CACE), the Georgia Association of Legal Externships (GALE), the New England Externship Consortium (NExt), the New York Area Consortium of Externship Directors, Faculty, and Administrators (NYACE), the Ohio Legal Externships Alliance (OLEA), and the Washington Consortium for Law Externships and Exchange (WCLEE). *See* LexternWeb, https://www.lexternweb.org/ externship-consortiums (last visited February 24, 2022).

28. Cole, *supra* note 10, at 165.

29. *See* Model Rules of Prof'l Conduct r. 5.3 (Am. Bar Ass'n) (responsibilities of managing attorneys regarding nonlawyer assistance); Model Rules of Prof'l Conduct r. 5.1 (Am. Bar Ass'n) (responsibilities of a partner or supervisory lawyer for other attorneys under their supervision).

a. Content of Supervisor Training

There are many important topics that should be addressed in training externship site supervisors. First and foremost, faculty should train supervisors on the externship course's objectives and expectations.[30] That training should include instruction on the learning outcomes for the externship program as a whole and the individual externship course in which the supervisor is participating, as well as ABA Standard 304's requirements regarding providing substantial lawyering experience, multiple opportunities for student performance and self-evaluation, and feedback from the site supervisor.[31] Externship faculty should provide a copy of their course syllabus to site supervisors, so supervisors can be aware of the topics that faculty are addressing in seminar classes or tutorials and look for opportunities to highlight and discuss those topics with students when they arise at the externship site. Faculty also should inform site supervisors of confidentiality protocols that are followed in seminars, tutorials, and student assignments to ensure that students do not disclose any confidential workplace or client information. Supervisors also should be trained on any teaching or administrative requirements they will need to satisfy for the course, such as working with students to set learning goals, approving weekly timesheets, meeting with students for a mid-semester evaluation, or completing a final performance evaluation for the student, if any of these tasks are required. Finally, supervisors should be made aware of the law school's non-discrimination policies, its sexual harassment policies, policies regarding accommodations for students with disabilities, and policies regarding the confidentiality of student educational records.

Faculty also should train site supervisors on effective techniques for providing feedback to students on their work. According to *Best Practices for Legal Education*, "[t]he guidance and feedback that students receive in experiential education courses influences the quality of the experience more than any other component."[32] Entire books and articles have been written on best practices for providing feedback, so a comprehensive discussion of this topic is beyond the scope of this book.[33] Indeed, Liz Ryan Cole, Barbara Blanco and Sandy Buhai, and Bernadette Feeley have published articles specifically about methods for training externship super-

30. Ogilvy, *supra* note 18, at 149.

31. ABA STANDARDS AND RULES OF PROCEDURE FOR APPROVAL OF LAW SCHOOLS 2022–2023, STANDARD 304(a) and (d).

32. BEST PRACTICES FOR LEGAL EDUCATION, *supra* note 7, at 175.

33. *See* DOUGLAS STONE & SHEILA HEEN, THANKS FOR THE FEEDBACK: THE SCIENCE AND ART OF RECEIVING FEEDBACK WELL (2015); *see also, e.g.*, Anne D. Gordon, *Better Than Our Biases: Using Psychological Research to Inform Our Approach to Inclusive, Effective Feedback*, 27 CLINICAL L. REV. 195 (2021); Paula J. Manning, *Word to the Wise: Feedback Intervention to Moderate the Effects of Stereotype Threat and Attributional Ambiguity on Law Students*, 18 U. MD. L. J. RACE, RELIGION, GENDER & CLASS 99 (2018); Paula J. Manning, *Understanding the Impact of Inadequate Feedback: A Means to Reduce Law Student Psychological Distress, Increase Motivation, and Improve Learning Outcomes*, 43 CUMB. L. REV. 225 (2013).

visors to provide feedback to students.[34] *Best Practices for Legal Education* offers the following guidelines, with accompanying explanations, for performing effective critiques of student work:

- Being prepared to critique,
- Being selective,
- Starting with a positive comment,
- Being specific,
- Being constructive,
- Being succinct,
- Being honest,
- Taking responsibility for your critique,
- Critiquing the performance, not the person,
- Making the student a partner in the critique, and
- Teaching by example.[35]

Faculty should consult these and other resources to determine the techniques that are most appropriate for their courses and then prioritize those techniques in their training.

Faculty also should consider discussing special considerations that apply to working with law students. Although externs need to be provided with substantial lawyering experiences at their placement sites, they do not have the knowledge and experience of first-year lawyers, with whom site supervisors may have more familiarity. Accordingly, students cannot be treated in the same way as junior associates or given the same responsibilities. In addition, the significant power imbalance inherent in the site supervisor/student relationship "can affect students' learning experiences and legal careers both subtly and overtly."[36] An externship, for example, may be a student's first work experience in a law office, which can cause the student to feel intimidated and even overwhelmed by the environment. These sorts of feelings can be particularly acute for students from historically marginalized backgrounds who have had negative experiences in law school, or for first-generation students whose parents did not graduate from college and who have not interacted with lawyers before.[37] Students who are uncomfortable in the work environment or too

34. Cole, *supra* note 10; Blanco & Buhai, *supra* note 2; Bernadette T. Feeley, *Training Field Supervisors to be Efficient and Effective Critics of Student Writing*, 15 CLINICAL L. REV. 211 (2009).

35. BEST PRACTICES FOR LEGAL EDUCATION, *supra* note 7, at 176.

36. Nancy M. Maurer & Robert F. Seibel, *Addressing Problems of Power and Supervision in Field Placements*, 17 CLINICAL L. REV. 145, 148 (2010).

37. *See* Alexi Freeman, *Don't Hire Me as a Token: Best Practices for Recruiting and Supporting*

intimidated to ask their supervisors for guidance and feedback will miss out on valuable opportunities to learn, improve, and develop new skills.[38] Accordingly, faculty should introduce site supervisors to these issues as part of their training.[39]

Finally, it also is advisable as part of supervisor training to discuss the inherent tensions that site supervisors face in working with externship students. "In an off-campus field placement, the primary concern of the supervising attorney must be the work of the agency or judicial chambers, while the concern for the education of the field extern must by nature be a secondary goal."[40] Externship faculty should acknowledge these competing demands on the supervisors' time and assure supervisors that they will provide whatever support they can to help supervisors in their teaching responsibilities. Resources that can help in this regard are discussed below.

b. Methods for Delivering Supervisor Training

Externship faculty have several ways of providing training for site supervisors. One of the most effective and common methods is conducting in-person training sessions in which site supervisors meet together with the externship faculty member to address the identified topics for training. Alternatively, training sessions can be provided via live videoconferences. Supervisors can be required to attend such training sessions as a condition for participating in the externship course. Externship faculty also can design their training sessions to provide additional benefits to the site supervisors, such as CLE credit and networking opportunities.[41] Multiple examples of materials for in-person training sessions, including PowerPoint slides, are posted and available on LexternWeb[42] and are shared regularly on the externship listserv.

Externship faculty also can provide training through the use of written materials or educational videos. At a minimum, each externship course should provide to site supervisors a written manual that includes information about its goals, expectations, and method of operation; guidance for selecting and assigning projects to students; the written externship learning agreement; the ABA Standards governing extern-

---

Externs from Historically Marginalized Backgrounds, 72 S. Car. L. Rev. 357 (2020); Russell A. McClain, *Helping Our Students Reach Their Full Potential: The Insidious Consequences of Ignoring Stereotype Threat*, 17 Rutgers Race & L. Rev. 1 (2016); Jacqueline M. Bryant & Katherine Traylor Schaffzin, *First-Generation Students in Law School: A Proven Success Model*, 70 Ark. L. Rev. 913 (2018).

38. Maurer & Seibel, *supra* note 36, at 148–49.

39. *Id.* at 167. Chapter 9 of this book includes additional information and resources on teaching about race and bias.

40. Blanco & Buhai, *supra* note 2, at 612; *see also* Building on Best Practices, *supra* note 2, at 231 ("In the field placement, the supervisor's emphasis on achieving student educational goals often (and understandably) ranks in precedence behind loyalty to the work of the host court or law office.").

41. Blanco & Buhai, *supra* note 2, at 629 (describing CLE program for supervisors followed by a reception).

42. Lexternweb, https://www.lexternweb.org/site-supervisor-materials-1 (last visited February 24, 2022).

ships; and the role and responsibilities of the site supervisor, including providing effective mentoring and feedback to students.[43] Chapter 13 of this book is designed to be a stand-alone chapter that can be provided to site supervisors as a training guide or used as a template for a supervisor handbook or other training tool. In addition, several externship manuals from various law schools are posted on LexternWeb, so there is no need to reinvent the wheel in creating a manual.[44] In addition to manuals, faculty can provide tip sheets answering frequently asked questions and providing examples of common problems that arise in externships and suggested solutions.[45] Another good practice is to provide short articles on supervision and other important issues that busy supervisors can benefit from and will actually have time to read.[46]

4. Communicating with Site Supervisors

"Externships are a result of a professional, collaborative relationship between the law student extern, the faculty advisor, and the supervising lawyer. Communication between and among these participants is essential."[47] ABA Standard 304(d)(ii) states that externship courses must have a method for communicating with site supervisors, including "regular contact between the faculty and site supervisors through in-person visits or other methods of communication that will assure the quality of the student educational experience."[48] The Standard, however, does not define the term "regular contact" or mandate any particular method of communication, so externship faculty have considerable flexibility regarding these requirements. Much communication about the objectives and operations of the externship course, as well as expectations for site supervisors, will be accomplished through the training techniques described above. Below are suggestions for communicating with supervisors after their training and introduction to the course, once they have actually started their work supervising students.

---

43. *E.g.*, Ogilvy, *supra* note 18, at 148–49; *see also* Circo, *supra* note 14, at 130 ("To promote and protect the educational quality of the externship, the faculty supervisor should provide written guidance to both the supervising attorneys and the students.")

44. LEXTERNWEB, https://www.lexternweb.org/site-supervisor-materials-1 (last visited February 24, 2022).

45. James H. Backman, *Where Do Externships Fit? A New Paradigm is Needed: Marshaling Law School Resources to Provide an Externship for Every Student*, 56 J. LEGAL EDUC. 615, 635 (2006).

46. *See, e.g.*, Nicole P. Dyszlewski & Laura Pickering, *9 Strategies for Improving the Legal Internship Experience at Your Office*, LAW LIBRARY STAFF PUBLICATIONS 4, https://docs.rwu.edu/ law_lib_sp/4 (last visited February 24, 2022).

47. Baker & Lancaster, *supra* note 22, at 96; *see also* Ogilvy, *supra* note 18, at 139 ("There must be regular and meaningful communication among the parties to ensure that the goals of each party are met.").

48. ABA STANDARDS AND RULES OF PROCEDURE FOR APPROVAL OF LAW SCHOOLS 2022–2023, STANDARD 304(d)(ii).

a. Communicating the Student's Goals to the Site Supervisor

"Good practice dictates that the student's learning goals and objectives and his or her skill levels be communicated to the placement prior to acceptance of the student as an extern, or as soon thereafter as is practicable."[49] Several methods exist for making site supervisors aware of students' learning objectives. One method is for the faculty member to send the student's externship application, including supporting materials such as a résumé and statement of interest, to the site supervisor. Another method is to have the site supervisor conduct a pre-placement interview with the prospective extern, during which they can discuss such matters.[50] The faculty member also can ask students to complete an individualized Learning Agenda or Goals Memo prior to or soon after starting their externship work, which the student then discusses with the site supervisor. Some externship courses ask students and their site supervisors to meet together and create the student's learning goals. Regardless of the particular method used, making supervisors aware of the student's goals facilitates the student's learning and can obviate misunderstandings about the opportunities available at the placement.[51]

b. Open Lines of Communication Between Faculty Members and Site Supervisors

It is critical for faculty members to have an open line of communication with all of the site supervisors who participate in their externship course. "Two-way input and feedback is particularly important at critical junctures during the term, such as immediately before the externs begin, during the first few weeks of the externship, and during the final days of the externship, including for purposes of the evaluations of student performance."[52] As noted above, the faculty member should share the course syllabus with the site supervisor.[53] Knowing the topics that students are encountering in assigned readings, class discussions, and journal assignments will heighten the site supervisor's awareness to these topics and help her raise and explore them with the extern when they arise in the student's work at the site. Faculty could "solicit suggestions, advice, or practical professional examples regarding how a particular topic that will be addressed in the externship course relates to supervising lawyers' work."[54] Faculty members also might invite site supervisors to participate in the seminar course as guest speakers or as co-teachers on a particular topic. Such

49. Ogilvy, *supra* note 18, at 142.
50. *Id.* at 143.
51. *Id.*
52. Circo, *supra* note 14, at 132.
53. *E.g.*, Adams et al., *supra* note 1, at 434.
54. Baker & Lancaster, *supra* note 22, at 97.

invitations acknowledge and respect the supervisors' expertise while also "serv[ing] to remind them that they have signed on to an educational enterprise."[55]

Externship faculty should make clear to site supervisors that the faculty member is available at any time to help resolve any problems that arise during the externship or to provide resources or support.[56] Faculty members should ensure that site supervisors have their contact information and also have contact information for a designated back-up person, such as the faculty member's administrative assistant, in case an emergency arises and the faculty member is unavailable.

Faculty also should communicate with site supervisors about any changes that are made to the externship course, including the reason for the change. When a change is implemented, such as adding summer externships, awarding credit for paid externships, or expanding externship placements to include private, for-profit law firms, "externship faculty should be assertive about communicating the pedagogical rationale for the change to peers, students and supervising attorneys."[57] These changes can be communicated via email, a newsletter, a blog, or law school social media platforms. Faculty also can foster communication with site supervisors by sending them short articles on developments in their particular practice areas, tips for working with law students, or changes in the ABA Standards governing externships. "Constant communication reminds all externship participants that nothing can be on autopilot."[58]

c. Written Agreement Among Student, Faculty Member, and Site Supervisor

Another method for communicating with site supervisors is the written agreement that the extern student, site supervisor, and faculty member must execute. ABA Standard 304(d)(i) requires that all externship courses must have

> a written understanding among the student, faculty member, and a person in authority at the field placement that describes both (A) the substantial lawyering experience and opportunities for performance, feedback and self-evaluation; and (B) the respective roles of faculty and any site supervisor in supervising the student and in assuring the educational quality of the experience for the student, including a clearly articulated method of evaluating the student's academic performance.[59]

A good externship agreement "sets the bounds" of an externship by articulating the student's expectations, the respective roles and responsibilities of the site supervisor

55. Eyster, *supra* note 12, at 392, *see also* Adams et al., *supra* note 1, at 434.

56. *E.g.*, Ogilvy, *supra* note 18, at 149.

57. Baker & Lancaster, *supra* note 22, at 97.

58. *Id.*

59. ABA Standards and Rules of Procedure for Approval of Law Schools 2022–2023, Standard 304(d)(i).

and the faculty member, the type of legal work that the student will perform, and the process for evaluating the student's work.[60] Examples of such agreements are available on LexternWeb, so externship faculty do not have to create them from scratch.[61] Rather, faculty can take one of the sample agreements and tailor it to their specific course. For reference, copies of externship agreements also are included in the Appendix.

d. Site Visits

There is much debate in the externship scholarship about the usefulness of in-person site visits for externship courses. ABA Standard 304(d)(ii) suggests them as one method for communicating with site supervisors, but it does not mandate them. Some externship teachers find site visits to be extremely valuable,[62] while others find that they "serve little, if any, pedagogical purpose[.]"[63] Some externship faculty conduct a site visit before accepting a new placement into the course, in order to vet both the prospective site supervisor and the office environment. Other externship teachers perform site visits at mid-semester to check on the extern's progress and relationship with the supervisor, or to model a good feedback session for the supervisor and student, build a relationship with the supervisor, and gather information for advising students on the supervisor and the work at the site. Professor Ogilvy asserts that while site visits generally are not necessary, they "should be mandatory in programs where students are responsible for client representation and where the program is unfamiliar with the abilities and conscientiousness of the fieldwork supervisor."[64]

Conducting an individual, in-person visit with the supervisor at each externship site certainly will consume a significant amount of the externship faculty member's time. Visits that require travel to placements outside of the law school's immediate geographical area also may be costly.[65] Thus, externship teachers should weigh the benefits and costs of in-person site visits and identify significant pedagogical reasons

---

60. Baker & Lancaster, *supra* note 22, at 96; *see also* Eyster, *supra* note 12, at 392 ("It is essential to have a fairly clear understanding between the field supervisor and the faculty member about the role of each in the oversight of student work.").

61. LEXTERNWEB, https://www.lexternweb.org/site-supervisor-materials-1 (last visited February 24, 2022).

62. Circo, *supra* note 14, at 132–33 (Site visits "can be integral to the success and evolution of a program" and "provide excellent opportunities to keep the educational partnership vibrant and dynamic.").

63. Robert F. Seibel & Linda H. Morton, *Field Placement Programs: Practices, Problems and Possibilities*, 2 CLINICAL L. REV. 413, 444 (1996). According to Professors Seibel and Morton, "Faculty directors have better uses of their time than to spend precious hours visiting placements." *Id. See also* Ogilvy, *supra* note 18, at 149 (site visits are "not necessary or even particularly effective" for monitoring externships).

64. Ogilvy, *supra* note 18, at 163. In other situations, Professor Ogilvy says, "the program should weigh the costs and benefits of conducting site visits in light of all the parties' goals." *Id.*

65. Backman, *supra* note 45, at 636; *see also* Seibel & Morton, *supra* note 63, at 444 ("For a law

for conducting them. If the faculty member decides against conducting site visits due to time or cost considerations, she can still arrange to have a discussion with the site supervisor via videoconference, telephone, or email. Indeed, since the coronavirus pandemic, videoconferencing technology has vastly improved, and most lawyers have become adept at using it. To avoid travel costs, externship teachers also have the option of asking faculty members at other law schools to conduct in-person visits at sites that are in their area and then report back on their findings.[66]

If an externship faculty member decides to use site visits, she should ensure that she has a clear plan for making them a valuable use of her time and the time of the site supervisor. According to Professor Ogilvy, externship faculty should consider the following questions in planning site visits:

- At what point in the semester will a site visit be most productive?
- Should the student extern be present during the site visit?
- What preparation for the site visit should be required of the fieldwork supervisor and other persons at the placement site?
- What topics should be discussed during the site visit?
- How can the faculty supervisor use the site visit to enhance the fieldwork supervisor's understanding of the goals and objectives of the externship program?
- How can the faculty supervisor use the site visit to deepen and broaden the learning that takes place at the placement site?
- How can the faculty supervisor enhance the fieldwork supervisor's supervisory skills, if necessary, and ensure that the fieldwork supervisor provides meaningful task assignments, oversight, and feedback to the student extern?[67]

Other questions to consider include asking the site supervisor how well he is balancing his supervisory responsibilities with his regular job responsibilities, whether the externship course works well in conjunction with the office's regular operations, and whether any improvements should be made to improve the functioning of the externship course.

---

school to allocate funds for faculty visits to out-of-town placements also touches the realm of absurdity.").

66. ABA Standards and Rules of Procedure for Approval of Law Schools 2022–2023, Standard 304, Interpretation 304-1 ("When appropriate, a school may use faculty members from other law schools to supervise or assist in the supervision or review of a field placement program.").

67. Ogilvy, *supra* note 18, at 162–63.

Site visits also can serve important pedagogical purposes for students. In her article *Learning How To Learn: Carnegie's Third Apprentice*,[68] Professor Laurie Barron explains how she uses mid-semester site visits with supervisors and their externs as a means to teach students lessons relating to the formation of professional identity. Through these three-way meetings, Professor Barron teaches students the skill of learning to be effectively supervised by others, the skill of being a self-directed and effective learner, and the skill of exhaustive preparation. Thus, site visits can be used as a teaching method, in addition to a means for monitoring placements and checking in with site supervisors.

e. Expressing Appreciation for the Site Supervisors' Work

Finally, faculty members should express their appreciation for the site supervisors' work early and often. Site supervisors contribute a considerable amount of time and effort to an externship course, and most are uncompensated for that work. The supervisors' efforts can be recognized in a variety of ways. Some externship courses, for example, host an end-of-semester reception or luncheon for the site supervisors to honor their contributions. Other forms of recognition might include awards for outstanding supervisors, awards for the best supervisor-extern team, or awards based on years of service as a supervisor. Supervisors also might be highlighted in publications such as bar journals or the law school's alumni newsletter, promotional materials, or website.

5. Evaluating Site Supervisors

Pursuant to ABA Standard 304(d)(ii), externship courses must have a method for evaluating site supervisors. The Standard does not mandate a particular method, however. A combination of informal and formal evaluation methods is advisable. It is crucial to evaluate the work of site supervisors throughout a student's externship experience and not wait until the conclusion of the student's experience to conduct the evaluation.

a. Informal Evaluation

The assignments that students submit to the externship faculty member throughout the externship experience are an excellent means of gaining insights about site supervisors and informally evaluating them. In most externship courses, students submit journals reflecting on their work experiences and timesheets documenting the tasks they have performed. Externship faculty should pay close attention to

68. Laurie Barron, *Learning How to Learn: Carnegie's Third Apprentice*, 18 CLINICAL L. REV. 101 (2011).

students' journals to see if the students disclose any concerns regarding their supervision at the site. Indeed, a faculty member could assign a specific journal prompt requiring students to reflect on their relationship and communication with their supervisor, the assignments they are receiving, and the feedback they are receiving on those assignments. Externship faculty also should closely review students' timesheets to ensure they are performing legal work that is appropriate for externships and not menial, administrative tasks. Class discussions and mid-semester meetings with students also are effective methods for determining whether students are receiving appropriate supervision and assignments.[69]

If students raise any concerns about their supervision, the externship faculty member should consult with the student immediately to determine the best mechanism for addressing the concerns. In some situations, it may be appropriate to use the situation as a "teachable moment" and counsel the student on how to raise and resolve concerns with the supervisor. In other situations, however, it may be necessary for the externship faculty member to intervene and address the matter with the supervisor. The decision about which approach to take largely will turn on the seriousness of the concerns, the student's comfort level in raising the issues with the site supervisor, and the teacher's professional judgment.

b. Formal Evaluation

Professor Ogilvy sets out the following guidelines for formal evaluations of site supervisors:

> Each program should develop and use a valid and reliable instrument for the extern to conduct a summative evaluation of the placement and fieldwork supervisor at the conclusion of the placement. Topics included in the instrument should include the extern's assessment of the adequacy of the physical environment; the appropriateness and clarity of assignments (both in terms of relevance to the work of the placement and relevance to the educational goals and objectives of the extern); the nature, extent, and effectiveness of feedback from the fieldwork supervisor; the accessibility of the fieldwork supervisor; unanticipated opportunities for learning; and the appropriateness of the fieldwork supervisor's attitude toward the extern.[70]

---

69. *See, e.g.*, Building on Best Practices, *supra* note 2, at 233 ("Teachers must implement consistent checks to ensure a high quality educational experience.... These checks should include monitoring the student work and supervision in field placement through a combination of site visits, student and supervisor evaluation tools, general supervisor outreach by phone call or email, and careful review of student timesheets and journals.") .

70. Ogilvy, *supra* note 18, at 150.

Externship faculty who are members of an externship consortium can use common evaluation instruments and share information about the effectiveness of site supervisors who participate in their courses. Even if externship faculty are not members of a consortium, they still may consult with each other to compare notes on site supervisors who participate in both of their courses. Likewise, externship faculty frequently share their supervisor evaluation forms with each other via the externship listserv and at conferences. Examples of supervisor evaluation instruments are included in the Appendix.

6. Terminating a Site Supervisor from an Externship Course or Program

At some point, an externship faculty member may have to consider whether to terminate a site supervisor or an externship site from participating in the course. "Field supervisors identified in periodic evaluations who are unable to consistently meet and address placement criteria for student feedback and evaluation should not be retained in a law school field placement program, as unpleasant a task to program faculty as terminating those field supervisors may be."[71] Likewise, site supervisors who engage in abusive behavior or harassment toward students; put students in any sort of dangerous situation with clients, witnesses, or others; fail to provide adequate supervision under a student-practice rule; or engage in any sort of professional misconduct, should be terminated from the course.

To prepare for situations like these, externship faculty should develop policies and procedures for terminating site supervisors and for making any other major changes, such as changing the student's placement prior to the end of the externship work.[72] In addition, students "should be made aware of the responsibility and authority of the faculty supervisor to intervene in the relationship between the student and the fieldwork supervisor to preserve the integrity of the program, to safeguard the physical or emotional health of the student, or to ensure the educational value of the experience to the student."[73] Removing a site supervisor, however, likely will have political repercussions, since site supervisors often have some sort of relationship to the law school, whether as alumni, donors, or supporters. Supervisors also may have relationships with the dean or other faculty members. In light of these relationships, the externship faculty member should inform the dean of any impending decision to terminate a site supervisor.[74] While these decisions are undoubtedly delicate, they

71. Blanco & Buhai, *supra* note 2, at 624.

72. Ogilvy, *supra* note 18, at 150.

73. *Id.*

74. *See* Blanco & Buhai, *supra* note 2, at 624 ("removing individual or unmotivated supervisors or judges rarely occurs in the absence of political ramifications to the director or other faculty in the law school who have a relationship with the supervisor, and commonly may involve the Dean or an Associate Dean as a final arbiter").

must be carried out when circumstances warrant because the student's educational experience is the paramount concern.

"Fostering effective and inspired field supervision is the most challenging and one of the most time intensive aspects" of externship teaching and program development.[75] It is crucial, however, because site supervisors play an indispensable role in the externship learning process. Fortunately, externship faculty members have many valuable resources to draw on, including their colleagues in the externship community, the considerable scholarship on this topic, and LexternWeb.

75. Building on Best Practices, *supra* note 2, at 233.

Chapter 5

Establishing and Assessing Student Learning Outcomes for Externship Programs

1. The Role of Student Learning Outcomes in an Externship Program[1]

The ABA Standards require law schools to establish and publish learning outcomes designed to prepare their students, "upon graduation, for admission to the bar and for effective, ethical, and responsible participation as members of the legal profession."[2] At a minimum, law schools must establish learning outcomes that include their graduates' competency in the following knowledge, skills, and values:

(a) Knowledge and understanding of substantive and procedural law;

(b) Legal analysis and reasoning, legal research, problem-solving, and written and oral communication in the legal context;

(c) Exercise of proper professional and ethical responsibilities to clients and the legal system; and

(d) Other professional skills needed for competent and ethical participation as a member of the legal profession.[3]

---

1. Parts of this chapter are adapted, with permission, from Kelly Terry, Gerald Hess, Emily Grant & Sandra Simpson, Assessment of Teaching and Learning: A Comprehensive Guidebook for Law Schools (2021).

2. ABA Standards and Rules of Procedure for Approval of Law Schools 2022–2023, Standard 301(a). The complete ABA Standards are available at www.americanbar.org/content/dam/aba/ administrative/legal_education_and_admissions_to_the_bar/standards/2022-2023/2022-2023-aba-standards-and-rules-of-procedure.pdf.

3. ABA Standards and Rules of Procedure for Approval of Law Schools 2022–2023, Standard 302.

Statements of learning outcomes such as these—that describe the general knowledge, skills, and values that a school's graduates should possess upon completing their J.D. degree—are known as "institutional"-level learning outcomes.[4]

After establishing these outcomes, schools must engage in a continuous and systematic process of assessment to determine whether their graduates are achieving competency in the outcomes and to make changes in the curriculum if they are not.[5] An assessment process typically is divided into a series of steps, such as these set forth by assessment expert Mary Allen:

1. Develop learning outcomes;
2. Ensure alignment between the curriculum and the outcomes;
3. Develop an assessment plan;
4. Collect the assessment data;
5. Evaluate the assessment data;
6. Use results to improve the program; and
7. Routinely examine the assessment process and revise, as needed.[6]

In addition to setting learning outcomes at the institutional level, educational experts recommend establishing and assessing learning outcomes at the program level and the course level, as well.[7] Program-level outcomes are statements of more particularized knowledge, skills, and values in which students should achieve competency as a result of completing a distinct academic component within the overall curriculum, such as an externship program, a legal-writing program, or a lawyering-

---

4. *See, e.g.*, Andrea Susnir Funk, The Art of Assessment: Making Outcomes Assessment Accessible, Sustainable, and Meaningful 41 (2017); Peggy L. Maki, Assessing for Learning: Building a Sustainable Commitment Across the Institution 90 (2d ed. 2010).

5. ABA Standards and Rules of Procedure for Approval of Law Schools 2022–2023, Standard 315 ("The dean and the faculty of a law school shall conduct ongoing evaluation of the law school's program of legal education, learning outcomes, and assessment methods; and shall use the results of this evaluation to determine the degree of student attainment of competency in the learning outcomes and to make appropriate changes to improve the curriculum.").

6. Mary J. Allen, Assessing Academic Programs in Higher Education 10 (2004) (hereinafter "Allen, Assessing Academic Programs").

7. Regional accreditors that regulate a law school's parent university also may require program outcomes. *See* Chapter 2, *supra* (discussing regional accreditors); *see also* ABA Section of Legal Education and Admissions to the Bar, Report of the Outcome Measures Committee 47 (2008), www. americanbar.org/content/dam/aba/administrative/legal_education_and_admissions_to_the_bar/reports/2008_outcome_measures_committee_final_report.pdf ("As the regional accreditors have begun holding accredited schools accountable for demonstrating educational effectiveness at all levels, law schools are no longer able to fly beneath the regional radar screen"); Lori E. Shaw & Victoria L. VanZandt, Student Learning Outcomes and Law School Assessment: A Practical Guide to Measuring Institutional Effectiveness 23 (2015) ("The current push for law schools to up their assessment game is, at least in part, the result of the tightening of the regional accreditors' standards over the past decade.").

skills program.[8] Program-level outcomes "will not be identical to the institutional outcomes, but will be more specific and tailored to the program's subject area."[9] For example, a law school's institutional outcomes might state that its graduates should be able to communicate effectively orally and in writing, while its externship program might have a complementary outcome stating that students who complete externship courses should be able to demonstrate effective verbal communication skills when speaking with a supervisor.

The ABA does not currently require law schools to adopt program-level learning outcomes for any distinct programs within the J.D. curriculum, such as legal-writing programs or experiential-education programs. Nevertheless, schools that offer multiple externship courses should consider adopting and assessing learning outcomes for their externship programs as a whole because such outcomes promote curricular integration and intentionality in teaching.[10] Program-level outcomes also provide another layer of data regarding student learning and allow externship faculty to evaluate whether the program is achieving its intended purposes. The remainder of this Chapter explains the benefits of program-level learning outcomes and methods for establishing and assessing them in externship programs.

2. The Benefits of Program-Level Learning Outcomes

Program-level learning outcomes promote the design of a cohesive and integrated curriculum that is intentionally structured to help students progress from novice to proficient during the course of their education.[11] Assessment expert Peggy Maki

---

8. *E.g.*, FUNK, *supra* note 4, at 43; *see also* MAKI, *supra* note 4, at 90 ("Outcome statements become more specific at the program or department level, reflecting the kinds of writing within a discipline, profession, or field of study.").

9. FUNK, *supra* note 4, at 43. Course-level outcomes are even more specific than program outcomes and describe the knowledge, skills, and values that students should develop from completing an individual course.

10. *Id.* (stating that specific academic programs within a law school, such as legal writing, lawyering skills, or bar preparation programs, as well as concentrations that focus on a particular substantive area, should have their own set of learning outcomes); *see also, e.g.*, Anthony Niedwiecki, *Law Schools and Learning Outcomes: Developing a Coherent, Cohesive, and Comprehensive Law School Curriculum*, 64 CLEVELAND ST. L. REV. 661, 678 (2016) (recommending that law schools develop "specific learning outcomes for each academic program"); ROY STUCKEY & OTHERS, BEST PRACTICES FOR LEGAL EDUCATION: A VISION AND A ROAD MAP 55 (2007) (hereinafter "BEST PRACTICES FOR LEGAL EDUCATION") ("Law schools should describe the specific educational goals of each course or other component of the program of instruction in terms of what students will know, understand, and be able to do, and what attributes they will develop by completing that component.").

11. Legal education reformers consistently have called for law schools to provide a more integrated and coherent curriculum based on principles of educational design and learning theory. *See, e.g.*, BEST PRACTICES FOR LEGAL EDUCATION, *supra* note 10, at 39–40, 93; BUILDING ON BEST PRACTICES: TRANSFORMING LEGAL EDUCATION IN A CHANGING WORLD 12 (Deborah Maranville, Lisa Radtke

explains how institutional, program, and course-level learning outcomes integrate with one another to create a coherent curriculum:

> In a cohesive curricular and co-curricular design, these institution-level outcomes are seeded into program or department-level outcomes; in turn, institution and program or department-level outcomes are seeded into the courses and educational experiences that altogether contribute to students' major program of study and to their institution-wide learning. Institution- and program- or department-level outcomes become more specifically stated as they are adapted to the context of courses; modules; [and] educational experiences[.][12]

The diagram below illustrates how an outcome for assessing one's own learning and professional development could be integrated across the levels of an institution, an externship program, and an individual externship course:

Figure 5-1. Integration of Institutional, Program, and Course Outcomes

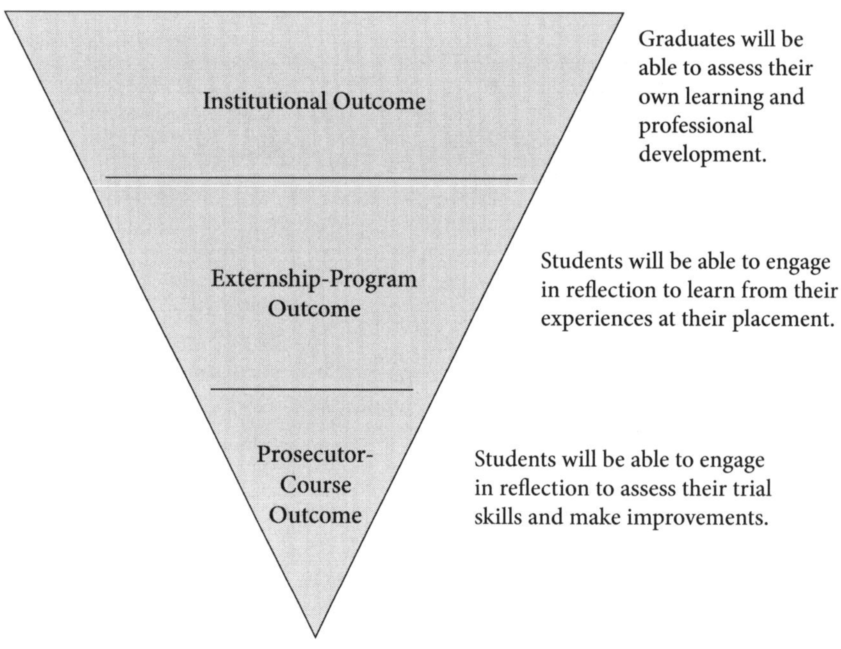

Bliss, Carolyn Wilkes Kaas & Antoinette Sedillo Lopez eds., 2015) (hereinafter "BUILDING ON BEST PRACTICES"); WILLIAM M. SULLIVAN, ANNE COLBY, JUDITH WELCH WEGNER, LLOYD BOND & LEE SHULMAN, EDUCATING LAWYERS: PREPARATION FOR THE PROFESSION OF LAW 180–81, 191–92 (2007) (hereinafter "EDUCATING LAWYERS").

12. MAKI, *supra* note 4, at 90. *See also* MARY E. HUBA & JANN E. FREED, LEARNER-CENTERED ASSESSMENT ON COLLEGE CAMPUSES: SHIFTING THE FOCUS FROM TEACHING TO LEARNING 107 (2000) ("Intended learning outcomes at the program level should reflect the type of knowledge and skills expected in members of the program's discipline, but they should be compatible with and support institutional outcomes.").

Through this integration, the outcomes build on one another from the institutional level to the course level, and the curriculum becomes a "pathway for learning" rather than just a collection of independent courses.[13]

In addition to this integrative effect, program-level outcomes have the added benefit of encouraging faculty to be more intentional in their teaching.[14]

> Knowing what students are expected to achieve at the end of their program helps individual faculty members decide, in part, what students should achieve *at the end of each course*. In turn, knowing what students are expected to achieve at the end of a course helps us decide what students should achieve at the end of each section of the course, or indeed, at the end of each class period.[15]

Thus, identifying learning outcomes for externship programs helps faculty to make deliberate and well-considered choices about the teaching methods, course content, and learning activities to include in their individual courses.[16]

3. Defining the Externship Program

As explained in Chapter 3, law schools structure their externship offerings in a variety of different ways. Some schools group all of the available externship placements together regardless of placement type and offer them within a single course, which is typically referred to as a "general placement" program. In this case, the externship program and the externship course are essentially one and the same, so there is no need for separate program-level outcomes and course-level outcomes. Other schools, however, sort the placements into multiple courses based on their common subject matter and group similar placements together in a single course, such as courses for students externing with prosecutors, courses for students externing with corporate counsel, courses for students externing with judges,[17] and so on. In this framework, the externship program consists of multiple courses that are centered on the common subject matter of the work at the placement sites. This structure typically is referred to as a "subject-specific" or "specific placement" program.[18]

---

13. Best Practices for Legal Education, *supra* note 10, at 95 (quoting *Principles of Good Practice in the New Academy*, in Ass'n of Am. Colleges and Universities, Greater Expectations: A New Vision for Learning as a Nation Goes to College 30 (2002)).

14. *See* Mary J. Allen, Assessing Academic Programs, *supra* note 6, at 28.

15. Huba & Freed, *supra* note 12, at 96 (emphasis in original).

16. *See* Allen, Assessing Academic Programs, *supra* note 6, at 48. *See also* Building on Best Practices, *supra* note 11, at 27 ("Identifying desired outcomes brings crucial focus to teaching and learning.").

17. Judicial-externship courses could be divided further into appellate-court externships and trial-court externships.

18. *See, e.g.*, Robert F. Seibel & Linda H. Morton, *Field Placement Programs: Practices, Problems, and Possibilities*, 2 Clinical L. Rev. 413, 423–24 (1996) (explaining differences between general and

Schools with a part-time division may create different courses based on whether the placement sites permit students to work remotely and complete externship work during nights and weekends.[19] Other schools may group externship students into different courses based on the number of credit hours students receive upon satisfactory completion of the externship requirements. Some schools, for example, offer "semester-in-practice" externships in which students work at their externship sites full-time during the semester and receive 12 to 16 hours of academic credit. [20] When a law school offers multiple externship courses, it essentially has created, whether by design or default, an externship program.[21]

4. Writing Learning Outcomes for an Externship Program

Student learning outcomes are simply statements that "describe what we want the result of obtaining an education at our institution to be: what our graduates will know, what they will be able to do, and what they will value." [22] Because learn-

---

specialized externship programs); *see also* Carl J. Circo, *An Educational Partnership Model for Establishing, Structuring, and Implementing a Successful Corporate Counsel Externship*, 17 CLINICAL L. REV. 99 (2010) (discussing externship programs specific to corporate legal departments); Hans P. Sinha, *Prosecutorial Externship Programs: Past, Present, and Future*, 74 MISS. L.J. 1297 (2005) (describing externship programs specific to prosecutors' offices).

19. For example, the University of Arkansas at Little Rock William H. Bowen School of Law has created "practicum" courses in which part-time students perform externship work remotely for judges and prosecutors who are located outside of the school's immediate vicinity. *See* https://ualr.edu/law/clinical-programs/judicial-practicum/ (last visited March 4, 2022).

20. *See* Lance Cole & Camile C. Marion, *Semester-in-Residence Programs: Design, Implementation, and Best Practices*, *in* EXPERIENTIAL EDUCATION IN THE LAW SCHOOL CURRICULUM 225–57 (Emily Grant, Sandra Simpson & Kelly Terry eds., 2018); Liz Ryan Cole, *Lessons from A Semester in Practice*, 1 CLINICAL L. REV. 173 (1994) (describing Semester-in-Practice program at Vermont Law School). Other schools offer externships for varying levels of credit, ranging most frequently from two to twelve credit hours. *See* ROBERT R. KUEHN, MARGARET REUTER & DAVID A. SANTACROCE, CENTER FOR THE STUDY OF APPLIED LEGAL EDUCATION, 2019–20 SURVEY OF APPLIED LEGAL EDUCATION 45 (2020), www.csale.org/#results (last visited February 24, 2022).

21. *See* BUILDING ON BEST PRACTICES, *supra* note 11, at 217 n.7 ("Schools differ with how many courses they offer and what they call each externship course, but often, when there are several courses, they are coordinated, and sometimes administered, as a 'program.'"). *See also id.* at 221–22 (Externships "should be categorized organizationally as courses (and collectively, programs) that are part of the overall clinical legal education program. It is a best practice to organize both the courses and the faculty structure to accomplish this."); Susan L. Brooks, Cynthia Adcock, Stephen Ellmann, Robert L. Jones, Jr., Christine Cimini & Margaret Berry, *Experience the Future: Papers from the Second National Symposium on Experiential Education in Law: Alliance for Experiential Learning in Law*, 7 ELON L. REV. 1, 18 (2015) (defining "externship program" as the "collection of courses within a school's clinical legal education program that provides students with the opportunity to integrate academic inquiry with work experiences in the law for academic credit").

22. SHAW & VANZANDT, *supra* note 7, at 8. *See also* BUILDING ON BEST PRACTICES, *supra* note 11, at 28 ("Learning outcomes emphasize the knowledge, skills, and attitudes to be evidenced by students

ing outcomes for a program are integrated across multiple courses, "they should be developed not in isolation but as the result of research, reflection, and informed collaborative discussion."[23] At a minimum, the leader of an externship program, such as a faculty director or an associate dean for experiential education, and the faculty who teach in the program should participate in the discussion to identify and determine program learning outcomes. If an externship program also employs adjunct professors, it could be helpful to include them in the discussion to have their perspective on the competencies that students need to develop for practice. If it is not practicable to include all of the adjuncts in the discussion, a school could survey them to get their input on the program learning outcomes.

Externship faculty also must decide the appropriate number of learning outcomes for their program. Program outcomes should "target only the most important goals" because addressing "a small number of well-focused outcomes enhances the cost effectiveness of the assessment program."[24] Assessment expert Linda Suskie recommends that institutions should focus on just three to six key learning outcomes for a program.[25]

Once externship faculty decide the number of outcomes a program should have, they must actually draft the language of the outcomes. Educational experts have identified several characteristics of effectively written outcomes. First, an outcome should focus on what students will learn and be able to do, and not on what professors will do or the material they will cover.[26] Second, program outcomes should reflect the law school's mission and align with its institutional outcomes.[27] Third, the outcomes should reflect "what is important in a particular area of law or for law practice, and focus on those skills or the knowledge that will endure."[28] Finally, outcomes should be "general enough to capture important learning but clear and specific enough to be measurable."[29] In this context, "measurable" does not

---

at the end of a particular period, and use a clear, active verbal framework about what students can be expected to do (analyze, explain, produce) rather than more passive ones (understand, appreciate).").

23. Linda Suskie, Assessing Student Learning: A Common Sense Guide 51 (3d ed. 2018). *See also* Huba & Freed, *supra* note 12, at 93 (Developing program outcomes is a task for faculty "to complete collectively, and it is a task that takes time and deliberation.").

24. Huba & Freed, *supra* note 12, at 73. *See also id.* ("Assessments at the program level should be as focused as possible on important aspects of learning in order to yield useful information without wasted effort.").

25. Suskie, *supra* note 23, at 50.

26. Niedwiecki, *supra* note 10, at 679; Huba & Freed, *supra* note 12, at 98–99.

27. Huba & Freed, *supra* note 12, at 100–07; *see also* Niedwiecki, *supra* note 10, at 679 ("[A] program's outcomes should be tied to the institution's outcomes.").

28. Niedwiecki, *supra* note 10, at 679.

29. Huba & Freed, *supra* note 12, at 116.

mean "objective decimal-point accuracy"[30]; rather, it means "a general judgment of whether students know, think, and can do most of what we intend for them."[31]

With these principles in mind, faculty can use a basic formula to draft outcome statements for an externship program. "Under this formula, each learning outcome should have a stem, an action verb, and outcome."[32] The learning outcome starts with the stem, which is "the part of the outcome that focuses on the students and when or what they should be able to do or know."[33] For example, the stem for an externship program learning outcome might state: "Upon completing a course in the externship program, students will be able to ______________________________."

The remaining parts of an outcome statement are a description of the type of learning that is intended and a verb that identifies actions students will take to demonstrate their learning. Educational theorists generally recognize three types (or "domains") of learning:

- "the cognitive domain (increasingly complex sorts of understandings and analytical processes),
- the psychomotor or performance domain (complex patterns of physical or motor activity such as lawyering activities), and
- the affective or feeling domain (values, attitudes, and beliefs)."[34]

Outcomes are not exclusive to one domain, however, and overlap often occurs.[35] For example, the practice skills of client interviewing, fact investigation, and oral argument certainly depend on cognitive abilities such as critical thinking and the ability to know and recall substantive law and procedure. The chart below provides some examples of learning within the three domains:

---

30. Best Practices for Legal Education, *supra* note 10, at 49.

31. *Id.* (quoting James O. Nichols, The Departmental Guide and Record Book for Student Outcomes Assessment and Institutional Effectiveness 22 (1995)).

32. Niedwiecki, *supra* note 10, at 679 (emphasis in original).

33. *Id.*

34. Best Practices for Legal Education, *supra* note 10, at 167. *See also* Trudy W. Banta & Catherine A. Palomba, Assessment Essentials: Planning, Implementing, and Improving Assessment in Higher Education 67 (2d ed. 2015) ("Educators distinguish between cognitive, affective, and psychomotor learning outcomes—what students know, value, and can do."). Thus, program-level assessment can measure student learning in all three of the apprenticeships identified in Educating Lawyers, *supra* note 11.

35. Susan P. Liemer, *Embodied Legal Education: Incorporating Another Part of Bloom's Taxonomy*, 95 U. Det. Mercy L. Rev. 69, 76 (2017) ("The fact that the domains may overlap or more than one may be relevant to a learning task has long been acknowledged.").

Figure 5-2. Examples of Learning Within the Three Domains

Types of Learning Within Cognitive Domain	Types of Learning Within Performance Domain	Types of Learning Within Affective Domain
Knowledge of legal doctrine	Self-directedness	Understanding cultural differences
Knowledge of ethical rules	Legal writing skills	Commitment to pro bono
Ability to apply substantive law and procedural rules to fact situations	Working collaboratively as part of a team	Demonstrating empathy in one's work
Capacity to learn through reflection	Negotiation skills	Formation of professional identity
Problem-solving	Trial-advocacy skills	Exemplifying integrity

The action verb should align with the domain of learning that an outcome addresses and describe some observable act that students will perform to demonstrate their knowledge of that domain. Learning taxonomies can be helpful in selecting appropriate action verbs. A learning taxonomy is simply a system that classifies educational objectives and usually includes guidelines for developing them.[36] The most well-known learning taxonomy is probably Bloom's Taxonomy, which was developed in 1956 and identifies six categories of learning within the cognitive domain.[37] The categories, which are arranged in ascending levels of difficulty, are knowledge (the least complex), comprehension, application, analysis, synthesis, and evaluation (the most complex).[38] Using this taxonomy, educators have developed lists of action verbs that correlate with the various levels of cognitive learning and can be used in writing outcome statements.[39] For example, action verbs such as "analyze," "distinguish," "identify," and "compare" relate to a cognitive-domain outcome such

---

36. *E.g.*, Huba & Freed, *supra* note 12, at 112; Shaw & VanZandt, *supra* note 7, at 66. *See also* Maki, *supra* note 4, at 91 ("Taxonomies also help educators identify the verbs that describe what students should chronologically represent or demonstrate.").

37. Shaw & VanZandt, *supra* note 7, at 66. Other learning taxonomies that can be helpful in crafting learning outcomes include Fink's "Taxonomy of Significant Learning"; Marzano, Pickering, and McTighe's "Dimensions of Learning"; and Marzano and Kendall's "Taxonomy of Educational Objectives." Suskie, *supra* note 23 at 52–53. *See also* Michael Hunter Schwartz, *Teaching Law by Design: How Learning Theory and Instructional Design Can Inform and Reform Law Teaching*, 38 San Diego L. Rev. 347, 395–98 (2001) (discussing Gagné's five domains of learning).

38. Shaw & VanZandt, *supra* note 7, at 66. Bloom's original taxonomy was subsequently revised, and the categories in the cognitive domain are now remembering, understanding, applying, analyzing, evaluating, and creating. Maki, *supra* note 4, at 91.

39. *See* Allen, Assessing Academic Programs, *supra* note 6, at 37; Shaw & VanZandt, *supra* note 7, at 67.

as critical thinking skills. Action verbs such as "present" or "engage" align with a psychomotor-domain outcome such as the ability to work collaboratively as part of a team. Action verbs such as "demonstrates," "adheres," or "integrates" can work well with outcomes in the affective domain.

5. Examples of Learning Outcomes for Externship Programs

In crafting learning outcomes for externship programs, faculty have many different options from which to choose.[40] One way for faculty to articulate and prioritize the intended learning outcomes is to try to describe the qualities of the ideal student who has completed the program.[41] "What does this person know? What can this person do? What does this person care about? Faculty also might find it useful to ask for input from important stakeholders, such as students, alumni, and employers. What do they believe that students should know, do and value by the end of the program?"[42] These questions align with the three domains of learning discussed above—cognitive, psychomotor, and affective—and suggest that an externship program should have outcomes in each of the three areas.

To some degree, the selection of program learning outcomes will depend on whether the program is a general-placement or subject-specific program.[43] If the program groups all placements together in a single course, then the program and course outcomes will be one and the same. However, if the program consists of multiple, subject-specific externship courses, then the program-level outcomes should be broad enough that all students, regardless of the particular course in which they are enrolled, will have the opportunity to achieve and demonstrate competency in each of the program outcomes. Accordingly, faculty who teach in programs with multiple, subject-specific courses should work together to develop program-level outcomes that are common to all of the externship courses and are not contingent on a particular area of law or type of practice.

When establishing program-level outcomes, the triad of the cognitive, psychomotor, and affective domains can be an effective organizing principle. What cognitive skills should all students who complete an externship within the program be able to perform? Are there any skills within the psychomotor domain that should be the focus of a learning outcome? Are there any affective skills that should be articulated in a learning outcome? A program outcome in the cognitive domain could

---

40. *See generally* Kelly S. Terry, *Embedding Assessment Principles in Externships*, 20 Clinical L. Rev. 467, 484–89 (2014).

41. Allen, Assessing Academic Programs, *supra* note 6, at 33.

42. *Id.*

43. *See generally* Terry, *supra* note 40, at 485–89 (discussing how the nature of subject-specific and general-placement externship programs can affect outcomes).

include the ability to engage in reflection to learn from one's experiences.[44] Other possible outcomes in this domain could include knowledge of ethical rules, the ability to engage in problem-solving, or the capacity to think critically about the work of lawyers and the operation of institutions within the legal system.[45] These outcomes are appropriate for the program as a whole because all students, regardless of their placements, should be able to practice and demonstrate competency in them.

Identifying program outcomes within the psychomotor domain may be more difficult, because the lawyering skills that externship students perform vary widely across the spectrum of placements. It is not necessary, however, to have an externship-program outcome in each of the three domains, and it may be more appropriate for skills within the psychomotor domain to be the focus of another program within the curriculum, such as a trial-advocacy program. Nonetheless, program outcomes within this domain might include effective communication skills and the ability to work well with supervisors, since all externship students should encounter and have the opportunity to practice these skills.

Potential program outcomes within the affective domain include the development of professional identity, an appreciation for the lawyer's pro bono obligation, the cultivation of well-being practices, and components of professionalism such as civility, diligence, and ethical conduct. The ABA's MacCrate Report identified four fundamental values of the legal profession, which include providing competent representation; promoting justice, fairness, and morality; striving to improve the profession; and developing professionally as a lawyer.[46] Researchers Shultz and Zedeck also have identified certain values that correlate with lawyer effectiveness, including passion and engagement, integrity and honesty, and self-development.[47] In addition, the *Foundations for Practice* study, which surveyed more than 24,000 lawyers, found that characteristics such as integrity, trustworthiness, conscientiousness, and common sense, as well as professional competencies such as active listening and punctuality, "were *far more important* in brand new lawyers than legal skills[.]"[48] Indeed,

---

44. *E.g.*, Rebecca B. Rosenfeld, *The Examined Externship Is Worth Doing: Critical Self-Reflection and Externship Pedagogy*, 21 Clinical L. Rev. 127, 130 (2014) ("[O]ne express goal of field placement classes should be to help students learn how to learn. These courses should teach self-assessment and critical reflection, so students gain the ability to learn throughout their careers."); *see also* Mary Jo Eyster, *Designing and Teaching the Large Externship Clinic*, 5 Clinical L. Rev. 347, 359–61 (1999) (discussing learning through reflection as primary goal of externship course).

45. *E.g.*, Best Practices for Legal Education, *supra* note 10, at 168–73; Building on Best Practices, *supra* note 11, at 226–28; Nancy M. Maurer & Liz Ryan Cole, *Design, Teach and Manage: Ensuring Educational Integrity in Field Placement Courses*, 19 Clinical L. Rev. 115, 143–44 (2012).

46. ABA Section of Legal Education and Admissions to the Bar, Legal Education and Professional Development—An Educational Continuum (Report of the Task Force on Law Schools and the Profession: Narrowing the Gap) 138–41 (1992) (hereinafter "MacCrate Report").

47. Marjorie M. Shultz & Sheldon Zedeck, *Predicting Lawyer Effectiveness: Broadening the Basis for Law School Admission Decisions*, 36 Law & Soc. Inquiry 620, 629–30 (2011).

48. Alli Gerkman & Logan Cornett, Foundations for Practice: The Whole Lawyer and the Character Quotient 3 (2016) (emphasis in original), https://iaals.du.edu/sites/default/

the ten qualities that the surveyed attorneys identified as the most important for new lawyers are: maintaining confidentiality; arriving on time for meetings, appointments, and hearings; honoring commitments; integrity and trustworthiness; treating others with respect and courtesy; listening attentively and respectfully; promptly responding to inquiries and requests; diligence; having a strong work ethic and putting forth one's best effort; and attention to detail.[49] Program outcomes could include the development of the professional values and attitudes identified in *Foundations for Practice*, the MacCrate Report, or the Shultz and Zedeck study.

In light of the renewed movement for racial justice following the police murder of George Floyd in May 2020 in Minneapolis,[50] externship programs also might consider learning outcomes focused on antiracist principles. According to Professor Ibram X. Kendi, an antiracist is one "who is expressing the idea that racial groups are equals and none needs developing, and is supporting policy that reduces racial inequity."[51] ABA Standard 303 now requires law schools to provide education on bias, cross-cultural competency, and racism to students at the start of law school and once again before graduation.[52] Importantly, this requirement specifies that "[f]or students engaged in law clinics or field placements, the second educational occasion will take place before, concurrently with, or as part of their enrollment in clinical or field placement courses."[53]

Below are examples of institutional-learning outcomes from the California Polytechnic State University that focus on racial-justice issues and might be adapted into learning outcomes for an externship program:

Graduates should be able to:

- Understand the history of issues related to diversity, social and economic inequities, and political power in the United States and across the world;
- Analyze the various institutions and structures that create and maintain social, economic, and political inequality in the United States and across the world; and, identify those that offer redress for these issues;
- Define and describe the various issues related to diversity, equity, and inclusion in their respective disciplines;

---

files/documents/publications/foundations_for_practice_whole_lawyer_quotient.pdf (last visited March 4, 2022) (hereinafter "Foundations for Practice").

49. *Id.* at 26.

50. *See, e.g*, Eliott C. McLaughlin, *How George Floyd's Death Ignited a Racial Reckoning That Shows No Signs of Slowing Down*, CNN (Aug. 9, 2020, 11:31 AM), http: //www.cnn.com/ 2020/08/09/us/george-floyd-protests-different-why/index.html.

51. Ibram X. Kendi, How to Be an Antiracist 24 (2019).

52. *See* ABA Standards and Rules of Procedure for Approval of Law Schools 2022–2023, Standard 303(c).

53. *Id.*

- Critically examine their own personal beliefs, attitudes, and biases about historically marginalized people and cultures in the United States and across the world.[54]

Similarly, Seattle University School of Law currently is considering a proposed institutional-learning outcome stating that its graduates "will demonstrate the ability to identify and address racism and other forms of structural and systemic inequality."[55]

Once externship faculty have established their program-level outcomes, they should articulate learning outcomes for their individual courses. The course-level outcomes should be consistent with and follow from the program outcomes, with a more specific focus on the particular learning that can be accomplished within the individual course. For example, an externship program consisting of multiple courses could have a program outcome stating that, at the end of their externships, students should be able to communicate effectively in writing in a professional setting. Consistent with that program-level outcome, individual courses within the program could have the following course-level learning outcomes:

- Judicial externship course: students will be able to write an effective bench memorandum;
- Prosecutor externship course: students will be able to write an effective response to a defense motion;
- Government agency externship course: students will be able to write an effective research memorandum.

These course-level outcomes more specifically express the program-level writing outcome within the context of the particular course. Chapter 7 on course design addresses course-level learning outcomes in more detail.

6. Assessing Externship Program Learning Outcomes

Once externship faculty have established the learning outcomes for the program as a whole, they should gather and evaluate the assessment data. Program-level assessment has a wider focus than course-level assessment, so program outcomes generally are assessed in a process that is in addition to the assessment of student learning that occurs within individual courses. While program-level assessment is a new endeavor for many law schools, it need not be overwhelming. It likely will entail reviewing the same externship assignments that students complete as part

54. California Polytechnic State University, Diversity Learning Objectives, www.academicprograms. calpoly.edu/content/academicpolicies/diversity_lo (last visited March 4, 2022).

55. Posting of Professor Lisa Brodoff, Dir. of Clinical Law Prog., lbrodoff@seattleu.edu, to LEXTERN@listserv.gsu.edu (Dec. 30, 2020) (on file with author).

of their regular coursework, simply from a different perspective. In addition, many universities have assessment offices staffed by experts in the field who can provide training, guidance, and resources.[56]

The differences in how assessment processes operate at the program level and the course level are best demonstrated with a hypothetical externship program. Assume that a law school has an externship program that consists of three individual externship courses: 1) a prosecutor externship; 2) a civil-litigation externship; and 3) a corporate-counsel externship. Assume further that the faculty teaching the various externship courses have established the following learning outcomes for the externship program as a whole:

Students who complete the externship program will be able to:

1. Draft a well-written practice-related document;
2. Effectively demonstrate verbal communication skills in a professional environment;
3. Effectively use problem-solving skills on behalf of a client;
4. Recognize ethical issues and effectively apply ethical rules in practice situations;
5. Explain the concept of a professional identity and articulate the elements of their own professional identity.

The sections that follow discuss how to develop an assessment plan for these program learning outcomes, collect and evaluate evidence of student achievement of the outcomes, and use information gathered from that evaluation to improve student learning.

7. Developing a Plan for Program Assessment

a. Designate a Leader for Program Assessment

Conducting an assessment process involves identifying, collecting, managing, and evaluating a significant amount of information over an extended period of time. To ensure that this process is effective, meaningful, and well-executed, it must have a designated leader. Depending on how a school structures its externship offerings, the leader could be an associate dean for experiential education, a faculty director of the externship program, a faculty member who teaches in the program, or a group of externship faculty members who form an assessment committee for program-level evaluation. The leader will be responsible for implementing the program-assessment process, documenting the steps of the process and the information it produces, and working with faculty to make program improvements based on the assessment data.

---

56. These experts typically are located in a provost's office or in an office of institutional effectiveness.

b. Create a Written Assessment Plan

The designated leader for program assessment should start by working with the externship faculty to create an assessment plan, which is simply a written document setting out the process for determining whether students are achieving the stated program learning outcomes.[57] The plan typically includes the learning outcomes at issue, an inventory of the courses in which the outcomes are addressed, a schedule specifying when and how often each outcome will be assessed, the type of evidence of student learning that will be used to evaluate student attainment of each outcome, and the number of measures of student learning that will be considered.

1) Inventory Externship Courses to Determine Where Program Outcomes Are Addressed

"For students to learn what is expected of them, the relevant subject matter must be addressed and reinforced in the curriculum."[58] Students can be expected to learn the knowledge, skills, and values described in a program outcome only if they are exposed to that content and provided the opportunity to apply and practice it. Thus, the assessment leader and the externship faculty should work together to inventory the content of all of the externship courses to ensure that they are providing students sufficient opportunities to develop competency in the program learning outcomes.[59] Using the hypothetical program outcomes described above, faculty teaching the prosecutor, civil-litigation, and corporate-counsel externships would review their courses to determine if all of their students have the opportunity to draft practice-related documents, demonstrate verbal communication skills, engage in problem-solving, recognize ethical issues and apply ethical rules, and explore the concept of professional identity. Externship courses are unique in that they provide two different settings that can potentially address the program outcomes: the placement site and the externship seminar.

In reviewing their courses, externship faculty should look for gaps and patterns in the treatment of the program outcomes.[60] For example, are all of the students in each of the externship courses receiving the opportunity to develop the knowledge, skills, and values associated with each of the five program learning outcomes? If the students are not being exposed to the program outcomes at their placement sites, are the outcomes being addressed in the externship seminars? Is there a program out-

---

57. *See, e.g.*, Banta & Palomba, *supra* note 34, at 20 ("An assessment plan captures agreement about what matters, gives direction for actions, and provides a means to determine if progress is being made."); Funk, *supra* note 4, at 30 (describing assessment plan); Shaw & VanZandt, *supra* note 7, at 54–57 (same).

58. Banta & Palomba, *supra* note 34, at 71.

59. This process is similar to the curriculum mapping that occurs in institutional assessment.

60. *See, e.g.*, Maki, *supra* note 4, at 61 (Curriculum maps "identify gaps in student learning opportunities or identify concentrations of learning experiences without further opportunity for students to transfer, build on, or apply learning.").

come that is addressed in some of the externship courses, but not all of them?[61] Do the courses address the program outcomes with sufficient depth to allow students to achieve competency in them? The results of this course-review process should be provided to and discussed with the program-assessment leader.

This process should reveal a great deal of information about the content of externship courses and how that content aligns with the broader program outcomes. Using this information, faculty should be able to make thoughtful decisions about the program outcomes, the design of individual courses, and teaching methods. For example, if the inventory process reveals that the skill of problem-solving is not addressed in all of the externship courses, then the faculty should ask if that outcome is truly critical to their students' learning. Is it essential for all students who complete an externship course to develop the skill of problem-solving?[62] If it is, then the faculty should change the content of the externship courses to ensure that all of them incorporate that skill. Those changes could involve working with site supervisors to ensure that students receive opportunities to engage in problem-solving at their placement sites, or they could mean restructuring the externship seminars to include teaching the skill of problem-solving. However, if faculty determine that problem-solving is not an essential skill for all students who complete an externship course, then problem-solving should be discarded as a program outcome. Similarly, changes to course content should be made if an outcome is merely introduced in externship courses, but students do not receive adequate opportunities to practice and achieve competency in it. This change could involve creating more assignments or in-class exercises relating to the outcome to broaden students' exposure to it.

2) Create an Assessment Schedule

Given the amount of work required, trying to assess every program outcome every year is likely not feasible, and it would make the assessment process unsustainable.[63] There is no established rule mandating how often program outcomes should be assessed. Accordingly, most experts recommend creating a cycle for assessing each outcome every few years on a repeating basis.[64] The schedule will be determined largely by the number of program outcomes, the amount of evidence that

61. *See, e.g.*, BANTA & PALOMBA, *supra* note 34, at 72 ("If a particular outcome is getting too much coverage or too little, the curriculum map will reveal the imbalance.").

62. Problem-solving might not be an essential outcome for the externship program if it is sufficiently addressed in another required course in the curriculum.

63. *See, e.g.*, FUNK, *supra* note 4, at 55; SHAW & VANZANDT, *supra* note 7, at 83.

64. SHAW & VANZANDT, *supra* note 7, at 83. *Cf., e.g.*, SUSKIE, *supra* note 23, at 99 (suggesting that key learning outcomes should be assessed at least every three years and preferably every two years). Assessing outcomes every few years provides ongoing evaluation of student learning, with opportunities to respond to deficiencies and implement corrective measures in a timely manner, while not being overly burdensome for faculty.

must be gathered and reviewed to assess them, and the faculty resources necessary to conduct the review.

Using the five hypothetical program outcomes described previously in this Chapter, the diagram below illustrates a possible timeline for assessing each outcome three times over the course of nine years:

Figure 5-3. Timeline for Assessing Program Outcomes

Learning Outcomes	2022–2023	2023–2024	2024–2025	2025–2026	2026–2027	2027–2028	2028–2029	2029–2030	2030–2031
Drafting Practice-Related Documents	X			X			X		
Verbal Communication Skills	X			X			X		
Problem-Solving Skills		X			X			X	
Recognizing Ethical Issues and Applying Ethics Rules		X			X			X	
Professional Identity			X			X			X

3) Decide the Types of Assessment Measures to Use

Assessment leaders also must decide the types of measures they will use to evaluate whether students are achieving the program learning outcomes. Assessment measures (also known as "instruments" or "tools") are simply "the means by which one gathers evidence to demonstrate learning or the achievement of learning outcomes; they are indicators of performance."[65] Educational experts typically categorize assessment instruments as either "direct measures" or "indirect measures."

Direct measures are based on actual student work or performance and require students to display their knowledge and skills to a trained evaluator.[66] Examples of direct assessment measures include journals, timesheets, quizzes, essays, drafting

65. Shaw & VanZandt, *supra* note 7, at 183.
66. *Id.* at 104; *see also* Banta & Palomba, *supra* note 34, at 23.

assignments, presentations, skills performances, portfolios, and evaluations by externship supervisors. "Direct assessment tools tend to be viewed with great favor because they do not involve guesswork. What the students can and cannot do or do and do not know is right there in front of the assessor[.]"[67] Assessment experts also suggest that direct measures are "more likely to yield meaningful data because we are evaluating students based on work they are heavily invested in, and for which they have incentives to do their best."[68]

Indirect measures, on the other hand, "are based upon opinion, either the student's opinion or any other observer's opinion."[69] Forms of indirect assessment include students' self-evaluation of their own knowledge, skills, and values, as well as surveys and focus groups of employers asking for their general perceptions about students' abilities.[70] While indirect evidence can provide useful information, it is based on opinions and self-reporting and therefore is less reliable than direct evidence. Accordingly, "*no assessment of knowledge, understanding, or thinking or performance skills should consist of indirect evidence alone*."[71] Assessment experts generally recommend using a combination of direct and indirect measures.

Program assessment generally relies on embedded assessments, which are assignments or learning activities that students complete as part of a regular course. In addition to being reviewed for specific courses, these same assignments also are reviewed for evidence of student learning with respect to the program learning outcomes. Experts recommend using embedded assessments whenever possible because they allow the gathering of assessment information through the use of assignments that have been created for other purposes, which saves faculty time and energy.[72] In addition, students are motivated to complete the course assignments on which their grades depend, so embedded assessments likely produce more accurate information about student learning than assignments that students are asked to complete solely for assessment purposes, such as surveys and interviews.[73] The

67. SHAW & VANZANDT, *supra* note 7, at 105.

68. Docia L. Rudley, *Bridging the Divide Between Assessment and Accreditation*, 62 N.Y.L. SCH. L. REV. 37, 45 (2017–2018).

69. SHAW & VANZANDT, *supra* note 7, at 104.

70. BANTA & PALOMBA, *supra* note 34, at 23; HUBA & FREED, *supra* note 12, at 11; SHAW & VANZANDT, *supra* note 7, at 104.

71. SUSKIE, *supra* note 23, at 26 (emphasis in original).

72. FUNK, *supra* note 4, at 29. *See also* BANTA & PALOMBA, *supra* note 34, at 25; SUSKIE, *supra* note 23, at 156.

73. *See* SHAW & VANZANDT, *supra* note 7, at 100 ("Using embedded tools is preferable because students tend to take assignments more seriously (and hence perform better) in the context of a class. Therefore, embedded tools may provide better evidence of student learning."); *see also, e.g.*, Rudley, *supra* note 68, at 45 ("When possible, use assessment that is already embedded in the curriculum to ensure that students are invested in their performance and that the results are genuinely of interest to them and to faculty members."); SUSKIE, *supra* note 23, at 279 ("Grades are a powerful incentive for students to participate in an assessment and to give it serious thought and effort.").

embedded assessments available for program review likely will include both direct and indirect measures.

Using the five hypothetical program outcomes discussed previously in this Chapter, the leaders of the program assessment process would review the externship courses to determine if any of the existing course assignments provide evidence of student learning with respect to the program outcomes. For example, for the outcome relating to drafting a well-written practice document, site supervisors might review the written work that students produce at the placement sites and report their findings to the externship faculty. Alternatively, if workplace confidentiality is protected and site supervisors grant permission, externship faculty might review the students' written work themselves for assessment purposes.[74] Simulated practice documents that students draft for a class assignment also might be considered. For the outcome relating to professional identity, student journals or a final reflective essay might be reviewed. Alternatively, there may be assignments in which students have been asked to evaluate their progress in developing a professional identity.

For each program outcome, the assessment leader, working in conjunction with faculty who teach the externship courses, will need to identify the assessments from each course that can be used for program assessment. This identification usually can be made when the courses are inventoried to determine how each program outcome is addressed in each course.[75] If there are no embedded assessments available to use for program evaluation, the externship faculty can decide whether they want to incorporate such assessments into their courses, or whether they want to ask students to complete "add-on" assessments, which are assignments given outside of a regular class that are used solely for program assessment. Once the assessment leader and externship faculty have decided which assessments will be used for program evaluation, the assessment leader should record that information in the assessment plan.

4) Decide the Number of Assessment Measures to Use

With a variety of direct and indirect measures from which to choose, the assessment leader must decide how many assessments to consider in evaluating whether students are achieving competency in the program outcomes. Assessment expert Barbara Walvoord recommends using a minimum of two measures for each outcome—one direct measure and one indirect measure.[76] For example, the program-assessment leader might choose students' final essays (a direct measure) and their self-evaluations of their achievement of the program outcomes (an indirect measure). Multiple measures are essential because no single assessment instru-

---

74. The site supervisor or the extern student would need to redact case-specific and identifying information from any written work prior to providing it to the externship teacher.

75. *See* Chapters 8, 9, and 10, *infra* (discussing topics for seminar classes, from which assignments for program assessment can be generated).

76. Barbara E. Walvoord, Assessment Clear and Simple: A Practical Guide for Institutions, Departments, and General Education 59–60 (2d ed. 2010).

ment, even if it is very well-designed and executed, "can provide the comprehensive view needed to determine whether a criterion is being achieved."[77] Students may perform better on one type of assessment than another, so using multiple assessments provides students with more opportunities to demonstrate their learning and produces a more accurate picture of whether students are achieving learning outcomes.[78] Using multiple measures also enhances credibility in the assessment process by allowing faculty to compare results from multiple methods.[79] When multiple methods of assessment produce similar findings, greater confidence may be placed in the results.[80]

An assessment process also must be sustainable to be effective. It does no good to collect a mountain of assessment data that faculty members do not have sufficient time to consider and analyze. Accordingly, assessment leaders are advised to start with a manageable number of assessment measures, following Dr. Walvoord's recommendation of two measures. If faculty later determine that they would like to have more information about student learning, and they have adequate time to evaluate it, then more assessment measures can be added to the program assessment plan as the process progresses.

8. Gathering Program Assessment Data

a. Determine the Amount of Data to Collect

1) The Use of Representative Samples

Once assessment leaders decide the type and number of assessment instruments to use, they will need to determine how many students will be asked to complete them. How many students need to be assessed in order to draw reliable conclusions about whether students are achieving an externship program's learning outcomes? No hard and fast rule exists to answer this question.

The reliability of results increases as larger numbers of students are assessed and more data are collected.[81] Accordingly, schools should strive to assess as many students as possible at the program level, and they may choose to assess all of the stu-

77. SHAW & VANZANDT, *supra* note 7, at 112.

78. *See* MAKI, *supra* note 4, at 157.

79. BANTA & PALOMBA, *supra* note 34, at 31. *See also, e.g.*, SUSKIE, *supra* note 23, at 327 ("Comparing evidence from various assessments against one another is called corroboration or triangulation.").

80. Susan Hanley Duncan, *They're Back! The New Accreditation Standards Coming to a Law School Near You—A 2018 Update, Guide to Compliance, and Dean's Role in Implementing*, 67 J. LEGAL EDUC. 462, 477 (2018) ("Greater accuracy and authority are achieved when several methods of assessment produce similar findings."); FUNK, *supra* note 4, at 74, n. 3 ("Taken together, information gleaned from multiple sources will strengthen your confidence in your observations and conclusions.").

81. *E.g.*, FUNK, *supra* note 4, at 37.

dents taking courses in an externship program. For schools with small externship programs, it should be possible to review assessment instruments completed by all of the students in the program. In addition, university policies may require assessment of all students, so program leaders should find out whether their parent university has such a mandate.

In the absence of such a requirement, assessment leaders will need to decide whether it is feasible for them to review and evaluate assessments completed by every student who has taken an externship course. For example, using the hypothetical program outcomes discussed above, assume that the program leaders have decided to use a ten-page reflective essay that all students complete at the end of their externships to assess students' development with respect to professional-identity formation. Assume further that the prosecutor externship course, the corporate-counsel externship course, and the civil-litigation externship course each have 40 students per year. It simply may not be feasible for a committee of externship faculty to review all 120 essays for program-assessment purposes.[82] Program assessment, however, does not require the measurement of each and every student's learning.[83] Rather, reviewing a representative sample of student work is an acceptable method of drawing conclusions about student learning as a whole.

If assessment leaders are going to use a representative sample, they must determine an appropriate sample size. While there is no established rule for determining an appropriate sample size, "[t]he sample must be representative and complete."[84] Some experts suggest as a rule of thumb that, at a minimum, the sample "should be **the greater of ten students or 10 percent of the student population being measured.**"[85] So, using the example of the reflective essays above, the assessment committee would need to review at least 12 of the essays as a representative sample. University assessment offices also may be able to provide guidance on determining an appropriate sample size.

Other experts suggest deciding the sample size based on the margin of error that is acceptable.[86] Using a formula, experts have calculated the following error margins based on sample size:[87]

---

82. The same time concerns apply to interviews and focus groups. While the financial costs of these assessment instruments typically are low, the time and effort required to conduct them with all students may be prohibitive. SUSKIE, *supra* note 23, at 158.

83. SHAW & VANZANDT, *supra* note 7, at 114.

84. *Id.*

85. *Id.* (emphasis in original).

86. SUSKIE, *supra* note 23, at 159–60.

87. This table is reproduced from SUSKIE, *supra* note 23, at 159.

Figure 5-4. Sample Sizes and Error Margins

Random Sample Size	Error Margin
9604	1%
2401	2%
1067	3%
600	4%
384	5%
264	6%
196	7%

Thus, sample size depends in large part on the error margin that faculty are willing to tolerate. According to assessment expert Linda Suskie, "[w]hile professional pollsters often aim for sample sizes of about 1,000 people, with an error margin of three percent, unless your assessments may lead to major (read expensive) changes, a sample of no more than 300 or 400 is probably sufficient."[88] If a sample that size is still too large to be practical, faculty may use a smaller sample that is more feasible, so long as they recognize that the error margin will increase.[89] According to Suskie, "[i]f the assessment will likely lead to only minor changes, such as adjusting the curriculum in a course or two, a smaller sample may be fine."[90] For example, if the assessment might cause teachers to supplement reading materials in classes or add some additional class exercises or assignments, a smaller sample size probably would suffice. However, if teachers are contemplating complete redesigns of courses, they probably would want to base their decisions on a larger sample size.

2) Methods for Choosing Representative Samples

A variety of methods exists for choosing representative samples, including simple random samples, cluster random samples, and convenience samples.[91] Simple random sampling requires that every student in the population being assessed has an equal chance to be selected for the sample.[92] When using simple random sampling, it is important to use methods that will reduce bias in the selection of students.[93] One method for reducing bias is to use a random number generator to select students based on their exam numbers and then assess the work product of

88. *Id.*
89. *Id.* at 159–60.
90. *Id.* at 160.
91. BANTA & PALOMBA, *supra* note 34, at 90–91; SHAW & VANZANDT, *supra* note 7, at 115.
92. SHAW & VANZANDT, *supra* note 7, at 115.
93. MAKI, *supra* note 4, at 258.

those students.[94] Another method might be to redact student names from assignments and then randomly select a certain number of assignments to review for program-level assessment.

Cluster random sampling "involves randomly selecting subgroups/sections and assessing everyone in that section."[95] This method could be used for the hypothetical reflective essays discussed above. If the externship program used this method, it would choose one of the three externship courses—either the prosecutor, corporate counsel, or civil-litigation course—and review all of the essays from that one course for program evaluation of the professional-identity formation learning outcome.[96]

If these sampling methods are not possible, information often is collected from what is known as a "convenience sample."[97] This type of sample occurs when faculty "cannot comply with the rules for appropriate sampling and have simply done the best they can in locating individuals to participate in the assessment."[98] In-class exercises, for example, are completed only by those students who attend the class on the day of the exercise, and the characteristics of those students may not be representative of all of the students in the externship program.[99] Assessment data, however, do not have to comply with empirical-research protocols, and information of this type is still quite meaningful and useful.[100]

b. Methods for Gathering the Assessment Data

Once the amount of data to collect has been decided, the program-assessment leader should design a system for gathering, protecting, and storing that data. Otherwise, the information may be inadvertently destroyed or discarded, or simply not made available in a timely manner. When designing this process, the assessment leader must ensure that it complies with the Family Educational Rights and Privacy Act (FERPA), which is a federal law that limits the disclosure of personally identifiable information in educational records.[101]

The nature of the assessment instruments likely will determine the method for collecting them. For example, if the assessment data are embedded assessments, such as journals or class presentations, the assessment leader will need to set up a process to work with the faculty administering the assessments to collect copies of them, a representative sample of them, or the rubrics used to evaluate them. The least complex process would probably require the faculty members to provide the

94. SHAW & VANZANDT, *supra* note 7, at 115.
95. *Id.*
96. *E.g.*, *id.*
97. BANTA & PALOMBA, *supra* note 34, at 90.
98. *Id.*
99. *E.g.*, *id.* at 90–91.
100. *See* FUNK, *supra* note 4, at 73–74.
101. 20 U.S.C. § 1232g; 34 C.F.R. Part 99. Chapter 7, *infra*, discusses FERPA requirements in more detail.

information directly to the assessment leader at a designated time of the year. Assessment data that originate outside of the law school may need to be obtained from the dean or another law school administrator. For example, if assessment of an externship program involves review of data from focus groups or surveys of employers conducted by outside consultants or other entities, the assessment leader should identify the law school administrator who receives that information and set up a process for obtaining the data from that person.[102]

Finally, assessment leaders should decide how long they will retain assessment data, such as rubrics and student assignments, after they have reviewed it. For guidance on this question, assessment leaders can look to the records-retention policy of their school or parent institution. Another suggestion is to keep the data until at least the next ABA accreditation inspection, in case any members of the site-inspection team ask to see it.

9. Evaluating Program Assessment Data

Once the evidence of student learning has been gathered, externship faculty must evaluate it to determine what it demonstrates regarding student achievement of the program outcomes. Depending on how the program-assessment process is structured, this evaluation might be performed by the externship program director, an associate dean for experiential education, a committee of the externship faculty, or all members of the externship faculty.[103] The fundamental question that faculty must answer is "On what basis do we decide that a sufficiently high percentage of our students have been shown to have learned a sufficient amount for us to say, 'This is good enough'?"[104] Answering this question is a subjective process that requires informed judgment.[105] The ABA Standards do not define minimum competence,

---

102. For example, many law school students participate in the annual Law School Survey of Student Engagement (LSSSE). *See* www.lssse.indiana.edu (last visited March 4, 2022). A school's LSSSE results typically are provided to its dean or associate dean for academic affairs.

103. If externship teachers review student work from another externship teacher's course as part of the program-assessment process, protocols should be established for maintaining the confidentiality of all student course work and externship work that are reviewed.

104. Cecilia L. López, *A Decade of Assessing Student Learning: What We Have Learned, and What Is Next*, *in* Outcomes Assessment in Higher Education: Views and Perspectives 67–68 (Peter Hernon & Robert E. Dugan eds., 2004). *See also* Suskie, *supra* note 23, at 288 ("Defining successful outcomes means having a clear sense of what is good enough.").

105. Suskie, *supra* note 23, at 290.

so externship faculty must establish their own definition of competence for their program learning outcomes.[106]

Defining competence requires faculty to answer three interrelated questions:

- What kind of standard will be used to evaluate student performance? For example, a criterion-referenced standard or a value-added standard?
- What is the minimum score for competence on an assessment instrument?
- How many students from the group being assessed must achieve that minimum score in order to declare that program learning outcomes have been successfully achieved?[107]

The process for answering each of these questions is explained in turn below.

a. Deciding the Standard for Measuring Student Performance

In isolation, a student's score on an assessment instrument, such as a journal, a skills performance, or a final reflective essay, is meaningless. A score of 80 on a final essay, for example, tells one nothing about how well the student did. For the score to have meaning, there must be a standard against which to compare it, such as a set of performance criteria, a grade scale, or scores achieved by other students on the same essay assignment.[108] Faculty must establish these standards[109] for the assessment instruments they use to measure student learning. There are various types of standards from which to choose, including criterion-referenced standards, norm-referenced standards, and value-added standards.[110] Faculty should choose the standard when

---

106. *See* Shaw & VanZandt, *supra* note 7, at 126 ("To date, the ABA has not set a threshold other than to state that students should be 'competent' in the learning outcomes. So, it will be up to you and your faculty to define 'competency' for your students."); *see also* Margaret Martin Barry, *Reflections on Identifying and Mapping Learning Competencies and Outcomes: What Do We Want Law Students to Learn?*, 62 N.Y.L. Sch. L. Rev. 131, 147 (2017–2018) ("Another aspect of adopting student learning outcomes and competencies is deciding what level of accomplishment should be achieved for each. Every competency should be learned at a level that the faculty believes is sufficient.").

107. Faculty and administrators must "ask what percentage of students completing a program should perform at what level and against what (or whose) standards for them to be satisfied with the evidence of students' learning generated by assessment practices across the academic program or major." López, *supra* note 104, at 67.

108. *See, e.g.*, Suskie, *supra* note 23, at 288–90.

109. Some commentators use the term "benchmark" rather than standard to describe this frame of reference. *See, e.g.*, Shaw & VanZandt, *supra* note 7, at 92–93. There is no consensus on terminology, so this book uses the term "standard."

110. Suskie, *supra* note 23, at 290–96. No particular standard is perfect, and none provides a complete picture of success or failure regarding student learning.

they are planning the assessment process, not when they have collected evidence and are ready to review it.[111]

1) Criterion-Referenced Standards

Criterion-referenced standards, also known as local standards, measure competency by comparing student performance against a set of absolute criteria established by those teaching in the program.[112] Program assessment almost always uses local, criterion-referenced standards for measuring competency,[113] because the purpose "is to learn something about the effectiveness of the educational program as measured against deliberately chosen benchmark outcomes and to gather and employ evidence that will help the school determine how to achieve those outcomes."[114] When a criterion-referenced standard is used, in theory at least, "every student could be found competent or every student could be found to be incompetent."[115] Assessment expert Linda Suskie recommends that faculty start by establishing a local, criterion-referenced standard to articulate the qualities of what they consider minimally competent student performance.[116] Local standards have the added advantage of faculty ownership because faculty "pay much closer attention to assessment results when they have played a role in establishing performance expectations."[117]

The performance expectations typically are set forth in a rubric,[118] which is a set of detailed written criteria that describe what students should learn and how they will be evaluated.[119] While rubrics vary considerably in complexity and design, they typically "divide an assignment into its component parts and provide a detailed description of what constitutes acceptable or unacceptable levels of performance for

---

111. *Id.* at 290.

112. *Id.*

113. SHAW & VANZANDT, *supra* note 7, at 93. *See also* ALLEN, ASSESSING ACADEMIC PROGRAMS, *supra* note 6, at 158 ("Faculty generally set their own standards when they do program assessment.").

114. BUILDING ON BEST PRACTICES, *supra* note 11, at 26.

115. SHAW & VANZANDT, *supra* note 7, at 93.

116. SUSKIE, *supra* note 23, at 297.

117. *Id.* at 290 (quoting S.L. Pieper, K.H. Fulcher, D.L. Sundre & T.D. Erwin, INTRODUCTION TO RUBRICS "What Do I Do with the Data Now?" *Analyzing Assessment Information for Accountability and Improvement,* 2(1) RESEARCH & PRACTICE IN ASSESSMENT 7 (2008), retrieved from www.rpajournal.com/dev /wp-content/uploads/2012/05/A11.pdf).

118. This discussion of rubrics is adapted from Terry, *supra* note 40, at 493–98.

119. Sophie Sparrow, *Describing the Ball: Improve Teaching by Using Rubrics—Explicit Grading Criteria,* 2004 MICH. ST. L. REV. 1, 6 (2004); *see also* BEST PRACTICES FOR LEGAL EDUCATION, *supra* note 10, at 244 ("Criteria-referenced assessments rely on detailed, explicit criteria that identify the abilities students should be demonstrating (for example, applying and distinguishing cases) and the bases on which the instructor will distinguish among excellent, good, competent, or incompetent performances."); DANNELLE D. STEVENS & ANTONIA J. LEVI, INTRODUCTION TO RUBRICS: AN ASSESSMENT TOOL TO SAVE GRADING TIME, CONVEY EFFECTIVE FEEDBACK AND PROMOTE STUDENT LEARNING 3 (2005) (hereinafter "INTRODUCTION TO RUBRICS") ("At its most basic, a rubric is a scoring tool that lays out the specific expectations for an assignment.").

each of those parts."[120] Reviewing a set of completed rubrics for a group of students will identify patterns in student learning, revealing areas of strength and weakness with respect to the stated learning outcomes.[121] Thus, externship programs that use criterion-referenced standards will need to create a rubric for each assessment instrument. Faculty should create rubrics that capture the knowledge, skills, or values of each program outcome and also work well with the embedded assessments that professors are already using in their courses.[122] Faculty will grade the course assessments as they normally do to assign course grades, and then either the faculty member or a program-level assessment committee can apply the rubric to the assessments to evaluate them for program-assessment purposes.

A rubric can be created for any type of assessment instrument. Professors Dannelle Stevens and Antonia Levi provide an excellent step-by-step guide for designing rubrics in their book *Introduction to Rubrics: An Assessment Tool to Save Grading Time*.[123] According to Stevens and Levi, "[r]ubrics are composed of four basic parts in which the professor sets out the parameters of the assignment."[124] Those four parts, which usually are set out in a grid, are a task description, the dimensions of the assignment, a scale of performance levels, and specific descriptions for each level of performance.[125]

The task description is simply the assignment itself that involves some sort of student performance, whether in the form of a journal, a presentation, or a skills demonstration.[126]

The dimensions of the assignment are the knowledge, skills, or values that must be demonstrated and are being assessed.[127] Dividing the assignment into such distinct dimensions allows "the components of the task [to be] clearly identified."[128]

The performance scale sets out the levels of achievement that students may attain on each dimension of the assignment, such as "exemplary," "competent," or

120. Introduction to Rubrics, *supra* note 119, at 3; Sparrow, *supra* note 119, at 7 (rubrics typically include benchmarks describing varying levels of student performance).

121. Maki, *supra* note 4, at 219.

122. Andrea A. Curcio, *A Simple, Low-Cost Institutional Learning-Outcomes Assessment Process*, 67 J. Legal Educ. 489, 493 (2018).

123. Introduction to Rubrics, *supra* note 119, at 5–15. For other helpful explanations of the process for creating rubrics, see Sparrow, *supra* note 119, at 32–37; Suskie, *supra* note 23, at 190–203. Resources for creating rubrics also are available online. *See, e.g.*, Institute for Law Teaching and Learning, www.lawteaching.org/resources (last visited March 4, 2022); Georgia State University, https://oie.gsu.edu/our-services/assessment/assessment-resources/ #1590504625036-234ba963-fad4 (last visited March 4, 2022).

124. Introduction to Rubrics, *supra* note 119, at 5.

125. *Id.* at 5–6.

126. *Id.* at 6.

127. *Id.* at 6, 9–10.

128. *Id.*

"unacceptable."[129] Since program assessment focuses on measuring competence, these three levels typically are sufficient for a rubric for program assessment. For course-level assessment that has a more formative purpose, faculty may want to make finer distinctions among student work and divide the rubric into additional levels of performance.[130] The rubric in Figure 5-5 below, for example, includes four performance levels: Needs Work, Developing, Competent, and Exemplary.

Finally, the performance descriptions set out the qualities that comprise each level on the scale. For example, in a scale that includes levels of exemplary, competent, and unacceptable, the rubric should describe the elements of a performance that is exemplary, a performance that is competent, and a performance that is unacceptable.[131] The performance elements should be described as specifically as possible so the evaluators using the rubric can apply it accurately and consistently across the student work they review.

Below is an example of a rubric[132] for an oral presentation in an externship course that illustrates the rubric components discussed above.

129. *Id.* at 8.

130. *Id.* at 8–9. Stevens and Levi recommend limiting a rubric to just three levels of performance when initially constructing it, and, if necessary, expanding it to include additional levels after it has been used on an actual assignment. *Id.* at 8.

131. *Id.* at 10–11.

132. Professors Kendall Kerew and Kinda Abdus-Saboor at Georgia State University College of Law created this rubric.

Figure 5-5. Sample Rubric

Criteria	Needs Work: 1	Developing: 2	Competent: 3	Exemplary: 4
Time	N/A	N/A	N/A	Presentation is long enough to effectively communicate the required content and research but does not exceed 6 minutes.
Forensics	Eye Contact			
	Does not make eye contact, relies heavily on notes, reading most of the presentation.	Inconsistent eye contact and reads directly from notes during some of the presentation.	Maintains generally consistent eye contact and reads from notes at several points during the presentation.	Maintains consistent and comfortable eye contact throughout the presentation and only occasionally references notes.
	Cadence and Verbal Fillers ("um," "like," "you know," etc.)			
	Speaks so fast or so slow and/or uses so many verbal fillers that it impedes the audience's ability to understand the presentation.	Speaks too fast or too slow and/or uses many verbal fillers.	Speaks with a steady pace that is at times too fast or too slow, and/or rarely uses verbal fillers.	Speaks with a varied, dynamic pace that is not too fast or too slow and avoids verbal fillers.
	Volume			
	Does not project voice.	Projects voice at a volume that varies and is not always appropriate for the size of the room/ audience.	Projects voice at a volume appropriate for the size of the room/audience throughout the presentation.	Projects voice at a volume appropriate for the size of the room/audience, and stylistically integrates varied intonation.

Structure and Content	Organization			
	Information is not presented in a logical sequence.	Information is presented in a somewhat logical sequence that is often difficult to follow.	Information is presented in a generally logical sequence that is occasionally difficult to follow.	Information is presented in a logical sequence that is easy to follow.
	Required Content			
	Does not address one of the Shultz-Zedeck Lawyering Effectiveness Factors.	Addresses a Shultz-Zedeck Lawyering Effectiveness Factor, but does not connect it to his/her externship experience or does not provide a new perspective on its relevance to future practice.	Discusses a Shultz-Zedeck Lawyering Effectiveness Factor and its connection to his/her externship experience and provides some insight regarding its relevance to future practice.	Connects a Shultz-Zedeck Lawyering Effectiveness Factor to his/her externship experience and provides a new perspective regarding its relevance to future practice.
	Research			
	Does not provide research/data.	Provides research/data but does not reflect a clear understanding of the research/data and/or does not connect the research to the topic presented.	Provides relevant research/data, indicates a working understanding of the research/data, and establishes some connection of the research to the topic presented.	Provides relevant research/data, demonstrates a clear understanding of the research/data presented, and clearly connects the research/data to the topic presented.

2) Norm-Referenced Standards

Norm-referenced standards, also known as peer standards, compare one student's performance against the performance of other students.[133] This type of standard is "designed to rank each student in relation to how she or he performs compared with other students in the same class, usually based on a curve."[134] While some ex-

133. Shaw & VanZandt, *supra* note 7, at 93; Suskie, *supra* note 23, at 291.

134. Rogelio A. Lasso, *Is Our Students Learning? Using Assessments to Measure and Improve Law School Learning and Performance*, 15 Barry L. Rev. 73, 76 (2010).

ternship faculty may be required to determine course grades on a curve pursuant to school grading policies, norm-referenced standards do not require students to meet an absolute level of achievement. For example, an "A" in a course that uses a norm-referenced standard just "means the student's performance ranked at the top of the class, without regard to whether this student or the class as a whole performed at an excellent, mediocre, or poor level."[135] For these reasons, norm-referenced standards are "inconsistent with sound assessment principles"[136] and should not be used in program assessment.

3) Value-Added Standards

Value-added standards, also known as longitudinal or growth standards, measure competency by comparing students' performance on an assessment, such as a skills demonstration or a self-evaluation, to their subsequent performance on the same assessment after they have completed some additional portion of their education.[137] Thus, this standard evaluates whether students have improved[138] and tries to measure learning growth over time. This type of standard may work well for certain kinds of program learning outcomes, such as those related to professional norms and values. Professor Neil Hamilton, for example, recommends using longitudinal standards to measure students' development of professionalism skills.[139] There are some disadvantages, though, to using this type of standard for program assessment. Using a value-added standard doubles the workload, because the same assessment must be administered and scored twice.[140] Value-added standards also are imprecise, because determining the cause of any demonstrated improvement is difficult; the improvement may be the result of external forces such as outside employment or normal maturation, rather than a particular pedagogical approach or curriculum.[141]

b. Setting Minimum Scores for Competence on Assessment Instruments

Once faculty decide the type of standard, they then must set a minimum score for each assessment instrument that is used to measure achievement of program learning outcomes. Often referred to as "benchmarks," "cutoff scores," or "cut-

135. Lynn M. Daggett, *All of the Above: Computerized Exam Scoring of Multiple Choice Items Helps to: (A) Show How Exam Items Worked Technically, (B) Maximize Exam Fairness, (C) Justly Assign Letter Grades, and (D) Provide Feedback on Student Learning*, 57 J. Legal Educ. 391, 399 (2007).

136. Gregory S. Munro, Outcomes Assessment for Law Schools 119–20 (2000).

137. Shaw & VanZandt, *supra* note 7, at 93; Suskie, *supra* note 23, at 293–95.

138. Suskie, *supra* note 23, at 296.

139. Neil Hamilton, *Assessing Professionalism: Measuring Progress in the Formation of an Ethical Professional Identity*, 5 U. St. Thomas L.J. 470, 500 (2008).

140. Suskie, *supra* note 23, at 295.

141. *Id.* at 294.

scores,"[142] these scores set the "minimally acceptable" level for student achievement or performance on an assessment.[143] Setting benchmarks is a subjective process that requires the use of informed judgment,[144] and there is no error-free approach.[145] Nonetheless, experts in the field have identified best practices to follow, which are discussed below.

According to assessment expert Linda Suskie, the most important rule to remember in setting benchmarks is that they must be justifiable.[146] "You must be able to convince your stakeholders that your standards are appropriately rigorous. You must be able to explain not only *what* minimally acceptable student achievement is but *why* you consider that level minimally acceptable."[147] To ensure this rigor, Suskie recommends that faculty setting benchmarks ask the following questions:

- What achievement level would earn the lowest possible passing grade at this point in the student's studies?
- What is the lowest achievement level that would nonetheless adequately prepare students for success in what comes next in their lives: the next course in a sequence, more advanced study, or employment?
- What is the lowest achievement level that wouldn't embarrass you, if people learned that a student passed this course or graduated performing at that level?[148]

These questions are useful because they help identify the performance level for minimum competence, which is what the benchmark reflects. A benchmark score is akin to the minimum score for awarding credit in a pass/fail course; it is not the level achieved by typical "B" students.[149]

Another factor to consider in setting benchmarks is how the evidence regarding student achievement of them will be used.[150] If the evidence will be used to identify areas for improvement in student learning, then Suskie recommends setting a relatively high measure so faculty can increase the chances of identifying the areas that need improvement.[151] The harm resulting from setting benchmarks too high or too low also should be considered. When benchmarks are set too high, which results in

---

142. *Id.* at 290. *See also* T. Dary Erwin, Assessing Student Learning and Development: A Guide to the Principles, Goals, and Methods of Determining College Outcomes 113–14 (1991); Michael J. Zieky, Marianne Perie & Samuel A. Livingston, Cutscores: A Manual for Setting Standards of Performance on Educational and Occupational Tests 1, 9–11 (2008).

143. Suskie, *supra* note 23, at 290.

144. *Id.* at 290, 298–99.

145. Erwin, *supra* note 142, at 114.

146. Suskie, *supra* note 23, at 299.

147. *Id.* at 299 (emphasis in original).

148. *Id.* at 297–98.

149. Erwin, *supra* note 142, at 115.

150. Suskie, *supra* note 23, at 298.

151. *Id.* at 298.

large numbers of students not reaching them, the benchmarks may not accurately represent whether students are minimally competent. Thus, faculty may spend time and effort working to improve student learning when that is not actually necessary.[152] When benchmarks are set too low, however, the risk is that schools will graduate students who are not competent for practice. This risk weighs in favor of law schools setting benchmarks that are higher rather than lower.

The process for setting benchmarks for program outcomes typically involves convening program faculty or the program-assessment committee to discuss the assessment instruments being administered and identify the level of minimally competent performance for them. Ideally, either a member of the externship faculty or the designated assessment leader has created a draft of a rubric for the assignment, as discussed in Section 9.a(1) above. Then, the program faculty or assessment committee would meet to discuss the elements of the rubric, whether it includes all of the essential performance criteria (*i.e.*, knowledge, skills, values) for the assignment, and the minimum score that a student should achieve on the rubric to demonstrate minimum competence. The goal of the discussion is to "decide what skill level is required of an entry-level lawyer."[153]

Several types of resources are available for those involved in setting benchmarks to consult and use to inform their thinking. A good starting point is to review samples of student work, compare them against the rubric for the assignment, and identify examples that constitute excellent, adequate, and inadequate work. From these examples, the group can articulate the qualities that differentiate the excellent examples from the ones that are merely adequate, and the adequate examples from the ones that are inadequate. With these specific qualities in mind, the group can determine whether the excellent examples should set the benchmark for minimum competence, or whether the adequate examples more accurately reflect minimum competence in program learning outcomes.[154]

Faculty also may look to benchmarks set by other law schools as examples to follow. Many law schools have developed rubrics as they have engaged more deeply in assessment. Professor Andrea Curcio, for example, has written about and provided examples of rubrics that Georgia State University College of Law has developed.[155] The Holloran Center for Ethical Leadership in the Professions at the University of St. Thomas School of Law has created rubrics specifically for assessing learning outcomes related to formation of professional identity.[156] The American Association of Colleges and Universities has designed rubrics for sixteen different learning out-

152. *Id.*

153. Shaw & VanZandt, *supra* note 7, at 143.

154. Suskie, *supra* note 23, at 299–300.

155. Curcio, *supra* note 122, at 515–29.

156. *See* www.stthomas.edu/hollorancenter/holloranccompetencymilestones (last visited March 4, 2022).

comes, including teamwork, problem-solving, and intercultural competence.[157] Examples of law school rubrics also are available on the website of the Institute for Law Teaching and Learning.[158] Externship faculty may be able to adapt the benchmarks set in these rubrics for use in their program-assessment process.

Once externship faculty reach agreement on the benchmarks, they must test the benchmarks by applying them to the assessments to determine if they set accurate expectations for minimum competence.[159] For example, if only 30% of students achieve the benchmark score for minimum competence on an oral presentation, does that mean that the students lack effective verbal communication skills, or does it mean that the benchmark score was set too high? To answer this question, faculty will need to think carefully about the assignment itself and the expectations they set for student performance. Subsequent modification of the benchmark may be necessary, because "[a]fter a trial exercise, many educators will find that the initial cut-off score or rating level needs adjusting to account for too high or too low expectations."[160]

c. Setting Performance Thresholds

Once the benchmarks for competence have been set for each instrument used in program assessment, assessment leaders then must determine the percentage of students who must achieve that benchmark in order to declare that the program learning outcomes have been met. This percentage is known as a "target"[161] or a "performance threshold."[162] These percentages describe the expectations for students' collective performance on direct or indirect assessment instruments in a quantifiable way.[163] For example, if an externship program is using the oral presentation rubric previously discussed in this Chapter to assess students' verbal communication skills, the faculty might set the performance threshold at 75%, which means that if 75% of the presentations achieve the rubric's benchmark score for minimum competence, then the externship faculty can state that the program outcome for verbal communication skills has been met. Conversely, if fewer than 75% of the

---

157. *See* www.aacu.org/value/rubrics (last visited March 4, 2022).

158. *See* lawteaching.org/resources/ (last visited March 4, 2022).

159. SUSKIE, *supra* note 23, at 300.

160. ERWIN, *supra* note 142, at 114. "Most faculty set the cutoff level too high initially, often having unrealistic expectations for their students." *Id.*

161. SUSKIE, *supra* note 23, at 300. *See also id.* at 290 ("A target is the proportion of students that should achieve at least that minimally acceptable level.").

162. SHAW & VANZANDT, *supra* note 7, at 125 (defining performance thresholds as "minimum expectation levels for the group as a whole").

163. *Id.* at 125.

presentations achieve the benchmark score, then the outcome has not been met, and the externship faculty must investigate to determine the cause of the shortcoming.[164]

In setting these percentages, Suskie recommends making a distinction between whether learning outcomes are essential or aspirational. For critical learning outcomes, faculty should aim for almost all student work to meet the benchmark. According to Suskie, "[s]ome learning goals are so basic, essential, or vital to health and safety that we want absolute assurance that *every* student graduates with minimally adequate achievement of them."[165] Suskie and other experts recognize, however, that a performance threshold of 100% is likely unrealistic.[166] Regardless of how well an assessment instrument is designed, it is "an imperfect, incomplete sample of what students have learned."[167] Moreover, it is possible for students who actually have mastered important learning outcomes to perform poorly on any given assessment because they misunderstand it, are ill, or are distracted by a personal issue.[168] Thus, Suskie asserts that for outcomes that have "grave consequences for students who don't achieve them at a minimally adequate level—a target close to, but not quite at 100 percent is often appropriate."[169]

To set performance thresholds, externship faculty can look to past student performance for a baseline.[170] For example, assume that an externship program is using the oral presentation rubric discussed above to evaluate students' presentations for competency in its learning outcome for verbal communication skills, and that it has set a score of 75 points (out of a possible 100 points) as the benchmark score for minimum competence. Assume further that the externship program has used the rubric for two years. In the first year of using the rubric, 70% of the students in the program achieved the benchmark score. In the second year of using the rubric, 80% of the students achieved the benchmark score. In setting a performance threshold for this assessment, the externship program has several options. First, it could simply set the threshold at 70%, since it has evidence that its students can meet that threshold. Second, it could set the threshold at 75%, since that is the average percentage for the two years the rubric has been used. Third, it could set the threshold at 80% or even higher, since that percentage seems attainable in light of past performance and the program likely wants to have high standards for its students. Lawyers need strong verbal communication skills, which weighs in favor of setting a high thresh-

164. *E.g.*, *id.* at 125.
165. Suskie, *supra* note 23, at 301 (emphasis in original).
166. *Id.*; *see also* Shaw & VanZandt, *supra* note 7, at 126.
167. Suskie, *supra* note 23, at 301.
168. *Id.*
169. *Id.*
170. Monica Stitt-Bergh, What's Good Enough? Setting Standards 34–36 (2014) (presentation at the 2014 Annual Conference of the Association for Assessment of Learning in Higher Education) (presentation materials on file with author).

old. There is no "perfect" threshold, however, so this question must be decided by the faculty's informed judgment and expectations.

Faculty also should understand that setting benchmarks and performance thresholds for program outcomes is an iterative process. Once the benchmarks and thresholds have been established, they must be applied to student work to gauge both how students are performing and whether the benchmarks and thresholds seem appropriate. It may take some time and a few cycles of applying the benchmarks and thresholds to identify the levels that are right for a particular externship program. Thus, setting benchmarks and performance thresholds is "a perpetual work in progress, something to be adjusted as you learn more about your goals, the assessment tools you're using, and your students' performance."[171]

Evaluating achievement of an externship program's learning outcomes also will likely depend to some degree on how well the program's learning outcomes, benchmarks, and performance thresholds align with those of the externship courses that comprise the program. If the program benchmark scores are consistent with the benchmark scores that program faculty have set for their individual courses, then the course results may be generalizable to the externship program as a whole, thus making it unnecessary to review the assessment data a second time solely for program review.[172]

The hypothetical program outcomes discussed above can illustrate this concept. One of the hypothetical program outcomes is that students completing the externship program will be able to "draft a well-written practice-related document." Assume that the three courses in the hypothetical externship program—the prosecutor externship, the corporate-counsel externship, and the civil-litigation externship—have the following course learning outcomes related to document drafting:

- Prosecutor externship: students will be able to draft an effective response to a defense motion;
- Corporate-counsel externship: students will be able to draft an effective client-advice letter;
- Civil-litigation externship: students will be able to draft an effective motion.

Each of these assignments, which is a regular part of an externship course, is an example of an "embedded assessment" discussed previously in this Chapter. Relying on either the site supervisors' review of students' written work, or the faculty members' review of redacted written work, the externship faculty will evaluate the students' written work according to the assessment criteria they have established for

---

171. Suskie, *supra* note 23, at 303.

172. *See* Mary J. Allen, Assessing General Education Programs 125 (2006) ("Assuming course outcomes are well aligned with program outcomes, results can be generalized to the program, as a whole.").

their individual courses. If the course-level criteria and benchmark scores for these assessments are similar to the criteria and benchmark score for the program-level outcome of a "well-drafted practice-related document," then the course-level results should be generalizable to the program level, thus making a second review of the students' work for program assessment unnecessary. However, if the course-level criteria do not align with the program-level criteria, then the externship faculty will need to create a rubric for assessing the students' written work for program-level assessment and then review the work using that rubric.[173]

Some variation may occur with respect to performance thresholds, however. At the course level, the professor teaching the course sets the percentage at which to declare that a sufficient number of students have successfully achieved the course learning outcomes, according to the professor's individual standards. At the program level, however, that percentage should be determined by the externship faculty as a whole to set the performance threshold for the entire program of courses. Thus, it is possible that a group of externship faculty might set a performance threshold for program assessment that is lower or higher than the percentage set by an individual professor for his or her own course.

10. Using Data to Improve the Externship Program

Finally, externship faculty should use the information produced by the program-assessment process to improve student learning. If the designated percentage of students is not achieving the minimum competency scores on the assessment instruments, then the externship faculty should review their program design, pedagogy, and assessments to try to determine the reasons for the shortcomings. Faculty should look for patterns of mistakes or common misunderstandings that reveal the areas of knowledge, skills, or values in which student learning fell short. If faculty can identify these areas, then they can decide whether to refine the learning outcomes or change teaching methods or other instructional approaches.[174] Using the hypothetical program outcomes discussed throughout this Chapter, the chart below provides examples of the evidence that program assessment might produce and actions that could be taken to improve student learning:

173. For example, if an externship faculty member's criteria for exemplary, competent, and unacceptable work in his or her course differ significantly from the program-level criteria for exemplary, competent, and unacceptable work, then it will not be possible to extrapolate the assessment data from that individual course to the program level.

174. *See, e.g.*, SUSAN BRYANT, ELLIOTT S. MILSTEIN & ANN C. SHALLECK, TRANSFORMING THE EDUCATION OF LAWYERS: THE THEORY AND PRACTICE OF CLINICAL PEDAGOGY 14 (2014) ("When the students fail to meet the goals, teachers can assess whether to refine or reject the goals or take a different approach to meeting them.").

Figure 5-6. Outcomes Evidence and Possible Corrective Measures

Program Outcome	Evidence of Student Learning	Possible Corrective Measures
Draft a well-written practice-related document	Supervisor evaluations reveal requisite number of students did not achieve minimum competency score when rated on writing practice documents.	• Add a class on drafting practice documents to seminar, or make changes to existing class. • Add a document-drafting assignment to seminar. • Ask supervisors to provide students more opportunities to draft practice documents.
Effectively demonstrate verbal communication skills in a professional environment	Review of rubrics for students' in-class presentations reveals requisite number of students did not meet minimum competency score when rated on verbal communication skills.	• Add a class on professional communication skills to seminar, and then require students to make a brief presentation recommending a proposed legal strategy to a hypothetical client. • Ask supervisors to provide students more opportunities to practice their verbal communication skills, such as making oral presentations of research findings and legal analysis.
Effectively use problem-solving skills on behalf of a client	Supervisor evaluations reveal requisite number of students did not meet minimum competency score when rated on using problem-solving skills.	• Add a class on problem-solving skills to seminar or change existing class. • Use in-class exercise in which students work in teams to devise a litigation strategy for a hypothetical client. • Ask supervisors to include students in strategy sessions and discuss potential strategies with them.

Recognize ethical issues and effectively apply ethical rules in practice situations	Supervisor evaluations reveal requisite number of students did not meet minimum competency score when rated on recognizing ethical issues and applying ethical rules.	• Increase emphasis in seminar on ethical issues and application of ethical rules. • Assign students to complete problems on ethics issues. • Ask supervisors to highlight ethical issues and discuss them with students.
Explain the concept of a professional identity and articulate the elements of their own professional identity	Review of students' final reflective essays on this topic reveals that the requisite number of students **did** achieve the minimum competency score.	No corrective measure needed. Celebrate!

Thus, the program-assessment process should reveal opportunities for making improvements in program design, pedagogy, or work opportunities at the placement sites that will enhance students' learning regarding the program outcomes. Externship faculty then should implement those changes and document in the assessment plan the changes that are made. The next time that a particular learning outcome is assessed, faculty will be able to compare the most recent results with prior results to determine if the changes have had a positive effect.

Chapter 6

Special Considerations Regarding Remote[1] Work Environments and Site Locations Away from the Geographic Area of the Law School

The increasing number of lawyers and judges working in a partially remote or virtual work environment has given those designing externships a broader array of choices regarding both type of externship work and site location. Prior to the 2019 coronavirus pandemic, many law schools allowed students to extern in locations physically distant from the law school, including other parts of the state, other states,[2] and outside the U.S.[3] Programs did this by offering full-time externships[4] and a way for the students to participate in a classroom or reflection component.[5] However, until the pandemic pushed many lawyers to work from home or remotely, most externship programs generally did not permit students to earn credit unless they were physically present at their externship sites. Because externship sites can now

1. Remote (also known as virtual) externships are defined as sites where the supervisor and student are physically distanced from one another and communicate through technology. The supervisor may or may not be physically located in a law office or judicial chambers.

2. *See* Lance Cole & Camille C. Marion, *Semester-in-Residence Programs: Design, Implementation, and Best Practices*, in Experiential Education in the Law School Curriculum 225–57 (Emily Grant, Sandra Simpson & Kelly Terry eds., 2018), for a discussion of the accreditation requirements, benefits, costs, and risks of a semester-in-residence externship program.

3. According to the 2019-20 CSALE Survey, 51% of schools offered international externships. Robert R. Kuehn, Margaret Reuter & David A. Santacroce, Center for the Study of Applied Legal Educ., 2019–2020 Survey of Applied Legal Education 10 (2020) (hereinafter "CSALE Survey"), www.csale.org/#results (last visited March 6, 2022).

4. According to the 2019–20 CSALE Survey, 54% of schools allowed students to extern full time. *Id.* Alternatively, students could do part-time externships in another state and enroll as a visitor at a local law school in order to earn a full semester's credits.

5. This was done by either offering a class in the location where the students were externing, whether Alaska, Washington D.C., or Geneva, or by allowing students to participate in class through the use of technology. For more on ways that programs can use technology to facilitate externship seminars, *see* Chapter 12.

be *both* remote and in a location away from the school, this Chapter addresses these design choices separately to better understand the challenges and benefits of each.

1. Remote Work Environments

Many lawyers and judges have experienced doing legal work while physically remote from their offices, so an important choice in externship design is whether to allow these opportunities for students as externships. Regardless of whether a remote site is approved, the best approach is to have a process for considering both the site and the student's externship arrangement individually, while prioritizing the student's pedagogical and professional learning outcomes. Reviewing both the benefits of and concerns about remote sites can help establish the elements of that process.

a. Benefits

Approving some remote sites, even if on a limited basis, has a number of benefits. The first one is that students will likely encounter the option or necessity of working remotely at some time in their professional careers.[6] By participating in a remote externship, students will gain skills in building professional relationships and in conducting legal work in a remote setting. For remote work to be successful, students must be intentional in communicating about their legal work and creating a plan to build a relationship through remote social interaction. Learning to do legal work in a remote environment teaches students to become adept with technology and helps them acquire a range of other new skills, from building rapport in a client interview conducted through a videoconference, to negotiating contracts through email and breakout rooms, to offering exhibits, cross-examining witnesses, and picking a jury in a videoconference setting.[7]

These skills are not just required in the current legal workplace; they are also part of the gradual evolution of the legal profession's use of technology. Lawyers' development and use of these skills may help increase access for those in remote and underserved areas[8] and provide services to persons whose physical and mental health

6. Bob Ambrogi, *87% of Law Offices Working Remotely, Survey Finds, as They Struggle to Maintain Financial Stability*, LawSites (Apr. 30, 2020), https://www.lawsitesblog.com/2020/04/87-of-law-offices-working-remotely-survey-finds-as-they-struggle-to-maintain-financial-stability.html (last visited March 6, 2022). *See also* David Dorion, *Working Remotely: How It's Impacting the Legal Industry and Your Firm*, LAWCROSSING, https://www.lawcrossing.com/ employers/article/ 900048761/ Working-Remotely-How-It-s-Impacting-the-Legal-Industry-and-Your-Firm/ (last visited Sept. 10, 2021).

7. Dorion, *supra* note 6.

8. Sara Sutton, *Why Remote Work Can Help Bridge the Hiring Gap, Especially for Rural Professionals*, Entrepreneur (Aug. 26, 2019) https://www.entrepreneur.com/article/331817.

disabilities prevent them from coming to an office.[9] Remote work enables parents and caregivers to participate in the workplace more easily after attending to other responsibilities at home.[10] The remote workplace offers the potential for addressing climate change by reducing pollution created by commuting and travel to meetings.[11] The elimination of commute time may also provide other benefits to physical and mental health, addressing issues of well-being relevant to both law students and the legal profession.[12]

While the benefits discussed above apply to all students, other benefits of remote work are particularly helpful for part-time students and those who cannot easily travel or relocate. Students who are juggling both a job and an externship can benefit from the flexibility remote work allows by giving them an opportunity to meet with a supervisor during a break or at the end of the workday before starting their externship work. This flexibility is helpful for students with busy schedules, especially if an in-person site is only open during regular work hours. Students who wish to extern in a site outside the area where they live also have the option to do so without needing to relocate.

Remote work options allow students to extern at sites that specialize in topics that interest them, in both private and public sectors, regardless of where they live. Externship sites have embraced these opportunities to recruit students more easily from outside their geographic area.[13] Remote work may also be particularly useful in efforts to increase diversity within the profession, allowing students who lack resources for travel and separate housing to gain access to opportunities throughout the U.S. and the rest of the globe.

b. Concerns

Balancing these benefits are a variety of concerns. Some of these concerns are ones that existed pre-pandemic and made externship program directors reluctant to approve remote work. Other concerns have arisen as more experience with remote

---

9. Neelam Bohra & AJ Willingham, *Remote work made life easier for many people with disabilities. They want the option to stay*, CNN (Aug. 10, 2021), https://www.cnn.com/2021/08/10/ health/ remote-work-disabilities-pandemic-wellness-trnd/index.html.

10. Courtney Connley, *Women with Child care Needs are 32% Less Likely to Leave Their job if They Can Work Remotely, According to New Report*, CNBC (June 17, 2021), https://www.cnbc.com/2021/06/17/working-moms-are-32percent-less-likely-to-leave-their-job-if-they-can-work-remote.html.

11. Jared Shein, *Is Working From Home Better for the Environment?*, CET (Sept. 11, 2020), https://www.centerforecotechnology.org/is-working-from-home-better-for-the-environment/.

12. For more on the importance of well-being in externship pedagogy, see Chapter 9.

13. One example of this is the supervising attorney at the Legal Aid at Work office in San Francisco, California, who explained that as a legal services organization focusing on employment-related issues, they were recruiting nationally and were particularly focused on increasing diversity within their extern pool. Notes of Seattle University Site Approval (on file at Seattle University School of Law).

work has exposed some drawbacks. The first category of concerns encompasses the worry that remote students will not have the same easy access to a supervisor's feedback, to observation of meetings and proceedings, or even to social gatherings, as their in-person peers. The degree to which this may be a problem depends on factors that are specific to each site. Such factors include the number of partly or fully remote judges and attorneys, the technological proficiency and access of the office, the number of other remote externs, and the amount of experience the site and the supervisors have had with remote work.[14] Considering these factors in deciding whether to allow remote work will help ensure a good learning experience for each student.

A second category of concerns stems from research that points to the potential for isolation and stress that comes with remote environments.[15] The best option for a good learning environment will generally be a hybrid of in-person and remote work. The practical implications of this concern are that even remote students should plan to visit the physical externship site and meet their site supervisor in person at least once during a semester and more if possible. Externship faculty should help students prioritize wellness and create peer support with other externs to address isolation. In addition, accommodations should be made to facilitate student attendance at events that are not accessible remotely. Ensuring that such opportunities are available requires extra planning, time, and resources; for this to occur, externship directors and site supervisors will need to prioritize this kind of planning and convince busy students of its importance.[16]

c. Trends

With both benefits and drawbacks, remote work is now a feature of the legal profession. Externship program directors who decide to offer the option of remote externships must have a process for counseling students on the pros and cons of a remote environment. Externship faculty should consider whether to include remote

---

14. For a guide to a set of questions for this inquiry with externship site supervisors, *see* Supplemental Template for Virtual and Remote Externship Placements, available at https://docs.google.com/document/d/1uJZCe5_YGq14c0OLKzANsINJT3An6UyzsU6ix_ulZ-4/edit. For a more general set of questions about remote work outside the legal sphere, *see* Tsedal Neeley, *15 Questions About Remote Work, Answered*, HARV. BUS. REV. (Mar. 16, 2020) https://hbr.org/2020/03/15-questions-about-remote-work-answered.

15. Marine Dobson Zimmerman & Pouran Faghri, *Blurred Boundaries: Work-Life Balance in the Time of COVID19*, HEALTHY WORK NOW (May 22, 2020), https://healthyworknow.medium.com/blurred-boundaries-work-life-balance-in-the-time-of-covid19-719e42e85cb5; *see also* Helen Pluut & Jaap Wonders, *Not Able to Lead a Healthy Life When You Need It the Most: Dual Role of Lifestyle Behaviors in the Association of Blurred Work-Life Boundaries With Well-Being*, FRONTIERS PSYCH. (Dec. 2020), https://www.frontiersin.org/articles/10.3389/fpsyg.2020.607294/full.

16. The same supervisor at Legal Aid at Work in San Francisco, California described their plans to enable remote students to come and visit by providing miles for air travel and other inexpensive lodging. Legal Aid at Work, *supra* note 13.

work as a seminar and reflection topic, given its important relationship to career choice, mentoring relationships, access to justice, and legal skills.

2. Site Locations Away from the Law School in the United States and Internationally

Locating externship sites away from the law school is another design choice that requires consideration of advantages and disadvantages, along with a process for approving sites, communicating with supervisors, and monitoring the student experience. When the site is located within the United States, these factors include the challenges and benefits of having students relocate to a different geographic area and the possible additional connections and skills the students may gain. When the site is located outside the United States, these factors include challenges of visa restrictions; language capacity of the student and site supervisor; communication with legal professionals who have a different legal background and training; and any issues that may arise for the student regarding housing, health, or travel outside the United States. This section will discuss the design options relevant to both kinds of placements, noting where there may be special considerations if the site is international. Although topics such as credits,[17] student counseling,[18] and selection and communication with sites[19] are discussed elsewhere in this book, design options specific to away placements are included here.

In the view of some legal educators in the United States, the challenges of maintaining connection with sites at a distance from the law school have often outweighed the benefits of such externships, especially those that are international. This has led to a disadvantage for many American students when compared to their peers in Europe, Australia, Asia, and Africa, who have had legal training outside their home countries.[20] To help address this deficit in American legal education, this section also offers some brief research on the importance of international legal education to prepare American students for global practice.

a. Benefits of Semester Away

Between a quarter and a half of externship programs throughout the United States offer externship placements distant from the law school.[21] This number is increasing

17. For a thorough discussion of credits, see Chapter 3.

18. For more on counseling students, see Chapter 8.

19. For a discussion of communication with site supervisors, see Chapter 13.

20. *See* Gillian Dutton, *International Experiences: A Path to Critical Legal Skills, Values, and Innovation for American Law Students*, 27 Clinical L. Rev. 1 (2020), for a thorough discussion of the benefits of international externships and the need to catch up to law students outside the U.S.

21. The number is an approximation because there is no precise question about the location of externships on the CSALE Survey. However, according to the 2019–20 Survey, 54% of schools allow

for a variety of reasons, many of which relate to student demand.[22] Some law schools are located in areas with smaller populations where local externship opportunities are limited. Approving externships away from the law school's geographic area allows programs to expand placement options, particularly as law schools increasingly recommend, guarantee, or require student completion of a clinic or externship before graduation.[23] Some law schools are expanding their curriculum in practice areas that can be learned best in specialized placements. For example, students wishing to learn about intellectual property issues specific to the technology industry may want to be in cities where that industry is located, and students hoping to gain skills in legislative advocacy will get the most hands-on experience by working in a state or national capital.

Other reasons for expansion relate to a law school's desire to optimize student admissions and the school's regional, national, and international reputation. A law school wishing to attract out-of-state students could allow students to complete law school with a final remote externship semester in their home state or the state where they plan to practice.[24] These students get practice experience in more than one jurisdiction and increase their post graduate job placement opportunities. Law schools that seek to increase the number of diverse and international applicants may allow students to extern in parts of the United States or in other countries that offer opportunities to work with diverse supervisors. As law schools continue to offer more courses online,[25] enrollment by students who are physically distant from the law school will increase the demand for externships located throughout the United States to meet experiential education requirements. Even students who wish to practice in the same state as their law school still benefit from the increased knowledge, skills, values, and creativity[26] that come from a semester away. Finally,

---

students to extern full time and, of those schools, 56% allow externships wherever the student has identified an eligible placement, while 44% only allow placements where the school has relationships or a designated program. Sixty percent of the schools with full-time externships (so 60% of 54%) allow full-time placements in other countries. CSALE SURVEY, *supra* note 3, at 10–11.

22. Student demand for field placement classes increased at 47% of schools surveyed in the 2019–20 Survey, remained constant at 46% of schools, and declined at only 7% of schools. Ninety-three percent of schools reported that demand increased or remained constant in the most recent period, up from 85% in the 2016–17 survey. *Id.* at 17.

23. As of the latest CSALE survey in 2019–20, 28% of schools guaranteed JD student enrollment in a law school clinic or field placement course before graduation. "Among these schools, 18% guarantee participation in a clinic, 4% in a field placement course, and 78% in a law clinic or field placement course." *Id.* at 12.

24. An example is Washburn University Law School's Third Year Anywhere program, which allows students to earn credit working 20 hours per week to complete their third year of law school in the geographic areas where they plan to practice. *See* https://www.washburnlaw.edu/admissions/thirdyearanywhere/index.html (last visited on March 6, 2022).

25. For an in-depth study of student experiences during the shift to online law school education, see ACCESSLEX, *Law School in a Pandemic: Student Perspectives on Distance Learning and Lessons for the Future* (June 16, 2021), https://www.accesslex.org/law-school-in-a-pandemic.

26. See Chi Yue Chiu, Adam Galinsky, Angela Ka-yee Leung & William Maddux, *Toward a More Complete Understanding of the Link between Multicultural Experience and Creativity*, AMERICAN

students preparing for global practice, including working with cases or clients that have crossed borders, can use an externship away from the law school to gain practical legal experience in another state or country.

Student interest and growing awareness of the skills and experience necessary for global practice[27] have led many law school externship programs to consider expanding their externships beyond the United States to international sites.[28] The increase of foreign-born individuals in the United States population[29] means that international experience is a benefit for all law students, because they have a high probability of encountering immigrant communities in their legal practice.[30] This is as true for lawyers in private practice as for those going into public interest.[31]

Another important but lesser-known benefit of international externships is the demonstrated effect of international experiences on improved creativity and cognitive skills. According to social science research, the extensiveness of multicultural experiences is positively related to the following factors: creative performance (insight learning, remote association, and idea generation), as well as creativity-supporting cognitive processes (retrieval of unconventional knowledge and recruitment of ideas from unfamiliar cultures for creative idea expansion).[32] Studies have found that the enhanced creativity and professional success of bicultural individuals compared to those who identify with only one culture is due to greater levels of integrative complexity, an information processing capacity that involves considering and combining multiple perspectives.[33] While many law students and even most lawyers may be unaware of such benefits, highlighting them for externs enables them to more effectively absorb such benefits as well as articulate them for future employers. These factors are also persuasive for faculty and law school administrators.

PSYCH. 156–58 (2009); *see also* Adam D. Galinsky, William Maddux & Carmit T. Tadmor, *Getting the Most Out of Living Abroad: Biculturalism and Integrative Complexity as Key Drivers of Professional and Creative Success*, 103 J. PERSONALITY & SOC. PSYCHO. 520–42 (2012).

27. *See* Carole Silver, *Getting Real About Globalization and Legal Education: Potential and Perspectives for the U.S.*, 24 STAN. L. & POL'Y REV. 457 (2013), for an authoritative discussion of the importance of globalization for legal education generally.

28. Just over half of law schools offer international externships. CSALE SURVEY, *supra* note 3, at 10 (data showing 51%).

29. Close to fourteen percent (13.7) of the U.S. population in 2019 was foreign born. MIGRATION POLICY INSTITUTE, *Frequently Requested Statistics on Immigrants and Immigration in the United States*, https://www.migrationpolicy.org/article/frequently-requested-statistics-immigrants-and-immigration-united-states#demographic-educational-linguistic (last visited September 25, 2022).

30. Silver, *supra* note 27.

31. *Id.*

32. Chi Yue Chiu et al., *supra* note 26.

33. Galinsky et al., *supra* note 26.

b. Challenges of Semester Away

1) Resources

The benefits of semester away externships are many, but challenges do exist. One factor that can limit away and international placements is the demand on externship faculty time and program resources. The best option when approving a new site is to visit in person, whether it be across the state, across the country, or across the globe. An in-person site visit provides the externship director with an understanding of not just the physical office space and culture, but also the surrounding area in which the student is likely planning to live and work. While these site visits and supervisor meetings can now be conducted through a videoconference, externship faculty will have greater difficulty in understanding the student learning environment in places with which they are not previously familiar. Traveling to a new site takes time and resources but can also be done as a follow up to a videoconference introduction or spread out at regular time intervals to optimize travel time and expenses.

Another approach to this challenge is to seek assistance from externship faculty at other schools.[34] They may be able to help with identifying good externship sites, and to offer joint seminars, share course syllabi, and give suggestions for student advising. The AALS Externship Subcommittee on International and Semester Away Placements often fields such questions through emails or on their quarterly video conference calls and offers a website to share resources.[35] Doing a site visit for a colleague involves some preparation but is a chance to share best practices and connect students from different institutions.

2) Credits

Another challenge in considering away placements is how externship credits are awarded; this includes whether full-time externships are available as well as whether credits are limited to fixed amounts or have a variable range up to a full-time semester.[36] Students in a placement far from the law school may have to enroll as visitors in another school if the law school does not offer a part-time remote or full-semester externship option. The decision to use variable rather than fixed credits relieves this pressure somewhat as it allows students the flexibility to earn credit based on the

34. ABA Standard 304 permits such collaborations. "When appropriate, a school may use faculty members from other law schools to supervise or assist in the supervision or review of a field placement program." ABA Standards and Rules of Procedure for Approval of Law Schools 2022–2023, Standard 304, Interpretation 304-1. The complete ABA Standards are available at https://www.americanbar.org/content/dam/aba/administrative/legal_education_and_admissions_to_the_bar/standards/2022-2023/2022-2023-standards-and-rules-of-procedure.pdf.

35. LexternWeb, *International & Semester Away*, https://www.lexternweb.org/remote-and-international-placements (last accessed Sept. 9, 2021).

36. Externship courses can either combine the fieldwork and reflection courses into one course (done by 61% of courses) or separate them into two separate components. CSALE Survey, *supra* note 3, at 44. Where the credits are separated out, 53% of courses offer variable credits, and 47% require a fixed number. *Id.* at 45.

hours they work as well as the credits they need to earn for the semester. Offering full-time externships is another helpful step in facilitating semester away externships; however, even if only part-time externships are offered, most programs can still permit an away placement using either fixed or variable credits.[37]

Another option for schools where credits may be limited is to offer semester away externships in summer.[38] This kind of program may also be attractive to part-time students who can sometimes take a combination of vacation and unpaid leave if they wish to pursue a semester away externship during the shorter summer semester.[39]

A final concern of away full-time externships is how these are affected by any restrictions on the total number of externship credits that can count toward graduation.[40] It is important to review the latest version of the ABA Standards and internal law school restrictions before expanding remote and international placements and when advising students.[41]

3) Selecting and Monitoring Placements

As discussed briefly above, communication to supervisors for training and site visits can be more difficult when increased distances require more resources, especially given ABA requirements for a structured and well-supported program.[42] Two strategies can alleviate this concern: one is to use existing externship networks to make connections with appropriate placements; the second is to use technology to adequately monitor placements and site supervisors.

The externship program faculty can reach out to law school externship programs in the desired state to get contact information about available sites that have a good reputation for student supervision.[43] While some externship directors may be reluctant to share site information, most are willing to provide it, as there are generally more sites looking for students than students applying for externships. Even where the externship faculty does not have an existing relationship with the other state's law

---

37. This is especially true if they allow the student to work remotely, which may permit attendance at in-person classes at the law school.

38. Fifty-seven percent of field placement courses in the 2019–20 Survey were offered during the summer term. CSALE SURVEY, *supra* note 3, at 49. Summer terms are appealing for students because they are shorter, but they also require more limited learning goals, and many organizations will be unable to host a student who is available for fewer than six weeks.

39. *See id.* at 50 for more details on how law schools apportion credits and seminars in the summer.

40. *See* Chapter 2 for a discussion on how the limits on distance education apply to externships. The 2019–20 Survey reported that 62% of schools limit the number of field placement (12 is the most common) credits a student can apply toward graduation, showing a decline from 71% in 2016–17 and 80% in 2013–14. *Id.* at 15.

41. For more on the differences that apply to externships where the seminar and field placements are combined, see Chapter 2.

42. *Id.*

43. *See* LEXTERNWEB, *International & Semester Away*, https://www.lexternweb.org/remote-and-international-placements (last accessed Sept. 9, 2021).

school program, a stated willingness to share information with that school's students in a reciprocal manner will usually establish a collaborative approach and help a student find a placement. Once the site in another geographic area has been established, keeping a copy of the placement description, contact person, and application process in a database can greatly facilitate future students going to the same site again.[44]

4) Seminar Component

A final challenge preventing law schools from expanding in these areas is concern about the externship seminar component, especially as many schools have all externs together in one general, on-campus class.[45] There are strategies to address this concern through a seminar or faculty guided reflection. In either, faculty should provide a framework to identify learning outcomes, guide reflection, and assist students in assessing their progress in reaching their goals. Designing a seminar for remote externships requires some attention to time zones and student access to the internet. However, even though students are not located in the same city, state, or country as the law school, providing a seminar is possible.[46] If the program is large enough to have separate seminars divided by practice area (e.g., criminal, judicial, civil, etc.), one option is to have remote students join those classes by videoconference. Where there is one general, in-person class, it may be more useful for students and more manageable for the professor to offer a separate class to all remote students, especially if the class is large.[47] Another possibility is to front load the semester with an in-person intensive experience, sometimes called an orientation or bootcamp, and follow it with videoconferencing or online communication.[48] This approach allows students to meet one another as well as the faculty member and facilitates more open communication throughout the rest of the course. A final option is to use reflection and other online asynchronous assignments in lieu of a seminar.[49]

---

44. It can be very beneficial to get student permission to share their names with future students, as establishing networks for job hunting can generally be a little harder for a student seeking employment outside a law school's geographic area. Students can be asked for this permission in the evaluation that they complete at the conclusion of the externship.

45. The classroom component was offered in only one section in 64% of field placement courses. Eight percent of field placement courses offered two sections of the classroom component, 6% offered three, and 14% offered four or more. CSALE SURVEY, *supra* note 3, at 46.

46. Seventy-five percent of field placement courses meet the ABA requirement for "a classroom instructional component...." *Id.*

47. The median enrollment in an externship seminar was 11–15 students, the same as in the 2016–17 and 2013–14 Surveys. Eight percent of field placement courses had enrollments of more than 26 students. *Id.*

48. The AALS Externship Subcommittee on Remote (Semester Away) and International Placements, a group that meets monthly via videoconference during the academic year, has also discussed collaborations for joint seminars for students in more than one school. The website includes forms, syllabi, and a database of pre-approved placements. *See* LEXTERNWEB, *International & Semester Away*, https://www.lexternweb.org/remote-and-international-placements (last accessed Sept. 9, 2021).

49. *See* Chapter 12 for more on using technology to provide asynchronous education.

c. Student Advising

1) National

Faculty preparing to advise students who wish to apply for placements away from the law school should start with an approach similar to advising students about any placement: what skills does a student already possess and how will the proposed placement build skills and values, develop experience, and establish networks relevant to a student's desired practice area? However, when considering available sites, faculty will usually face the problem that the number of sites that the school is in contact with outside of the local area is usually small. The student should thus start planning and applying early because of the necessity of both finding a site and confirming an offer before making travel and lodging arrangements.

Once students have identified the desired kind of placement, they can look at a description of local sites to get a sense of the kinds of opportunities that can also be found in another state or country. For instance, a student wishing to extern in criminal law can review local options to work in either state or federal prosecution or defense agencies and at the trial or appellate level. The student can also determine any state-specific differences regarding student-practice rules. To find out more about sites in a distant location, the student can search online, as many offices list internship or externship openings on their websites. Helping students develop a plan for externships, clinics, classes, and jobs to build a series of skills prior to application is also useful if the student is looking for a remote placement that may require specialized knowledge.[50]

2) International

The first part of advising students about international externships also involves encouraging students to assess their previous experience and identify their goals. Some students' prior exposure to international travel and study abroad will have resulted in comfort and knowledge around foreign travel. For students who have such familiarity, faculty will need to confirm that the site has enough resources to supervise students and give them adequate work. For other students who may be new to international travel, faculty encouragement and knowledge can provide the support needed to embark on a rewarding externship experience.

Many colleges and universities have an undergraduate office responsible for study abroad and foreign exchange programs; these offices are good sources of information for visas, health information, and travel restrictions. Faculty who do not have an office at the undergraduate or graduate level outside of the law school should still

---

50. Advising is a special topic discussed elsewhere in Chapter 8. There are also useful forms available on the Lextern website for remote and international placements at LexternWeb, *International & Semester Away*, https://www.lexternweb.org/remote-and-international-placements (last accessed Sept. 9, 2021).

consider developing an international program, using the resources from the International and Semester Away Externship Subcommittee available on LexternWeb[51] and keeping in mind that issues of liability can be addressed with careful preparation.[52]

A student's language preparation and background will influence which externships are a good fit. Unless the externship teacher is fluent in the language of the externship site, gauging a student's ability to speak a language other than English requires an independent and knowledgeable assessment of how well the student speaks, understands, reads, and writes the other language. As competency in each area can vary, students should be encouraged to recognize that work in law requires a sophisticated level of vocabulary, grammar, and punctuation; students should also be realistic about their capabilities. Some sites may be able to provide interpreters to help students complete externship tasks, but this must be confirmed if needed. Where helpful, externship faculty should advise students to undertake additional language preparation in either individual tutoring or immersion courses. Reminding students that language study will give them insight into the culture, demonstrate respect for their future colleagues, and prove useful in everyday life outside of work, can provide strong motivation to study another language. Even if a student may not be able to become fluent in another language, their native or near native fluency in English can be of great benefit to an international externship site. Helping an organization produce English-language legal documents can be part of a substantial legal experience, even if the student may need to learn the differences between American and English conventions to successfully edit and produce final documents.

Additional preparation for students may include taking international and comparative law courses or working as a research assistant for professors teaching international law. Both can provide the foundation needed for a successful externship. Enrolling in international human rights or international transactional clinics also helps make student applications more competitive and gives them relevant practical experience necessary for an international externship.

d. Approval of Sites and Supervisors

Once a site has been selected, faculty should be aware of special considerations for communicating with supervisors and arranging for mid-semester visits. Where possible, faculty should visit distant sites in the United States or abroad at least once in person,[53] but if resources and time do not permit this, faculty should conduct the

51. LexternWeb, *International & Semester Away*, https://www.lexternweb.org/remote-and-international-placements (last accessed Sept. 9, 2021).

52. *See* Kathleen M. Burch, *Going Global: Managing Liability In International Externship Programs—A Case Study*, 36 J.C. & U.L. 455 (2010), and Vincent R. Johnson, *Americans Abroad: International Educational Programs and Tort Liability*, 32 J. C. & U. L. 309 (2006), for a thorough review of the issue of liability.

53. Some programs include an average amount per student for site visits in their budgets. Members of the AALS Subcommittee on Semester-Away and International Externships have also assisted

initial site visit via a video conference call. A video conference call, rather than a phone call or emailing back and forth, allows the faculty member to get a sense of the culture of the site.[54] An in-person visit can uncover any issues regarding safety of the surrounding area and give the externship director relevant experience for designing course topics and responding to reflections. Meeting the site supervisor also allows for assessment of that person's qualifications for mentoring and promotes the development of a relationship for ongoing communication and collaboration around teaching.[55] These relationships with remote sites are even more important than for local sites, since the student will be physically distant from the law school and possibly in a very different cultural, social, and physical environment.

For site approval and communication to sites in countries where English is not the national language, faculty should take the time to engage an interpreter if the site supervisor is not proficient in English.[56] Forms should be translated if sent to those who are not English speakers.[57] Inquiries based on mutual respect and learning[58] are critical for establishing good communication. Successful cross-cultural communication must also be grounded in an awareness of the impact of American domination in international settings with a colonial history. Interactions with supervisors at international sites go best when faculty prepare by a brief review of the history and mission of the site.

e. International Seminar or Guided Reflection

Technology for the international externship seminar is like that described above for remote students, with the additional complication of international time zones. Certain time zone differences can be handled with a morning class for the professor and an evening class for the students.[59] Others will require students to do asynchro-

---

each other in doing a site visit, especially at a local site. To find out who could do this nationally, use the LexternWeb resources to locate the law school's externship director. *See* LEXTERNWEB, *International & Semester Away*, https://www.lexternweb.org/remote-and-international-placements (last accessed Sept. 9, 2021), for resources for international visits.

54. The benefits to faculty of traveling for these visits include a different perspective on their students' experiences, and increased opportunities for professional development and advancement.

55. "The most common methods of training field placement supervising attorneys are through written materials (86%) and individual discussions with the supervisor (85%). Twenty-three percent of courses do live/in person training, while 8% do some form of online training (either asynchronous or synchronous). CSALE SURVEY, *supra* note 3, at 4.

56. Most states have a process for certifying interpreters in many languages and an office that manages language access within the state court. A good source for such resources is the National Center for State Courts Language Access Services Section at NCSC, *Language Access Programs by State*, https://www.ncsc.org/Services-and-Experts/Areas-of-expertise/Language-access/Resources-for-Program-Managers/LAP-Map/Map.aspx (last accessed Sept. 14, 2021).

57. *Id.*

58. *See* the section in Chapter 9 on cultural humility and bias for a more complete discussion of the respect, curiosity, and empathy needed for good cross-cultural communication.

59. Daylight savings goes into effect on different dates.

nous work to be successful. Externship directors should check the resources of the AALS International and Semester Away Placements Sub-Committee for possible joint seminars offered by colleagues in other law schools.

The seminar topics can be varied according to the kind of legal work done at the sites and the number of students.[60] Some that may be useful to students in international externships include international legal research, comparative law, impact of colonialism, secondary trauma, restorative justice, cultural humility or competence, tips for working with interpreters and translators, presentations at conferences, preparation of policy documents, and international practice resources.[61] Faculty who lack relevant expertise in these topics can also reach out to others to guest lecture, with the added benefit of creating additional connections within the law school. With this in mind, all faculty should feel confident in expanding their programs to include these important opportunities for their students.

60. CSALE data on classroom topics shows some similarities that may be useful if there are not adequate resources to create a separate class for students at remote placements. "The greatest amount of classroom time is devoted to fieldwork discussion/rounds (21% of total classroom time), followed by professional identity formation (15%), ethics/professional responsibility (12%), skills instruction (12%), substantive law (8%), career development (8%), simulation (6%), and procedural law/rules (5%)." CSALE Survey, *supra* note 3, at 47. "Eighty percent of courses devote some portion of classroom time to fieldwork discussion/rounds, 77% address ethics/professional responsibility, 67% address professional identity, 62% include skills instruction, and 59% include career development. In contrast, 64% of courses spend no class time on procedural law/rules, 59% spend no time on simulation, and 58% spend no time on substantive law." CSALE Survey, *supra* note 3, at 47.

61. *See* Dutton, *supra* note 20, for a more thorough description of providing international externships.

Chapter 7

Designing Individual Externship Courses

"Fundamental principles about learning, teaching, and instructional design should guide the development of any course."[1] In addition to heeding these principles, faculty designing externship courses must satisfy the specific ABA Standards governing externships and other experiential courses. As explained in Chapter 2, ABA Standard 304(a)[2] sets out requirements for experiential courses, and Standard 304(d)[3] sets out particular requirements for externship courses. This Chapter discusses how externship faculty can structure their courses to meet these ABA Standards and comply with best practices in instructional design.[4]

"Instructional design is a reflective, systematic, and comprehensive approach to creating instruction."[5] The primary components of instructional design include "learning objectives, teaching and learning methods, instructional materials, feedback, and assessment."[6] A core concept of instructional design is "congruence," which means that all of the elements of instruction—the learning outcomes, the teaching and learning methods, the instructional materials, and the feedback and assessment methods—are consistent and in alignment with each other.[7] In achiev-

1. Gerald F. Hess, *Blended Courses in Law School: The Best of Online and Face-to-Face Learning?*, 45 McGeorge L. Rev. 51, 70 (2013) (hereinafter "Hess, *Blended Courses*").

2. ABA Standards and Rules of Procedure for Approval of Law Schools 2022–2023, Standard 304(a). The complete ABA Standards are available at www.americanbar.org/content/dam/aba/ administrative/legal_education_and_admissions_to_the_bar/standards/2022-2023/2022-2023-aba-standards-and-rules-of-procedure.pdf.

3. ABA Standards and Rules of Procedure for Approval of Law Schools 2022–2023, Standard 304(d).

4. Parts of this Chapter are adapted, with permission, from Kelly Terry, Gerald Hess, Emily Grant & Sandra Simpson, Assessment of Teaching and Learning: A Comprehensive Guidebook for Law Schools (2021).

5. Michael Hunter Schwartz, *Teaching Law by Design: How Learning Theory and Instructional Design Can Inform and Reform Law Teaching*, 38 San Diego L. Rev. 347, 383 (2001).

6. Gerald F. Hess, *Value of Variety: An Organizing Principle to Enhance Teaching and Learning*, 3 Elon L. Rev. 65, 70–71 (2011) (hereinafter "Hess, *Value of Variety*").

7. *Id.* at 71.

ing congruence, the learning outcomes provide the foundation, and all subsequent design decisions flow from and support those outcomes.[8]

In their seminal book *Teaching Law by Design: Engaging Students from the Syllabus to the Final Exam*, Michael Hunter Schwartz, Sophie Sparrow, and Gerald Hess explain how law teachers can apply instructional design principles in creating their courses. Following these principles, Schwartz, Sparrow, and Hess set out a seven-step recursive design process that is depicted in the following diagram:[9]

Figure 7-1. Recursive Course Design Process

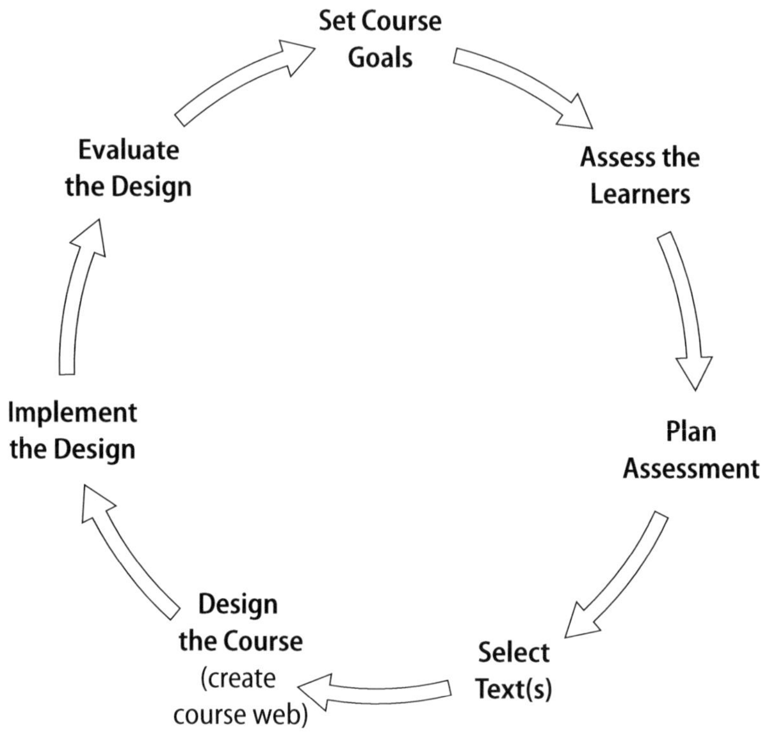

This process provides an excellent roadmap for designing externship courses, including courses taught face-to-face, online, or in a hybrid format.

8. *See, e.g.*, Hess, *Blended Courses*, *supra* note 1, at 70–71 ("The learning objectives then should drive the subsequent decisions on teaching and learning methods, materials, feedback, and assessment."). *See also* Susan Bryant, Elliott S. Milstein & Ann C. Shalleck, Transforming the Education of Lawyers: The Theory and Practice of Clinical Pedagogy 14 (2014) (goals in clinical courses "help teachers make choices about topics to pursue, ideas to reinforce, or experiences to encourage") (hereinafter "Transforming the Education of Lawyers").

9. Michael Hunter Schwartz, Sophie M. Sparrow & Gerald F. Hess, Teaching Law by Design: Engaging Students From the Syllabus to the Final Exam 34 (2d ed. 2017) (hereinafter "Teaching Law by Design") (Illustration 3.1: the Recursive Design Process, reprinted with permission). For another excellent resource on course design, see Carwina Weng, Danielle R. Cover, Margaret E. Reuter & Chris Roberts, Learning Law Through Experience & By Design (2019).

1. Setting Course Learning Outcomes[10]

Applying the recursive design process to externship courses, the first step is to set outcomes for students' learning. Learning outcomes are concise, declarative statements of what students should be able to do as a result of completing the course.[11] They should identify "the important doctrine, theory, thinking skills, performance skills, and values that students should learn[.]"[12] As explained briefly in Chapter 5, course-level outcomes focus on the learning that students should accomplish within an individual course, and they should be consistent with any program-level outcomes that have been adopted for an externship program comprised of multiple courses.[13] Schwartz, Sparrow, and Hess recommend establishing no more than three or four overarching learning outcomes per course.[14]

Course learning outcomes are most effective when they have the following three characteristics: (1) they "focus on the student—not the teacher"; (2) they "identify high-level intellectual activities or important values, not just knowledge"; and (3) they "are concrete and not abstract."[15] Outcomes are student focused when they describe what students will be able to do or what values they will appreciate as a result of the course, rather than what a teacher will do or say in class.[16] While identifying specific topics to cover is a frequent concern in course design, "coverage" is not a student-centered learning outcome, because "the attention is on the teacher and a march through topics without any unifying themes."[17] In a student-focused course, "the attention is on the students' learning."[18]

Course outcomes identify high-level intellectual activities or important values when they focus on "having students apply learning to new problems."[19] Some examples of higher-level skills in legal education include "drafting law-related documents, analyzing and solving legal problems, evaluating cases, [and] conducting client and

10. The assessment literature uses different terms for the knowledge, skills, and values that teachers want students to learn. Some authors use "goals," while others use "objectives" or "outcomes." These terms are not used consistently in the literature, and there is not an accepted consensus regarding their meaning. According to assessment expert Linda Suskie, "[u]nless an agency or accreditor requires otherwise, use whatever terms work best with your college's culture." LINDA SUSKIE, ASSESSING STUDENT LEARNING: A COMMON SENSE GUIDE 40 (3d ed. 2018). This book generally uses the term "outcome" unless a quotation from another source or context requires otherwise.

11. TEACHING LAW BY DESIGN, *supra* note 9, at 34.

12. Hess, *Value of Variety*, *supra* note 6, at 71.

13. As explained in Chapter 5, course-level outcomes are tailored to a particular course and are more specific than program-level outcomes, which identify knowledge, skills, and values that are common to all of the individual externship courses that comprise an externship program.

14. TEACHING LAW BY DESIGN, *supra* note 9, at 35.

15. *Id.*

16. *Id.*

17. BUILDING ON BEST PRACTICES: TRANSFORMING LEGAL EDUCATION IN A CHANGING WORLD 95 (Deborah Maranville, Lisa Radtke Bliss, Carolyn Wilkes Kaas & Antoinette Sedillo Lopez eds., 2015) (hereinafter "BUILDING ON BEST PRACTICES").

18. *Id.*

19. TEACHING LAW BY DESIGN, *supra* note 9, at 35.

witness interviews[.]"[20] These tasks build on and require students to apply foundational skills, such as case reading, recall of legal doctrines, and knowledge of closed and open-ended questions.

Outcomes are concrete if they have sufficient clarity to allow a teacher to measure whether students have attained them.[21] Outcomes framed as students "appreciating" or "understanding" certain ideas or values typically lack such clarity because they do not include a way for students to demonstrate that appreciation or understanding.[22] Measuring attainment, however, "does not require statistical precision—good, better, and best are forms of measurement that, so long as the rater applies the same criteria consistently, can provide plenty of information about student learning and permit comparisons across time or classes."[23]

It is a best practice to articulate learning outcomes in externship courses.[24] In designing externship course outcomes, ABA Standards 304(a)(1) and (2) come into play, as faculty should consider how they can create course learning outcomes that will accomplish the integration of doctrine, theory, skills, and legal ethics; engage students in the performance of professional skills; and develop the concepts underlying the professional skills being taught.[25] This consideration, in turn, will require faculty to determine which outcomes might be best accomplished at the placement site, and which outcomes are better addressed through an accompanying seminar class or faculty tutorial. It may be more feasible to accomplish certain outcomes, such as the performance of professional skills, through students' work at their placement sites. The identification of course learning outcomes also will affect the types of placements that externship faculty include in the course.[26] For example, if the outcomes focus specifically on learning related to practice in the public-service or public-interest sector, then placements in private firms or for-profit corporations likely must be excluded. Conversely, if the course outcomes are broad enough to encompass learning arising from any type of practice setting, then placements in private practice or for-profit corporations likely could be included.[27]

As discussed previously in Chapter 5, educational theorists generally recognize three types (or "domains") of learning that outcomes can encompass: cognitive, psy-

---

20. *Id.*

21. *Id.*

22. *Id.*

23. Building on Best Practices, *supra* note 17, at 96–97.

24. *Id.* at 226. *See also* Roy Stuckey & Others, Best Practices for Legal Education: A Vision and a Road Map 55 (2007) (hereinafter "Best Practices for Legal Education").

25. ABA Standards and Rules of Procedure for Approval of Law Schools 2022–2023, Standard 304(a)(1) and (2).

26. *See* Building on Best Practices, *supra* note 17, at 225–26 (explaining that choice of learning outcomes will affect the range of placement opportunities available to students).

27. Externship teachers who inherit courses that already include particular placements that need to be continued should identify the knowledge, skills, and values that they want students to take away from those placements and articulate course outcomes that focus on that learning.

chomotor, and affective. Scholars in externship and clinical pedagogy have identified a wide variety of possible learning outcomes that fall within these categories, such as the ability to learn from experience, being able to engage in metacognition, the ability to perform particular practice skills, and the development of professional identity and professionalism. For example, *Building on Best Practices: Transforming Legal Education in a Changing World* identifies the following learning outcomes regarding professional-identity formation and the development of ethical capacities that externship faculty might consider for their courses:

- The ability to explain the concept of professional identity and articulate the facets of one's own professional identity;
- The ability to "perform ethically with attentiveness to all relevant rules of professional conduct and self-awareness";
- The ability to "identify the fundamental values of the legal profession and recognize the presence or absence of those values in practice situations";
- The ability to "recognize and articulate the elements of competent practice, and how knowledge, skill, and values are woven together in service of a client or cause"; and
- The ability to articulate the "role of lawyers and identify changes to the profession that are occurring[.]"[28]

Similarly, *Transforming the Education of Lawyers: The Theory and Practice of Clinical Pedagogy* identifies over 25 possible learning outcomes, including, among others:

- The ability to "connect with and serve clients while respecting dual loyalty to the profession";
- The ability to develop "a personal commitment to achieve justice and providing access";
- The ability to "develop and use critical insights about how the law functions";
- The ability to "see clients and problems in context";
- The ability to engage in effective problem-solving;
- The capacity to engage in "role-based legal analysis";
- The capacity to "learn through reflection";
- The ability to understand the perspective of another; and
- The ability to perform selected practice skills.[29]

28. Building on Best Practices, *supra* note 17, at 227.
29. Transforming the Education of Lawyers, *supra* note 8, at 14–31.

Another source for potential learning outcomes is the *Australian Best Practices in Clinical Legal Education*, which includes outcomes centered on students' development of their:

- "Ability to work collaboratively";
- "Interpersonal skills; emotional intelligence; and self-awareness of their own cognitive abilities and values";
- "Awareness of lawyering as a professional role in the context of wider society";
- "Developing a preference for an ethical approach to legal practice and an understanding of the impact of that preference in exercising professional judgment"; and
- "Awareness of the social issues of justice, power, and disadvantage and an ability to critically analyze entrenched issues of justice in the legal system."[30]

Faculty also can draw inspiration for learning outcomes from the fundamental lawyering skills and values set forth in the *MacCrate Report*,[31] the 26 lawyering-effectiveness factors identified by Shultz and Zedeck,[32] the competencies identified in the *Foundations for Practice study*,[33] and competencies suggested in *Best Practices for Legal Education*.[34]

Faculty who want to focus specifically on learning outcomes related to racial-justice issues might consider adapting the following learning outcomes that Professor Carwina Weng created for her "Anti-Racism and Beyond: Equitable Lawyering Skills" course:

> By the end of the course, you will be able to use antidiscrimination and equity strategies and habits in culturally uncomfortable situations. To achieve this goal, you will be able to:

---

30. Linda F. Smith, Jeff Giddings & Leah Wortham, *Risks and Rewards of Externships: Exploring Goals and Methods*, 24 Int'l J. Clinical Legal Educ. 30, 43 (2017) (citing Adrian Evans et al., Best Practices in Australian Clinical Legal Education: The Final Report of the Project *Strengthening Australian Legal Education by Integrating Clinical Experiences: Identifying and Supporting Effective Practices* (2013)).

31. *See* American Bar Association Section of Legal Education and Admissions to the Bar, Legal Education and Professional Development—An Educational Continuum (Report on the Task Force on Law Schools and the Profession: Narrowing the Gap) 138–41 (1992).

32. Marjorie M. Shultz & Sheldon Zedeck, *Predicting Lawyer Effectiveness: Broadening the Basis for Law School Admission Decisions*, 36 Law & Soc. Inquiry 620, 630 (2011).

33. Alli Gerkman & Logan Cornett, Foundations for Practice: The Whole Lawyer and the Character Quotient (2016), iaals.du.edu/sites/default/files/ documents/publications/foundations_ for_practice_whole_lawyer_quotient.pdf (last visited March 6, 2022).

34. Best Practices for Legal Education, *supra* note 24, at 168–73.

- Recognize actions by yourself and others that cause discrimination to occur;
- Recognize supports and barriers to anti-discriminatory behavior;
- Practice habits and strategies to increase supports and overcome barriers to anti-discriminatory behavior;
- Choose intentionally the kind of response you make to discriminatory behavior;
- Evaluate your own learning of equitable behavior; and
- Explain your learning to others.[35]

The outcomes discussed in the preceding paragraphs are broad enough that they would work well in a general externship course that includes different types of placements, because all students in the course would encounter the identified knowledge, skills, and values, regardless of their placement type, and would have the opportunity to focus on their development in those areas. Faculty whose courses are limited to certain types of externship placements have the opportunity to consider more specific learning outcomes related to the focus of their students' common work. For example, the teacher of an appellate externship course might set an outcome relating to the ability to identify and appropriately apply different standards of review or an outcome related to the ability to write a bench memorandum. The teacher of a prosecutor externship course might have learning outcomes related to the ability to interview a witness, conduct a direct examination, or draft a jury instruction. The discrete nature of subject-specific externship courses allows for the creation of more narrowly tailored course learning outcomes.[36]

As this discussion demonstrates, externship faculty have a multitude of outcomes they can use as a starting point, and there is no need to "reinvent the wheel." Externship courses, however, cannot teach anything and everything, so faculty must make intentional choices about the knowledge, skills, and values they want their students to learn. The key is to prioritize the most important learning that students should take away from the course and draft outcomes that encompass that learning. In crafting the actual language of their course outcomes, faculty should use the "stem-action verb-outcome" formula explained previously in Chapter 5.

Once established, course learning outcomes should be communicated to students. Making students aware of the course outcomes has many benefits, including creating interest in the instruction, establishing the teacher's expectations for the students' learning, allowing students to monitor and direct their own learning, and allowing students to communicate what they have learned to others, such as employers.[37] This

35. Posting of Professor Lisa Brodoff, Dir. of Clinical Law Prog., lbrodoff@seattleu.edu, to LEXTERN@listserv.gsu.edu (Dec. 30, 2020) (on file with author).

36. *See, e.g.*, Building on Best Practices, *supra* note 17, at 229.

37. *See* Mary J. Allen, Assessing Academic Programs in Higher Education 44 (2004);

transparency is especially important in experiential education because the outcomes "articulate what students need to learn to be excellent beginner practitioners and lifelong learners."[38] To achieve these benefits, the ABA requires teachers to include their course learning outcomes in their syllabi.[39]

Externship faculty also should communicate the course learning outcomes to the site supervisors and "take steps to ensure that the supervisor structures the field experience and assigns tasks in alignment with those goals."[40] Since the site supervisor is a co-teacher in the externship process, and probably interacts with the student more frequently and for longer periods of time than the externship faculty member, it is imperative that the site supervisor and externship faculty share a common understanding regarding the student's intended learning. Externship faculty can communicate course outcomes to site supervisors through a variety of means, such as initial discussions with prospective supervisors to determine if placements are appropriate for the course, informational materials about the course, the course website, training sessions for supervisors, supervisor manuals, and the course syllabus.

2. Assess the Learners

Once externship faculty have established their course outcomes, the next step in the instructional design process is to assess the learners and evaluate their incoming knowledge, skills, and values.[41] Law students are not blank slates, and they enter law school with knowledge drawn from their undergraduate education, prior work history, and general life experience. In addition, extern students will have completed some part of the law school curriculum, including any specified prerequisites, and

Schwartz, *supra* note 5, at 403–04 ("[I]f communicated to the learners, objectives can arouse interest in the instruction and enable the learners to engage in metacognitive self-assessment; students can ask themselves whether they have learned to do what they were supposed to learn to do"); Transforming the Education of Lawyers, *supra* note 8, at 14 ("If we set clear expectations, students will be motivated to meet them.").

38. Transforming the Education of Lawyers, *supra* note 8, at 14. *See also* Best Practices for Legal Education, *supra* note 24, at 168 ("In order to maximize the effectiveness of instruction, both faculty and students must be aware of and share a common set of instructional goals and objectives, which should be explicit, published, and widely disseminated.").

39. ABA Section of Legal Education and Admissions to the Bar, Managing Director's Guidance Memo: Standards 301, 302, 314, and 315 at 4 (June 2015), www.americanbar.org/content/dam/aba/ administrative/ legal_education_and_admissions_ to_the_bar/ governancedocuments/ 2015_learning_outcomes_guidance.pdf (last visited March 6, 2022).

40. Building on Best Practices, *supra* note 17, at 225.

41. Teaching Law by Design, *supra* note 9, at 33.

will bring the knowledge, skills, and values from that experience into the externship course.[42]

These factors have design implications for an externship course. For example, information about students' undergraduate backgrounds and previous work experiences can reveal particular skills that students bring with them to the course and on which the externship teacher can build. Externship faculty can gather this information by asking their students to complete a brief extern profile or questionnaire prior to or at the beginning of the course.[43] Using this information, externship faculty can design authentic, practice-based learning experiences to which students can relate and in which they will be motivated to learn.[44]

Externship faculty also should consider the components of the required law school curriculum that students have completed when they begin externships. For example, what types of writing assignments, and how many such assignments, did students complete during their first year? Did they write only legal memoranda and appellate briefs, or did they also write documents such as contracts, complaints, and discovery requests? Do any of the required law school courses use team-based learning and thus expose students to aspects of collaborative learning and teamwork skills? What, if any, instruction have students received in fundamental practice skills, such as client interviewing, fact investigation, and negotiation? Does any aspect of the required curriculum include instruction in professionalism skills and the formation of professional identity? Have the students completed any upper-level law-practice simulation courses or clinical courses prior to the externship course, and if so, what skills did they learn in those courses? Externship faculty can obtain this information by talking to their faculty colleagues, reviewing their school's required curriculum, or reviewing syllabi from other courses. Having this information can help externship faculty avoid incorrect assumptions about the knowledge of their incoming stu-

---

42. Extern students "shall have successfully completed sufficient prerequisites or shall receive sufficient contemporaneous training to assure the quality of the student educational experience." ABA STANDARDS AND RULES OF PROCEDURE FOR APPROVAL OF LAW SCHOOLS 2022–2023, STANDARD 304(f).

43. *See, e.g.*, Sandra Simpson, *Getting to Know Your Students*, (September 4, 2016), http:// lawteaching.org/2019/09/04/getting-to-know-your-students/ (last visited March 6, 2022) (providing example of brief questionnaire students are asked to complete at beginning of semester).

44. Educational psychologist Malcolm Knowles' research in adult learning theory, known as "andragogy," has demonstrated that "adults' greater reservoir of personal experience can be used as a basis for learning" and that "adults' readiness to learn is quite high if the subject of learning is related to their developmental tasks, i.e., the performance expected of them in their social role." Fran Quigley, *Seizing the Disorienting Moment: Adult Learning Theory and the Teaching of Social Justice in Law School Clinics*, 2 CLINICAL L. REV. 37, 47 (1995) (citing and discussing MALCOLM KNOWLES, THE ADULT LEARNER: A NEGLECTED SPECIES (4th ed. 1990)).

dents, design a course that builds on students' existing knowledge, skills, and values, and introduce new knowledge that students have not yet encountered.

3. Plan Assessment

After establishing course outcomes and assessing one's learners, the next step is to design the process for assessing student learning in the course. Assessments are simply the "tools used to obtain and document information about student achievement, skills, and ability,"[45] and they can take various forms, such as journals, quizzes, exams, papers, in-class exercises, group projects, presentations, or skills performances. While it may seem counterintuitive to plan assessments at this point in the design process, educational experts recognize that "creating an assessment plan right after you have articulated your objectives ensures that your assessment instruments, class sessions, and syllabus are congruent with your goals."[46] It is a best practice to assess learning outcomes in externship courses.[47] The subsections below explain how to design an assessment process for an individual course.

a. Create an Assessment Plan

Externship faculty should create a comprehensive assessment plan that lists all of their course learning outcomes and identifies the assessment instruments they will use to measure student achievement of those outcomes. For example, an outcome relating to the ability to engage in reflection could be measured using students' journals or a reflective essay at the end of the semester. An outcome relating to verbal communication skills could be measured by in-class presentations. An outcome related to the development of teamwork skills could be evaluated through the use of an in-class exercise using small groups. Students' weekly timesheets could be used to measure a learning outcome relating to professionalism and punctuality. Other externship learning outcomes may be measured through supervisor evaluations of students' work products or skills performances at their placement sites. A wide variety of externship assignments exists to measure learning outcomes; the key is to ensure that each outcome is being measured through some sort of instrument that allows the faculty member or site supervisor to determine whether students are meeting the outcome. Externship faculty should assess all of their outcomes each time they teach the course.

---

45. Rogelio Lasso, *Is Our Students Learning? Using Assessments to Measure and Improve Law School Learning and Performance*, 15 Barry L. Rev. 73, 76 (2010).

46. Teaching Law by Design, *supra* note 9, at 39.

47. Building on Best Practices, *supra* note 17, at 226.

In planning assessments, externship faculty also must keep in mind the ABA Standards governing experiential education and externship courses. To satisfy the requirements for an experiential course, an externship course must provide "multiple opportunities for performance" and "opportunities for student performance, self-evaluation, and feedback" from a faculty member or a site supervisor.[48] In addition, Standard 304 requires that externship courses must have "a clearly articulated method of evaluating the student's academic performance" that is set forth, along with other agreements about externship content, structure, and management, in a written understanding among the externship student, the externship faculty member, and a person in authority at the placement site.[49] Externship faculty must be mindful of these requirements and ensure that their assessment plans satisfy them.

b. Decide the Types of Assessment Measures to Use

Externship faculty must decide the types of measures they will use to assess whether students are achieving the course learning outcomes. Assessment measures (also known as "instruments" or "tools") are simply "the means by which one gathers evidence to demonstrate learning or the achievement of learning outcomes; they are indicators of performance."[50] As explained in Chapter 5, educational experts typically categorize assessment instruments as either "direct measures" or "indirect measures." Examples of direct assessment measures in externship courses include journals, timesheets, quizzes, essays, drafting assignments, presentations, skills performances, portfolios, and evaluations by externship supervisors. Types of indirect measures in externship courses include students' self-evaluations of their own knowledge, skills, and values, as well as surveys and focus groups of employers asking for their general perceptions about the abilities of a cohort of students.[51] While indirect evidence can provide useful information, it is based on opinions and self-reporting and therefore is less reliable than direct evidence. Accordingly, externship

---

48. ABA Standards and Rules of Procedure for Approval of Law Schools 2022–2023, Standard 304(a)(3) and (a)(4).

49. ABA Standards and Rules of Procedure for Approval of Law Schools 2022–2023, Standard 304(d)(i).

50. Lori F. Shaw & Victoria L. VanZandt, Student Learning Outcomes and Law School Assessment: A Practical Guide to Measuring Institutional Effectiveness 183 (2015).

51. Trudy W. Banta & Catherine A. Palomba, Assessment Essentials: Planning, Implementing, and Improving Assessment in Higher Education 23 (2d ed. 2015); Mary E. Huba & Jann E. Freed, Learner-Centered Assessment on College Campuses: Shifting the Focus from Teaching to Learning 11 (2000); Shaw & VanZandt, *supra* note 50, at 104. In the assessment context, surveys generally ask for employers' or supervisors' perceptions of graduates or students as a group. Conversely, supervisor evaluations of externship students focus on the performance of individual students.

faculty should always include some form of direct assessment for evaluating each of their course learning outcomes.

c. Decide Whether Assessments Will Be Formative, Summative, or Both

In selecting which direct and indirect measures to use, externship faculty also should consider whether the purpose of the assessment is formative or summative.[52] An assessment is formative if its primary purpose is to provide feedback to students and faculty on student performance. ABA Standard 314 defines formative assessments as "measurements at different points during a particular course or at different points over the span of a student's education that provide meaningful feedback to improve student learning."[53] This feedback is important because it provides students opportunities to identify weaknesses in their performance and make improvements before a final evaluation is made. Formative assessments often are ungraded, but teachers may choose to assign grades to them.

Summative assessments, on the other hand, are used for assigning a grade or otherwise indicating a student's level of achievement at the end of a course or unit of study. ABA Standard 314 defines summative assessments as "measurements at the culmination of a particular course or at the culmination of any part of a student's legal education that measure the degree of student learning."[54] "In contrast to formative evaluation, which looks forward to ways in which students might continue to learn, summative evaluation looks back and judges how much students have learned."[55] The table below summarizes the primary differences between formative and summative assessments:

52. This discussion of formative and summative assessment is adapted from Kelly S. Terry, *Embedding Assessment Principles in Externships*, 20 Clinical L. Rev. 467, 476–78 (2014).

53. ABA Standards and Rules of Procedure for Approval of Law Schools 2022–2023, Standard 314, Interpretation 314-1.

54. *Id.*

55. Lynn M. Daggett, *All of the Above: Computerized Exam Scoring of Multiple Choice Items Helps to: (A) Show How Exam Items Worked Technically, (B) Maximize Exam Fairness, (C) Justly Assign Letter Grades, and (D) Provide Feedback on Student Learning*, 57 J. Legal Educ. 391, 397 (2007) (emphasis in original).

Figure 7-2. Formative and Summative Assessment

What	When	Where	Why	How
Formative Assessment	Ongoing throughout the course Looks forward	In class or outside of class	Provides feedback to students (to improve learning) and faculty (to improve teaching) regarding student progress in meeting course outcomes	Graded or ungraded assignments, exercises, or other assessment tools
Summative Assessment	At the end of the course or unit Looks back	In class or outside of class	Measures what students have learned and whether they have met course outcomes	Generally, graded final assignments, projects, or exams

Externship faculty should use both formative and summative assessment methods.[56] A single assessment instrument can serve both formative and summative purposes. For example, many externship faculty assign students to complete a self-evaluation at mid-semester. This assignment is summative in that it measures the self-evaluation skills that students have developed up to that point in the semester. The assessment also is formative because the teacher's feedback identifies ways that students can further improve their self-evaluation skills during the remainder of the semester.

d. Decide Whether Assessments Will Be Norm-Referenced or Criterion-Referenced

Externship faculty also should decide whether their assessments will be norm-referenced or criterion-referenced.[57] Norm-referenced assessments evaluate student performance in relation to the performance of all the students in the class and rank students based on how they perform in comparison to each other, usually based on a curve. Norm-referenced evaluation does not require students to meet an

56. Building on Best Practices, *supra* note 17, at 230.

57. This discussion of norm-referenced and criterion-referenced assessments is adapted from Terry, *supra* note 52, at 478–80.

absolute standard of achievement. Thus, an "A" on a norm-referenced assessment "means the student's performance ranked at the top of the class, without regard to whether this student or the class as a whole performed at an excellent, mediocre, or poor level."[58]

Criterion-referenced assessments, in contrast, measure student performance in relation to established standards and evaluate whether students have met particular levels of performance. Scores are based on students' individual performance in relation to these specific standards, and there is no curve or pre-set distribution of grades. Thus, an "A" on a criterion-referenced assessment "means the student demonstrated excellent mastery of the course concepts and skills, without regard to how other students did."[59] Educational experts recommend the use of criterion-referenced assessments because they are more reliable and because they measure student proficiency in acquiring knowledge and skills instead of merely sorting students.[60]

Criterion-referenced assessment generally uses rubrics,[61] which are detailed written criteria that describe what students should learn and how they will be evaluated.[62] According to Professor Sophie Sparrow, a recognized assessment expert, using rubrics causes professors to focus on the most meaningful aspects of their courses:

> To develop explicit criteria that will be distributed to students in writing, we must necessarily be clear about what we expect students to learn; we must identify the core skills and knowledge that are necessary to be competent or proficient in the particular area of law. These are fundamental questions focusing not on what we will "cover" in class and how we will fill up the time, but on what we want students to take away with them, hold on to, and return to in the future.[63] Rubrics also increase fairness because

---

58. Daggett, *supra* note 55, at 399.

59. *Id.*

60. Best Practices for Legal Education, *supra* note 24, at 243–44; William M. Sullivan, Anne Colby, Judith Welch Wegner, Lloyd Bond & Lee Shulman, Educating Lawyers: Preparation for the Profession of Law 168–71 (2007) (hereinafter "Educating Lawyers").

61. This discussion of rubrics is adapted from Terry, *supra* note 52, at 493–96.

62. Dannelle D. Stevens & Antonia J. Levi, Introduction to Rubrics: An Assessment Tool to Save Grading Time, Convey Effective Feedback and Promote Student Learning 3 (2005) (hereinafter "Introduction to Rubrics") ("At its most basic, a rubric is a scoring tool that lays out the specific expectations for an assignment."); *see also* Best Practices for Legal Education, *supra* note 24, at 244 ("Criteria-referenced assessments rely on detailed, explicit criteria that identify the abilities students should be demonstrating (for example, applying and distinguishing cases) and the bases on which the instructor will distinguish among excellent, good, competent, or incompetent performances."); Sophie Sparrow, *Describing the Ball: Improve Teaching by Using Rubrics—Explicit Grading Criteria*, 2004 Mich. St. L. Rev. 1, 6 (2004).

63. Sparrow, *supra* note 62, at 18.

they cause teachers to evaluate each assignment according to the same criteria, thus creating consistency in assessment.[64]

Chapter 5 provides a detailed explanation of a process for creating rubrics, based on Dannelle Stevens' and Antonia Levi's *Introduction to Rubrics: An Assessment Tool to Save Grading Time*. In creating rubrics used at the course level, it is helpful to keep in mind a few additional guiding principles. First, the terms used to describe the level of performance "should be tactful but clear."[65] Some professors use grades or numbers for their levels of achievement, while others use descriptors such as "high level," "middle level," and "beginning level."[66] Stevens and Levi also recommend limiting a rubric to just three performance levels when initially constructing it; if the teacher subsequently wants to make finer distinctions among student work, she can expand the rubric to include additional performance levels after she has applied it to the actual assignment.[67] Finally, the performance criteria should be described as specifically as possible so students will be able to see the areas in which they are doing well and the areas in which they need improvement.[68] For the lower levels of the performance scale, Stevens and Levi recommend articulating performance criteria that describe "the most common ways in which students fail to meet the highest level of expectations."[69]

Below is an example of a rubric for evaluating a reflective journal assigned in an externship course.[70]

64. *See, e.g.*, Suskie, *supra* note 10, at 195 ("Rubrics make scoring more accurate, unbiased, and consistent. They ensure that every assignment is assessed using the same criteria.") (internal citation omitted); Teaching Law by Design, *supra* note 9, at 179 ("[W]hen teachers have explicit criteria, such as rubrics, they grade consistently and reliably."); Best Practices for Legal Education, *supra* note 24, at 243 (encouraging law professors "to develop and apply explicit grading criteria to minimize the risk of unreliability in assigning grades").

65. Introduction to Rubrics, *supra* note 62, at 8.

66. *Id.*

67. *Id.*

68. *E.g.*, Sparrow, *supra* note 62, at 9.

69. Introduction to Rubrics, *supra* note 62, at 11.

70. This rubric is an updated version of the rubric that is included in Terry, *supra* note 52, at 495–96. Examples of rubrics for other externship assignments, including timesheets, rounds discussions, professional development plans, class participation, oral presentations, and essays, are included in the Appendix to this Chapter.

Figure 7-3. Rubric for Externship Journal

Task Description:	**Students shall write a journal entry reflecting on their learning from their externship experiences.**		
	Needs Work	**Competent**	**Excellent**
Professionalism: **Punctuality** ______2	☐ Submitted late. **(0 pts)**	☐ Submitted by deadline or requested extension for good cause prior to deadline. **(2 pts)**	N/A
Professionalism: **Compliance w/ Instructions** ______8	☐ Not submitted in Word. **(0 pts)** ☐ Not double-spaced in 12-point font. **(0 pts)** ☐ Less than 750 words. **(0 pts)** ☐ Lacks word-count certification. **(0 pts)**	☐ Submitted in Word. **(2 pts)** ☐ Double-spaced in 12-point font. **(2 pts)** ☐ At least 750 words. **(2 pts)** ☐ Includes word-count certification. **(2 pts)**	N/A
Reflection: **Clarity and Relevance of Topic to Writer's Learning** ______8	☐ Journal topic and writer's rationale for choosing it are not clear; journal provides little or no detail to provide context for the reader to understand the relevance of the topic to the writer's learning. **(0–3 pts)**	☐ Journal topic can be discerned, but journal provides minimal rationale for choosing topic, or discussion lacks connection to topic; journal includes some background information that provides minimal context for the reader to understand the relevance of the topic to the writer's learning. **(4–6 pts)**	☐ Journal clearly articulates the chosen topic and the writer's rationale for choosing the topic; journal includes sufficient background information that provides a clear context for the reader to understand the relevance of the topic to the writer's learning. **(7–8 pts)**

Reflection: **Introspection** _______8	☐ Journal lacks self-examination of writer's own thoughts and feelings in response to an externship experience, class discussion, or reading assignment; for example, it merely describes an experience or reading in narrative form, summarizes work performed, or summarizes case law or legal analysis from an externship work product. **(0–3 pts)**	☐ Journal explores an externship experience, class discussion, or reading assignment with some self-examination of writer's own thoughts and feelings in response to the experience or reading. Writer engages in analysis sufficient to allow reader to respond with comments or questions to prompt additional insights or thoughts by the writer. **(4–6 pts)**	☐ Journal explores an externship experience, class discussion, or reading assignment with meaningful self-examination of writer's own thoughts and feelings in response to the experience or reading. Writer engages in deep analysis of issues raised, insights gained, or changes in writer's knowledge, values, or beliefs in response to experience or reading. **(7–8 pts)**
Reflection: **Self-Assessment of Writer's Learning or Understanding** _______8	☐ Journal lacks self-assessment of the writer's learning from the topic discussed; writer does not evaluate his or her present knowledge/understanding and what writer still needs to learn for professional development. **(0–3 pts)**	☐ Journal shows some self-assessment of the writer's learning from the topic discussed; writer engages in superficial evaluation of his or her present knowledge/understanding and identifies general steps to take for further learning and professional development. **(4–6 pts)**	☐ Journal shows significant self-assessment of the writer's learning from the topic discussed; writer engages in deep evaluation of his or her present knowledge/understanding and identifies individualized and meaningful steps to take for further learning and professional development. **(7–8 pts)**

Reflection: **Understanding Multiple Perspectives** _______8	☐ Journal lacks complexity; it considers experiences from only the writer's perspective. **(0–3 pts)**	☐ Journal shows some complexity; writer demonstrates an awareness of others' perspectives, but does not consider the experiences from the others' perspectives, or considers the others' perspectives only superficially. **(4–6 pts)**	☐ Journal shows significant complexity; writer demonstrates an awareness of others' perspectives, considers the others' perspectives, and evaluates experiences from the others' perspectives in a deep and meaningful way. **(7–8 pts)**
Reflection: **Gaining New Knowledge** _______8	☐ Journal lacks "reflection on action"; writer makes few or no connections between prior knowledge and new knowledge gained from externship experience, reading assignment, or class discussion. **(0–3 pts)**	☐ Journal shows some "reflection on action"; writer makes some connections between prior knowledge and new knowledge gained from externship experience, reading assignment, or class discussion. **(4–6 pts)**	☐ Journal shows meaningful "reflection on action"; writer explains how he or she applied new knowledge gained from externship experience, reading assignment, or class discussion to a new situation, or writer explores how such new knowledge could be applied to a new situation. **(7–8 pts)**

e. Course Grades Are Not Acceptable Outcomes Measures

When designing an assessment plan, externship faculty should understand the distinctions between assessment and grading. While assessment and grading are related processes, and often are used in conjunction with one another, they serve different purposes and should not be conflated or viewed as interchangeable. Several crucial differences exist between assessing student learning and assigning course grades, which render course grades of limited, if any, value in an assessment process.

First, awarding grades and assessing student learning serve entirely different purposes. "[G]rading is evaluative—designed to sort and classify students, to confer distinction or channel students."[71] It often is used primarily to reward exemplary performances, penalize poor performances, and stratify students for employers.[72] Assessment, on the other hand, "is ameliorative—designed to improve student learning and faculty teaching."[73] Course-level assessment measures an individual student's performance on the basis of explicit criteria, with the teacher providing contemporaneous feedback to the student on his or her progress in achieving the course's learning outcomes.[74] It is "the process of determining what a student understands, how that student can improve that understanding, and how she can apply that understanding to future experiences."[75]

Second, assessment focuses on student learning with respect to individual learning outcomes, while grades reflect student performance with respect to multiple outcomes. In a course-level assessment process, each learning outcome is analyzed separately and independently. The learning outcome is identified, the evidence relating to that outcome is gathered, that evidence is evaluated, and a conclusion is reached regarding the level of student learning achieved with respect to that outcome. Thus, there is a laser-like focus on one outcome at a time that allows faculty to pinpoint specific areas of strength and weakness.[76]

Assigning a course grade does not have this singular focus. Professors typically weigh several factors in determining course grades, such as multiple assessments keyed to different learning outcomes. Professors also may base grades on factors unrelated to students' mastery of course learning outcomes, such as attendance, class participation, punctuality, penalties for late assignments, and opportunities for extra credit.[77] Thus, a grade is an aggregation based on a combination of inputs,

---

71. Building on Best Practices, *supra* note 17, at 94.

72. Stacy L. Brustin & David F. Chavkin, *Testing the Grades: Evaluating Grading Models in Clinical Legal Education*, 3 Clinical L. Rev. 299, 306 (1997). *See also, e.g.*, Philip C. Kissam, *Law School Examinations*, 42 Vand. L. Rev. 433, 436 (1989) ("[T]he immediate function of law school grading practices is to establish a highly disaggregated class ranking system" that "is an efficient device, or at least a rational one, for sorting students in ways that serve the hiring purposes of many law firms."); Jeffrey Evans Stake, *Making the Grade: Some Principles of Comparative Grading*, 52 J. Legal Educ. 583, 584 (2002) ("Grades generally purport to tell only who performed better and who performed worse on an instrument of assessment, usually a single exam or paper" and sort students for employers).

73. Building on Best Practices, *supra* note 17, at 94.

74. *E.g.*, Gregory Munro, Outcomes Assessment for Law Schools 12 (2000) (citing Alverno College Faculty, Student Assessment-as-Learning, at Alverno College 3 (1994)).

75. Steven J. Johansen, *"What Were You Thinking?": Using Annotated Portfolios to Improve Student Assessment*, 4 Legal Writing: J. Legal Writing Inst. 123, 125 (1998).

76. *See* Shaw & VanZandt, *supra* note 50, at 13.

77. Thus, when factors such as these are considered in a final grade, students who do not achieve the course learning outcomes might still receive a fairly high grade by attending classes and participating in discussions, submitting their assignments on time, and taking advantage of opportunities for extra credit. Conversely, students who do achieve the course learning outcomes may receive a lower grade if they miss classes, fail to participate in discussions, or submit late assignments. *See, e.g.*, Suskie, *supra* note 10, at 10.

and it does not provide disaggregated information regarding student learning with respect to any particular outcome. A student's grade of "B" in an externship course, for example, implies that the student probably learned a good deal in the course, but it does not indicate which learning outcomes were mastered and which were not. An assessment process focusing on each course learning outcome, however, would provide that information.

In sum, a grade is "essentially an artificial construct designed to compare the performance of one student to another and rank them accordingly."[78] Thus, while grades may provide some indirect evidence about student learning, they "are not acceptable outcome measures."[79] A discussion of the pros and cons of grading students' assignments in externship courses is included later in this Chapter.

f. Decide the Number of Assessment Measures to Use

To obtain the most comprehensive and accurate picture of student performance, externship faculty should use more than one assessment instrument, and different types of instruments, to measure student learning.[80] Multiple measures are recommended because no single assessment instrument, even if it is very well-designed and executed, "can provide the comprehensive view needed to determine whether a criterion is being achieved."[81] Students may perform better on one type of assessment than another, so using multiple assessments of different types provides students with more opportunities to demonstrate their learning and produces a more accurate picture of whether they are achieving learning outcomes.[82] Using multiple measures also enhances credibility in the assessment process by allowing faculty to compare results from multiple methods.[83] When multiple methods of assessment produce similar findings, greater confidence may be placed in the results.[84]

In deciding how many assignments are necessary to obtain an accurate picture of students' learning, teachers should consider the time demands of the students' externship placements and their other courses. Another important consideration

---

78. Shaw & VanZandt, *supra* note 50, at 13.

79. *Id. See also* Building on Best Practices, *supra* note 17, at 422 ("[T]raditional grading practices do not inform the law school in evaluating the effectiveness of its program.").

80. *See* Terry, *supra* note 52, at 482.

81. Shaw & VanZandt, *supra* note 50, at 112.

82. *See* Peggy L. Maki, Assessing for Learning: Building a Sustainable Commitment Across the Institution 156–57 (2010).

83. Banta & Palomba, *supra* note 51, at 31. *See also*, Suskie, *supra* note 10 at 327 ("Comparing evidence from various assessments against one another is called *corroboration* or *triangulation*.").

84. Susan Hanley Duncan, *They're Back! The New Accreditation Standards Coming to a Law School Near You—A 2018 Update, Guide to Compliance, and Dean's Role in Implementing*, 67 J. Legal Educ. 464, 477 (2018) ("Greater accuracy and authority are achieved when several methods of assessment produce similar findings."); Andrea Susnir Funk, The Art of Assessment: Making Outcomes Assessment Accessible, Sustainable, and Meaningful 74, n.3 (2017) ("Taken together,

in determining the types and number of assessments may be whether the externship course has a classroom seminar component, which provides opportunities for assessments to occur during class time, or uses some other method to provide contemporaneous, faculty-guided reflection. Finally, faculty should also consider their own capacity to evaluate multiple assessments over the course of the semester and provide timely feedback on them. Administering assessments that the teacher does not have sufficient time to review and critique is not useful to an assessment process.

g. Assessment Instruments Must Be Valid, Reliable, and Fair

Finally, externship faculty must design their assessment instruments to ensure that they are valid, reliable, and fair.[85] Validity means that the assessment measures the knowledge, skills, or values that the teacher taught and intended for students to learn. If an assessment measures something other than that, it is not valid. For example, if journals are used to measure students' skills in reflection, then the journal rubric should include criteria that correlate with the elements of the reflective process, such as introspection and self-evaluation. The journal rubric should not include criteria such as grammar and writing skills, unless those skills relate to a learning outcome for the course and the teacher has addressed those skills in the course. If the journals are meant to assess reflection, but the rubric evaluates composition instead, then there is a "mismatch," and the journal is not a valid assessment of students' skills in reflection.

Reliability means that the assessment instrument is consistent and "yields the same results on repeated trials."[86] Thus, an assessment is reliable if a teacher can evaluate a student's performance on it multiple times and award the same score each time. Again using the example of a journal rubric, the rubric is reliable if the teacher can assess the same journal with it multiple times and reach a similar score each time. Reliability reduces the impact of subjective influences in the assessment process, such as whether a student's performance is assessed first or last.

Fairness in assessment means that "students are given equitable opportunities to demonstrate what they know."[87] To ensure fairness, assessments should have clear instructions that are easily understood, and they should not include cultural references that reflect biases or favor students from a particular background.[88] Fairness

---

information gleaned from multiple sources will strengthen your confidence in your observations and conclusions.").

85. This discussion of validity, reliability, and fairness is adapted from Terry, *supra* note 52, at 480–82.

86. BEST PRACTICES FOR LEGAL EDUCATION, *supra* note 24, at 239.

87. Linda Suskie, *Fair Assessment Practices: Giving Students Equitable Opportunities to Demonstrate Learning*, 52 AAHE BULLETIN, Issue 9, 7–10 (May 2000), http://citeseerx.ist.psu.edu/viewdoc/download?doi=10.1.1.540.9919&rep=rep1&type=pdf (last visited March 6, 2022).

88. SUSKIE, *supra* note 10, at 30–31.

also is enhanced when faculty administer multiple assessments of different types, so all of the assessments do not favor students with a particular set of skills.[89] In an externship course, for example, a teacher might include both writing tasks and class presentations, so that students who excel at writing and students who excel at speaking both have equal opportunities to demonstrate what they know and can do.

h. Decide Whether to Assign Letter or Number Grades to Assessments and for the Course

In conjunction with their assessment planning, externship faculty also should consider whether they should assign letter or number grades to formative assessments or assign overall letter or number grades for the course.[90] As explained above, grades are not a substitute for genuine assessment. Nonetheless, it is worthwhile to consider whether to award letter or number grades on assessments because grades can affect student motivation.[91] It is undeniable that grades operate as a "powerful incentive" for students because they determine rewards and punishments such as Dean's list, graduation honors, law review membership, academic probation and dismissal, and career opportunities.[92] While grades are not essential to student motivation, they "may be one of the most efficient methods to induce learning behaviors[.]"[93] Indeed, a survey of clinical students at the Catholic University Columbus School of Law found that 61% of the students responded that a numerical grading system "had a significant positive impact on their motivation in their clinical courses."[94] Conversely, the absence of letter or number grades can negatively affect student effort. As one law school administrator has noted, "Pass-fail leads students not to

---

89. Suskie, *supra* note 87, at 7–10.

90. Parts of this discussion of grading are adapted from Terry, *supra* note 52, at 472–73, 511–15.

91. Douglas A. Henderson, *Uncivil Procedure: Ranking Law Students Among Their Peers*, 27 U. Mich. J.L. Reform 399, 402 (1994) (stating that grades serve motivational, diagnostic, informational, and administrative purposes) (citing Moshe Zeidner, *Key Facets of Classroom Grading: A Comparison of Teacher and Student Perspectives*, 17 Contemp. Educ. Psychol. 224, 225 (1992)).

92. Barbara Glesner Fines, *Competition and the Curve*, 65 UMKC L. Rev. 879, 883 & n.19 (1996–97); *see also* Kissam, *supra* note 72, at 463 (Employers "use class ranks and law review status to screen and select law students for the more prestigious and lucrative employment opportunities that the legal profession has to offer."); Steve Sheppard, *An Informal History of How Law Schools Evaluate Students, with a Predictable Emphasis on Law School Final Exams*, 65 UMKC L. Rev. 657, 686 (1996–97) (stating that grades place students "into strata, including those unfit for graduation, those fit for graduation, those who are outstanding, and many gradations among them, including individual location in a class rank").

93. Fines, *supra* note 92, at 884. *See also, e.g.*, Teaching Law by Design, *supra* note 9, at 174 ("g]rades are among the most powerful learning and motivating tools we have"); Sparrow, *supra* note 62, at 5 (calling grading "the most effective tool a teacher has to promote learning").

94. Brustin & Chavkin, *supra* note 72, at 314. Students also admitted that "if faced with the choice of preparing for a number-graded course or a pass/fail course, they would focus their efforts on the number-graded course." *Id.* at 315.

work hard. No grades, no standards. When students must make decisions about time allocation, they do what's needed to 'only pass.'"[95]

Despite these motivational effects, a consideration of grades also should weigh their negative consequences. "Grades can influence the ways students think about themselves, swelling their heads or shaking their confidence."[96] Grades often can significantly affect the career tracks available to students and even eliminate them from some employment opportunities.[97] In addition, an externship course may be subject to a school's mandatory grade curve, which would require the externship teacher to limit the best grades to only a small percentage of students, despite students' actual performance on class assignments.[98] In light of these considerations, externship faculty might choose to grade student assessments and the course on a pass/fail basis and use timely and well-crafted feedback as a means for promoting engagement and motivation.

The dual-supervision model of externship pedagogy also presents a wrinkle in awarding letter grades that is unique to externships. In externships, students typically have two supervisors: a practicing attorney or judge who directs their day-to-day work at the placement site, and a faculty member who arranges the placements, reviews student journals and timesheets, and teaches the seminar class. Because the faculty member does not supervise the student's work at the placement site, the faculty member has little or no basis for evaluating the quality of that work. Likewise, the students' work at the different placement sites often varies widely, making it difficult for the faculty member to measure the students' work against the same standards.

This complication, however, is not insurmountable. If the student's placement work and classroom work are combined in a single course, a possible solution is to award an identical amount of points for each student's fieldwork, relying on the placement supervisor's evaluation of the student's work, and to award additional

---

95. EDUCATING LAWYERS, *supra* note 60, at 169. *See also* Leslie M. Rose, *Norm-Referenced Grading in the Age of Carnegie: Why Criteria-Referenced Grading Is More Consistent with Current Trends in Legal Education and How Legal Writing Can Lead the Way*, 17 LEGAL WRITING: J. LEGAL WRITING INST. 123, 129 (2011) ("a pass-fail system can decrease student motivation by eliminating the reward of a higher grade for more work").

96. Stake, *supra* note 72, at 584. According to Professor Lawrence Krieger, students who "succeed in the grades race are likely to experience a performance-based boost in their sense of personal worth, confidence, and security." Lawrence S. Krieger, *Institutional Denial About the Dark Side of Law School, and Fresh Empirical Guidance for Constructively Breaking the Silence*, 52 J. LEGAL EDUC. 112, 118 (2002). Conversely, students "who falter in the competition by receiving less-than-stellar grades often become thoroughly deflated; their sense of confidence, security, and personal worth plummets." *Id. See also* Fines, *supra* note 92, at 883 ("Students use grades to define themselves in positive or negative fashion, as in 'I am a B student.'").

97. Stake, *supra* note 72, at 585.

98. *See, e.g.*, BEST PRACTICES FOR LEGAL EDUCATION, *supra* note 24, at 244 ("Mandatory grade curves are not consistent with best practices for assessing student learning. A bell curve outcome actually reflects a failure of instruction.").

points for the seminar portion of the externship, relying on the faculty member's evaluation of the student's work in the seminar class. Accordingly, an externship teacher could award points for just the course elements that he or she directly evaluates, such as the seminar class, student journals, and final essays, and award a uniform amount of points for the students' fieldwork, based on a positive evaluation from the site supervisor. The sum of these points then would determine each student's final letter grade in the course. Alternatively, a teacher might factor in a site supervisor's evaluation for a small percentage of a student's overall grade in the course.

Another option is to split the placement work and the classroom work into separate credit units, with the placement work receiving a pass/fail grade and the classroom work receiving a letter grade. The most recent data from the Center for the Study of Applied Legal Education (CSALE) indicate that some schools use this method. According to the data, 83% of the schools responding to the survey award a pass/fail grade for students' fieldwork, while 12% of schools award a letter or number grade for the fieldwork.[99] Conversely, 53% of schools award pass/fail grades for the classroom work, while 42% of schools award a letter or number grade for that work.[100]

4. Select Texts

After planning assessment, the next step in the course-design process is to select texts. It may seem counter-intuitive to select texts at this point, because selecting a textbook is the place that many teachers start in planning a course. Starting with the selection of course materials, however, violates the important instructional-design principle of having congruence among course outcomes, teaching methods, assessments, instructional materials, and design of class sessions. As noted above, the learning outcomes establish the foundation for a course, and they should drive all other decisions regarding course design. Accordingly, externship faculty should select a text only after they have established their course outcomes, and the selected text should align with those outcomes and support instruction that will foster student achievement of those outcomes.

According to Schwartz, Sparrow, and Hess, '[n]o textbook will meet all of your needs," so the priority "is finding the book that best furthers as many of your goals

99. Robert R. Kuehn, Margaret Reuter & David A. Santacroce, Center for the Study of Applied Legal Educ., 2019–2020 Survey of Applied Legal Education 45 (2020) (hereinafter "CSALE Survey"), www.csale.org/#results (last visited February 24, 2022). *See also* J.P. "Sandy" Ogilvy, *Guidelines for the Self-Evaluation of Legal Education Clinics and Clinical Programs*, 15 T.M. Cooley J. Prac. & Clinical L. 1, 155 (2013) (stating that when externships are graded on a number or letter system, frequently only the student's work in the seminar or tutorial portion receives a letter or number grade, and the fieldwork portion is graded on a pass/fail basis).

100. CSALE Survey, *supra* note 99, at 47.

as possible."[101] However, there may not be a textbook suited to the learning outcomes of a particular externship course. If that is the case, the teacher should compile his or her own materials rather than adopt a textbook. Compiling one's own materials also keeps the course content fresh and ensures that it is timely and relates to the practice of law in ways that are meaningful to students. LexternWeb is a valuable resource for course materials, as it contains both course syllabi with reading assignments and teaching exercises.[102] In addition, Chapters 9, 10, and 11 discuss topics for general and subject-specific externship seminars, resources on those topics, and suggestions for teaching techniques.

5. Design the Course

Once the externship teacher has established the course learning outcomes, assessed the learners, created an assessment plan, and selected instructional materials, it is time to synthesize all of those elements into a coherent and comprehensive design for the course. The ABA Standards will have a large impact on this stage of the process, because they set out certain mandatory requirements that govern all externship courses.

a. The Nature of the Course

ABA Standard 304(d) mandates, among other requirements, that externship courses must provide "substantial lawyering experience" that is "reasonably similar to the experience of a lawyer advising or representing a client or engaging in other lawyering tasks in a setting outside of a law clinic under the supervision of a licensed attorney or an individual otherwise qualified to supervise[.]"[103] In addition, for a course to qualify as "experiential" under ABA Standard 303(a), it must be "primarily experiential" in nature.[104] These Standards necessarily will guide course design

101. Teaching Law by Design, *supra* note 9, at 41.

102. *See* LexternWeb, www.lexternweb.org/externship-teaching (last visited March 6, 2022). In addition, textbooks available for externship courses include the following: Rebecca Cochran, Judicial Externships: The Clinic Inside the Courthouse (4th ed. 2016); Mary Dunnwold et al., Judicial Clerkships: A Practical Guide (2010); Aliza Milner, Judicial Clerkships: Legal Methods in Motion (2011); Abigail Perdue, An All-Inclusive Guide to Judicial Clerking (2017); Jennifer L. Sheppard, In Chambers: A Guide for Judicial Clerks and Externs (2012); Learning From Practice: A Text for Experiential Legal Education (Leah Wortham, Alexander Scherr, Nancy Maurer, Susan L. Brooks eds., 3d ed. 2016).

103. ABA Standards and Rules of Procedure for Approval of Law Schools 2022–2023, Standard 304(d).

104. ABA Standards and Rules of Procedure for Approval of Law Schools 2022–2023, Standard 304(a).

decisions about the selection of externship placements and the amount of fieldwork that students must complete for a course to be "primarily experiential."

A placement site that provides students with opportunities to engage in work that lawyers typically perform should be sufficient to satisfy Standard 304(d). Accordingly, representative examples of externship placements include the legal departments of government agencies and nonprofit organizations, prosecutor and public defender offices, corporate counsel offices, legal aid organizations, regulatory compliance departments, judicial chambers, and private law firms. As stated previously, externship faculty must keep their course outcomes at the forefront in selecting placements, and they should select and recruit those placements that will engage students in authentic lawyering tasks.[105]

b. Selecting and Working with Site Supervisors

The course design also must include processes for selecting and working with site supervisors. According to ABA Standard 304(d)(ii), an externship course must include "a method for selecting, training, evaluating, and communicating with site supervisors, including regular contact between the faculty and site supervisors through in-person visits or other methods of communication that will assure the quality of the student educational experience." These requirements are discussed extensively in Chapter 4, so please refer to that Chapter for guidance on this topic.

c. Methods for Providing Faculty-Guided Reflection

Another significant decision in the course design process is the method by which students will engage in reflection on their externship experiences. It is a best practice in externship pedagogy for courses to include "a planned program requiring student reflection."[106] ABA Standard 304(a)(5) mandates that externship courses that qualify as "experiential" must include "a classroom instructional component, regularly scheduled tutorials, or other means of ongoing, contemporaneous, faculty-guided reflection."[107] Chapter 8 provides specific guidance on how to teach the skill of reflection in externship courses.

The 2019–2020 CSALE survey found that 75% of externship courses include a "classroom instructional component,"[108] which is often referred to as an externship seminar. This overwhelming majority is not surprising, since a seminar class pro-

---

105. *See, e.g.*, Best Practices for Legal Education, *supra* note 24, at 201 ("The range and nature of placements offered in a given externship program should relate to articulated educational goals for that program. Placement sites should be committed to providing students opportunities to observe or engage in activities that are consistent with the educational goals of the program.").

106. Building on Best Practices, *supra* note 17, at 233.

107. ABA Standards and Rules of Procedure for Approval of Law Schools 2022–2023, Standard 304(a)(5).

108. CSALE Survey, *supra* note 99, at 46.

vides an excellent vehicle for faculty to integrate doctrine, theory, skills, and legal ethics and to develop concepts underlying the professional skills being taught both in the classroom and at the placement site.[109] According to Building on Best Practices, an externship seminar also provides four primary advantages over individual student-faculty tutorials:

- Opportunities to reflect on and critique field experiences with fellow students and the teacher;
- Opportunities for students who are in placements by themselves to find colleagues and a sense of community;
- Opportunities for students to learn from each other about the practice of law, including placements different from their own; and
- Opportunities for the delivery of knowledge and classroom experiences such as skills simulations.[110]

In addition to lacking these benefits, tutorials may not be feasible if an externship course has a large number of students. "It is a best practice to have student-teacher contact for the equivalent of at least one semester credit, or roughly fourteen contact hours."[111] In a course with 20 to 30 students, it seems highly unlikely that a teacher could conduct 14 hours of individual meetings with each student over the course of a semester. Tutorials might work well, however, for externship faculty working with a small number of students in a full-time externship course.

Teachers who decide to include an externship seminar should follow best practices for seminars, which include establishing learning outcomes for individual class sessions[112] and having an appropriate faculty-to-student ratio. While the ABA has not established a faculty-student ratio for externship seminars, Professor Sandy Ogilvy, a recognized expert in externship pedagogy, asserts that enrollment in a seminar "should be limited to no more than 16 students in order to give each student sufficient supervisor attention and opportunity to participate in the seminar, especially where student presentations are part of the course design."[113] Faculty may want to organize the seminar into several learning units based on broad topics and

---

109. ABA Standards and Rules of Procedure for Approval of Law Schools 2022–2023, Standard 304(a)(1) and (a)(2).

110. Building on Best Practices, *supra* note 17, at 236–37. *See also* Best Practices for Legal Education, *supra* note 24, at 205 (recommending that externship courses provide "sufficient opportunities for students to interact with externship faculty and other students in the course" and recognizing that, in many courses, a regularly scheduled on-campus classroom meeting is the best way to provide these opportunities).

111. Building on Best Practices, *supra* note 17, at 237.

112. *E.g.*, Building on Best Practices, *supra* note 17, at 237; Hess, *Value of Variety*, *supra* note 6, at 71.

113. Ogilvy, *supra* note 99, at 154. *See also* James H. Backman, *Where Do Externships Fit? A New Paradigm Is Needed: Marshaling Law School Resources to Provide an Externship for Every Student*, 56 J. Legal Educ. 615, 620 (2006) (suggesting that faculty-to-student ratio "should not exceed one

then subdivide those topics into more specific topics that will comprise the individual class sessions.[114] For example, faculty could create a learning unit on "Relational Skills in Law Practice" and then subdivide that unit into individual classes on communication skills, emotional intelligence, and cultural awareness. Faculty also will need to plan the reading assignments, if any, for each class, in-class exercises they want to include, and post-class assignments, such as reflection papers, that can help students integrate existing knowledge and new knowledge. Specific teaching techniques and ideas for class topics are discussed in detail in Chapters 8, 9, 10, and 11.

Faculty will need to consider other factors, such as distance and differences in time-zones, for students who are in remote and international placements. It is often not feasible for students in these types of placements to attend a seminar class on site at the law school. Accordingly, faculty may need to design an online seminar class for these students that meets either synchronously or asynchronously.[115] Chapter 6 discusses special design considerations for remote and international externships, and Chapter 12 discusses design considerations for online and hybrid courses.

d. Setting Credit Hours for Externship Courses

Another design consideration is the number of credit hours to award for externship courses. According to ABA Standard 304(e), the academic credit granted for an externship course "shall be commensurate with the time and effort required and the anticipated quality of the educational experience of the student."[116] This Standard, however, does not establish a minimum number of credit hours. *Building on Best Practices* recommends that externship courses should be offered for "enough credits to provide students with sufficient experience to generate meaningful reflection and learning."[117] In determining the amount of credits to award for an externship course, faculty must comply with ABA Standard 310 and the Managing Director's Guidance Memo on Standard 310, which are discussed extensively in Chapter 2.

Pursuant to Standard 310, to justify an award of three credit hours for an externship course, the students should spend a minimum of 127.5 hours of time working

---

faculty to fifteen or twenty students"). Chapter 3, *supra*, also discusses appropriate faculty-student ratios.

114. *See, e.g.*, Teaching Law by Design, *supra* note 9, at 43–49.

115. "When learners participate in a learning course at the same time but in different locations, it is known as synchronous learning. Synchronous learning allows learners to interact with the instructor and other participants. This is done through software that creates a virtual classroom[.]" University of Liverpool, www.liverpool.ac.uk/languages/open-languages/what-you-need-to-know/what-is-blended-learning/ (last visited March 6, 2022). "When learners participate in an online learning course at different times, it is known as asynchronous learning. Asynchronous learning allows learners to go through a course at their own pace and on their own schedule." *Id. See also* Chapter 12, *infra* (discussing distance learning in externship context).

116. ABA Standards and Rules of Procedure for Approval of Law Schools 2022–2023, Standard 304(e).

117. Building on Best Practices, *supra* note 17, at 180.

at their externship sites, preparing for and attending classes or tutorials, and completing class assignments.

Data from the 2019–2020 CSALE survey indicate that a wide range of credit hours exists for externship courses. According to the survey responses, 53% of externship courses offered variable credits for student work, rather than a fixed number of credits.[118] In externship courses where the credit hours were variable, the most frequent minimum numbers of credits were two per term (40%), one per term (23%), and three per term (22%); the most frequent maximum numbers of credits were five per term (19%), two per term (17%), four per term (17%), and twelve per term (17%).[119] In courses where the number of credits is fixed, the most common numbers of credits awarded were two per term (38%), three per term (29%), and four per term (9%).[120] The most common number of hours students must work during the term per fieldwork credit is 42.5 hours per credit.[121]

e. Special Course-Design Considerations for Part-Time Students

According to *Building on Best Practices*, "it is a best practice to provide at least one supervised practice opportunity to all students[.]"[122] A significant number of law schools are trying to satisfy this recommendation, as 23% of the 185 ABA-accredited schools that responded to the 2019–2020 CSALE survey indicated that they require students to participate in a law clinic or externship as a condition of graduation.[123] In addition, 89% of the externship courses at schools with part-time J.D. students allow part-time students to enroll in the courses.[124] Part-time students who have sufficient flexibility in their schedules should be able to participate in externship courses with full-time students.

However, designing externship courses for part-time students who have limited availability can present unique challenges. If part-time students work full-time jobs during the day, they often have less time to devote to work at an externship site, and the time they do have often is limited to evenings and weekends. Students with full-time jobs also may have to travel out-of-town for their work or may experience unexpected work demands, which can affect their schedules and cause their availability for externship work to be unpredictable. Even part-time students who have flexible work schedules may face constraints if changing their work schedule would cause them to lose income from their paid job. These factors will affect pedagogical

118. CSALE Survey, *supra* note 99, at 45. *See also* Chapter 3, *supra*.
119. *Id.*
120. *Id.*
121. *Id.*
122. Building on Best Practices, *supra* note 17, at 179.
123. CSALE Survey, *supra* note 99, at 12.
124. *Id.* at 44.

decisions such as the choice of externship sites, whether an accompanying seminar course should be taught online or in-person, the number of credit hours to award, and the selection of site supervisors who are willing to work with part-time students with time and scheduling limitations.[125] To inform these decisions, it can be helpful to survey part-time students to gather information regarding the amount of time they have available for externship work, the externship experiences they seek, and the type of externship work that would be most compatible with their jobs and work schedules.[126]

Several law schools have overcome the design challenges and created meaningful externship opportunities for their part-time students. Brooklyn Law School, for example, has a large evening division and has placed its part-time students with prosecutors, public defenders, and judges in local family and criminal courts that have evening and weekend sessions.[127] Brooklyn also has created externships with local public schools that have evening sessions to provide legal advice to students and parents, with unions and government agencies that have evening intake sessions for clients with legal issues, and with victim-advocacy organizations that are open on nights and weekends.[128] Similarly, Catholic University Columbus School of Law has created externships with service organizations that are open on nights and weekends and with a local court-based mediation program.[129] The University of Arkansas at Little Rock William H. Bowen School of Law has created practicum courses in which part-time students telecommute and perform work remotely for judges and prosecutors.[130]

Georgia State University College of Law has created a two-credit externship option that is limited to and specifically designed for part-time students. Under this option, part-time students must work 6.5 hours per week at their externship sites over a fourteen-week regular semester, or 13.5 hours per week over the seven-week summer term. The externship director has identified placement sites that will allow part-time students flexibility in their work schedules, and she individually counsels part-time students regarding these opportunities. Students also have flexibility to complete some of their work hours away from the site, so long as they have regular

125. *See, e.g.*, Building on Best Practices, *supra* note 17, at 239. When training externship supervisors who will work with part-time students, externship teachers should ensure that supervisors are aware of the students' time limitations, job demands, and limited schedule flexibility. Knowledge of these constraints should help to minimize potential conflicts between students and supervisors regarding externship expectations.

126. *See, e.g.*, David F. Chavkin, *Clinic Under the Stars: Giving Part-Time Students Their Due*, 13 Clinical L. Rev. 719 (2007) (discussing survey of part-time students conducted prior to creating a clinical course in which part-time students could enroll).

127. Sudeb Basu & J.P. "Sandy" Ogilvy, *Externship Demographics Across Two Decades With Lessons for Future Surveys*, 19 Clinical L. Rev. 1, 11 (2012).

128. *Id.* at 11–12.

129. *Id.* at 12.

130. *See* https://ualr.edu/law/clinical-programs/judicial-practicum/ (last visited March 6, 2022).

communication with their supervisor and meet with their supervisor for at least one hour per week to check in on their progress and learning. Part-time students may be allowed to extern at the same location where they currently work, but only if they can: (1) perform externship work that is substantially different from their regular paid work; (2) the externship work will provide "substantial lawyering experience" within the meaning of ABA Standard 304(d); and (3) they will be supervised by a licensed attorney who does not supervise them in their regular job. Thus, some creativity and flexibility may be required to create externship positions for part-time students. Nonetheless, the effort is worthwhile because these positions may be one of the few opportunities that part-time students have to gain exposure to the legal profession and work in the field prior to graduation.[131]

f. Maintain Records to Demonstrate Compliance with ABA Standards

Externship faculty must create systems for maintaining records as part of their course design. ABA Standard 304(d) mandates that law schools "must maintain records to document the steps taken to ensure compliance with the Standard, which shall include, but is not necessarily limited to, the written understandings described in Standard 304(d)(i)."[132] Accordingly, externship faculty should maintain not only the required written understandings among faculty, site supervisors, and students,[133] but also records documenting the lawyering experiences being offered in the course, the method by which a faculty member evaluates each student's educational achievement, and the methods for selecting, training, evaluating, and communicating with site supervisors. Law schools and universities often have policies setting out the length of time that student records must be maintained and the methods for maintaining them. Faculty should determine if their law schools and universities have such policies and comply with them if they do. In the absence of any express policies, faculty should retain student records for at least one year after students' graduation.[134]

Externship teachers also must ensure that the recordkeeping systems they implement comply with the federal Family Educational Rights and Privacy Act, which is

---

131. *See* Chavkin, *supra* note 126, at 750 (discussing benefits part-time students gain from clinical experiences). *Cf. also, e.g.*, Martin H. Malin, *Constructing a Comprehensive Curriculum in Labor and Employment Law*, 58 St. Louis U. L.J. 111, 120 (2013) (describing need-based scholarships awarded to part-time students who quit jobs or reduced work hours to participate in externships).

132. ABA Standards and Rules of Procedure for Approval of Law Schools 2022–2023, Standard 304(d)(iv).

133. These records also are discussed in Chapter 5, *supra*.

134. This recommendation is based on the ABA Site Evaluation Questionnaire, which requires law schools to make available to site visit teams "[f]ormative and [s]ummative assessments and course syllabi for the previous academic year." *See* www.americanbar.org/content/dam/aba/

commonly known as "FERPA."[135] Under FERPA, law students' educational records are deemed private, and such records may not be disclosed unless the student consents to the disclosure or the disclosure is to another school official and is necessitated by a "legitimate educational interest."[136] The statute takes a broad view of educational records, defining them as "records, files, documents, and other materials which—(i) contain information directly related to a student; and (ii) are maintained by an educational agency or institution or by a person acting for such agency or institution."[137] In addition to the federal statute, universities often issue guidance regarding FERPA compliance across their various units and departments.[138] Externship faculty should design their recordkeeping system to comply with both federal and university FERPA requirements, and they should train their administrative assistants and the site supervisors who participate in their externship courses to comply with these requirements as well.[139]

6. Implement the Design and Then Evaluate It

The final steps in the recursive design process are to implement the design, i.e., teach the course, and then evaluate how it went. In evaluating the design, faculty should return to their foundation—the course learning outcomes—and review the multiple assessments administered throughout the semester to determine if their students' learning achieved those outcomes. In the assessment process, this step is known as "closing the loop." As explained in Chapter 5, the fundamental question faculty must answer at this point is "On what basis do we decide that a sufficiently high percentage of our students have been shown to have learned a sufficient amount for us to say, 'This is good enough'?"[140] To answer this question, externship

---

administrative/legal_education_and_admissions_to_the_bar/Questionnaires/21-22-seq-onsite.pdf (last visited March 6, 2022).

135. 20 U.S.C. § 1232g.

136. 20 U.S.C. § 1232g(b)(1).

137. 20 U.S.C. § 1232g(a)(4)(A).

138. *See, e.g.*, www.registrar.gsu.edu/academic-records/records-access/#ferpa (last visited March 6, 2022) (describing FERPA policy at Georgia State University); www.registrar.northwestern.edu/records/student-information-privacy/privacy-policy-ferpa.html (last visited March 6, 2022) (describing Northwestern University's FERPA policies); www.ualr.edu/records/ferpa (last visited March 6, 2022) (describing students' rights under FERPA at the University of Arkansas at Little Rock).

139. Site supervisors likely will have educational records in their possession, such as students' timesheets; the written agreements among externship faculty, site supervisors, and students; and the supervisors' evaluations of students at the end of their externships. Accordingly, externship teachers should address FERPA requirements in their training programs for site supervisors. *See generally*, Chapter 4, *supra* (discussing training for site supervisors).

140. Cecilia L. López, *A Decade of Assessing Student Learning: What We Have Learned, and What Is Next*, *in* Outcomes Assessment in Higher Education: Views and Perspectives 67–68 (Peter Hernon & Robert E. Dugan eds 2004); *see also* Suskie, *supra* note 10, at 288 ("Defining successful outcomes means having a clear sense of what is good enough.").

faculty will need to (1) set benchmark scores for minimum competence on the assessment instruments they administer; and (2) establish performance thresholds for how many students in the course must achieve the benchmark scores in order to conclude that the course learning outcomes have been achieved. The processes for setting benchmark scores and performance thresholds are discussed in detail in Chapter 5 regarding program assessment. The sections below explain the application of these processes to individual externship courses.

a. Setting Scores for Minimum Competence on Assessment Instruments

Externship faculty likely will develop and assign several different assessments to measure their students' learning, such as journals, class presentations, mid-semester self-evaluations, and final essays. As explained above, faculty should develop rubrics they can use to evaluate and score those assessments. For a score to have meaning, however, there must be a standard against which to compare it, such as a scale set by the teacher. For example, if a student scores 35 points on a journal, when 50 points were available, what information does that score provide about the competencies the journal is measuring? To make such scores meaningful for assessment purposes, externship faculty need to set a minimum score for each assessment they administer that denotes competence in the knowledge, skills, or values that are being measured. These minimum scores, which often are referred to as "benchmark" scores, must be appropriately rigorous and justifiable to stakeholders.[141]

In determining benchmark scores for assignments in an externship course, a good starting point is for faculty to review samples of student work, compare them against the rubric for the assignment, and identify examples that they consider inadequate, adequate, and excellent. Alternatively, faculty might use the categories of below expectations, meets expectations, and exceeds expectations. From these examples, faculty can articulate the qualities that differentiate the three categories of student work. With these specific qualities in mind, faculty then can determine whether the excellent/exceeds expectations examples should set the benchmark for minimum competence, or whether the adequate/meets expectations examples more accurately reflect minimum competence.[142]

Once the externship teacher has determined a benchmark score for an assignment, he or she must test it by applying it to the assignment to see if the expectations for minimum competence are accurate.[143] For example, if only 40% of students achieve the benchmark score for minimum competence on a reflective journal, does that mean that the students lack adequate reflection skills, or does it mean that the benchmark score was set too high? To answer this question, faculty will need to

141. SUSKIE, *supra* note 10, at 299.
142. *Id.* at 299–300.
143. *Id.* at 300.

think carefully about the assignment itself and their expectations for student performance. Subsequent modification of the benchmark score may be necessary, because "[a]fter a trial exercise, many educators will find that the initial cut-off score or rating level needs adjusting to account for too high or too low expectations."[144]

b. Setting Performance Thresholds for the Students Being Assessed

Once externship faculty have set the benchmark score for an assessment instrument, they then should determine the percentage of students in the course who must achieve that score in order to declare that the course learning outcome has been met. This percentage is known as a "target"[145] or a "performance threshold."[146] For example, if an externship teacher is using a rubric to assess students' reflection skills in a final essay, the teacher might set the performance threshold at 75%, which means that if 75% of the essays achieve the rubric's benchmark score for minimum competence, then the teacher can state that the course learning outcome for reflection skills has been met. Conversely, if fewer than 75% of the essays achieve that score, then the outcome has not been met.

To set performance thresholds for assessment instruments like journals, essays, and mid-semester evaluations, externship faculty can look to past student performance for a baseline.[147] For example, assume that an externship teacher is using a rubric to assess students' mid-semester self-evaluations for competency in a learning outcome for self-directedness, and that she has set a score of 75 points (out of a possible 100 points) as the benchmark for minimum competence. Assume further that the teacher has used the rubric for two years. In the first year of using the rubric, 70% of the students in the course achieved the benchmark score. In the second year of using the rubric, 80% of the students achieved the benchmark. In setting a performance threshold for this assessment, the teacher has several options. First, she could simply set the threshold at 70%, since she has evidence that students can meet that threshold. Second, she could set the threshold at 75%, since that is the average percentage for the two years she has used the rubric. Third, she could set the threshold at 80% or even higher, since that percentage seems attainable in light of past

---

144. T. Dary Erwin, Assessing Student Learning and Development: A Guide to the Principles, Goals, and Methods of Determining College Outcomes 114 (1991).

145. Suskie, *supra* note 10, at 300. *See also id.* at 290 ("A target is "the proportion of students that should achieve at least that minimally acceptable level.").

146. Shaw & VanZandt, *supra* note 50, at 125 (defining performance thresholds as "minimum expectation levels for the group as a whole").

147. Arizona State University Office of Evaluation and Educational Effectiveness, Effective Program Assessment Planning, Reporting, and Decision Making 20–21, https// uoeee.asu.edu/sites/default/ files/docs /Plan%20Handbook%202018.pdf (last visited March 6, 2022); National Center for the Improvement of Educational Assessment, Inc., Using Baseline Data and Information to Set SLO Targets, https.www.nciea.org/ sites/default/ files/slo-tools/7_ Using-Baseline-Data-and-Information_7.15.13.pdf (last visited March 6, 2022).

performance, and the teacher wants to have high standards for her students. Self-directedness is certainly an important skill for lawyers, which is a factor that weighs in favor of setting a high threshold. However, there is no "perfect" threshold, so this question must be decided by the teacher's informed judgment and her expectations regarding the percentage of her students who should demonstrate competency in the course learning outcome for self-directedness.

c. Analyzing the Assessment Data

Finally, externship faculty must evaluate the information they learn from applying the benchmarks and performance thresholds to their students' work. If the designated percentage of students meets the established level of competence on the assessment instruments, then the teacher has good evidence that students are achieving the learning outcomes and that the course design is sound. Course design is a continuous process of improvement, though, so the teacher should not stop there. Rather, he or she should examine positive results to determine why the particular materials, teaching methods, and assessments were effective and how they might be refined to produce even better learning in the future.

On the other hand, if the requisite percentage of students did not achieve the benchmark score on an assessment instrument, then the teacher needs to examine the instrument to determine if it was an accurate measure of student learning and also consider whether any outside factors might have affected student learning.[148] If poorly designed assessments or outside factors do not appear to be the cause, then the teacher must try to determine if there are patterns of mistakes or common misunderstandings that reveal the areas of knowledge, skills, or values in which student learning fell short. If faculty can identify these areas, then they can decide whether to refine the learning outcomes or change teaching methods or other instructional approaches.[149] The teacher also may want to add more formative assessments earlier in the semester as a means to identify deficiencies in student learning prior to the end of the course.[150] For example, if student performance on final reflective essays in the course is lower than expected, the teacher might consider adding short reflective

148. BUILDING ON BEST PRACTICES, *supra* note 17, at 97.

149. *See, e.g.*, TRANSFORMING THE EDUCATION OF LAWYERS, *supra* note 8, at 14 ("When the students fail to meet the goals, teachers can assess whether to refine or reject the goals or take a different approach to meeting them.").

150. BUILDING ON BEST PRACTICES, *supra* note 17, at 97–98.

essay assignments the next time the class is taught so the students can practice their writing skills and receive more feedback on them prior to writing their final essay.

d. Using Data from Externship Courses for Institutional Assessment

Finally, the assessment data that externship faculty collect from their individual courses also can provide valuable information for a law school's institutional-assessment process. For example, the externship program at Georgia State University College of Law has designed its end-of-semester supervisor review form to evaluate student competency in both the course learning outcomes and the law school's institutional learning outcomes.[151] The learning outcomes for the GSU externship course state that, after completing the course, students will be able to:

- Define the concept of professional identity formation and articulate its relevance to the practice of law;
- Draft written reflective narratives, identifying pivotal experiences and assessing the impact of those experiences on the formation of your professional identity;
- Identify relationships within your network and devise a networking strategy to sustain those relationships;
- Outline your role as a team member, list skills that help you to contribute to collaborative efforts, and describe potential roadblocks to effective teamwork;
- Describe the competencies necessary to be an effective communicator and the tools necessary to navigate inherent challenges in communication;
- State the complexity of cross-cultural interactions, specifically as it relates to lawyering, and discuss approaches to managing cross-cultural lawyering;
- Exhibit essential skills in professional responsibility including timeliness, office demeanor, diligence, and lawyering ethics;
- Use time management tools for timekeeping, meeting deadlines, and managing multiple assignments; and
- Critique your externship experience, including the intricacies of your externship site and its role in the legal profession and justice system.

At the end of the externship semester, the site supervisors complete a review form evaluating the performance of each student who externed for them. (A copy of this form is included in the Appendix.) The form lists the school's seven institutional

151. Professor Kendall Kerew directs the externship program at Georgia State University College of Law, designed the supervisor review form, and provided both her course learning outcomes and her school's institutional outcomes.

learning outcomes and their performance criteria, and it includes rubrics for each of the institutional outcomes.[152] The form asks supervisors to rate students on a scale of 1 to 4 on each of the elements that comprise those outcomes. From each individual form, the externship director obtains specific information about that particular student's achievement of the course learning outcomes. The externship director then combines the aggregate data from all of the forms, which provide information about how the group of students as a whole performed with respect to both the course and institutional outcomes. Thus, the review form serves two purposes, generating assessment data at both the course level and the institutional level.

152. The rubrics are the same as those used by the faculty teaching other courses charged with assessing student achievement of institutional learning outcomes. While the externship course is not a required course that all students must complete, it is the only course that provides data regarding student achievement as to all seven institutional learning outcomes.

Section III

Teaching the Externship Course

Section 2 of this book details how to design both externship programs and externship courses. This Section—consisting of five chapters—provides information about topics to teach in externship courses and techniques for teaching those courses after a careful and comprehensive design process. Chapter 8 explains essential elements of all externship courses: goal setting, meaningful learning experiences, and reflection. Chapter 9 reviews topic ideas and resources for general externship courses. Chapter 10 gives ideas about targeted class topics for subject-specific externship courses. Chapter 11 provides information on teaching techniques for externship courses. Finally, Chapter 12 gives information on using online technology to teach externship courses.

As the following chapters will make clear, there is no one recommended syllabus for externship seminars. In fact, it may be hard to find two that are the same. The syllabus and teaching methods will depend on program goals and course objectives, assessment methods, resources (one class or many), externship settings, time available for the class, and a range of other factors. This Section aims to give faculty many options from which to choose in order to teach courses appropriate for their students and externship program.

Within these pedagogical options, however, there are three components that are essential to all forms of experiential education, including externships: goal setting, meaningful learning experiences, and reflection.[1] Each component empowers and challenges students to take responsibility for their own learning and to develop habits of self-direction,[2] which are essential to successful law practice.

1. LEARNING FROM PRACTICE: A TEXT FOR EXPERIENTIAL EDUCATION 9 (Leah Wortham, Alexander Scherr, Nancy Mauer, Susan L. Brooks eds., 3d ed. 2016) (referring to these steps as "plan, do, reflect, and integrate"). "Experiential learning requires the active processing of experiences. This process is cyclical." *Id.*

2. "Self-directedness is perhaps the foundational component on which students begin their growth as professionals. It begins with a commitment to evaluate oneself and accept evaluation of others on skills and competencies crucial to professional excellence." Benjamin Madison, *Self-Directed Growth*, BEST PRACTICES FOR LEGAL EDUCATION BLOG, https://bestpracticeslegaled.com/2018/02/27/self-directed-growth/ (last visited March 20, 2022).

Chapter 8

Student Goal Setting, Meaningful Learning Experiences, and Reflection

1. Goal Setting

Before an externship begins, students should identify what they want to learn while at their externship placement. When students set their own learning agenda or professional development plan, they are more likely to take ownership of their externship experience and be proactive about accomplishing their goals. Student goal setting can be facilitated by student review of a concrete list of lawyering competencies,[3] such as Shultz and Zedeck's 26 Lawyering Effectiveness Factors[4] or the Institute for the Advancement of the American Legal System's (IAALS) Foundations for Practice Study.[5] After examining the list, students can identify competencies they want to develop or strengthen. Externship teachers also may want to focus students on setting goals in the three contexts of legal education: knowledge ("thinking like a lawyer"), skills ("doing like a lawyer"), and values ("being a lawyer").[6] Students might want to think about their past work and learning experiences and career goals to narrow down those goals they wish to develop through their fieldwork.

In developing learning goals, students often start with a broad articulation. To narrow the learning goals and make them more meaningful, it is helpful to introduce students to the concept of "SMART goals." The acronym SMART is used to facilitate the development of goals that are specific (focused and concrete), measurable (capable of producing evidence that can indicate progress), achievable (within the student's abilities and the work available at the externship site), relevant (important

3. Learning From Practice, *supra* note 1, at 18.

4. *Id.* at Appendix 1.3.

5. https://iaals.du.edu/sites/default/files/documents/publications/foundations_handout.pdf.

6. *See* William M. Sullivan et al., Educating Lawyers: Preparation for the Profession of Law (2007) (hereinafter "Educating Lawyers"); Louis D. Bilionis, *Professional Formation and the Political Economy of the American Law School*, 83 Tenn. L. Rev. 895 (2016).

to what the student wants to accomplish), and time bound (able to be accomplished by the end of the semester or other finite time period).[7]

A version of the "Backwards Resume" exercise described in Chapter 26 of *Learning From Practice* provides an effective method for setting SMART goals. "Because students will necessarily update their resumes to include their externship experience at the end of the semester, students see practical value in completing the exercise."[8] The exercise, which is done before students have settled on learning goals, has students list three bullet points they hope to add to their resumes to describe the work they performed at their externships.[9] "This helps students see the difference between a general goal and one that is measurable. For example, a goal of wanting to improve research and writing skills will not translate easily to a resume. In the context of a resume, students must specifically communicate the work they did to improve their research and writing skills (*e.g.*, writing memos, bench briefs, draft legislation, etc.)."[10]

Once students have articulated their learning goals, it is helpful to have students record them as part of a goals form, learning agenda, or professional development plan.[11] In this exercise, students should identify potential assignments and observational opportunities that will facilitate their achievement of the specific goals articulated in each category. Students can be asked to identify actions they can take to evaluate accomplishment of their goals. In addition, students should set up a meeting to discuss these goals with their site supervisor and/or supervising attorney. This discussion helps to confirm that the student's goals are attainable and to facilitate meaningful assignments and feedback in furtherance of the student's articulated goals. A mid-semester self-evaluation can serve as a helpful tool for students to consider whether they have made progress toward achieving their goals and to facilitate the identification of new goals. Chapter 2 in *Learning From Practice* provides additional information for students to consider in setting learning goals, meeting with supervisors, and evaluating progress toward achieving those goals.

---

7. University of California, SMART Goals: A How To Guide, https://www.ucop.edu/local-human-resources/_files/performance-appraisal/How%20to%20write%20SMART%20Goals%20v2.pdf.

8. Timothy W. Floyd & Kendall L. Kerew, *Marking the Path from Law Student to Lawyer: Using Field Placement Courses to Facilitate the Deliberate Exploration of Professional Identity and Purpose*, 68 Mercer L. Rev. 767, 790 (2017).

9. *Id.*

10. *Id.*

11. *See* Learning From Practice, *supra* note 1. Examples of a Goals Form and Mid-Semester Self-Assessment can be found in the Appendix to this Chapter.

2. Meaningful Learning Experience

Once their goals are set, students must learn by doing. By performing fieldwork and taking on the role of a lawyer, externs achieve "learning while engaged in legal experience rather than in a classroom."[12] Through the legal work and interaction with their supervisors, externs see and experience the practice of law as it really is. Moreover, "[e]xternships [] offer an optimal opportunity for students to learn the skill of being effectively supervised by another lawyer not trained in the art of supervision."[13] Because the realities of law practice do not center around the student in the same way classroom learning does, externs must be proactive about both seeking assignments that further their goals and securing meaningful feedback.[14] After having discussed learning goals and possible assignments with the extern, a supervisor can assign work that advances those goals and gives the extern an opportunity to practice relevant lawyering skills. In addition, the supervisor can facilitate observations of certain lawyering activities.

In receiving assignments, externs must be sure they understand not only the nature of the task but also the relevant contextual facts and procedural background. Clarifying assignments can be difficult for externs, especially those who have not had much previous work experience. "If a supervisor assigns a task without much explanation, an extern can fill in possible gaps and be sure there has been a 'meeting of the minds' by summarizing the extern's understanding of the assignment and asking follow-up questions that address five points: What, How, Why, Who, and When."[15] It can be helpful for externship faculty to discuss a hypothetical assignment[16] and have students ask these clarifying questions during an externship orientation session or early seminar class. Another approach, especially with part-time students or students with a lot of work experience, is to facilitate a discussion about how they have dealt with unclear assignments in their work and techniques they have used to gain clarity. In addition, externs should identify a plan for how to communicate with their supervisor about any additional questions they have regarding the assignment.[17] The mid-semester meeting externship teachers have with students

12. *Id.* at 33.

13. Laurie Barron, *Learning How to Learn: Carnegie's Third Apprenticeship*, 18 CLINICAL L. REV. 101, 104 (2011).

14. *Id.* at 111 ("While in-house clinical programs provide excellent, all-encompassing supervision from experienced clinicians who are trained educators, externship programs require students to obtain quality supervision from a variety of different lawyers who are understandably not focused primarily on the education of law students. Externship students are required to be more proactive about seeking supervision and must often be primarily responsible for ensuring that they receive the supervision they crave and need.").

15. LEARNING FROM PRACTICE, *supra* note 1, at 37.

16. The deeded septic easement assignment in *Learning From Practice* is a helpful hypothetical to use with students.

17. Barron, *supra* note 13, at 115 ("Because externships often require students to set their own distinct learning goals and plan a course of action to achieve these goals, students must learn the skill

(and their supervisors, if the decision is made to include them) is a good time to check in regarding the types of assignments externs are receiving and whether the extern needs to brainstorm other ways to seek assignment clarification.

In addition to meaningful assignments, externs must be sure to secure meaningful feedback to maximize their learning experience. There are "three primary types of feedback sometimes given and often desired by potential feedback receivers: appreciation (thanks and other forms of acknowledgment); coaching (comments directed toward learning and improving performance); and evaluation (information on 'where one stands,' *e.g.*, a grade or rating, prospects for promotion)."[18] Most supervisors regularly give appreciative feedback. This is usually the feedback externs are most comfortable receiving and supervisors are most comfortable giving. Because supervisors are acting as the teachers at the externship site, specifically describing the supervisor's role as the teacher in the field can empower them to also provide coaching and evaluative feedback. In addition, it is helpful to remind supervisors of the three-way agreement required under Standard 304(d)(i) that:

> [D]escribes both (A) the substantial lawyering experience and opportunities for performance, feedback and self-evaluation; and (B) the respective roles of faculty and any site supervisor in supervising the student and in assuring the educational quality of the experience for the student, including a clearly articulated method of evaluating the student's academic performance.[19]

This reminder can empower supervisors to embrace their roles as an integral part of the externship teaching process. Chapters 4 and 13 provide specific ideas for how to facilitate site supervisor feedback.

---

of assessing their own strengths, weaknesses, and abilities to meet challenges in light of their individual goals for their externships. Students must then be able to effectively communicate their goals to their supervisors and be able to evaluate both their work product and the progress of their greater educational and professional goals, with the help of both placement supervisor and faculty member, along the way.")

18. Learning From Practice, *supra* note 1, at 37 (citing Douglas Stone & Sheila Heen, Thanks for the Feedback: The Science and Art of Receiving Feedback Well (2014)).

19. ABA Standards and Rules of Procedure for Approval of Law Schools 2022–2023, Standard 304.

Chapter 3 of *Learning From Practice* provides seven ways students can solicit useful feedback:

1. Be ready with your own critique;
2. Ask questions;
3. Look for ways to get timely feedback and keep reminding your supervisor that you want feedback;
4. Try and read more than necessary into your supervisor's style;
5. Ask for examples to make sure you understand your supervisor's comments;
6. Learn from the final work product; and
7. Share your learning goals and ask for your supervisor's help from the beginning.[20]

Externship teachers should consider discussing feedback and these techniques with students during an orientation session or a seminar class at the beginning of the semester.

In addition to the assignment-level feedback students receive throughout the semester, it is important for students to receive a formal evaluation of their work at the middle and end of the semester. Before receiving feedback, it is helpful for students to conduct a self-assessment of their performance and their progress toward meeting their goals. Some externship teachers meet at mid-semester with the student to review the self-assessment. Others meet individually with the student and then again with the student and supervisor. By incorporating the supervisor into the meeting, Professor Laurie Barron finds that "students [have] a unique opportunity to receive real-time assessments about their performances as professionals-in-training, to articulate their own assessments of their progress, and to receive formative assessments from their supervising judges or lawyers about their skills at self-evaluation."[21] "The formality of a scheduled, on-site meeting requires everyone to be prepared: the student must draft, edit, and revise the self-evaluation with feedback from the externship teacher, the supervisor must read it in advance of the meeting and be prepared to respond to it, and the externship teacher must be prepared to facilitate the meeting after understanding the student's goals for the meeting."[22]

Externship teachers should ensure that externs receive a formal end-of-semester evaluation from their supervisor. If possible, externs should meet with the supervisor to discuss the evaluation. This provides externs with the opportunity to ask questions and discuss their work holistically throughout the semester. While

20. Learning From Practice, *supra* note 1, at 51–55.
21. Barron, *supra* note 13, at 116.
22. *Id.* at 119.

end-of-semester evaluation forms vary, an evaluation form that also ties in an assessment of the school's institutional learning outcomes may provide another point of feedback from outside practitioners, as opposed to internal law faculty, about how well students are progressing toward those competencies.[23]

3. Reflection

As described above, reflection is a key component of experiential learning. Donald A. Schön, a leading scholar on the issue of reflective professional practice, described it as "the conscious practice of naming what you have observed or experienced and connecting it to the professional identity you are forming."[24] Without reflection, students are not able to fully process what they are learning while they are learning it. It is for this reason that reflective practice is one of the key components of externship pedagogy and specifically required under Standard 304(a)(5), which mandates that externships provide "a classroom instructional component, regularly scheduled tutorials, or other means of ongoing, contemporaneous, faculty-guided reflection."[25] The explicit inclusion of reflection presumes that faculty will guide students in reflective practice and facilitate student development of this important lawyering skill. Reflection allows externs to think deeply about what they are learning in their externship by closely examining the work they do, the broader lessons they learn about lawyering, and their application of those lessons to future practice.[26] In addition, "it forces the student to think about making decisions in context and allows the student to maximize the learning experience."[27] To introduce students to the concept of reflective practice and its benefits, it can be helpful to assign and point to some real world examples of why reflection matters.[28] It also can be helpful to point

---

23. *See* the Appendix to this Chapter for a Sample Supervisor Evaluation Form.

24. Learning From Practice, *supra* note 1, at 204 ("As you reflect, you act; observe what happens after you act; analyze those observations—often seeking input from others about your assessment; identify what you have learned as the basis for new knowledge; and use the new knowledge as basis for future actions.").

25. ABA Standards and Rules of Procedure for Approval of Law Schools 2022–2023, Standard 304(a)(5).

26. Learning From Practice, *supra* note 1, at 203 ("Reflective lawyering is a process in which you evaluate your work as a lawyer to develop professional expertise. It is a skill that helps you identify successful actions, avoid prior mistakes, adjust current conduct based on past learning, and apply current lessons to future practice.").

27. Tim Casey, *Reflective Practice: A Critical Habit for Successful Lawyers* (Jan. 17, 2019), https://www.cwsl.edu/news/newsroom/faculty-news/2019/01/17/reflective-practice-a-critical-habit-for-successful-lawyers (last visited March 6, 2022).

28. Kate Murphy, *No Time to Think*, N.Y. Times (July 25, 2014), https://www.nytimes.com/2014/07/27/sunday-review/no-time-to-think.html; Camille Sweeney & Josh Gosfield, *Secret Ingredient for Success*, N.Y. Times (Jan. 19, 2013), http://www.nytimes.com/2013/01/20/ opinion/sunday/secret-ingredient-for-success.html; *see* Floyd & Kerew, *supra* note 8, at 791 ("The first article highlights how technology has decreased our level of comfort with reflection and the second highlights the positive impact reflection can have on our ability to learn from mistakes and achieve success.").

out that reflection is a skill used across professional disciplines and is not unique to lawyers. For example, athletes watch film of their performance after a game, doctors conduct "mortality and morbidity" conferences to review patient outcomes, and members of the military conduct "after-action reviews" to evaluate performance.

In its most basic form, the process of reflection can be encompassed by three questions:

> First, students must ask and answer the question, "What?" This inquiry requires students to think about and describe the details of an experience related to their own work, observation of others, etc. while at their externship site. Second, students must ask and answer the question, "So What?" This inquiry requires externs to describe why they picked that experience to discuss. The inquiry consists of two steps: a personal reaction in which externs must identify how the experience described made them feel and a general reaction in which students must identify the overall lesson learned about lawyering and any conclusions that can be drawn about the legal profession. Third, students must ask and answer the question, "Now What?" This inquiry requires students to think about both the individual and lawyering lessons learned and how to apply those lessons to future practice.[29]

In their book, *Expert Learning for Law Students*, Professors Michael Hunter Schwartz and Paula J. Manning break down self-reflection into four "facets" that include: 1. Self-evaluation; 2. Attribution; 3. Reaction; and 4. Adaptation.[30] In the self-evaluation facet, students evaluate their own performance, compare their performance to an external, objective evaluation, and consider the accuracy of their self-assessment.[31] In the attribution facet, students develop explanations for their performance ("why they performed well or poorly").[32] In the reaction facet, students react to the results of performance and adopt a growth mindset.[33] In the adaptation facet, students "identify solutions and make adjustments for future learning."[34] These facets are part of a continuing cycle of self-regulated learning, which guides practitioners in legal decision-making.[35]

Rather than describing reflection as a cycle, Professor Tim Casey articulates reflection as six progressive stages that allow "the teacher to guide the student to the higher stages of reflection by passing through the earlier stages. Students should ad-

---

29. Floyd & Kerew, *supra* note 8, at 791.

30. Michael Hunter Schwartz & Paula J. Manning, Expert Learning for Law Students 34 (3d ed. 2018).

31. *Id.* at 35–37.

32. *Id.* at 37.

33. *Id.* at 40.

34. *Id.*

35. *Id.* at 35–36, 41.

vance along a continuum by developing increasingly complex modes of reflection."[36] In the first stage, "the student must compare her performance to the standard of professional competence."[37] In the second stage, the student "must identify different, equally successful ways to accomplish the lawyering performance."[38] In the third stage, "the student must explain *why* she made specific decisions in the context of a professional performance," with the goal of increasing student self-awareness.[39] The internal context focuses on "the lawyer's own experiences, preferences, biases, and characteristics and how those affect the lawyer's decision-making in terms of choosing ways to accomplish a task."[40] In the fourth stage, the student must examine the external context and "be aware of the preferences, experiences, biases and characteristics of other people involved in the lawyering performance. These other people include clients, other lawyers, judges, and third-party neutrals."[41] In the fifth stage, "the student should be identifying societal forces and factors that influenced his professional decision making process."[42] Finally, in the sixth stage, the student reflects on the process of reflection and considers "how they think differently, or, how their thinking has changed, as a result of reflection on the lawyering activity."[43]

Building on Professor Casey's model, Professors Capulong, King-Ries, and Mills posit that "[t]he integration of racial identity development models into the reflective process presents important opportunities to deepen the reflective process."[44] Reflection can "render bare the connection among racial identity, structural racism, and professional purpose."[45] "Antiracist reflection prompts the law student to explore a richer conception of role and a more inclusive consideration of legal relevance while

36. Timothy Casey, *Reflective Practice in Legal Education: The Stages of Reflection*, 20 Clinical L. Rev. 317, 331 (2014). Professor Casey provides specific prompts to ask the students at each of these six phases.

37. *Id.* at 334. "Specific prompts could be any of the following: What would a competent lawyer do in this situation? What would be necessary to achieve a basic level of competence in performance? Did you meet the standard of competence?" *Id.*

38. *Id.* at 338. "A Stage Two reflection should be matched with a task where the experience of performing the assignment will demonstrate to the student that there is more than one way to accomplish the assignment." *Id.* at 339.

39. *Id.* at 339 (emphasis in original).

40. Casey, *supra* note 27.

41. Casey, *supra* note 36, at 341. "Stage Four reflections can be paired with any interactive lawyering task." *Id.* at 344.

42. *Id.* at 344. "The best opportunities to develop Stage Five reflection occur in live-client experiences." *Id.*

43. *Id.* at 346.

44. Eduardo R.C. Capulong, Andrew King-Ries, & Monte Mills, *Antiracism, Reflection, and Professional Identity*, 18 Hastings Race & Poverty L.J. 3, 21 (2021).

45. *Id.*

also allowing consideration of the dangers of a reductionist view that essentializes race and racism and robs individuals of agency and possibility."[46]

All of these models provide a possible framework for reflection in an externship course. Once the framework is selected, faculty need to choose the means by which reflection will be facilitated and assessed. In addition to the reflection questions outlined by Professors Casey and Capulong, King-Ries, and Mills, Chapter 8 of *Learning From Practice* sets forth a range of possible topics for reflection including: class readings and discussions; substantive law or legal process; the non-legal realities of legal work; relationships among lawyers; standards of practice; supervising attorneys as mentors and role models; defining and negotiating the lawyer's role; ethical awareness, ethical action and ethical decision making; critical assessment of power and politics; identity and bias; and life balance and career satisfaction.[47] Externship teachers will need to decide whether they will assign specific topics for all students to reflect on, allow students to reflect on topics of their own choosing related to their particular externships, or use a combination of guided and student-selected reflections.

One of the most common ways students engage in the reflective process is through reflection papers or journals. As Professor Kelly Terry states:

> [A] journal is a tool that students can use to reflect upon their externship experiences and that teachers can use to assess whether students are learning the skill of reflection. In the educational context, a journal is "a regular, written communication from a student to a teacher, related to the course of study, that is authored by the student at the request of the teacher and to which the teacher may respond in writing." ... Journal writing fosters reflection by giving students an opportunity "to take a step away from the cases, clients, and legal issues with which they have been engaged and to think about them objectively."[48]

A journal can facilitate student engagement in the reflective process through writing, but it also can be used as a tool to assess student learning of the skill of reflec-

---

46. *Id.* (positing that "Professor Casey's reflective stages can be deepened by asking racial identity development model questions."); *see* Monika Batra Kashyap, *Rebellious Reflection: Supporting Community Lawyering Practice*, 43 N.Y.U. Rev. L. & Soc. Change 403 (2019) (providing first-hand accounts from students, now lawyers, regarding how the reflection in their externship class helped them be better lawyers).

47. Learning From Practice, *supra* note 1, at 220–26. For additional reflection exercises that could be used in an externship course, see Thiadora A. Pina, Laura E. Jacobus, and Rupa Bhandari, Essential Lawyering Skills: A Companion Guide for Neil W. Hamilton's ROADMAP (2021).

48. Kelly S. Terry, *Embedding Assessment Principles in Externships*, 20 Clinical L. Rev. 467, 490 (2014) (internal citations omitted).

tion. A sample rubric is provided and discussed in Chapter 7. Several articles have provided rubrics for assessing written reflection.[49]

In addition to or instead of reflection papers, externship teachers may choose to assign a Professional Development Plan, which can serve as a guided reflection and provides a basis for class discussion. The Professional Development Plan[50] is assigned by sections to focus students on only one portion of the plan at a time. In addition, at the end of the semester, externship teachers may have students "complete and submit a Final Professional Development Plan, which requires students to revisit their responses in each section, make revisions based on their experiences, and answer some additional questions."[51] The process of reviewing previous responses in light of the entirety of the student's externship experience can provide an opportunity for a metacognitive exploration of the reflective process to prompt the student to examine what they learned about learning.

Finally, class discussion and oral presentation assignments can prompt students to engage in reflection. Employing a variety of formats can reinforce the reflective process and challenge students to think deeply about the conclusions they reach after engaging in it. Like the decisions regarding written reflection, externship faculty will want to consider how and if they will assess students in these other aspects of reflection.

---

49. Floyd & Kerew, *supra* note 8, at Appendix; Jodi S. Balsam, Susan L. Brooks & Margaret Reuter, *Assessing Law Students as Reflective Practitioners*, 62 N.Y.L. Sch. L. Rev. 49 (2017–18).

50. *See* the Appendix to this Chapter for a Professional Development Plan.

51. Floyd & Kerew, *supra* note 8, at 792.

Chapter 9

Topic Ideas for the General Seminar

This Chapter and the following one cover topics that can be included in externship seminars and guided reflections. Chapter 9 focuses on topics to include in a general externship seminar with students at all sites in one class,[1] and Chapter 10 covers topics for subject-specific seminars including judicial, criminal, corporate counsel, public interest, and civil government.[2] Chapter 9 begins with a brief comparison between general and subject-specific externship seminars and then covers a range of topics that can be included: orientation; ethics; professional identity formation; values and well-being; bias, racism, and cross-cultural humility; social justice; time management; networking and business development; teamwork and collaboration skills; and professional communication. These topics can be used in combination with each other; most can also be expanded into a full quarter or semester's worth of classes. Even if teaching a subject-specific seminar like the ones discussed in Chapter 10, it may be useful to include some of the topics in Chapter 9. Regardless of what type of seminar is offered, both chapters offer suggestions for ways to achieve the learning goals established.[3]

General externship seminars present several benefits.[4] First, they are practical, allowing the externship faculty member to provide a seminar for every student even if there are a small number of externs in a particular practice area. Second, they provide students in one kind of externship a window into other areas of practice that they might not pursue due to a lack of knowledge. Finally, they encourage the choice

1. According to the 2019–20 CSALE Report, 64% of field placement courses offer one general seminar. Robert R. Kuehn, Margaret Reuter, & David A. Santacroce, Center for the Study of Applied Legal Education, 2019–20 Survey of Applied Legal Education 46 (2020) (hereinafter "CSALE Survey"), www.csale.org/#results (last visited March 6, 2022).

2. *See id.* at 43 for information on the percentages of schools offering each kind of seminar.

3. Deciding which topics to include in any seminar should follow the process described in Chapter 7.

4. *See* Spring Miller, *The Generalist Externship Seminar: A Unique Curricular Opportunity to Teach About the Legal Profession*, 27 Clinical L. Rev. 279 (2021), for an article arguing that the generalist externship seminar provides an opportunity to teach students about the legal profession.

of topics that are relevant to all students but may be unintentionally neglected in the regular law school curriculum or even in other clinical courses.

General externship seminars also have some disadvantages. When students wish to do a second externship, they must either repeat the seminar or complete an alternative to the seminar such as a guided reflection or tutorial.[5] Repeating the seminar is less engaging for the student and may create pressure on the faculty member to develop new content just for repeating students. Completing an alternative to the seminar usually means that the student is without the benefit of group exercises or a learning community. Creative options to address these challenges exist,[6] and an alternative to the general seminar may not be necessary if most students do only one externship.

Subject-specific externship seminars likewise offer benefits and challenges. They can cover discrete knowledge, skills, and values[7] more tailored to the work in the narrower category of placements. For example, a judicial seminar could cover topics including judicial ethics, opinion writing, judicial selection and qualifications, and the role of the judge in criminal cases.[8] Criminal procedure, prosecutorial discretion, plea bargains, sentencing, and racial disparities are all examples of topics for a criminal seminar. A subject-specific seminar can feel more meaningful for students accustomed to law classes divided by topic and can create bonds among future colleagues in a practice area. If the externships are divided into different seminars by type of experience, students can participate in a number of different kinds of seminars and take a class tailored to each kind of externship. However, fielding a full slate of subject-specific seminars requires more faculty and may only be possible in a larger program.[9]

In suggesting ways to teach the topics in a general seminar, this Chapter focuses on exercises and active learning. Resources include law review articles; practice materials found in bar journals; articles and exercises from other disciplines such as

---

5. According to the 2019–20 CSALE report, half of field placement courses permit students to enroll two or more times in the same course. CSALE Survey, *supra* note 1, at 47.

6. "The reflection component for repeat enrollments is most often handled (51%) by a classroom component (perhaps with modifications such as different content, assignments, or attendance rules). Twenty-two percent of schools handle the reflection component for repeat students with regularly scheduled tutorials, while 28% handle it in other ways such as journals or reflective writings." *Id.* at 48.

7. *See* Alexi Freeman & Katherine Steefel, *Uniting the Head, Hands, and Heart: How Specialty Externships Can Combat Public Interest Drift*, 25 Clinical L. Rev. 325 (2019) (arguing that specialized public interest externships can help keep students connected to their public interest career goals).

8. *See* Chapter 10 for a detailed discussion of topics to cover in specialized seminars; *see* LexternWeb, *Course Syllabi and Resources*, www.lexternweb.org/course-syllabi (last visited Jan. 9, 2021), for more examples of syllabi and of textbooks.

9. According to the CSALE 2019–20 Survey, most seminars are general and include students at a variety of different placements (70% of courses) rather than placing all students in a specialized course (29%). CSALE Survey, *supra* note 1, at 42.

psychology, sociology, business, and economics; as well as externship texts such as *Learning From Practice*[10] that cover skills such as building client relationships, working as part of a team, writing for practice, and making presentations.[11] Resources are continually being developed as new issues arise in each of these topics; checking for updated resources on LexternWeb[12] and in the Clinical Law Review can help supplement those provided here and keep them current.

1. Orientation

Many externship seminars begin with a whole or half-day orientation, also known as an intensive, or bootcamp, offered at the start of the semester and designed to prepare the student for the transition to practice. Deciding what to put in the orientation is determined partly by necessity and partly as a matter of emphasis. For example, topics such as extern ethical obligations, requirements on recording time, knowledge about growth mindset, assessment forms due in the first week of class, information on what to do if facing sexual harassment or discrimination, and how to cultivate a good relationship with a supervisor, must be offered before or when the extern starts in order to be useful. Other topics, such as social justice, race equity, and professionalism, may form part of the intensive as a way to establish a central theme to a particular externship seminar or program.

Front-loading hours in an orientation also allows faculty to create a break in classes at the middle of the semester for time to conduct site visits or individual student meetings. The ability to eliminate some classes also gives students more time at their sites, especially if the class is weekly and in-person, requiring students to leave their sites during the workday and spend time commuting.

2. Incorporating Ethics

The ABA Standards require that every law student take at least one course in professional responsibility, including "substantial instruction in rules of professional conduct... and the values and responsibilities of the legal profession and its members...".[13] Teaching students about ethical issues must be a part of every externship

10. *See* LEARNING FROM PRACTICE: A TEXT FOR EXPERIENTIAL EDUCATION 203 (Leah Wortham, Alexander Scherr, Nancy Mauer, Susan L. Brooks eds., 3d ed. 2016).

11. *Id.* (Chapters 15, 16, 17, and 18).

12. *See* LEXTERNWEB, *Externship Teaching*, www.lexternweb.org (last visited Jan. 8, 2022).

13. ABA STANDARDS AND RULES OF PROCEDURE FOR APPROVAL OF LAW SCHOOLS 2022–2023, STANDARD 303(a)(1). Those values and responsibilities of the legal profession include "the importance of cross-cultural competency to professionally responsible representation and the obligation of lawyers to promote a justice system that provides equal access and eliminates bias, discrimination, and racism in the law[.]" ABA STANDARDS AND RULES OF PROCEDURE FOR APPROVAL OF LAW SCHOOLS 2022–2023, INTERPRETATION 303-6.

course,[14] regardless of whether the students have previously taken a course in professional responsibility. ABA Standard 304 requires that all experiential courses, including externship courses, "integrate doctrine, theory, skills, and legal ethics...."[15] Incorporating ethics into externship courses makes sense because the students will be working on actual cases and projects in real-life settings where lawyers are bound by ethical rules. In fact, lawyers who serve as supervisors for externs may be held responsible for unethical conduct by an extern.[16] In addition, externship students who are licensed under state student practice rules are required to act in accordance with that state's ethical rules for lawyers. While other students are not yet technically bound by the rules, they should make every effort to understand and follow them.

Schools may require students to have completed a course in professional responsibility before enrolling in an externship course, but many do not. Without such a requirement, the teacher must provide enough instruction and materials on the ethical rules to allow students to understand the rules and their own responsibilities. That instruction should start prior to or during the first class. A good place to start is to assign students to read the state's professional conduct rules, at least those most relevant to the externship. The orientation or first class should include a discussion of the importance of ethics to the profession and to their externship. Some faculty may choose to have an intensive longer session focused on ethics prior to the start of class.

Externship teachers should remind students that while it is important to reflect on the morality of various situations they will encounter in their externships, morality is different from the written rules that govern the actions of lawyers.[17] Faculty should stress the importance of reading and understanding the rules by explaining that students need to be able to spot potential ethical issues on their own, and that they need to understand the rules in order to do so. Students should also understand that while they will need to identify potential ethical issues, they should not attempt to resolve them on their own. If they think they have identified an ethical issue, they should raise it with their supervisor and let the supervisor decide how to address it.

Ethical issues are so important to externships that one could design an entire seminar focused on ethical issues, and indeed some externship faculty do just that. *Learning From Practice*[18] devotes three chapters to ethical issues that can arise in externships and is an excellent place to look for seminar design in this area. Some of the basic ethical concepts that arise in most externships and should arguably be taught in any externship seminar include: confidentiality; conflict of interest; com-

---

14. *See* ABA Standards and Rules of Procedure for Approval of Law Schools 2022–2023, Standard 304(a)(1).

15. *Id.*

16. *See* Model Rules of Prof'l Conduct R. 5.3 (1983).

17. Students' values matter of course, and using the externship classroom as a place to develop those values is discussed in more detail below in the sections on professional identity formation and core values.

18. Learning From Practice, *supra* note 10.

petence and diligence; candor to the tribunal and truthfulness with others; and the unauthorized practice of law.

Protecting confidential client information is a central duty of lawyers in the U.S. legal system,[19] and one that all externs need to study and understand. It is helpful for students to understand that the rule is meant to encourage clients to be candid so that the lawyer may provide accurate and helpful advice.[20] Given that the faculty member teaching the externship seminar and most of the students in the class are not part of each extern's workplace, externs must be careful not to disclose any confidential information when discussing their work. Helping students understand what is confidential (client names and identifying facts, discussion of legal strategy, information communicated by the client, etc.) and what is not (observations on the record in open court, what the student is learning about themselves and about the law, personal reflections on the justice system, etc.) should start before or at the very beginning of the seminar.[21] Many parts of the externship seminar, including rounds, class discussions, and journal entries, often call for students to discuss some aspect of their work, so the need to exclude confidential information will continue throughout the course. Learning how to discuss their work without revealing confidential information is a skill that students will continue to need throughout their careers to navigate conversations with friends, family, and others. Faculty may need to remind students that their confidentiality obligation applies to conversations with friends and postings on social media. Judicial externs need to be particularly careful of what they post on social media, as their posts may be seen as an extension of the court.[22] It is also helpful for students to discuss confidentiality with their externship supervisor to ensure that the students have a clear understanding of what should be treated as confidential.

Recognizing potential conflicts of interest is another ethical concept that is important for every extern. While the rules on conflicts can be complicated,[23] and a full exploration may be more appropriate in a course on professional responsibility, at a minimum, students need to identify prior, current, or future work that might be a conflict with their work at the externship. Faculty should explain that any prior or current legal work may be a source of a conflict, including paralegal work prior to law school, summer jobs, current jobs, and work in an in-house clinic or a prior

---

19. *See* Model Rules of Prof'l Conduct R. 1.6 (1983).

20. *See id.*, Comment 2 (confidentiality encourages the client to communicate fully and frankly with the lawyer so that the lawyer can represent the client effectively).

21. *See* Learning From Practice, *supra* note 10, at 286–92 (guidance and classroom exercises to help students identify what they may discuss in class).

22. *See, e.g., Committee on Codes of Conduct Advisory Opinion No. 112: Use of Electronic Social Media by Judges and Judicial Employees*, at https://www.uscourts.gov/sites/default/files/guide-vol02b-ch02-2019_final.pdf (2019) (last viewed March 7, 2022).

23. The Model Rules devote six separate rules to dealing with conflicts of interest. *See* Model Rules of Prof'l Conduct R. 1.7, 1.8., 1.9, 1.10, 1.11, 1.12 (1983).

externship.[24] It is important to identify potential conflicts in advance, before the extern starts work on a project that involves a conflict. It is much easier to keep externs away from assignments that include potential conflicts than it is to try to untangle a conflict situation once the student has started work on a case. Many externship sites have conflict procedures for lawyers that can be used for externs. In addition to requiring students to talk to their supervisors about potential conflicts, faculty may want to provide students with a conflicts form to complete prior to the start of the externship.[25] The completed form can be shared with the supervisor to help identify potential conflicts. If a potential conflict is identified, students can work with their supervisor to determine next steps to ensure compliance with ethical rules.

While most students recognize that they should approach their externship assignments seriously and try to do good work, they may not recognize that competence and diligence are part of a lawyer's ethical responsibilities.[26] Understanding these duties can help students develop resilience and determination in the face of difficult projects. It can also help them understand the importance of their relationship with their supervisor and when to seek guidance and clarification from them.[27] Students should seek input from their supervisor on what diligence and competence look like in their externship setting. While externships are an educational experience for students to develop lawyering skills, students must also recognize that cases are ultimately for the clients.

As externs start to assume the role of a zealous advocate, they also need to understand the ethical rules regarding truthfulness. In their eagerness to advocate for their client, they might be tempted to "bend" the truth or reach too far with an argument. Learning where to draw the line between vigorous advocacy and not making false statements of fact or law is an important skill for any lawyer. Faculty can review the rules on candor to the tribunal and truthfulness with others to help students start to understand where to draw the line.[28] Faculty should also encourage students to explore these issues with their supervisors.

---

24. Chapter 12 of LEARNING FROM PRACTICE, *supra* note 10, contains many exercises and examples of conflicts that can arise for externs.

25. For a good sample Conflicts of Interests Inventory form, *see* LEARNING FROM PRACTICE, *supra* note 10, at 332–33.

26. *See* MODEL RULES OF PROF'L CONDUCT R. 1.1 and 1.3 (1983).

27. Chapter 4 contains guidance on training supervisors, and Chapter 13 provides guidance for site supervisors.

28. Chapter 13 of LEARNING FROM PRACTICE, *supra* note 10, contains good guidance and examples for externs on duties to tribunals and third parties. *See also* MODEL RULES OF PROF'L CONDUCT R. 3.3, 3.4, 4.1 (1983).

Finally, students must understand the rules regarding the unauthorized practice of law. Students are not yet licensed lawyers, and absent authorization under student practice rules, they may not give legal advice, appear in court, or otherwise engage in the practice of law. The unauthorized practice of law is generally regulated under state law, and faculty should provide students with the relevant statutes and cases and ensure that they understand what is prohibited. Externs should always identify themselves as students to clients, judges, witnesses, and anyone else involved in their work. Both faculty and supervisors can work with students to identify what they may do with supervision and what is reserved for licensed attorneys.

Externship faculty should also be aware of the student practice rules in their jurisdiction. Most states have provisions that under certain conditions allow students to perform some of the duties generally reserved for licensed attorneys. Each state has its own requirements, and faculty should provide the application information to students before the externship course starts. It takes time for students to gather the required information and for the state to grant permission for the student to practice under supervision. Not all students or all externships will qualify. Faculty should be familiar with the rules in their state to help guide the students. The site supervisors must also be involved and be willing to provide the supervision required under the rules.

Some externship settings have ethical rules or a code of conduct in addition to the state rules of professional responsibility. For example, there are separate codes of conduct that apply to people who work in judicial chambers.[29] Prosecutors and other government attorneys often are bound by additional ethical restrictions. Students in those practice settings should review and be familiar with these rules. Supervisors can help students understand the rules and how they apply to externs.

It is generally insufficient in an externship class to simply assign students to read the rules of professional responsibility. They need to think about the rules as they apply to the legal work in their externships. Hypotheticals are a teaching technique that most students are accustomed to and that lend themselves well to an externship seminar, where the ethical rules may not allow students to share details of their own ethical dilemmas with the class. Hypotheticals allow faculty to focus on issues that often arise in externships, without singling out any individual student or externship site. Faculty can draw on many sources for fact patterns and hypothetical situations to explore in class, including past externships, the faculty's own practice experience, cases from the news, cases in published ethical opinions, and many others.

---

29. *See, e.g.*, Code of Conduct for Judicial Employees, *at* https://www.uscourts.gov/rules-policies/judiciary-policies/code-conduct/code-conduct-judicial-employees (last visited March 7, 2022).

The chapters in *Learning From Practice* that cover ethical rules have many relevant hypotheticals and exercises.

Rounds are another good place for students to practice identifying and protecting confidential information.[30] Students need to describe their work in a general way without revealing identifying information, strategy, work product, or client confidences. The teacher may need to step in and point out when a student is getting too close to identifying confidential information. Faculty should also ask all students to be alert and step in if they sense a presenting student is discussing confidential information. In general externship classes, it is possible that students are working on the same case on different sides (prosecution and defense) or from different perspectives (advocate and judge). It may be easier for students to recognize those sensitive areas even before the faculty member does.

Quick write and reporting back[31] is another good way to get the whole class thinking about an ethical issue and then to learn from each other. For example, the faculty could assign students to make a list of the sources of their potential conflicts. Comparing and discussing these lists helps students learn from each other and identify additional sources of potential conflicts.

3. Professional Identity Formation

Because externship courses orient students in real-world practice settings, they are a natural place to explore each student's emerging professional identity as a lawyer. Whether students have had previous professional lives or have come straight from another academic program, they rarely take the time without prompting to intentionally think about the transformative process of law school or what they want their lives as lawyers to look like.

a. Professional Identity Formation Defined

Professional identity formation is a concept that was first articulated in the 2007 Carnegie Report[32] as one of the three essential apprenticeships of legal education. "The apprenticeship of professional identity and purpose is the means through which law schools teach students the legal profession's guiding values and principles

30. See Chapter 11 for a more thorough discussion of how to use rounds as a teaching technique in an externship class.

31. Chapter 11 has more information on how to use quick write as a teaching method.

32. William M. Sullivan et al., Educating Lawyers: Preparation for the Profession of Law (2007).

.... [It] also extends to deeper, more philosophical questions, such as what it means to be a lawyer and the special obligations that lawyers have to society."[33]

Professional identity formation is distinct from but related to the concept of professionalism. Professionalism involves expected norms of behavior in dealing with clients, courts, legal adversaries, and others.[34] It "goes beyond compliance with the Rules of Professional Conduct and other statutory or regulatory standards.... [It] includes good judgment, effective problem solving, and leadership."[35] Many externship courses include a component on professionalism as part of an orientation class or as a discrete seminar topic. In that instance, teachers should consider assigning Chapter 9, entitled "Professionalism," from *Learning From Practice.*

The "educational goal of professional formation recognizes that legal education is a transformative process, a process law schools should consciously shape by integrating professional identity formation into curricular and pedagogical design in a way that will assist students in becoming competent, ethical, and fulfilled attorneys."[36] Professors Neil Hamilton and Lou Bilionis identify four goals that comprise a lawyer's professional identity: "1. Ownership of continuous professional development toward excellence at the major competencies that clients, employers, and the legal system need; 2. a deep responsibility and service orientation to others, especially the client; 3. a client-centered problem-solving approach and good judgment that ground each student's responsibility and service to the client; and 4. well-being practices. These four goals taken together state what it means for an individual to think, act, and feel like a lawyer."[37] Thus, professional identity formation requires students to develop self-awareness and self-direction regarding their professional futures.

Over the past decade, law schools have started to recognize the goals of legal education should expand beyond the learning of knowledge and skills, to include what is often referred to as "'values' or 'the formation of professional identity.'"[38] ABA Standard 303(b)(3) now requires law schools to "provide substantial opportu-

33. Learning From Practice, *supra* note 10, at 244.

34. *Id.* at 237.

35. *Id.* at 239–40.

36. Timothy W. Floyd & Kendall L. Kerew, *Marking the Path from Law Student to Lawyer: Using Field Placement Courses to Facilitate the Deliberate Exploration of Professional Identity and Purpose*, 68 Mercer L. Rev. 767, 769 (2017).

37. Neil W. Hamilton and Louis D. Bilionis, Law Student Professional Development and Formation: Bridging Law School, Student, and Employer Goals 2–3 (2022) (last visited June 30, 2022). Prior to describing professional identity as four integrated goals, Professor Hamilton defined professional identity formation as "a change from thinking like a student (where he or she learns and applies routine techniques to solve well-structured problems) toward acceptance and internalization of responsibility to others (particularly the person served) and for the student's own pro-active development toward excellence as a practitioner at all of the competencies of the profession." Floyd & Kerew, *supra* note 36, at 775.

38. Floyd & Kerew, *supra* note 36, at 769. *See also* Kendall Kerew, *Building Your Professional Identity* (Chapter 6), *in* Lawyering from the Inside Out (2018).

nities" to students for "the development of a professional identity"[39] with the expectation that the exploration of professional identity will take place throughout the law school experience. Interpretation 303-5 to ABA Standard 303(b)(3) employs the following definition: "Professional identity focuses on what it means to be a lawyer and the special obligations lawyers have to their clients and society. The development of professional identity should involve an intentional exploration of the values, guiding principles, and well-being practices considered foundational to successful legal practice...."[40]

b. Teaching Professional Identity Formation in the Externship Seminar

While professional identity formation should be addressed in classes across the curriculum, externships are a "signature pedagogy"[41] for the apprenticeship of professional identity and purpose. The very nature of externships exposes students to the realities of the legal profession and prompts students to consider their emerging professional identities. In their externship placements, students see firsthand the decisions lawyers and judges make, consider the impact their work has on individual clients and parties to a lawsuit, as well as the justice system and society, and grapple with inherent values conflicts. Moreover, the requirements of an externship course necessarily prompt students to be self-directed in their professional development; they must evaluate their strengths and areas for growth, set learning goals, seek meaningful assignments and feedback, and engage in self-reflection.[42] Accordingly, an externship seminar or a class or two centered on professional identity "can help students actively and intentionally engage in the transformative process of moving from law student to lawyer."[43] Moreover, because this transformative process happens in every externship regardless of the type of placement, professional identity formation is a valuable focus of a general externship seminar.[44]

---

39. ABA Standards and Rules of Procedure for Approval of Law Schools 2022–2023, Standard 303(b)(3); see Chapter 2 for a full discussion of the ABA Standards.

40. *See* Interpretation 303-5, *supra* note 39.

41. Kelly S. Terry, *Externships: A Signature Pedagogy for the Apprenticeship of Professional Identity and Purpose*, 59 J. Legal Educ. 240 (2010). "Signature pedagogies are the 'typical practices of teaching and learning by which schools induct new members into the field....' Through signature pedagogies, 'the novices are instructed on the fundamental dimensions of professional work—*to think, to perform, and to act with integrity*.' Such teaching methods are considered 'signature' because they are 'readily identifiable and unique to the field.'" *Id.* at 247 (internal citations omitted).

42. *See* ABA Standards and Rules of Procedure for Approval of Law Schools 2022–2023, Standard 304.

43. Terry, *supra* note 41.

44. *See* Megan Bess, *Transitions Unexplored: A Proposal for Professional Identity Formation Following the First Year* (February 4, 2022), http://dx.doi.org/10.2139/ssrn.4026976 (last visited March 20, 2022). In fact, professional identity formation has become the predominant learning objective for a number of different externship courses and programs. *See, e.g.*, Georgia State University College of Law, Mercer Law School, and University of Arkansas at Little Rock William H. Bowen School of Law.

There are a variety of seminar topics that can be explored through the lens of professional identity formation. Many topics focus students on developing self-awareness about their strengths, areas for growth, values, and career goals and aspirations.[45] Other seminar topics help students to frame the values and obligations of the profession such as the duties of lawyers, including pursuing justice, professionalism, and civility in the law.[46] An externship seminar need not be entirely devoted to professional identity formation, however. In the event an externship seminar focuses on skills specific to a particular practice area or covers a wide range of topics, it is worth considering intentionally addressing professional identity formation through the reflection and self-evaluation components of the course. If a seminar can support only one or two class sessions on professional formation, teachers can consider assigning the *Learning From Practice* chapter on this topic.[47]

Because professional identity formation necessarily involves self-exploration, students may initially resist a class addressing their emerging professional identities. After all, law school rarely asks students to conduct a subjective analysis of any topic but, rather, an objective analysis of the law. There are several ways to counter any initial student resistance. First, be straightforward about how the class is different from those they have encountered in law school. To do this, the externship teacher will want to "acknowledge that professional identity formation is necessarily personal and involves self-exploration to achieve the level of self-awareness necessary to determine personal and professional values."[48] To engage in self-exploration, students will have to determine what they think about a topic; this is a wholly different approach than they are used to in many doctrinal classes where they have been asked to predict an outcome, engage in objective analysis, or argue an assigned position.[49] Second, it is helpful to explain why professional identity formation matters and how it relates to the students' externships by using data and studies such as the IAALS Foundations for Practice Report and the Shultz-Zedeck 26 Lawyering Effectiveness Factors.[50] Third, provide a concrete definition of professional identity formation.[51]

45. Terry, *supra* note 41, at 256–80 (describing assignments and readings on these topics).

46. *Id.*

47. *See* Daisy Hurst Floyd & Tim W. Floyd, *Professional Identity and Formation* (Chapter 24), *in* Learning From Practice, *supra* note 10.

48. Floyd & Kerew, *supra* note 36, at 772.

49. *Id.*

50. *Id.*

51. *Id.*

4. Values and Well-Being

In a seminar, there are a number of different ways to approach values and well-being; they may be the subject of two separate class discussions, part of a single class discussion, or woven throughout the course of the seminar. These topics are well-suited to a seminar devoted to ethics or professional identity formation.

a. Values

An externship seminar can facilitate the intentional exploration of a student's personal and professional values. Although students acquire new professional values during law school, they do not lose their personal values.[52] "The well-integrated lawyer can fulfill both personal and professional values at the same time."[53]

Exercises that facilitate identification of personal values provide students with a starting point to consider if and how their personal values may have changed since entering law school.[54] As part of the values discussion, it is helpful for students to examine whether their values involve intrinsic or extrinsic motivations.[55] "Intrinsic values and motivations are fulfilled when a person chooses an action she genuinely enjoys or which furthers a fundamental purpose. In contrast, extrinsic values and motivations drive a person to choose an action because of external rewards, such as money, grades, or honors; the avoidance of fear; or to please or impress others."[56] A broad approach to values focuses on all of the things a person may find important and is not necessarily limited by ethics or morals. A more focused approach is that of concentrating on moral or ethical values. The central moral or ethical values most individuals identify include "five widely shared values: honesty, respect, responsibility, fairness, and compassion."[57]

In addition to personal values, exercises that help students identify professional values promote an intentional exploration of what values are involved and how they are playing out at their externship placements. "'There are some core values that derive from the fact that professionals in law and other fields hold a privileged position within society with obligations to people whose lives and well-being are at stake.' Such core values in the legal profession include 'confidentiality, competence, continued learning, and respect for the people you are serving and commitment

---

52. Chapter 24, Learning From Practice, *supra* note 10, at 691.

53. *Id.* at 692. Some experts argue that there is really only one set of values. *See* Brene Brown, Dare to Lead: Brave Work. Tough Conversations. Whole Hearts. (2018) (stating that you bring the entirety of yourself to all you do).

54. Floyd & Kerew, *supra* note 36, at 793–94.

55. *Id.* at 692.

56. *Id.* at 693. *See also* Lawrence Krieger & Kennon Sheldon, *What Makes Lawyers Happy?: A Data-Driven Prescription to Redefine Professional Success*, 83 Geo. Wash. L. Rev. 554, 566–69 (2015).

57. Mary C. Gentile, Giving Voice to Values: How to Speak Your Mind When You Know What's Right 30 (2012).

to service.'"[58] It may be helpful to use a list of core values that directly relates to the way lawyers exercise discretion in professional decision-making such as the one set forth in *Building on Best Practices*.[59] This list includes integrity, honesty, diligence, fairness, courage/honor, wisdom/judgment, compassion/service/respect for others, and balance.[60]

In an externship, students may struggle with values conflicts that present themselves in the practice setting. The externship seminar can be a productive forum to facilitate thought and practice in how to speak one's values. In her book *Giving Voice to Values* (GVV), Mary Gentile provides a skills and practice-based approach to dealing with values conflicts. "GVV is all about... building the skills, the confidence, the moral muscle, and, frankly, the *habit* of voicing our values. It begins with the assumption that most of us will encounter values conflicts in our careers, when the way we want to live and the things we want to accomplish seem in conflict with the expectations of our clients, our peers, our bosses, or our organizations."[61] In particular, this framework could be used as a single class session or throughout a seminar focused on ethics or professional identity formation.

To employ the GVV framework, students must know what their values are. Once they have identified their values through a core values exercise such as that outlined above, students can begin to learn and employ the GVV framework. After reviewing the starting assumptions of GVV,[62] students can engage in "A Tale of Two Stories" exercise that encourages reflection regarding "workplace situations when your values conflicted with what you were asked to do...."[63] The exercise has the following two objectives for participants: "1. To reflect on your previous experiences, successful and less so, at effectively voicing and acting on your values in the workplace; and 2. To discover which conditions and problem definitions empower you to effectively voice your values, and which tend to inhibit that action."[64] In addition, "[i]nsightful and supportive feedback on discussants' proposed 'scripts' and strategies for responding to values conflicts is an essential part of the Giving Voice to

58. Terry, *supra* note 41, at 256. In the context of complying with required professional responsibility courses, Interpretation 303-6 to ABA Standard 303 states that, "the importance of cross-cultural competency to professionally responsible representation and the obligation of lawyers to promote a justice system that provides equal access and eliminates bias, discrimination, and racism in the law should be among the values and responsibilities of the legal profession to which students are introduced." Interpretation 303-6, https://www.americanbar.org/content/dam/aba/administrative/legal_education_and_admissions_to_the_bar/standards/2022-2023/2022-2023-standards-and-rules-of-procedure.pdf (last visited Sept. 30, 2022).

59. Larry O. Natt Gantt & Benjamin V. Madison III, *Teaching the Newly Essential Knowledge Skills, and Values in a Changing World*, *in* BUILDING ON BEST PRACTICES: TRANSFORMING LEGAL EDUCATION IN A CHANGING WORLD 255 (Deborah Maranville et al. eds., 2015).

60. *Id.*

61. GENTILE, *supra* note 57, at xviii.

62. *Id.* at Appendix A.

63. *Id.* at Appendix B.

64. *Id.*

Values approach."[65] This provides a means of "joint problem-solving" that "includes noting strengths of a proposed response (so they can be retained) as well as identifying the remaining questions (so that the group can collaborate on more effective solutions)."[66] Using the GVV approach, externship teachers can help students to work though hypothetical or actual values conflicts the students experience during the course of their externship.

b. Well-Being

Externships often allow students to see how lawyers and judges handle the pressures of law practice and help students to become more self-aware about the need to do so. Some externship supervisors will model how to successfully integrate work and life to achieve well-being, but others will not. The externship seminar can help students become more aware of the profession's struggle with well-being and think about the strategies, or lack thereof, being used by their supervisors and other attorneys. An externship teacher can help students explore their well-being as both a professional and as an individual and provide strategies to achieve integration of work and life.[67] Topics could include imposter syndrome, secondary trauma,[68] growth mindset,[69] ways to manage stress and anxiety, and mindfulness practice.[70]

There are several studies that can be used to introduce the concept of well-being and the issue of substance abuse in the profession. The 2017 National Task Force on Lawyer Well-Being[71] report, entitled "The Path to Lawyer Well-Being: Practical Recommendations for Positive Change,"[72] provides a helpful definition of well-being:

> [L]awyer well-being is a continuous process whereby lawyers seek to thrive in each of the following areas: emotional health, occupational pursuits,

---

65. *Id.* at Appendix E. Appendix E provides a template to use for the peer coaching process.

66. *Id.*

67. *See* Marjorie A. Silver, *Work & Well-Being* (Chapter 25), *in* LEARNING FROM PRACTICE (providing reading and exercises for use in a seminar focused on well-being). *See also* NATHALIE MARTIN, LAWYERING FROM THE INSIDE OUT (2018).

68. This topic is addressed in Chapter 9.

69. *See* Megan Bess, *Grit, Growth Mindset, and the Path to Successful Lawyering*, 89 UMKC L. REV. 493 (2021) for ideas on how to address this topic.

70. *See* Janet Thompson Jackson, *Wellness and Law: Reforming Legal Education to Support Student Wellness*, 65 How. L.J. (2021), http://dx.doi.org/10.2139/ssrn.3839050 (last visited March 20, 2022) (describing the concept of the stool, which represents the components of professional identity, and the floor, which represents the foundation) for ideas of how to talk about and teach well-being and wellness practices.

71. The National Task Force on Lawyer Well-Being consisted of the National Organization of Bar Counsel (NOBC), the Association of Professional Responsibility Lawyers (APRL) and the ABA Commission on Lawyers Assistance Programs (CoLAP). This group led to the creation of the Institute for Well-Being in Law whose mission is "to lead a culture shift in law to establish health and well-being as core centerpieces of professional success." https://lawyerwellbeing.net/ (last visited March 20, 2022).

72. https://lawyerwellbeing.net/wp-content/uploads/2017/11/Lawyer-Wellbeing-Report.pdf.

> creative or intellectual endeavors, sense of spirituality or greater purpose in life, physical health, and social connections with others. Lawyer well-being is part of a lawyer's ethical duty of competence. It includes lawyers' ability to make healthy, positive work/life choices to assure not only a quality of life within their families and communities, but also to help them make responsible decisions for their clients. It includes maintaining their own long term well-being.[73]

This definition is a helpful starting point to discuss professional well-being. In addition, the report identifies six dimensions of well-being: Emotional,[74] Occupational,[75] Intellectual,[76] Spiritual, Physical,[77] and Social.[78] These dimensions can prompt reflection questions, student action plans, and other exercises to facilitate each student's individual exploration and assessment of their own well-being. In addition, individual self-assessments[79] can be a helpful tool to begin this discussion.[80]

On the topic of substance abuse, externship teachers could use two studies. The first is a 2016 study entitled *The Prevalence of Substance Use and Other Mental Health Concerns Among American Attorneys*,[81] which concluded that there is "a concerning amount of behavioral health problems among attorneys in the United States. Our most significant findings are the rates of hazardous, harmful, and potentially alcohol dependent drinking and high rates of depression and anxiety symptoms."[82] The second, which is specific to law students, is the *Survey of Law Student Well Being*.[83]

---

73. *Id.* at 9.

74. "Recognizing the importance of emotions. Developing the ability to identify and manage our own emotions to support mental health, achieve goals, and inform decision-making. Seeking help for mental health when needed." *Id.*

75. "Cultivating personal satisfaction, growth, and enrichment in work; financial stability." *Id.*

76. "Engaging in continuous learning and the pursuit of creative or intellectually challenging activities that foster ongoing development; monitoring cognitive wellness." *Id.*

77. "Striving for regular physical activity, proper diet and nutrition, sufficient sleep, and recovery; minimizing the use of addictive substances. Seeking help for physical health when needed." *Id.*

78. "Developing a sense of connection, belonging, and a well-developed support network while also contributing to our groups and communities." *Id.*

79. *See, e.g.*, Self-Care Assessment at http://socialwork.buffalo.edu/content/dam/socialwork/home/self-care-kit/self-care-assessment.pdf; University at Buffalo School of Social Work: Self-Care Starter Kit, http://socialwork.buffalo.edu/resources/self-care-starter-kit/developing-your-self-care-plan.html; ABA Well-Being Toolkit: https://www.americanbar.org/content/dam/aba/ administrative/lawyer_assistance/ls_colap_wellbeing_toolkit_for_lawyers_legal_ employers.pdf; Designing and Living an Integrated Life, Georgia Bar Journal, http://digitaleditions.walsworthprintgroup.com/publication/?m=15035&i=699200&p=52.

80. A rubric for assessing student learning outcomes relating to well-being is included in the Appendix to this Chapter.

81. Patrick R. Krill, Ryan Johnson & Linda Albert, *The Prevalence of Substance Use and Other Mental Health Concerns Among American Attorneys*, 10 J. Addict. Med. 46 (2016).

82. *Id.* at 51.

83. Jerome M. Organ, David B. Jaffe, & Katherine M. Bender, *Suffering in Silence: The Survey of Law Student Well-Being and the Reluctance of Law Students to Seek Help for Substance Use and Mental Health Concerns*, 66 J. Legal Educ. 116 (2016). The authors are working on an updated version of this study, *It is Okay to Not Be Okay: The 2021 Survey of Law Student Well-Being*.

The survey was designed to answer four research questions. These questions include: "1) to what extent are law students drinking alcohol, using prescription and nonprescription drugs, and engaging in nonmedical use of prescription drugs (taking prescription drugs without a prescription); 2) to what extent do law students experience mental health issues; 3) to what extent are law students with substance use or mental health issues inclined to seek assistance or treatment for such issues; and 4) what factors discourage law students from seeking help for substance use and/or mental health concerns."[84]

Another aspect of well-being that can be explored in externship seminars is imposter syndrome.[85] "Imposter syndrome can be defined as a collection of feelings of inadequacy that persist despite evident success. 'Imposters' suffer from chronic self-doubt and a sense of intellectual fraudulence that override any feelings of success or external proof of their competence."[86] This definition derives from the concept of "Impostor Phenomenon"[87] developed by Dr. Pauline Clance. The Imposter Phenomenon "interferes with the psychological well-being of a person"[88] and "limits the acceptance of success as an outcome of one's own ability and influences feelings of self-doubt and anxiety."[89]

There are a number of helpful resources to develop a class on this topic. For example, an externship teacher might want to assign Elizabeth Cox's TED Talk entitled *What Is Imposter Syndrome and How Can You Combat It?*[90] In addition, students could take the Imposter Test, which "was developed to help individuals determine whether or not they have IP characteristics and, if so, to what extent they are suffering,"[91] complete assigned readings that help students to focus on imposter syndrome in women and BIPOC students,[92] and reflect on the topic both in class and in written reflections.

Mindfulness theory and practice could also provide students with a way to facilitate well-being. "Mindfulness is present awareness of one's thoughts as they arise

---

84. *Id.*

85. Professors Amanda Rivas and Nira Geevargis have developed and shared imposter syndrome class materials, which have informed the discussion of this topic.

86. Gill Corkindale, *Overcoming Imposter Syndrome*, Harv. Bus. Rev. (May 7, 2008), https://hbr.org/2008/05/overcoming-imposter-syndrome); *see also* https://www.dcbar.org/ getmedia/bbcd750f-329b-4646-af84-82479ff95b3c/ImposterSyndromeKnowItNameItTameIt (last visited March 20, 2022) (providing several different definitions of imposter syndrome).

87. Jaruwan Sakulku & James Alexander, *The Impostor Phenomenon*, 6 Int'l J. of Behav. Sci. 75, 77 (2011), https://so06.tci-thaijo.org/index.php/IJBS/article/view/521/pdf. Professor Nira Geevargis assigns a portion of this article to her students to read.

88. *Id.*

89. *Id.*

90. https://www.ted.com/talks/elizabeth_cox_what_is_imposter_syndrome_and_how_can_you_combat_it (last visited March 20, 2022).

91. https://paulineroseclance.com/pdf/IPTestandscoring.pdf (last visited March 20, 2022). Professor Geevargis uses this survey as a class exercise.

92. Professor Geevargis assigns the following articles: Jeanne Crouteau, *Imposter Syndrome—Why*

and minute-to-minute awareness of one's existence. The concept of mindfulness can also include non-thinking or simply clearing the mind. In either case, mindfulness allows you to pay clear and particular attention to the things around you, so you can do what is best for yourself, those you care about, and the world at large, if you take it that far."[93] Mindfulness practices are well-known for improving peace of mind by relieving stress.[94] Externship teachers can introduce students to mindfulness and incorporate short exercises into their seminar teaching. For example, the 5-4-3-2-1 Exercise focuses students on their five senses and has them end with a good thing about themselves.[95] Playing a Headspace video[96] can facilitate a minute of meditation before each class. Asking students to complete an anonymous well-being check-in using polling software can provide an opportunity for students to see how they are doing with well-being as a class, and it can allow the externship teacher to address student well-being issues as they arise.

The use of class discussion, rounds, and student presentations can facilitate both individual and group reflection on these seminar topics by asking students to consider how they feel about a topic and sharing those thoughts in a group setting.[97] To the extent the seminar is graded, consider making class discussion and/or presentations a significant percentage of the grade. Class size is also an important consideration. Because these classes are often dependent on class exercises and discussion, an ideal class size is around 16 students.[98] Teachers who have a larger number of students should consider dividing the class into sections.

It's Harder Today Than Ever, FORBES (Apr. 4, 2019), https://www.forbes.com/sites/ jeannecroteau /2019/04/04/imposter-syndrome-why-its-harder-today-than-ever/ ?sh=356aac3b9ac5; Jolie A. Doggett, *Imposter Syndrome Hits Harder When You're Black*, HUFFINGTON POST (Oct. 10, 2019), https://www.huffpost.com/entry/imposter-syndrome-racism-discrimination_l_5d9f2c00e4b06ddfc514e-c5c; Kristin Wong, *Dealing with Imposter Syndrome When You're Treated as an Imposter*, N.Y. TIMES (June 12, 2018), https://www.nytimes.com/2018/06/12/smarter-living/dealing-with-impostor-syndrome-when-youre-treated-as-an-impostor.html. The following article, which challenges the framing of imposter syndrome, also might be helpful to assign and discuss with students: Ruchika Tulshyan & Jodi-Ann Burey, *Stop Telling Women They Have Imposter Syndrome*, HARV. BUS. REV., Feb. 11, 2021, https://hbr.org/2021/02/stop-telling-women-they-have-imposter-syndrome?fbclid=IwAR-3rizzHkGwQ0kq31SIKYzqC7TBqj4AJ9nxHDsuxUj6elYftB2lrfDFyFak.

93. Nathalie Martin, *Think Like a (Mindful) Lawyer: Incorporating Mindfulness, Professional Identity, and Emotional Intelligence Into the First Year Law Curriculum*, 36 U. ARK. LITTLE ROCK L. REV. 413, 416 (2014).

94. *Id.* at 427.

95. Jackson, *supra* note 70.

96. https://www.youtube.com/watch?v=c1Ndym-IsQg (last visited March 20, 2022).

97. See Chapter 11 for more information on the use of these techniques in a seminar class.

98. Chapter 3 provides a more detailed discussion of the ideal externship class size for optimal learning.

5. Bias, Racism, and Cross-Cultural Humility

a. Rationale for Including Instruction About Bias, Racism, and Cross-Cultural Humility[99] in the Seminar

The expansion of the Black Lives Matter movement following the murder of George Floyd in Minneapolis, Minnesota, on May 25, 2020, led to a nationwide reexamination of the ways in which institutionalized racism pervades American society and its system of justice.[100] Awareness of the devastating effects of racism was nothing new to the non-white community, but cell phone recordings and other social media allowed many white Americans a window into a world that they had never personally experienced.[101] The Black Lives Matter movement had been founded after the murder of 17-year-old Trayvon Martin in 2012,[102] but the brutality of George Floyd's death, following the deaths of countless other individuals, including women and young children,[103] fueled the movement, and it spread worldwide.[104]

This racial justice reckoning had a strong impact on legal educators and on the attorneys and judges supervising student externs. Law school faculty around the country responded to student calls for action with letters acknowledging the need for change; they committed to reviewing their institutions to identify and remove racism embedded in law school structures, from law school applications, through classroom instruction, to bar admission.[105] Externship faculty met in conferences

---

99. The term cultural competence is used in the ABA Standards, but "cross-cultural humility" places a greater emphasis on avoiding dominance or superiority by one particular group. For a more thorough discussion, *see* Gillian Dutton, *International Experiences: A Path to Critical Legal Skills, Values, and Innovation for American Law Students*, 27 Clinical L. Rev. 1, 26 (2020).

100. Alex Altman, *Why The Killing of George Floyd Sparked an American Uprising*, Time (June 4, 2020), https://time.com/5847967/george-floyd-protests-trump/.

101. *Id.*

102. *See Herstory*, https://blacklivesmatter.com/herstory/ (last visited Jan. 8, 2022), for more on the origins of the Black Lives Matter Movement.

103. Tamir Rice, a 12-year-old playing with a toy gun in Cleveland, was fatally shot by a police officer in November 2014. Michale Balsamo et al., *Feds Decline Charges Against Officers in Tamir Rice Case*, Associated Press (Dec. 29, 2020), https://apnews.com/article/politics-race-and-ethnicity-shootings-tamir-rice-timothy-loehmann-19724be26194ae75d259d1f54f7992f8. Breonna Taylor, a medical worker in Louisville, Kentucky, was shot by police in a botched drug enforcement raid. Richard A. Oppel Jr. et al., *What to Know About Breonna Taylor's Death*, N.Y. Times (Apr. 26, 2021), https://www.nytimes.com/article/breonna-taylor-police.html.

104. Jason Silverstein, *The Global Impact of George Floyd: How Black Lives Matter Protests Shaped Movements Around the World*, CBS News (June 4, 2021), https://www.cbsnews.com/ news/george-floyd-black-lives-matter-impact/.

105. Dean Annette Clark, *Dean Annette Clark Issues Call to Action on Racial Justice*, Seattle Univ. Sch. Law (June 2, 2020), https://law.seattleu.edu/newsroom/2020-news/dean-annette-clark-issues-call-to-action-on-racial-justice. Seattle University School of Law is a good example of the variety of voices that engaged in this process, which included the Dean, faculty, Black Law Student Association, editors of the Seattle Journal for Social Justice, and those who signed a change.org petition.

and workshops with themes focusing on addressing race equity,[106] not just within the law school[107] but within the broader community where the racism externs regularly encountered received renewed attention.[108]

Many legal educators, particularly Black, indigenous, and people of color (BIPOC),[109] exhausted from fear and anger, nonetheless worked hard to communicate the message that they, their sons, daughters, and other family members lived each day in fear of being arrested or shot by police simply by virtue of being in the wrong place at the wrong time. Their message not only underscored the need to address racism as a fundamental task of American society and, by extension, the legal system; it also showed the challenging complexity of teaching these skills to the next generation of lawyers.[110] Many legal educators, aware that racism had persisted so tenaciously, and had grown in terms of hate crimes and other attacks[111] despite the

---

106. The Clinical Legal Education Association (CLEA) held its New Clinicians Conference virtually in 2020 (https://www.cleaweb.org/new-clinicians) and included a section on Racial Justice in the Classroom and in Practice. *See* https://drive.google.com/drive/folders/1-EmveQRztlSPbQnWs-eG8yh2ZfRn427dI. The Externships 10 conference, held October 21–23, 2020, also continued in an online format with a focus on racial justice. The first plenary of the conference was entitled "Toward An Anti-Racist Future," http://law.syr.edu/academics/ conferences-symposia/externships-10-conference/wednesday-october-21; Professor Vernillia R. Randall (Professor Emerita of Law, The University of Dayton School of Law) shared her website—"Race, Racism, and the Law"—that examines the role of domestic and international law in promoting or alleviating racism. *See* Racism, https://racism.org/ (last visited Jan. 8, 2022).

107. Professors Gillian Dutton (Seattle University School of Law) and Janet Thompson Jackson (Washburn University School of Law) developed an anti-racism audit that encouraged externship faculty to audit their programs in several different categories including students, field placement location and supervisor, faculty supervisor, seminar, monitoring, program design and policies, and institutional and program culture. Gillian Dutton & Janet Thompson Jackson, *Anti-Racism Audit* (October 19, 2020) https://www.dropbox.com/sh/ jvlwcbavisebuwh/AADDiYeTbj4nlpf4yKqAQ6S-ba?dl=0&preview=Anti-Racism+Audit+Document+Dutton+Jackson+Final.docx.

108. Dr. Bridget Ortega (Atlanta's John Marshall Law School) and Professor Kinda Abdus-Saboor (Georgia State University School of Law) developed "Self-Check: A Guide to Antiracist Supervision" for externship supervisors who wanted to both assess themselves and create an antiracist organization; the guide also contains a list of reading recommendations. Bridget Ortega & Kinda Abdus-Saboor, *Self-Check: A Guide to Antiracist Supervision* https://www.dropbox.com/sh/t0duqnv7h5jdwv0/AABqZ5Vvg3g43ZN2px8kseCfa?dl=0&preview=2020.09.05+Final+Self-Check+for+Antiracist+-Supervision+-+edited-v1.1-1.pdf (last visited Jan. 11, 2022).

109. The term BIPOC began to be used in place of the term "people of color" to acknowledge that not all groups face equal levels of injustice and to explain that Black and indigenous groups are more severely impacted by systemic racism. Sandra E. Garcia, *Where Does Bipoc Come From?* N.Y. Times (June 17, 2020), https://www.nytimes.com/article/what-is-bipoc.html.

110. Kristen Rogers, *Dear anti-racist allies: Here's how to respond to microaggressions*, CNN (June 6, 2020), https://www.cnn.com/2020/06/05/health/racial-microaggressions-examples-responses-wellness/index.html. The focus on centering the experience of BIPOC individuals and ensuring that individuals with privilege lend their support as allies without focusing the attention on themselves and their feelings of responsibility and guilt highlighted the ways in which lawyers, law professors, and law students needed to learn to listen carefully to the lived experience of their BIPOC colleagues.

111. In November 2020, the Southern Poverty Law Center called on the federal government to mandate hate crime data collection after the recently released FBI report showed that hate crimes

struggles of the Civil Rights Movement, agreed that inaction equaled acquiescence. They believed they could not teach law students to follow laws that functioned as part of a system that had institutionalized racism throughout its components, but instead needed to teach students to be anti-racist[112] and actively working to dismantle that system.

Throughout the rest of 2020, the legal profession outside of academia responded with calls of their own to engage in the work of undoing institutionalized racism, from state supreme courts,[113] to legislatures,[114] legal aid organizations,[115] government agencies,[116] criminal justice organizations,[117] private law firms,[118] and in-house counsel at large and small corporations.[119] These changes were expressed in many ways, through the recruitment of more employees of color, the creation of many internal

---

had reached their highest level since 2008. *See* https://www.splcenter.org/presscenter/ splc-responds-new-fbi-report-showing-increase-hate-crimes-2019. The Southern Poverty Law Center monitors hate groups and keeps a yearly list. *See* https://www.splcenter.org/ 20200318/frequently-asked-questions-about-hate-groups#hate%20group.

112. *See* Ibram X. Kendi, How to Be an Antiracist 24 (2019) (discussing internalized racism and arguing for going beyond awareness of racism to fighting actively against it).

113. The Washington State Supreme Court issued a letter on June 4, 2020, recognizing the role the courts had played in devaluing Black lives and calling for the development of "a greater awareness of our own conscious and unconscious biases in order to make just decisions in individual cases" and committing to "administer justice and support court rules in a way that brings greater racial justice to our system as a whole." *See* https://www.courts.wa.gov/ content/publicUpload/Supreme%20 Court%20News/Judiciary%20Legal%20Community%20SIGNED%20060420.pdf.

114. On December 14, 2020, Washington State Governor Jay Inslee introduced a list of equity measures designed to address race equity issues in civil matters, education, criminal justice, employment, recreation, environment, insurance, and access to technology. *See Inslee Announces Washington's Historic Commitment to Diversity, Equity, Inclusion* (Dec. 14, 2020), https://www.governor.wa.gov/news-media/inslee-announces-washingtons-historic-commitment-diversity-equity-and-inclusion.

115. *Newsom Administration Announces First-of-its-Kind Diversity Initiative for California State Government*, (Jan. 18, 2019), https://www.gov.ca.gov/2019/01/18/inclusv/; *Oregon Governor's Office of Diversity, Equity and Inclusion*, (2019) https://www.racialequityalliance.org/jurisdictions/oregon-governors-office-of-diversity-equity-and-inclusion/.

116. Boulder Cnty., *Our Commitment to Diversity, Equity, and Inclusivity*, https://assets.bouldercounty.org/wp-content/uploads/2019/09/Our-Commitment.pdf (last visited Jan. 13, 2022); Boston Police Dept., *Commitment to Diversity, Equity, and Inclusion*, https://bpdnews.com/diversity-equity-and-inclusion (last visited Jan. 13, 2022).

117. The Washington State Race Equity and Justice Initiative is an example of a state-wide effort to address racial justice whose list of partners includes state institutions and nonprofits. Washington Race Equity & Justice Initiative, *Washington Race Equity & Justice Initiative: Our Partners*, www.wareji.org (last visited Jan. 9, 2022).

118. Sara Merken, *New Law Firm Commitments Include Goal that Ties Partner Pay to Diversity*, Reuters (Sept. 30, 2021), https://www.reuters.com/legal/legalindustry/new-law-firm-commitments-include-goal-that-ties-partner-pay-diversity-2021-09-30/; Keller Rohrback's Commitment to Diversity, https://www.kellerrohrback.com/diversity-equity-inclusion (last visited Jan. 9, 2022); Our Commitment to Diversity, Equity, and Inclusion, https://www.cojk.com/our-commitment-to-diversity-equity-and-inclusion (last visited Jan. 9, 2022).

119. *Id.*

task forces, and the implementation of internal monitoring for racially disproportionate outcomes. Most had a common approach that called for increased awareness of individual bias, particularly unconscious or implicit bias, as well as a corresponding examination of systems and structures.[120]

Some educators worried about whether these efforts would be sustained, and others began to experience a backlash against calls for racial justice,[121] but efforts to implement concrete steps toward change began to materialize.[122] Many law schools added a racial justice learning outcome to their law school mission.[123] In February of 2022, the ABA adopted Standard 303(c) requiring that "a law school shall provide education to law students on bias, cross cultural competency, and racism: (1) at the start of the program of legal education, and (2) at least once again before graduation."[124] Of particular importance to an externship general course design is the ABA's inclusion of the following direction at the end of 303(c): "(f)or students engaged in law clinics or field placements, the second educational occasion will take place before, concurrently with, or as part of their enrollment in clinical or field placement

---

120. *Id.*

121. Palash Ghosh, *A Year After George Floyd Killing, Fewer Americans Support Black Lives Matter Movement Poll Finds*, FORBES (May 25, 2021), https://www.forbes.com/sites/palashghosh/2021/05/25/a-year-after-george-floyd-killing-fewer-americans-support-black-lives-matter-movement-poll-finds/?sh=6a08d08053a2; Jack Dutton, *Critical Race Theory is Banned in These States*, NEWSWEEK (June 11, 2021), https://www.newsweek.com/critical-race-theory-banned-these-states-1599712.

122. *Charlottesville Removes Confederate Statues*, EQUAL JUSTICE INITIATIVE (June 13, 2021), https://eji.org/news/charlottesville-removes-confederate-statues/; Isidoro Rodriguez, *Stop Turning Your Head: Black Cops Speak Out Against 'Blanket of Racism,'* THE CRIME REPORT (Mar. 2, 2021), https://thecrimereport.org/2021/03/02/stop-turning-your-head-black-cops-speak-out-against-blanket-of-racism/.

123. Seattle University School of Law's Learning Outcome 7 is representative: "Graduates will be able to perform their lawyering tasks consistent with professional ethical requirements and with the cultural competence necessary for effective, respectful interaction with individuals from diverse backgrounds." SEATTLE UNIV. SCHOOL OF L., *Curriculum Outcomes*, https://law.seattleu.edu/academics/curriculum/outcomes (last visited Jan. 10, 2022); *see also* Tiffany Atkins, *#Fortheculture: Generation Z and the Future of Legal Education*, 26 MICH. J. RACE & L. 115, 151–55 (2020). Atkins argues for adopting learning outcomes that identify cultural competence and awareness of diversity as core features of legal education.

124. ABA STANDARDS AND RULES OF PROCEDURE FOR APPROVAL OF LAW SCHOOLS 2022–2023, STANDARD 303(c).

courses."[125] The Interpretations to Standard 303 explain that these topics should be integrated throughout the curriculum.[126]

b. Assessing Existing Curriculum and Developing Learning Outcomes

Before deciding how to teach these topics in the general externship seminar, faculty should determine how they have been covered elsewhere in the law school curriculum. For example, if students have already learned how America's legacy of racism has contributed to the systematic deprivation of the voting, economic, employment, educational, political, professional, financial, and housing opportunities for African Americans and many other non-white groups, they can build on this knowledge to more advanced skills. If this material has not been covered elsewhere, the general externship seminar should contain at least a brief orientation on this foundational knowledge.[127]

Assessing one's law school curriculum in the area of bias, racism, and cultural competence is most easily done by looking at three separate categories: knowledge,

---

125. ABA Standards and Rules of Procedure for Approval of Law Schools 2022–2023, Standard 303.

126. The Interpretations to Standard 303 state as follows:

> Interpretation 303-6
>
> With respect to 303(a)(1), the importance of cross-cultural competency to professionally responsible representation and the obligation of lawyers to promote a justice system that provides equal access and eliminates bias, discrimination, and racism in the law should be among the values and responsibilities of the legal profession to which students are introduced.
>
> Interpretation 303-7
>
> Standard 303(c)'s requirement that law schools provide education on bias, cross-cultural competency, and racism may be satisfied by, among other things, the following:
>
> (1) Orientation sessions for incoming students;
> (2) Lectures on these topics
> (3) Courses incorporating these topics; or
> (4) Other educational experiences incorporating these topics.
>
> While law schools need not add a required upper-division course to satisfy this requirement, law schools must demonstrate that all law students are required to participate in a substantial activity designed to reinforce the skill of cultural competency and their obligation as future lawyers to work to eliminate racism in the legal profession.
>
> Interpretation 303-8
>
> Standard 303 does not prescribe the form or content of the education on bias, cross-cultural competency, and racism required by Standard 303(c).

Id.

127. *See* the documentary *Who We Are: A Chronicle of Racism in America with Jeffery Robinson*, https://thewhoweareproject.org/the-film (last visited Jan. 11, 2022), for one example of a thorough overview of the history of slavery and its incorporation into American legal institutions.

skills, and values. Knowledge can include information such as: the history of slavery; its impact on legal codes and penal institutions; data on the unequal distribution of wealth, housing, access to education, medical care, and other services; and differences in cultural norms.[128] Skills encompass actions such as: responding to implicit or explicit bias as a target, perpetrator, or witness; practicing techniques to reduce bias in negotiation, litigation, and other forms of dispute resolution; seeing the world through another's eyes; and communicating effectively based on awareness of human psychology and behavior. Attitudes or values include awareness of emotions of anger, empathy, sadness, trauma, and guilt; commitment to equity; and recognition of harm.

Law schools have added curriculum on bias, racism, and cross-cultural competence in varied ways: including it in orientation, requiring it in stand-alone first year courses, or folding it into the core curriculum where relevant to the covered materials. The incorporation of bias, racism and cultural competence into many schools' institutional learning outcomes is helpful for externship faculty; the need to assess the learning outcome will likely mean that relevant curriculum has already been identified. Determining how knowledge, skills, and values on these topics are covered earlier in the curriculum also enables externship faculty to connect material in the externship seminar with curriculum previously taught. Teaching in the externship seminar reinforces this prior learning and helps students transfer the knowledge for real world application in law practice settings.[129]

As discussed in Chapter 7, the next step is to decide on the race, bias, and cultural humility learning outcomes for the seminar.[130] Examples of these types of learning outcomes could include:

- Explain the benefits of interacting with people from different cultures and perspectives;
- Assess your own knowledge and skill in cultural humility and awareness of bias (race, gender, sexual orientation, etc.) focusing on your role as a lawyer;

128. *See Hofstede Insights*, https://hofstede-insights-com/product/compare-countries/ (last visited Jan. 10, 2022), for information on a series of studies by psychologist Dr. Geer Hofstede on six dimensions of culture (Power Distance Index (high versus low); Individualism Versus Collectivism; Masculinity Versus Femininity; Uncertainty Avoidance Index (high versus low); Long-Versus Short-Term Orientation; and Indulgence Versus Restraint) expressed in different countries.

129. *See* Shaun Archer et al., *Reaching Backward and Stretching Forward: Teaching for Transfer in Law School Clinics*, 64 J. Legal Educ. 258, 258–59 (2014), for more on the concept of teaching for transfer.

130. One example of a school-wide learning outcome is Seattle University Law School's Learning Outcome adopted in 2020: graduates will be able to "[d]escribe the primary formal structures and processes of the American legal system and identify and work to eliminate the ways in which legal doctrine, institutions, and practices are beset by and complicit in racism and other forms of structural and systemic inequity." *See* https://law.seattleu.edu/academics/degree-programs/jd/learning-outcomes/ (last visited Jan. 11, 2022).

- Identify concrete skills and strategies to reduce bias and communicate across culture;
- Describe systemic strategies to reduce bias in the justice system; and
- Practice an approach that can help you explore your own biases and respond to biases when you observe them.

The externship general seminar, which covers both the law in practice and the student's individual personal and professional development, could include one learning outcome in each of the three topics and could expand to covering more advanced outcomes depending on the number of credits in the seminar and weeks in the semester.

Once the learning outcomes are determined, the externship faculty can decide which materials to include. Fortunately, the increased focus on bias in legal institutions and in legal education has led to a proliferation of materials on these topics.[131] Rather than providing an exhaustive list of resources, the following section first describes some common principles of pedagogy and then identifies some challenges to teaching these topics. The list of challenges is offered to help faculty prepare to teach the material and to build confidence in an area where every practitioner will make mistakes in order to learn and teach. The challenges should be shared with students as part of the learning process, both to remind them of the inevitability of mistakes, and to model a transparent process that builds community and encourages mutual accountability. Together, the principles and challenges serve as a guide for faculty to pick and choose among resources to ensure successful coverage of the topic.

c. Principles of Pedagogy in Teaching About Bias, Racism, and Cultural Humility

1) Addressing Bias and Racism and Practicing Cultural Humility Are Core Lawyering Skills

Gaining knowledge, skills, and values in the areas of bias, racism, and cultural humility is fundamental to the core lawyering skills of client representation and advocacy. It is also critical to professional development in a self-regulated profession concerned with the resolution of disputes within a multi-cultural and multi-ethnic society.[132] The dispersion of students at different sites, legal offices, and judicial

---

131. *See* LEXTERNWEB, *Anti Racist Teaching Materials*, https://www.lexternweb.org/anti-racism-teaching-materials (last visited Jan. 10, 2022), for the most up to date information; *see also* Margaret Reuter and Carwina Weng, *Navigating Cultural Difference* (Chapter 6), and Stacy L. Brustin and Carmia N. Caesar, *Bias in the Legal Profession* (Chapter 7), *in* LEARNING FROM PRACTICE, *supra* note 10.

132. U.S. Census data show that by the year 2043, non-Hispanic Whites will no longer be a majority in the US population. *See* https://www.census.gov/newsroom/blogs/random-samplings/2014/06/nation-to-become-a-plurality-but-some-areas-already-are.html (last visited Jan. 19, 2022).

chambers heightens the students' ability to compare and contrast how law practice depends on the "ability to see the world through other's eyes."[133] This contrast is further magnified in seminars that include remote students elsewhere in the state or throughout the United States, and in those programs that have international externships.

2) Knowledge, Skills, and Values Must Be Connected

Successful learning in these areas includes acquisition of knowledge (about history of racism, differences in culture), development of attitudes (curiosity, empathy, and respect), and building of skills (the ability to raise and address bias and racism, see the world from another's eyes, and engage in client centered lawyering). Scholars in the field of social anthropology have developed a number of frameworks that categorize how different societies around the world view relationships, communication, and the development of social norms.[134] Like medical school courses that focus on a practitioner perspective,[135] law school externship seminars are most successful when they show how attitudes, knowledge, and skills[136] are inter-connected for effective lawyering. By relating these topics to the work of students in their field placements, the general seminar shows students how to address race and bias in their work as future lawyers.[137]

3) Transformation Takes Place at Personal, Interpersonal, and Systemic Levels

Teaching students about racism, bias, and culture involves transformation on three different levels: personal (knowledge of oneself and one's own biases), inter-

133. *See* Factor Number 5 in the list of Lawyering Effectiveness Factors developed by Marjorie Shultz and Sheldon Zedeck, https://www.albanylaw.edu/media/user/faculty_scholarship/ wkshops/ Presentation_Materials/Lawyering_Effectiveness.pdf (last visited Jan. 11, 2022).

134. Geert Hofstede's country comparison, although it has been criticized, may be useful information for students in each country. *See* Geert Hofstede, http://www.geerthofstede.nl/ (last visited July 7, 2019); *see also Hofstede Insights*, *supra* note 128. Cultural differences are important to identify and respect. *See* Julia Ann Gold, *ADR Through a Cultural Lens: How Cultural Values Shape Our Disputing Processes*, 2005 J. Disp. Resol. 289 (2005).

135. *See* Cultural Competence Education for Medical Students, https://www.aamc.org/ download/54338/data (last visited Jan. 11, 2022).

136. *See* Andrea Curcio et al., *A Survey Instrument to Develop, Tailor, and Help Measure Law Student Cultural Diversity Education Learning Outcomes*, 38 Nova L. Rev. 177 (2014).

137. *See* Michelle Silverthorn, *5 Ways Law Students Can Interrupt Implicit Bias*, ABA Student Lawyer Blog (May 29, 2018), https://abaforlawstudents.com/2018/05/29/5-ways-law-students-can-interrupt-implicit-bias/; *see also* L. Song Richardson & Phillip Atiba Goff, *Implicit Racial Bias in Public Defender Triage*, 122 Yale L.J. 2626 (2013).

personal (interactions with others), and systemic (changes in the legal, economic, social, educational, and institutional framework of society).

Assessment tools such as the implicit association tests that track the test taker's positive and negative associations with race, gender, religion, weapons, weight, etc.,[138] are a good way to identify biases at the personal level. Students can also use self-assessments to develop a sense of their own cultural norms. There are a number of ways to assess student attitudes about culture. Adapting the questions from the survey instrument designed by Professor Andrea Curcio and her co-authors, Professor Gillian Dutton created an assessment that she uses to identify areas where students feel comfortable and uncomfortable; students then reflect on how they developed comfort in the first category to gain insight on how to strengthen their skills in the second. This *Advanced Cross-Cultural Communication Assessment* is available in the Appendix to this Chapter.

Finally, documents that assess and establish student goals for growth in all areas of the externship can incorporate consideration of bias, racism, and cultural humility. This allows for a holistic approach to developing a plan for the semester discussed more fully in Chapter 7. The Seattle University Law School "ABA Values & Skills Initial Student Survey" provides one example of how to do this. Gillian Dutton incorporated the Washington Race Equity and Justice Initiative Commitments[139] into the assessment students use to communicate with their supervisors and to create a "Goals Chart & Supervision Agreement" at the start of the semester. Both documents are available in the Appendix to this Chapter.

Once students can identify their own biases and cultural norms, the next level of transformation is to recognize and interrupt bias in interpersonal interactions.[140] Learning to raise observations about bias in a way that allows others to mitigate its effects rather than becoming defensive is an advanced skill. It is particularly critical to the work of lawyers who will need to be able to address bias in decision makers, opposing parties, and their own clients, not just in themselves.[141]

The third level of transformation is institutional. The externship seminar can introduce students to the use of racial justice reviews of legal institutions with the goal of reform and transformation.[142] Many nonprofits, as well as state and local govern-

138. *See* https://implicit.harvard.edu/implicit; *see also* Curcio et. al., *supra* note 136.

139. The Washington Race Equity and Justice Initiative Commitments are available at https://wareji.org/commitments/ (last visited Jan. 11, 2022).

140. *See* Silverthorn, *supra* note 137.

141. One free resource for showing students how to plan these conversations is available at Fringe Development LLC, https://info.fringepd.com/difficult-convos?utm_content=135094017&utm_medium=social&utm_source=linkedin&hss_channel=lcp-11039575 (last visited Jan. 11, 2022).

142. For an example, *see* the Washington State Race Equity & Justice Initiative Toolkit at https://justleadwa.org/learn/rejitoolkit/ (last visited Jan. 11, 2022). *See also* Bradley L. Hardy & Trevon D. Logan, *Racial Economic Inequality Amid the COVID-19 Crisis*, https://www.brookings.edu/wp-content/uploads/2020/08/EA_HardyLogan_LO_8.12.pdf (last visited Jan. 11, 2022).

ments, now apply diversity equity and inclusion (DEI) reviews to assess their client intake processes, prosecution recommendations, and other public interactions. The private sector, including law firms and companies, from small to multi-national, has followed suit.[143] Students can thus apply the skills of identifying and addressing bias on the personal, interpersonal, and systemic level in any externship site, no matter whether public or private, small or large, domestic or international.

4) Reflection Is a Key Component in Identifying and Addressing These Topics

Reflection, long a hallmark of clinical education and discussed more fully in Chapter 8, allows students to interrogate their own views as well as those of the people around them.[144] It reinforces the three levels of personal, interpersonal, and systemic development by breaking down the thought process into more manageable components and allowing students to reflect more deeply and successfully on each part. Professor Tim Casey's stages of reflection model takes the student through an analysis of a task in a similar step by step approach.[145] Casey's six stages include a (1) definition of competence, (2) awareness of difference and choice, (3) evaluation of internal factors (*e.g.*, personality), (4) external factors (*e.g.*, the law office environment), (5) societal factors (systemic issues), and finally (6) the meta level of awareness about the reflection process itself.[146] For reflecting on bias, race, and culture, the three middle levels (internal, external, and systemic) combined with the last "meta" stage reinforce the process of continual assessment, review, and growth that is key to successful learning.[147] Professor Gillian Dutton has incorporated reflection on bias, racism, and cultural humility in her externship seminars through the use of three separate reflection assignments that ask the students to consider the influence of bias in the performance of a skill, in achieving wellness and balance, and in future career development. This series of exercises is available in the Appendix to Chapter 8, as Seattle University School of Law Reflection Topics.

---

143. *See, e.g.*, https://stories.starbucks.com/stories/equity-inclusion/ (last visited Jan. 11 2022); https://www.forbes.com/sites/forbesbusinesscouncil/2020/12/01/why-your-managers-are-key-to-diversity-and-inclusion/ (last visited Jan. 11, 2022); https://www.weforum.org/agenda/ 2019/04/business-case-for-diversity-in-the-workplace/ (last visited Jan. 11, 2022).

144. *See* Alexi Nunn Freeman & Lindsey Webb, *Positive Disruption: Addressing Race in a Time of Social Change Through A Team-Taught, Reflection-Based, Outward-Looking Law School Seminar*, 21 U. Pa. J.L. & Soc. Change 121, 141–47 (2018) (discussing the use of student reflection and feedback on it in their Critical Race Reading Seminar).

145. Tim Casey's Stages of Reflection are discussed in Chapter 8.

146. *See* Monika Batra Kashyap, *Rebellious Reflection: Supporting Community Lawyering Practice*, 43 N.Y.U. Rev. L. & Soc. Change 403 (2019), for ways to tie this even more explicitly to cross-cultural competence.

147. *See* the Seattle University School of Law Reflection Topics in the Appendix to Chapter 8 for an example of how to use this process in a series of assigned reflections throughout a semester long externship.

5) Engage in Difficult Conversations and Use Appreciative Inquiry

Students who engage in self-assessment and interruption of racism and bias will need the skill of engaging in difficult conversations. The book by the same name, *Difficult Conversations: How to Discuss What Matters Most*, focuses on the elements of conversations that involve feelings and identity, not just the factual information exchanged.[148] It provides useful framing for the difference between impact and intent, and ways in which a conversation of mutual inquiry can be used to determine future changes in behavior.[149] Remaining curious, rather than judgmental, about oneself and others helps uncover hidden assumptions and discover shared values.

Another technique that can be employed effectively at both the personal and the systemic level is that of "appreciative inquiry" first developed by David Cooperrider and Ronald Fry at Case Western Reserve University in the late 1980s.[150] This strengths-based approach to problem solving seeks to solicit information on what is working and use this to stimulate further change through positive reinforcement. By "asking questions that elevate a system's cooperative capacity to apprehend strengths and positive potentials, unite around greater meanings and shared goals, and activate the kind of generative design that serves to open those systems to better and more valued possibilities,"[151] appreciative inquiry provides a technique for transformation at all three levels.

Skills must be practiced repeatedly at an individual and interpersonal level before students become comfortable employing them in a professional setting as lawyers. Introducing students to the concept of micro-messages, although there is some overlap with micro-aggressions, helps them see that these micro-messages are often more subtle and may occur as many as 2000 times a day. These messages are at the subconscious level and include things such as: whether and how one is acknowledged upon entering a room; whether one is welcomed into a conversation underway; whether one is introduced by name, with positive attribution, or not introduced at all; whether one's name is pronounced fluently, mispronounced and even forgotten; whether one is mistaken for another person from their cultural group; and whether one's opinion is solicited or not.[152] Once students have learned to be aware of these differences in everyday interaction, externship faculty can introduce them to how these issues arise in a professional setting. The 21-Day Racial

---

148. Sheila Heen, Bruce Patton, & Douglas Stone, Difficult Conversations: How to Discuss What Matters Most (2010).

149. *Id.*

150. David L. Cooperrider & Ronald Fry, *Appreciative Inquiry in a Pandemic: An Improbable Pairing*, 56(3) J. Applied Behav. Sci. 266–71 (2020). For more resources on appreciative inquiry, *see* https://weatherhead.case.edu/centers/fowler/business/appreciative-inquiry.

151. Cooperrider & Fry, *supra* note 150, at 267.

152. *See* European Institute for Gender Equality, *Gender Stereotypes and Education* (Aug. 17, 2017), https://www.youtube.com/watch?v=nrZ21nD9I-0 (last visited Jan. 11, 2022), for an interesting video of the impact of these messages in gender stereotypes.

Equity Habit-Building Challenge provides one example of how to take these skills to the professional level and gives students a choice of readings and materials to work through in their own 21-day process.[153]

Faculty should encourage students to practice the skills of curiosity, empathy, and respect in interactions with colleagues, opposing counsel, and clients.[154] This is another area where students can build on their interactions with other students or even other professors before practicing them in a legal setting. One simple example is how a student might raise an issue with a professor who is not pronouncing the student's name correctly in class. Professor Gillian Dutton uses the conversation mapping approach from the Difficult Conversations Series[155] to help students plan how they might address a microaggression, starting first by talking about shared values, then anticipating possible negative reactions, and ending with a discussion of the advantages and disadvantages of various solutions. For a script that she developed with a student who had experienced the name pronunciation problem, see the Appendix to this Chapter.

For more culturally complex situations, such as in international externships, cross-cultural awareness can include discussion of such skills as the use of cultural expert witnesses in litigation, the use of medical evaluations from culturally sensitive practitioners, and the use of mediation and other dispute resolution techniques in situations where solutions from the dominant legal culture may not be successful.

d. Explaining Bias, Racism, and Cultural Humility

1) Bias

Using the pedagogical techniques described above, externship faculty can lead students in an exploration of bias, racism, and cultural humility. This section offers information that may be helpful in those discussions. Faculty should explain that bias is both implicit and explicit and is part of the cognitive process. Recent advances in neuroscience have expanded the knowledge of psychological and cognitive development and provided new insights into human behavior relevant to the legal system.[156] Studies have shown bias to exist throughout the world; they have underscored that learning to understand our environment involves the development of schema, or organization of experiences, and that our minds associate both negative and positive characteristics with different schema in order to protect us from harm

---

153. *See* Syllabus, *21-Day Racial Equity Habit-Building Challenge*, https://www.americanbar.org/groups/labor_law/membership/equal_opportunity/ (last visited Jan. 10, 2022).

154. *See* Gold, *supra* note 134.

155. *See* Fringe Professional Development, *Difficult Conversations Series*, https://info.fringe-pd.com/difficult-convos (last visited March 13, 2022).

156. *See* Claude Steele, Whistling Vivaldi, How Stereotypes Affect Us and What We Can Do About Them (2010), for a thorough discussion of the impact of bias. *See also* Stacy L. Brustin & Carmia N. Caesar, *Bias in the Legal Profession* (Chapter 7), *in* Learning From Practice, *supra* note 10.

so that we may survive.[157] Bias is thus a natural part of cognitive development, and all human beings have it. When societies develop false characterizations around race, gender, or sexual orientation, these biases have negative consequences for justice and the legal system as an institution. Because each new experience is interpreted through the lens of prior interactions, new biases are constantly being generated, and reaffirmed. Students must learn that working to reduce bias is a lifelong skill.

Bias exists in many different forms (gender, religion, disability, age, nationality, etc.) and can be experienced by anyone who is external to another group. However, bias does not have the same impact on all individuals and is different from the racism that is built into the legal system at all levels.[158] Teachers can help students understand these differences by using tools that show areas in which they are privileged and areas in which they are marginalized.[159]

The concept of intersectionality helps students see that individuals who are members of more than one marginalized group (for example, women of color) experience increased bias and discrimination.[160] This concept also encourages students to develop empathy as they explore the different perspectives of individuals in marginalized groups and connect with their own experiences of emotion. Social worker and educator Brene Brown describes the four qualities necessary to express empathy: recognizing the perspective of another person as their truth, not judging that perspective, recognizing emotion in other people, and communicating that recognition.[161]

Every student will experience different treatment at one point or another in their lives. Enabling them to draw on that experience increases the connections that they feel with others and can be done while still acknowledging that these marginalized identities are not all equivalent and that their experience is not the same as those individuals who experience marginalization in multiple identities. Professor Gillian Dutton has adopted an approach from the Southern Poverty Law Center *Just Speak Up* Series that allows participants to break down the impact of bias and prepare to discuss it. She has used this exercise for over ten years with students, judges, parents

---

157. Jerry Kang et al., *Implicit Bias in the Courtroom*, 59 UCLA L. Rev. 1124 (2012).

158. *See* Michele Alexander, The New Jim Crow: Mass Incarceration in the Age of Colorblindness (2010), for a description of how racism has affected the criminal justice system. *See also* Tryon P. Woods, *The Implicit Bias of the Implicit Bias Theory*, 10 Drexel L. Rev. 631 (2018).

159. One example of a tool like this is the Social Identity Worksheet that is part of the National Museum of African American History and Culture Resources on Social Identities and Systems of Oppression, which is available at https://timeandplace.ubc.ca/files/2014/06/Appendix-2.pdf (last visited Jan. 11, 2022).

160. For a discussion of intersectionality, *see* Kimberle Crenshaw, *"What is Intersectionality?"* available at https://www.youtube.com/watch?v=-DW4HLgYPlA (last visited Jan. 11, 2022).

161. *See Brene Brown on Empathy*, (Dec. 10, 2013), https://www.youtube.com/ watch?v=1Evwgu-369Jw (last visited Jan. 11, 2022).

of refugees, public interest lawyers, and students. This "Exercise Reflecting on Impact of Bias" is available in the Appendix to this Chapter.

2) Racism

Race is just one of the ways in which human beings differ. It is a social construct, and research has found that genetic differences between members of the same race can be greater than those between individuals from two different races.[162] Nonetheless, while human beings of different races do not differ from one another in a biologically important way, racial differences have huge implications for human beings, as they affect the way different groups are treated by society.

Racism is the expression of bias connected to the power of the state and its institutions to award benefits to one group and exclude other groups from those benefits. The ABA,[163] many states' minority and justice commissions,[164] and other institutions such as the National Center for State Courts[165] have published guidelines and studies documenting the impact of racism in every aspect of the legal system.

Being anti-racist requires action. The skill of actively fighting racism requires the ability to listen with empathy, to communicate, and to advocate for transformation at the personal, interpersonal, and systemic level. Given the particular role of lawyers in society, believing that equity will prevail in a multicultural society and get better with time, or simply observing without taking action is, in the end, to be complicit.[166] Similar to their role in teaching the skills of cultural awareness, faculty covering racism in the externship seminar must teach students to apply their skills as part of their work at their sites. In addition to using the resources provided in this section, faculty can also look to public interest organizations such as the Southern

---

162. Alan Goodman, *Race Is Real but It's Not Genetic*, DISCOVER (Jun. 25, 2020), https://www.discovermagazine.com/planet-earth/race-is-real-but-its-not-genetic.

163. ABA resources on Racial Equity in the Justice System are available at https://www.americanbar.org/advocacy/justice-system/ (last visited Jan. 11, 2022).

164. *See* WASHINGTON COURTS GENDER AND JUSTICE COMMISSION, 2021: HOW GENDER AND RACE AFFECT JUSTICE, https://www.americanbar.org/advocacy/justice-system (last visited Sept. 15, 2022); *see also* SANTA CRUZ COUNTY COMMISSION ON JUSTICE AND GENDER, https://www.co.santa-cruz.ca.us/Government/Commissions/Committees/AdvisoryBodies/CommissionJusticeandGender.aspx (last visited Jan. 14, 2022); OR. JUST. RES. CTR., *Women's Justice Project*, https://ojrc.info/womens-justice-project (last visited Jan. 14, 2022).

165. NATIONAL CENTER FOR STATE COURTS, *Helping Courts Address Implicit Bias*, http://www.ncsc.org/~/media/Files/PDF/Topics/Gender%20and%20Racial%20Fairness/IB_report_033012.ashx (last visited Jan. 10, 2022).

166. This idea is not new. Pastor Martin Niemoller's famous statement highlighting the perils and inevitable consequences of letting injustice happen to others without intervention showed that an altruistic act is often one of self-preservation. HOLOCAUST MEMORIAL DAY TRUST, Pastor Martin Niemoller, *First They Came*, https://www.hmd.org.uk/resource/first-they-came-by-pastor-martin-niemoller/ (last visited Jan. 10, 2022).

Poverty Law Center[167] for exercises to help students respond to microaggressions and other expressions of bias.

3) Cultural Humility

Cultural humility includes awareness of differences between cultures (using an expansive definition of culture) and respect for and curiosity about those differences. The term is preferable to cultural competence because it avoids the concept that one can become "competent" in a culture and substitutes the notion of humility as a way to address the history and legacy of one culture's dominance over others.[168] Humility also includes the warning not to become complacent or assume one is immune to bias; students, as future lawyers, will need to continue learning throughout their professional lives. Other terms that are useful to emphasize these concepts are "cross-cultural awareness" and "cultural sensitivity."[169]

Teaching about cross-cultural communication allows students to understand the many ways in which differences in ability, religion, culture, gender, sexual orientation, and education, in addition to race, have led to different treatment. Cross-cultural awareness is one of the core skills of a lawyer, often described as the ability to see the world through another's eyes.[170] Lawyers' professional organizations such as the ABA have also recognized cross-cultural awareness as one of the crucial lawyering skills,[171] and many law schools now include it in their learning outcomes.[172]

---

167. *See* Southern Poverty Law Center, *Learning for Justice* (formerly Teaching Tolerance), materials available at https://www.splcenter.org/learning-for-justice (last visited Jan. 11, 2022).

168. *See* Psych Hub, *What Is Cultural Humility?* (Oct. 5, 2020), https://www.youtube.com/watch?v=cwOnJJEfxE (last visited Jan. 11, 2022), for a helpful resource to explain the difference to students.

169. Carole Silver, *Getting Real About Globalization and Legal Education: Potential and Perspectives for the U.S.*, 24 Stan. L. & Pol'y Rev. 457, 460 (2013) ("Put another way, inter-cultural competency can be understood as involving three elements: cognitive, which 'refers to possessing knowledge about cultural norms, values, behaviors and issues'; affective, which 'relates to the flexibility to adapt to new situations and open-mindedness to encounter new values'; and behavioral, which includes 'resourcefulness, problem-solving skills and culturally appropriate people skills.'") (footnotes omitted).

170. Susan Bryant and Jean Koh Peters are the authors of a rich source of books and articles on cultural competence. Susan Bryant, *The Five Habits: Building Cross-Cultural Competence in Lawyers*, 8 Clinical L. Rev. 33 (2001). *See also* Jeff Blumberg, *Sitting by the Well: The Case for Intercultural Competency Training in International Experiential Learning*, 43 U. Balt. L. Rev. 395 (2014); Mary A. Lynch, *The Importance of Experiential Learning for Development of Essential Skills in Cross-Cultural and Intercultural Effectiveness*, 1 Touro J. Experiential Learning 129 (2014–15); Margaret Reuter & Carwina Weng, *Navigating Cultural Difference* (Chapter 6), *in* Learning From Practice, *supra* note 10.

171. Aastha Madaan, *Cultural Competency and the Practice of Law in the 21st Century*, ABA Probate & Property Mag. (March 2017), https://www.americanbar.org/groups/real_property_trust_estate/publications/probate-property-magazine/2016/march_april_2016/2016_aba_rpte_pp_v30_2_article_madaan_cultural_competency_and_the_practice_of_law_in_the_21st_century/ (last visited Jan. 11, 2022).

172. As one example, a Seattle University Law School Learning Outcome states "[g]raduates will be able to perform their lawyering tasks consistent with professional ethical requirements and with

Despite this focus, relatively few law schools teach these topics as an actual course, underscoring the need for inclusion of the topic in the externship general seminar.[173]

Perhaps the least appreciated aspect of cross-cultural awareness is the fact that acquiring knowledge of other cultures leads to increased creativity and innovation.[174] This happens through a process known as recombination, in which ideas and approaches from one culture are modified and adapted for use in another.[175] This process, and the knowledge of how other cultures solve legal problems, provides future lawyers with an increased range of legal problem-solving skills. For all students who are at placements with diverse judges, clients, co-counsel, and opposing counsel, learning about cross-cultural communication is a critical skill.

e. Challenges of Teaching about Bias, Racism, and Cultural Humility

Long standing challenges in teaching about bias, racism, and cultural humility have been impacted by the Black Lives Matter movement in both positive and negative ways. The movement has increased awareness of the experience of Black people throughout the United States and throughout the globe, resulting in greater understanding for those with privilege who do not experience the same reality as BIPOC individuals. It has also focused attention on the issue of racism in a way that is leading to gradual change in some areas.[176] On the other hand, ongoing oppression of BIPOC communities after heightened attention to the problem has led to increased

---

the cultural competence necessary for effective, respectful interaction with individuals from diverse backgrounds." SEATTLE UNIV. SCH. L., https://law.seattle.edu/academics/degree-programs/jd/learning-outcomes (last visited March 13, 2022). For other examples, *see* UNIV. OF WASH., https://www.law.uw.edu/academics/jd/curriculum/student-learning-outcomes (last visited Jan. 11, 2022), and SOUTHWESTERN UNIV., Learning Outcomes, https://www.swlaw.edu/ curriculum/learning-outcomes (last visited Jan. 11, 2021).

173. UCLA offers a course. *See* https://www.uclalawreview.org/pdf/discourse/62-7.pdf (last visited Sept. 15, 2022). *See also* Serena Patel, *Cultural Competency Training: Preparing Law Students for Practice in our Multicultural World*, 62 UCLA L. REV. DISC. 140 (2014) (discussing the need for cultural competence training courses in law school); Andrew King-Ries, *Just What the Doctor Ordered: The Need for Cross-Cultural Education in Law School*, 5 TENN. J. L. & POL'Y 27 (2009); Cynthia M. Ward & Nelson J. Miller, *The Role of Law Schools in Shaping Culturally Competent Lawyers*, MICH. BAR J. (Sept. 2011).

174. *See* Dutton, *supra* note 99, at 24–26 for a discussion of this benefit.

175. Angela Ka-yee Leung et al., *Multicultural Experience Enhances Creativity: The When and How*, 63 AMERICAN PSYCH. 169–81 (2008). *See also* Adam D. Galinsky, William Maddux, & Carmit T. Tadmor, *Getting the Most Out of Living Abroad: Biculturalism and Integrative Complexity as Key Drivers of Professional and Creative Success*, 103 J. PERSONALITY & SOC. PSYCHO. 520–42 (2012).

176. Enoka Herat & Mina Barhimi Martin, *Police Killings Are Down 62% in 2021, and Policing Legislation Is a Key Driver of the Decline*, ACLU WASH. (Dec. 15, 2021), https://www.aclu-wa.org/story/police-killings-are-down-62-2021-and-policing-legislation-key-driver-decline.

anger, resentment, and frustration.[177] This pent-up emotion can be exhausting for those most impacted and can lead to a backlash in those who feel responsible.[178] This section covers these challenges and advocates for describing them at the start of the seminar; in this way, faculty can build empathy and resilience in both students of color and in white students.

Students will have a wide range of awareness about these topics and will be at different places along their personal journey of transformation, varying from ignorance or even rejection of the concepts of bias and racism all the way to sophisticated understanding and deep commitment to change. Students who have been the targets of racism and other kinds of discrimination will have a range of responses to the topic, including anger, weariness, and a feeling of lack of psychological and physical safety.[179] For individuals who have borne the effects of racism and discrimination all their lives, trauma can include not just their own trauma but that of previous generations. To help students see themselves as survivors rather than victims, successful teaching about racism should include the skills of trauma-informed lawyering.[180]

Students with privilege may have responses that include defensiveness,[181] guilt, and ignorance[182] when exposed to the idea that racism has benefitted those with privilege even if they have not personally participated in exploitation of others due to their race. A helpful concept in addressing these feelings is described as the compass of shame based on the work of psychologist Donald Nathanson, who examined human responses to shame and found that they could be categorized as "attack other," in which individuals blame others for their actions; "attack self," in which individuals blame themselves; "avoidance," in which individuals ignore the feeling or make light of it; and "withdrawal," in which individuals refuse to interact with

177. Clarity Clinic, *The Impact of Racism on Mental Health* (Dec. 8, 2021), https://www.claritychi.com/the-impact-of-racism-on-mental-health/.

178. *See* Safia Samee Ali & Associated Press, *Florida Board of Education Passes Rule Banning Critical Race Theory in Classrooms*, NBC (June 10, 2021), https://www.nbcnews.com/news/us-news/florida-board-education-passes-rule-banning-critical-race-theory-classrooms-n1270363 (last visited March 23, 2022).

179. Ali Vingiano, *63 Black Harvard Students Share Their Experiences in a Powerful Photo Project*, BuzzFeed News (March 3, 2014), https://www.buzzfeednews.com/article/alisonvingiano/21-black-harvard-students-share-their-experiences-through-a (last visited March 23, 2022); Sean Darling-Hammond & Kristen Holmquist, *Creating Wise Classrooms to Empower Diverse Law Students: Lessons in Pedagogy from Transformative Law Professors*, 25 Berkeley La Raza L.J. 1 (2015); Doggett, *supra* note 92; Wong, *supra* note 92.

180. A helpful resource for students on this topic is LegalEdWeb, Jessica Den Houter, *Trauma Informed Lawyering* (Sept. 1, 2020), https://www.youtube.com/watch?v=_t5lpeIwOLE (last visited March 23, 2022).

181. *See* Robin DiAngelo, White Fragility (2018), for a full discussion of the defensiveness that many white people exhibit when grappling with the benefits they have received from a system that affords them privileges not available to people of color.

182. *See* Peggy McIntosh, *White Privilege: Unpacking the Invisible Knapsack* (July/Aug. 1989), https://psychology.umbc.edu/files/2016/10/White-Privilege_McIntosh-1989.pdf.

others.[183] Teaching students to identify their own individual responses to shame in challenging conversations around race and bias can help them move from personal to professional discussions of race and culture. It can also help them see the ways in which dismantling systems of oppression has benefits for all within a society.

Creating a climate in which discussions of race and other biases can occur requires establishing a climate of trust and the ability to be vulnerable. Many educators will be familiar with mistakes that can occur when this is not done: students who are frustrated when a professor fails to notice a micro-aggression; students who speak up and don't feel supported; and students who have made mistakes unintentionally and then feel attacked, leading to withdrawal rather than increased awareness. Educating oneself about how to manage these interactions at the beginning is crucial to a successful seminar on the topics of bias, racism, and cultural humility. According to Professor Erin C. Lain, "studies show that faculty who demonstrate attunement, authenticity, and power-sharing generate the most effective class dialogues about race."[184] Developing ground rules (such as using "ouch" when someone has said something that might be hurtful, or "oops" when one recognizes one has made a mistake) and building a sense of community, before these conversations take place, are essential to a successful seminar. Many faculty invite students to generate these rules as part of the class. During introductions where students give their names and pronouns, Professor Gillian Dutton invites her students to "think of a time you realized you made a mistake or said something that reflected an unwanted bias," and then asks, "What agreements would you have liked to have in place? How would you define what it is to be a good ally?" She then uses student responses to these questions in class to add other useful agreements to create a safe learning environment, such as not sharing details about who says what in class, even if the general topic is discussed.

Educators must prepare themselves and their students to be uncomfortable, to make mistakes, and to know how to apologize when they make mistakes that harm others, even if unintentional.[185] This discomfort can be tied to learning theory which

---

183. INT'L INSTITUTE RESTORATIVE PRACS., *Restorative Practices and Discipline Chapter 2*, https://www.iirp.edu/images/pdf/Affect_and_Compass_of_Shame.pdf (last visited Jan. 8, 2021).

184. *See* Erin C. Lain, *Racialized Interactions in the Law School Classroom: Pedagogical Approaches to Creating a Safe Learning Environment*, 67 J. LEGAL EDUC. 780, 792 (2018) (citations omitted).

185. Sam Dylan Finch, *9 Phrases Allies Can Say When Called Out Instead of Getting Defensive*, EVERYDAY FEMINISM (May 29, 2017), https://everydayfeminism.com/2017/05/allies-say-this-instead-defensive/ (last visited March 23, 2022). Interestingly enough, another resource used often to illustrate seeing the world through another's eyes also demonstrates that each of us has blind spots. Chimamanda Adichie's Ted Talk, *The Danger of a Single Story*, https://www.ted.com/talks/chimamanda_adichie_the_danger_of_a_single_story/transcript?language=en, is widely used to demonstrate how easy it is to be influenced by biased media portrayals (using her own experience of visiting Mexico after living in the United States). Chimamanda Adichie was later criticized for both remarks she made about the trans community and her inability to convince members of that community that her apology was sincere. Emily Crockett, *The Controversy Over Chimamanda Ngozi Adichie and*

describes three zones of awareness and learning: the comfort zone, the stretch zone, and the panic zone.[186] This concept is expressed as a circle with a set of three concentric rings: the comfort zone at the center, the stretch or learning zone just outside it, and the panic zone as the outermost ring. German educator Tom Senniger attempted to distinguish between the stretch zone, where we move away from the familiar and can take some risks to learn, and the panic zone, where learning is blocked by a sense of fear and possible triggers of painful traumatic memories, resulting in a search for protection and safety rather than a focus on learning.[187]

Another underappreciated approach to the challenges of teaching about bias, racism, and cultural humility can be found in the concept of restorative justice.[188] The process of truth, justice, and reconciliation provides a path to possible transformation because those who have been harmed are able to tell their stories and feel that they are truly heard. The transformative justice approach seeks to have all parties participate (target, witnesses, and perpetrators) in the healing process. This acknowledges the harm and emphasizes commemorating the survival of those harmed, providing appropriate reparations, and avoiding repetition of future harm, rather than simply punishing the perpetrators and witnesses who have failed to act. This framework is especially promising for the issues of racism and bias, since it provides a path toward reconciliation and collaboration for future action.

6. Social Justice

Many externship courses include some teaching about the role of social justice in the practice of law, and some incorporate it as a unifying theme for the course. Schools and externship programs focus on these topics for a range of reasons. Some law schools have a public interest focus or mission, and including social justice concepts in experiential and other courses is a way of furthering that mission. Other externship programs are part of clinics that focus on public interest topics and

---

Trans Women, Explained, Vox (Mar. 15, 2017), https://www.vox.com/identities/ 2017/3/15/14910900/chimamanda-ngozi-adichie-transgender-women-comments-apology.

186. The "Learning Zone Model" was developed by Tom Senninger, a German educator and adventurer, based on the Lev Vygotsky Zone of Proximal Development. *See* Moments of Freedom, *Learning Zone Model*, https://www.momentsoffreedom.org/learning-zone-model (last visited Jan. 8, 2022).

187. *Id.*

188. Some examples of truth, justice, and reconciliation approaches to racism in the United States are the Maryland Lynching Truth & Reconciliation Commission, https://msa.maryland.gov/lynching-truth-reconciliation/ (last visited March 13, 2022); the Maine Wabanaki State Child Welfare Truth and Reconciliation Commission, https://www.mainewabanakireach.org/maine_wabanaki_state_child_welfare_truth_and_reconciliation_commission (last visited March 13, 2022); and the Greensboro Truth & Reconciliation Commission, https://greensborotrc.org (last visited March 13, 2022). *See also* Truth, Justice & Reconciliation Commission (tjrc.org) (last visited March 1, 2022) for a short video that gives students the power of this concept.

cases. Regardless of mission, helping students understand the inequalities in the legal system, the need for lawyers to help address those issues, and the satisfaction that comes from giving back are important topics in legal education. In fact, experts in legal education have stated that "it is a best practice for law schools to assure that every student learns the integral nature of social justice to the practice of law...."[189] Externship courses provide excellent opportunities for students to study and reflect on this important topic.

While "social justice" has become a popular term in the law and other contexts, there is no one accepted definition. Professor Deborah Archer, a longtime clinical professor and social justice advocate, has described social justice as "the recognition of marginalized groups in society and the empowerment of those groups to decrease power disparities."[190] Professor William Quigley, a leading law school clinical educator, defines social justice as "the commitment to act with and on behalf of those who are suffering because of social neglect, social decisions or social structures and institutions."[191] Helping students come to their own understanding of social justice and how it relates to their externship, the legal system, and their future work as a lawyer can be impactful topics for externship classes.

One of the challenges of including social justice concepts in an externship seminar is figuring out how to break down the concepts into smaller topics suitable for class sessions. The following section provides a few examples aimed at a general externship class, where student externship sites may range from judicial chambers to criminal defense and prosecution to law firms. Note that no discussion of social justice issues is complete without the inclusion of the role of structural racism, racial discrimination, and other race-based inequities in society and in the justice system, which was discussed earlier in this Chapter.

A great topic to begin a discussion of social justice concepts as they relate to the work of lawyers is the justice gap. This term is generally used to measure the difference between the need for civil legal services by low-income people and the legal resources available to them.[192] A recent national survey revealed that low-income people in the United States do not get any or enough legal help for 92% of their substantial civil legal problems.[193] These legal issues often involve crucial needs, including housing, health care, income maintenance, education, and child custody. Law students often incorrectly assume that free legal services are as available in civil cases

189. Building on Best Practices, *supra* note 59, at 360.

190. Deborah N. Archer, *Open to Justice: The Importance of Student Selection Decisions in Law School Clinics*, 24 Clinical L. Rev. 1, n. 1 (2017).

191. William P. Quigley, *Letter to a Law Student Interested in Social Justice*, 1 DePaul J. Soc. Just. 7, 13–14 (2007).

192. Legal Services Corporation, *The Justice Gap: The Unmet Civil Legal Needs of Low-Income Americans* (April 2022), https://lsc-live.app.box.com/s/xl2v2uraiotbbzrhuwtjlgi0emp3myz1 (last visited Sept. 15, 2022).

193. *Id.*

as they are in criminal cases. Helping them understand that there is currently no federal constitutional right to counsel in civil cases involving basic human needs,[194] as there is in most criminal cases,[195] is a good way to sharpen their focus on these issues. This understanding can lead to good class discussions on the inadequacy of funding for civil legal services for low-income people,[196] the special challenges for rural populations caused by a concentration of lawyers in urban areas,[197] and whether there should be legislation to create a right to counsel in civil cases where basic human needs are at stake.[198]

A discussion of the justice gap can naturally lead to consideration of what happens when people try to represent themselves. Many externships provide opportunities for students to observe court proceedings, and pro se parties appear in many of these courtrooms. Faculty may want to assign all students to observe proceedings involving pro se parties and discuss those observations in class or reflect on them in their journals. Those reflections can include the perspective of their externship site—judicial chambers, prosecutors' offices, legal aid offices, law firms, and others. Faculty also might want to engage students in a discussion of the role that rules against the unauthorized practice of law play in the justice gap. Students may want to consider the motivations for the prohibition[199] and whether the rules should be relaxed in certain circumstances.[200]

The criminal justice system is another place where student observations can inform class discussions of social justice issues. In many criminal courts, the majority of the defendants are BIPOC.[201] Student observations and presentations of statistics about the racial composition of criminal defendants are a good starting place for discussions about racial disparities in prosecutions, policing, and sentencing. Students

---

194. *See Lassiter v. Dept. of Social Services*, 452 U.S. 18 (1981).

195. *See Gideon v. Wainwright*, 372 U.S. 335 (1963).

196. *See The Justice Gap*, *supra* note 193; Alan Houseman, *The Justice Gap: Civil Legal Assistance Today and Tomorrow*, (June 2011), https://www.americanprogress.org/ issues/courts/reports/2011/06/22/9824/the-justice-gap/.

197. *See* Danielle M. Conway, Hannah Haksgaard, Amanda Kool, Lisa Pruit, Lauren Sudeall, & Michele Statz, *Legal Deserts: A Multi-State Perspective on Rural Access to Justice*, 12 Harv. L. & Pol'y Rev. 15 (2018); Robin Runge, *Addressing the Access to Justice Crisis in Rural America*, 40 ABA Hum. Rts. Mag. No. 3 (July 1, 2014), https://www.americanbar.org/groups/crsj/ publications/human_rights_magazine_home/2014_vol_40/vol_40_no_3_poverty/access_justice_rural_america/.

198. *See* National Coalition for a Civil Right to Counsel, http://civilrighttocounsel.org/; ABA Resolution on Civil Right to Counsel (2006), https://www.americanbar.org/content/dam/ aba/administrative/legal_aid_indigent_defendants/ls_sclaid_06A112A.authcheckdam.pdf.

199. *See* Deborah L. Rhode & Lucy Ricca, *Unauthorized Practice Enforcement: Protection of the Public or the Profession*, 82 Fordham L. Rev. 2587 (2014).

200. *See* Richard Zorza & David Udell, *New Roles for Non-Lawyers to Increase Access to Justice*, 41 Fordham Urb. L.J. 1259 (2014).

201. *See* The Sentencing Project, *Report to the United Nations on Racial Disparities in the U.S. Criminal Justice System* (April 19, 2018), https://www.sentencingproject.org/publications/un-report-on-racial-disparities/.

can also discuss the topics from the point of view of their various externship sites, including prosecutor offices, public defenders, and judicial chambers.

Another avenue for approaching social justice topics is discussing the role of pro bono representation.[202] Law firm and corporate pro bono work is one answer to helping to close the justice gap. Some externs in law firms work exclusively on pro bono cases, so this is a good chance for them to bring their experiences back to the classroom. This topic also allows students to explore the benefits of giving back and the value that corporations and law firms see in doing the work. Faculty might also want to expose students to some criticism of pro bono work. While firms have altruistic reasons for engaging in pro bono work, they also are motivated by factors including associate recruitment, training and retention, public relations, and law firm rankings that include pro bono.[203] Firms may prefer high-profile or short-term cases over cases that address the most acute needs of the client population.[204] In addition, law firm lawyers may disappear from pro bono cases when their paying work is pressing, and public interest agencies invest significant time training and mentoring young law firm lawyers on cases that the agencies could have handled more efficiently without the pro bono lawyers.[205]

Interest in corporate social responsibility, which impacts a variety of social justice issues, is growing in many corporations.[206] Understanding these efforts is helpful for many law students, especially those working as externs in corporate legal departments or as externs in law firms serving corporate clients. Similar to the classroom exploration of pro bono work, it may be helpful to examine both altruistic and other motivations for corporate social responsibility efforts.

Social justice issues are often in the headlines, and discussing current cases or issues is another way to help students understand them. Faculty can also develop hypotheticals and role plays around high profile cases or issues. For example, the faculty could design a role play exercise based on sexual harassment allegations at a large corporation. Students could play the role of in-house lawyers from the corporation, the law firm representing the corporation, the EEOC, a non-profit legal office representing the workers, and the union at the worksite. Students could start with one role and then change to another to see the issues from different perspectives.

---

202. *See* Scott L. Cummings, *The Politics of Pro Bono*, 52 UCLA L. Rev. 1 (2004).

203. *See* Leonore F. Carpenter, *"We're Not Running a Charity Here": Rethinking Public Interest Lawyers' Relationships with Bottom-Line-Driven Pro Bono Programs*, 29 Buff. Pub. Int. L.J. 37, 38 (2010–2011); Scott L. Cummings & Deborah L. Rhode, *Managing Pro Bono: Doing Well by Doing Better*, 78 Fordham L. Rev. 2357, 2371–72 (2010).

204. Carpenter, *supra* note 204, at 39.

205. *See id.*

206. *See* Rebecca M. Henderson, *More and More CEOs Are Taking Their Social Responsibility Seriously,* Harv. Bus. Rev. (Feb. 12, 2018), https://hbr.org/2018/02/more-and-more-ceos-are-taking-their-social-responsibility-seriously.

Such an exercise also allows them to reflect on the role of lawyers in these disputes and consider the kind of role that is most appealing to them.

7. Time Management

Externships often present students with time pressures that they may not have experienced in law school outside of a clinical course or program. Students may struggle with managing the work assigned by their externship site and their schoolwork, classes, and co-curricular activities. Because externship work involves real clients with real legal problems, time may be of the essence. While students "bemoan the pressures of law school," the "time restraints of legal education are minimal compared to life in practice. The time famine problems that start in law school continue to plague attorneys throughout their career."[207] An externship allows students to see this time struggle firsthand and often leaves students wondering how to begin a legal career that allows for greater control of time both for their well-being and to allow for opportunities to engage in pro bono work and avoid malpractice claims.[208]

Externship supervisors may provide good models for how to integrate work and life priorities or they may provide cautionary tales as to how work can take ahold of life priorities. In either instance, the externship seminar can be a good forum for focusing students on how to integrate their work and professional life in a way that will lead to a meaningful and fulfilling professional career. Exercises and TED Talks can focus students on time management and values priorities.[209] For these reasons, it is helpful to devote a class session or a portion of an orientation class to this topic.

Professor Camille Lamar Campbell identifies two aspects of time management: "(1) stress management and (2) project management. Stress management acknowledges the psychological obstacles that preclude effective time management. Project management requires students to realistically assess their time and then devise a strategy for maximizing time."[210] Professor Christine Bartholomew sets forth a more nuanced approach that groups time management into "subscales," which are "related aptitudes that can be broken down and quantified."[211] Though psychologists disagree on the total number of subscales, the bulk of the research suggests there are nine separate subscales: "Sense of Purpose, Structured Routine, Present Orientation, Effective Organization, Persistence, Setting Goals and Priorities, Mechanics, Perceived

207. Christine P. Bartholomew, *Time: An Empirical Analysis of Law Student Time Management Deficiencies*, 81 U. Cin. L. Rev. 897, 909 (2013).

208. *Id.* at 912 ("The problems of time famine go beyond harm to the attorneys themselves. Time is the most cited justification for attorneys failing to take pro bono cases. Poor time management is also one of the primary causes of malpractice. Hence, the harm is spreading from practitioners to the community needing the services.")

209. *See generally* Floyd & Kerew, *supra* note 36.

210. Camille Lamar Campbell, *Timing Is Everything: Teaching Essential Time Management Skills for "Real-World" Legal Writing*, 22 Perspectives: Teaching L. Res. & Writing 125 (2014).

211. Bartholomew, *supra* note 208, at 918.

Control of Time,[212] and Preference for Organization."[213] Professor Bartholomew suggests time management instruction should "fall into three categories: teaching students to break down tasks, teaching time allocation skills, and teaching techniques to implement those allocations."[214]

Many externship programs require students to set learning goals at the beginning of an externship. As part of that goal-setting exercise, an externship teacher could focus on teaching time management by having students set both short term and long-term goals. As part of that exercise, students can identify concrete tasks[215] or assignments that can facilitate the student meeting those goals and can "formulate a plan for allocating time to complete those tasks."[216]

In addition to goal setting, many externship seminar courses require that students track their time using time sheets.[217] Depending on the method and reasons for requiring time sheets, students can learn several lessons about time management in tracking their externship hours. In the most basic sense, students can reflect on the tasks they performed and the amount of time they spent on each task.[218] They can also gain a cumulative sense of where they are in achieving the requisite externship hours needed per credit. Another way to teach time management is through the use of reflective exercises and discussion. For example, before, during, or after class, or after completing research and writing assignments for their externship placements,[219] students could be asked to complete a time management quiz to assess their current time management practices. Students could be asked to answer open-ended questions that prompt them to "critically evaluate their performance in areas such as scheduling, prioritization, managing interruptions, and procrastina-

---

212. "Perceived Control may be the most important of all the subscales, so at least some substantive aspect of time management training needs to focus on helping students control time. Perceived Control measures an individual's subjective view of whether there is sufficient time to meet a deadline." *Id.*

213. *Id.* at 916.

214. *Id.* at 941.

215. "Generating tasks requires students to convert goals into concrete tasks. While a goal is abstract, a task is more a 'to do' list item that ensures the goal is achievable." *Id.* at 945.

216. *See* Chapter 8 for an additional discussion of setting goals.

217. Time can be tracked using cloud-based client management programs such as CLIO or Toggl. Some externship programs also require the site supervisors to sign off on the time sheets. A supervisor signature can facilitate discussion with the site supervisor regarding the student's time management practices.

218. "Generally, students will under-record the hours they spent on a project because they think they have spent too much time on it due to their inexperience. A professor should emphasize the importance of accuracy when it comes to timesheet recordation to these students. Students are not experienced lawyers, so it is expected that the time they spend on a given assignment would be greater than that of an experienced lawyer." Marie A. Monahan, *Towards a Theory of Assimilating Law Students into the Culture of the Legal Profession*, 51 CATH. U.L. REV. 215, 239 (2001).

219. In addition to time management themes explored during the externship seminar, it might be helpful to introduce students to or require them to draft a written time management plan that focuses on the following "three steps: (1) compute the net completion time, (2) identify intermediate tasks, and (3) prioritize intermediate tasks." *Id.*

tion."[220] In addition, "a cognitive protocol question might ask students to circle the time management quote that best summarizes their experiences."[221] Another idea would be to "ask students to identify two things they would change about their time management process, time management techniques that they found particularly effective, and the total number of hours that they spent revising, editing, and drafting a particular assignment."[222] The externship teacher could then facilitate a group discussion regarding the themes revealed in the reflections.[223]

Once students have reflected on their time management, they can identify ways to implement proposed solutions to their challenges. TED Talks and other assignments designed to facilitate self-assessment of time management challenges can help students develop solutions. Time famine and work-life balance are two other topics an externship teacher might want to explore with students. "[L]awyers identify time famine as a 'significant cause' of the diminishing quality of lawyers' health and lives."[224]

8. Networking and Business Development

An externship is a valuable opportunity to build a professional network; an opportunity that can be overlooked by students. In part, students do not make the most of the opportunity because they enter their first externship experience with a narrow view of what networking is and how they can develop their networks while at their externships. Prior to beginning an externship, students most likely have had an introduction to networking through programming and networking events provided by the law school's career services office. As a result, students may have preconceived notions of the purpose of networking, the utility of networking, and how they feel about it. They may decide that they are not good at networking, that it is uncomfortable, or that they cannot network effectively because they are introverts. Others may find networking enjoyable. Rarely do students see the value of networking beyond their job search. Another reason students do not make the most of networking at their externship is that they do not know where to begin.

The externship seminar is a helpful place for students to expand their understanding of networking purposes and strategies and to see their externship as a valuable networking opportunity. An intentional exploration of networking theory in the externship seminar can give students a theoretical framework that answers the "why?" of networking. The seminar need not teach networking theory in order to be

220. *Id.*
221. *Id.*
222. *Id.*
223. *Id.*
224. *Id.* at 912.

effective. However, the concepts underlying the theory can be explained: to "connect people to others, move in more than one community or social circle, and develop meaningful relationships that provide mutual benefit."[225]

Students focused on networking to get a job do not always see the necessity of networking as a means to develop their professional future. No matter their interest, students should understand that networking has many different functions. As Professor Avis Sanders describes in Chapter 26 of *Learning From Practice*, "[c]reating a legal network can help [students] feel a part of a larger community and give meaning to [their] work. It can help [students] become a more effective attorney as [they] have access to information and assistance. It can build [their] social network to give [them] a fuller life outside of work, and, perhaps most importantly, it can make [their] work more enjoyable." In addition, networking can facilitate student exploration of different practice areas through informational interviews and can be a source of advice on getting through law school, what classes to take to further their career goals, and how to prepare for the bar exam. Networking can facilitate connections that provide opportunities to participate in professional development programs or pro bono, nonprofit boards, and other community service. Using an exercise to determine a student's current network is a helpful place to begin. Students may not realize the extent of their existing networks and areas where their networks could grow. Providing students with a renewed perspective of their network can facilitate a change in mindset toward networking altogether.[226] In addition, reflective exercises can prompt students to think about the networking opportunities and affirmative steps they could take at their externship and, at the conclusion of the externship, how well they took advantage of those opportunities.

The externship seminar can also help students understand that networking is an important precursor to business development. "Networking is the mechanism for positioning a lawyer to get business, over time, based on his or her relationships. Business development, on the other hand, involves developing an expertise, asking for business [or donations in the case of non-profit work], and closing the deal."[227] While in law school, students can begin to think about what they enjoy, what they are good at, and how they plan to get themselves out into the community to develop that expertise. Among other things, students can explore the possibility of writing an article for a local bar journal, presenting at CLE programs, or becoming active

225. SUSAN R. SNEIDER, A LAWYER'S GUIDE TO NETWORKING 27 (2006). *See also* Avis L. Sanders, *Externships and Career Development* (Chapter 26), *in* LEARNING FROM PRACTICE, *supra* note 10, for teaching ideas.

226. For instance, the "12 Magic Circles" exercise has students map out their current network using 12 circles, with each circle representing a different sphere of their lives and 10 people included within each sphere. SNEIDER, *supra* note 226, at 32–39. This results in a list of 120 people in each student's current network.

227. *Id.* at 91–92.

in community organizations, and talk to lawyers and judges about how to pursue those opportunities.

9. Teamwork and Collaboration Skills

Teamwork and collaboration skills are another topic to consider teaching in a general externship seminar. Research demonstrates that teamwork skills are crucial for lawyers. According to the *Foundations for Practice* study, 72.9% of the surveyed attorneys said the ability to work "cooperatively and collaboratively as part of a team" is a foundational skill that new lawyers must have immediately upon entry into practice to be successful in the short term.[228] An additional 17.7% of the survey respondents rated this skill as an ability that new lawyers must acquire for continued success over time.[229] Similarly, the Shultz and Zedeck study identifies "developing relationships within the legal profession" as one of its 26 lawyering-effectiveness factors.[230] Law firms often evaluate new lawyers on their teamwork skills as part of their annual performance reviews.[231]

Based on his review of teamwork competency models provided by eight of the ten largest law firms in Minnesota, Professor Neil Hamilton identified the following sub-competencies of teamwork skills that firms expect of new lawyers:

1. Actively listening and communicating with empathy;
2. Initiating and maintaining respectful relationships and communication;
3. Encouraging cooperation, collaboration, and respectful candor within the team;
4. Keeping senior attorneys informed and knowing when to seek guidance;
5. Valuing inclusion;
6. Willingly sharing information and knowledge;
7. Actively seeking and incorporating the views of others;
8. Working for common ground within the team;
9. Dealing effectively with interpersonal conflict within the team;
10. Being open to feedback;

---

228. Alli Gerkman & Logan Cornett, Foundations for Practice: The Whole Lawyer and the Character Quotient 20 (2016), https://iaals.du.edu/sites/default/files/documents/ publications/ foundations_for_practice_whole_lawyer_quotient.pdf.

229. *Id.*

230. Marjorie M. Shultz & Sheldon Zedeck, *Predicting Lawyer Effectiveness: Broadening the Basis for Law School Admission Decisions*, 36 Law & Soc. Inquiry, 620, 630 (2011).

231. *See* Neil Hamilton, *Fostering and Assessing Law Student Teamwork and Team Leadership Skills*, 48 Hofstra L. Rev. 619, 625 (2019).

11. When one is a team leader, effectively (a) identifying tasks to be done by others; (b) delegating tasks clearly to them; and (c) supervising them; and
12. When one is a team leader, effectively maximizing the contributions of team members and enhancing the professional development of others.[232]

Externship faculty might choose to teach some or all of these aspects of teamwork skills in a class session or a series of classes. For example, faculty might design a specific class on emotional intelligence[233] or dealing with conflict.[234] While resources for teaching teamwork skills are abundant, some that are specific to legal education include Chapter 16 of *Learning From Practice*[235] and *Working Together in Law: Teamwork and Small Group Skills for Legal Professionals* by Eileen Scallen, Sophie Sparrow, and Cliff Zimmerman.[236] Scallen, Sparrow, and Zimmerman, for example, discuss group and team dynamics, the characteristics of highly effective teams, and decision-making processes available for teams to follow.

After a reading assignment and class discussion related to teamwork skills, externship faculty could engage students in an exercise allowing them to practice the skills discussed. For example, faculty might design an in-class or out-of-class assignment in which a pair or small group of students must work together to produce a deliverable, such as a research strategy for a legal issue, a fact-investigation plan, a discovery strategy, or an outline for a client interview. Having students apply the teamwork skills they have read about and discussed to an actual lawyering task will deepen their learning of those skills.

10. Professional Communication

While students come to an externship with varying levels of work experience, it is helpful for all students to consider how they interact with others in a professional environment. "Most lawyers spend a lot of their time communicating, so whether or not they succeed in their work depends largely on the effectiveness of their communication."[237] For this reason, professional communication is another topic to consider addressing in the externship seminar. Because professional communication is such a broad topic, there are many different ways to address it. In addition, it

232. *Id.* at 625–26.

233. *See, e.g.*, Harv. Bus. Rev., On Emotional Intelligence (2015).

234. See, e.g., Amy Gallo, HBR Guide to Dealing with Conflict (2017).

235. Learning From Practice, *supra* note 10.

236. Eileen Scallen, Sophie M. Sparrow, & Cliff Zimmerman, Working Together in Law: Teamwork and Small Group Skills for Legal Professionals (2014). *Cf. also* Cooperative Learning Inst., www.co-operation.org (last visited March 20, 2022) (discussing the Cooperative Learning Institute and research and resources related to cooperative learning).

237. Susan Brooks & Inga Laurent, *Effective Communication and Professional Relationships* (Chapter 6), *in* Learning From Practice, *supra* note 10, at 83.

is a topic that can be incorporated throughout the externship seminar when discussing the other topics mentioned in this Chapter.

One way to begin a discussion about communication is to focus on it as a broad concept and to intentionally explore the components of an interaction (context, intention, perception, interpretation, feelings, and action).[238] As part of or in addition to this discussion, students can explore methods of communication (speaking, listening, writing, and non-verbal/body language) and the communication cycle (sender, transmission, receiver, and response).[239]

A class could be spent on exploring the ways writing for practice is different from the legal writing students have done in their first-year legal writing course. Students can explore strategies to approaching legal research and approaching a writing assignment, along with special considerations applicable to emails and writing for non-lawyers. Chapter 17, *Writing for Practice*, in *Learning From Practice,* addresses this topic in more detail.[240]

In addition, an externship seminar could incorporate oral presentations. In *Making Presentations*, Chapter 18 *Learning From Practice*, Leah Wortham provides a number of ideas and methods for incorporating student presentations into the seminar. Students can be asked to not only make a presentation, but also to assess their peers during their presentations using an oral presentation rubric.[241] As an added element, student presentations can be recorded and watched by the students, who must self-assess their presentation in addition to providing peer assessments.[242]

---

238. *Id.*

239. *See* Floyd & Kerew, *supra* note 36, at 797–99 for exercises to address these topics.

240. For externship teachers teaching a judicial externship seminar, Mariana Hogan and Michael H. Roffer, *Judicial Externships* (Chapter 19), *in* Learning from Practice, *supra* note 10, also provide some guidance on researching and writing for judges.

241. *See* Floyd & Kerew, *supra* note 36, at 798–99. A sample oral presentation rubric is provided in the Appendix.

242. *Id.*

Chapter 10

Topics for Subject-Specific Seminars

When all students in an externship class are in one type of placement, the externship professor may want to design a syllabus that focuses on issues specifically related to that kind of placement.[1] Approximately one-third of law schools offer at least one externship course focused on a particular subject matter.[2] In such a course, the professor may choose to only include topics related to the placement or may combine those specific topics with some of the general topics discussed in Chapter 9. Subject-specific topics can also be taught in general externship courses, either by focusing on one type of placement each week or by dividing the class into subgroups by type of placement.

This Chapter contains seminar ideas for the following kinds of externship sites: judicial, public interest, civil government, criminal law, and legal departments of corporations.[3] These categories overlap with the majority of externship opportunities currently offered by law schools,[4] but are not exclusive. Externship teachers can also design subject-specific courses for any area of legal practice—such as health care law, intellectual property, or real estate. Similarly, externship faculty could create different courses focusing on specific types of practice, such as transactional or legislative work.[5]

---

1. Chapter 9 detailed some of the advantages of subject-specific courses.
2. ROBERT R. KUEHN, MARGARET REUTER & DAVID A. SANTACROCE, CENTER FOR THE STUDY OF APPLIED LEGAL EDUC., 2019–2020 SURVEY OF APPLIED LEGAL EDUCATION 42–43 (2020), https://www.csale.org/#results (last viewed March 7, 2022) (hereinafter "2019–20 CSALE REPORT").
3. Chapter 6 contains subject-specific course ideas for international externship sites. For additional seminar ideas focused on the subjects addressed in this Chapter, see LEARNING FROM PRACTICE: A TEXT FOR EXPERIENTIAL EDUCATION (Leah Wortham, Alexander Scherr, Nancy Mauer, Susan L. Brooks eds., 3d ed. 2016) (hereinafter "LEARNING FROM PRACTICE") (offering separate student-focused chapters and teaching materials for judicial externships, criminal law placements, public interest sites, public service externships, and transactional work).
4. *See* 2019–20 CSALE REPORT, *supra* note 2, at 10.
5. Seattle University School of Law's Externship Program has a Legislative Externship Seminar in the spring semester for students at nonprofits, government agencies, and legislatures. The seminar provides practical skills and tools to develop political strategies for influencing public policy debates, including coalition building, policy analysis, advocacy, implementation, and evaluation.

1. Judicial Externships

Judicial externship courses are one of the most common types of subject-specific seminars.[6] Externships with judges are available in most areas where law schools are located. They are also a likely choice for a separate course because the work is unique from other kinds of externships. Researching and writing for a judge is different from the client-centered representation that happens at most other externship sites. There are numerous articles focusing on teaching judicial externship courses[7] and at least one textbook.[8]

Chapter 9 discussed why every externship course must include instruction on ethics. Teaching students about the ethical rules governing judges and their application to externs is a good place to start a judicial externship course. Students should read the judicial code of conduct that applies to their court[9] and consider how the provisions apply to their work.[10] Faculty should draw students' attention to restrictions on their political activity while they are in a judicial externship[11] and their need to be particularly cautious when posting to social media sites.[12] Some chambers may have particular policies on social media use or written codes of conduct for externs.

Confidentiality is an area of particular concern for work in judicial chambers.[13] Teachers may need to be very explicit about what is considered confidential and therefore may not be shared in class discussions, journals, and with anyone outside the judicial chambers. In addition to reviewing the judicial and ethical rules

---

6. *See* CSALE Report, *supra* note 2, at 43 (24% of law schools offer externship courses where the judiciary is the subject matter of the course).

7. *See, e.g.*, Amany Ragab Hacking, *Jumpstarting the Judicial Externship Experience: Building Upon Common Themes for Student Success in the Classroom and in the Judge's Chambers*, 21 Clinical L. Rev. 29 (2014); Linda Smith, *The Judicial Clinic: Theory and Method in a Live Laboratory of Law*, 1992 Utah L. Rev. 429 (1993); Stacy Caplow, *From Courtroom to Classroom: Creating an Academic Component to Enhance the Skills and Values Learned in a Student Judicial Clerkship Clinic*, 75 Neb. L. Rev. 872 (1996).

8. Rebecca A. Cochran, Judicial Externships: The Clinic Inside the Courthouse (4th ed. 2016) (hereinafter "Judicial Externships").

9. *See, e.g.*, Code of Conduct for Judicial Employees, https://www.uscourts.gov/sites/ default/files/code_of_conduct_for_judicial_employees_effective_march_12_2019.pdf (2019) (last visited March 7, 2022).

10. For example, the *Federal Code of Conduct for Judicial Employees* states explicitly that it applies to "interns, externs, and other volunteer court employees." *Id.* at Sec. 310.10(a). Another good resource for students is *Maintaining the Public Trust: Ethics for Federal Judicial Law Clerks* (4th ed. Fed. Jud. Ctr. 2013), http://oscar.uscourts.gov/assets/Maintaining Public Trust.pdf (last visited March 7, 2022).

11. *See, e.g., Committee on Codes of Conduct Advisory Opinion No. 92: Political Activities Guidelines for Judicial Employees*, www.uscourts.gov/sites/default/files/guide-vol02b-ch02-2019_final.pdf (2019) (last visited March 7, 2022).

12. *See, e.g., Committee on Codes of Conduct Advisory Opinion No. 112: Use of Electronic Social Media by Judges and Judicial Employees*, www.uscourts.gov/sites/default/files/guide-vol02b-ch02-2019_final.pdf (2019) (last visited March 7, 2022).

13. *See* Judicial Externships, *supra* note 8, at 8–21.

on the topic, the externship teacher should help students understand what is said privately in chambers stays in chambers,[14] even if it is not technically covered by an ethical rule. Comments that a judge or clerk makes in chambers or other settings outside open court about cases, lawyers, or any other sensitive information may not be shared with anyone. Students are of course free to discuss and reflect on what they heard and saw in open court where the proceedings are on the record. Faculty should instruct students to talk about assignments from chambers in class and elsewhere only in general terms, without any identifying information about the particular case or opinion. It helps to remind students to focus on what they are learning about research, writing, organization, legal analysis, time management, and other skills, as opposed to the details of the assignment.

Conflicts are another important issue to address with students in judicial externships. In addition to making sure they inform chambers of any conflicts under the ethical rules,[15] externs also need to be aware of the importance of avoiding even the appearance of impropriety. When students receive an assignment, they should immediately check to see whether they have a connection to any of the lawyers or parties in the case. They should inform chambers when a relative, close friend, or future or past employer appears in court before the judge or is otherwise involved in a case before the judge. Students should also inform chambers when they are interviewing for other legal jobs during the externship. The judge can then decide how to deal with any potential conflicts or appearance of impropriety.

Judicial qualifications and selection are topics that often generate lively discussion. Externship faculty may want to assign each student to research their judge's qualifications and path to the bench. Students may find the assignment helpful as an "excuse" to interview the judge about their life and get to know them better. Sharing the information in class and mapping out law schools attended, prior work and volunteer experiences, age, gender, race and ethnicity, and other categories helps students see that there is no singular profile or career path that leads to the judiciary. Faculty may also want to help students consider the benefits of a diverse judiciary and impediments to that diversity.[16] Students may also enjoy debating whether ideology is an appropriate area to consider in judicial selection.[17] Another good area to explore in the judicial externship seminar is the different methods of judicial selection, including appointment, election, retention, and different hybrids.[18] Externship faculty could ask students to develop a list of pros and cons for each method and

---

14. *See* John Paul Jones, *Ethics for Judicial Clerks*, 4 GEO. J. LEGAL ETHICS 771, 775 (1991).

15. See Chapter 9 for a more thorough discussion of teaching externs about conflicts of interest.

16. *See, e.g.*, Theresa M. Beiner, *White Male Heterosexual Norms in the Confirmation Process*, 32 WOMEN'S RTS. L. REP. 105 (2011); BRENNAN CENTER FOR JUSTICE, *Improving Judicial Diversity* (2010), www.brennancenter.org/publication/improving-judicial-diversity (last visited March 7, 2022); Harry T. Edwards, *Race and the Judiciary*, 20 YALE L. & POL'Y REV. 325 (2002).

17. *See, e.g.*, Erwin Chemerinsky, *Ideology and the Selection of Federal Judges*, 36 U.C. DAVIS. L. REV. 619 (2003).

18. *See generally* JUDICIAL EXTERNSHIPS, *supra* note 8, at 102–17.

facilitate a debate about what constitutes the best selection system. Current news stories about federal nominations or local elections can be helpful in this discussion. While students are often aware of the political overtones of the federal appointment system, they may not have considered issues that arise when judges run for office—what they can promise, who funds the campaigns, backlash for unpopular decisions, and other relevant topics.[19]

Many judicial externs are interested in exploring the role of the law clerks and the selection process for becoming a clerk. Guest speakers can be helpful here, including a federal judge, a state court judge, current or former law clerks, and perhaps the person at the law school who assists students with clerkship applications.[20] Faculty may want to ask students to interview the law clerks in their chambers about the selection process they went through and what qualifications they brought to the job. Students can then share their findings with the class. Seeing the range of answers can help students see that clerkships are possible for students from many different schools and at different points in their careers.

It is helpful early in the semester to have at least one class on judicial writing. Law school writing courses usually teach students to write as advocates, so writing as a neutral judicial decision-maker is often new for them. There is a variety of written materials on this subject,[21] including a number written by judges.[22] Having judges, law clerks, former law clerks, or faculty members who have clerked as guest speakers to outline some basic concepts for students can be helpful. Of course students should also be receiving strong guidance and feedback on their writing from their externship supervisors. The heavy editing of student work that is typical in many judicial chambers is sometimes stressful for students. The externship faculty should encourage students to welcome this feedback and remember that it is part of their learning experience. Having students share in class helpful feedback given by supervisors about judicial writing can be a useful exercise that highlights common writing issues judicial externs face and helps students learn from each other.

Another topic that generally leads to engaged classroom discussion is judicial philosophy and decision-making. To what extent do judges simply call balls and strikes?[23] The judicial externship seminar is a good place to explore the role that ide-

19. *See* Martin Siegel, *In Defense of Judicial Elections (Sort of)*, 36 No. 4 Litig. 23 (2010); A.G. Sulzberger, *Ouster of Iowa Judges Sends Signal to the Bench*, N.Y. Times (Nov. 3, 2010), http://nytimes.com/2010/11/04/us/politics/04judges.html.

20. At schools that use judges as adjunct professors to teach judicial externship courses, those professors can share their own process for selecting clerks. *See also* Todd C. Peppers, Michael W. Giles & Bridget Tainer-Parkins, *Inside Judicial Chambers: How Federal District Court Judges Select and Use Their Law Clerks*, 71 Alb. L. Rev. 623 (2008); Judicial Externships, *supra* note 8, at 48–53.

21. *See, e.g.*, Judicial Externships, *supra* note 8, at 58–80; Jennifer Sheppard, *The "Write" Way: A Judicial Clerk's Guide to Writing for the Court*, 38 U. Balt. L. Rev. 73 (2008).

22. *See, e.g.*, Charles G. Douglas, *How to Write a Concise Opinion*, 22 Judges' J. 4 (Spring 1983); Patricia Wald, *How I Write*, 4 Scribes J. Legal Writing 55 (1993).

23. Chief Justice John Roberts famously said during his confirmation hearing that "I will remember that it's my job to call balls and strikes, and not to pitch or bat." *Confirmation Hearings on the*

ology or political preferences play in judicial decision-making.[24] One good question to spur class discussion is whether judges should use their personal experiences in making decisions.[25] Another topic for class discussion is how judicial philosophy and approach might vary depending on the court (trial level or appellate, federal or state). The externship teacher may also want to help students identify institutional checks on judges that help prevent them from simply following their own instincts and views of what the law should be.[26] Students often see firsthand how carefully clerks and judges base their opinions only on the facts presented by the parties and the controlling law, without regard to personal ideology or political persuasion. The experiential insights can help enrich the class discussion.

Sentencing is another topic that is often in the news that is of interest to many judicial externs. Faculty may want to assign every student to observe a sentencing hearing in their own chambers or elsewhere if their judge does not impose criminal sentences. For classes with students externing in federal court, it is helpful to give students an overview of the history of the federal sentencing system, including the Sentencing Guidelines and mandatory minimums.[27] Faculty can also review state and local sentencing practices for students working in state courts or assign students to do this and have them report back to the class. Having a judge come to class to explain the sentencing process and all the factors they consider is often helpful. There are many resources in the popular press and elsewhere that explore issues of racial disparities in sentencing, mass incarceration, punishment for drug addiction, and other timely issues.[28]

The role of settlement in the judicial system is another good topic for a judicial externship course. If possible, assign students to observe a settlement hearing and reflect on what they learned about judicial settlement techniques (without revealing confidential or identifying information) in class.[29] One issue to explore in class is why the number of trials in federal court is declining and more parties and judges

---

Nomination of John G. Roberts, Jr. to be Chief Justice of the United States: Hearings Before the Committee on the Judiciary, United States Senate, 109th Cong. 55–56 (2005), www.uscourts.gov/educational-resources/educational-activities/chief-justice-roberts-statement-nomination-process (last visited March 7, 2022).

24. For an interesting contrast on this topic by two well-known judges, see Richard A. Posner, How Judges Think (2008), and Jeffrey S. Sutton, *A Review of Richard A. Posner, How Judges Think*, 108 Mich. L. Rev. 859 (2010).

25. *See* Alex Kozinski, *Teetering on the High Wire*, 68 U. Colo. L. Rev. 1217 (1997) (advocating for judges drawing on their own experience and giving examples).

26. *See* Sutton *supra* note 24, at 868–75.

27. *See, e.g., U.S. v. Booker*, 125 S. Ct. 738 (2005); United States Sentencing Commission, *Quick Facts Mandatory Minimum Penalties* (2018), www.ussc.gov/sites/default/files/pdf/research-and-publications/quick-facts/Quick_Facts_Mand_Mins_FY18.pdf (last visited March 7, 2022).

28. *See, e.g.*, Lynn Adelman, *What the Sentencing Commission Ought to Be Doing: Reducing Mass Incarceration*, 18 Mich. J. Race & L. 295 (2013); The Sentencing Project, *Racial Justice Issues*, www.sentencingproject.org/issues/racial-disparity (last visited March 7, 2022).

29. *See also* Morton Denlow, *Settlement Conference Techniques: Caucus Do's and Don'ts*, 49 Judges' J. of the American Bar Assn. 21 (Spring 2010).

are resolving cases through settlement.[30] What effect do private sources of settlement like arbitration have on courts? Externship faculty may also want to raise questions regarding how an increasing reliance on settlements, especially confidential settlements, affects the development of the law, pro se parties, and public resolution of legal issues.[31]

Judicial ethics, misconduct, and discipline are topics that allow students to explore the boundaries of judicial power and conduct. Faculty may want to start with an overview of the various judicial codes of ethics and disciplinary procedures for judges or assign students to research these issues and report their findings to the class. Issues surrounding judicial impartiality, recusal, and disqualification may be new to the students and are worth taking some time to explore in class.[32] Another topic under the canopy of judicial misconduct that students often enjoy debating is whether judges should be active on social media sites including Facebook and Twitter and what issues that activity could raise.[33] The class can discuss why some judicial misconduct goes unreported[34] and limitations on disciplining judges for misconduct, short of removal from office.

The use of technology in court and by judges is a rapidly developing topic that often interests students. Students who grew up with easy access to information on a wide range of topics through the internet often wonder whether judges should turn to internet research to better understand factual issues before them.[35] Technology in the courtroom, including whether cameras should be allowed and how technology can be used in trials, is another evolving topic. During the 2020–22 global pandemic, most courts operated remotely out of necessity. It is likely there will be lasting effects

---

30. *See* Patrick E. Higgenbotham, *The Present Plight of the United States District Courts*, 60 Duke L.J. 745, 752–55 (2010); Judicial Externships, *supra* note 8, at 201, 229–30.

31. *See, e.g.*, Owen M. Fiss, *Against Settlement*, 93 Yale L.J. 1073 (1984).

32. *See* Judicial Externships, *supra* note 8, at 141–96.

33. *See* American Bar Association, *Formal Opinion 462: Judge's Use of Electronic Social Networking Media* (2013), www.americanbar.org/content/dam/aba/administrative/professional_responsibility/formal_opinion_462.authcheckdam.pdf (last visited March 7, 2022); *Herssein & Herssein, P.A. v. United Services Automobile Association*, 271 So. 3d 889 (Fla. 2018) (Facebook friendship with attorney alone is not enough to require judicial disqualification); *U.S. v. Sierra Pacific Industries, Inc.*, 862 F.3d 1157, 1174–75 (9th Cir. 2017) (judge not required to recuse himself because he followed prosecutor office on Twitter and tweeted links to news articles about the case).

34. *See* David Pimental, *The Reluctant Tattletale: Closing the Gap in Federal Judicial Discipline*, 76 Tenn. L. Rev. 909 (2009).

35. *See* Judicial Externships, *supra* note 8, at 321–41.

of this experience, including more remote hearings, more cameras in the courtroom, and better public access to the courts through technology.[36]

2. Public Interest Externships

What work qualifies as "public interest" lawyering has long been a topic of debate.[37] In the world of law school externships, public interest externship sites often include nonprofit organizations that work on civil (and sometimes criminal) cases and projects on behalf of low-income and other marginalized clients and communities.[38] It may be helpful in a public interest externship seminar to explore various definitions of public interest lawyering and how it applies to each of the students' externship sites.[39]

This section will focus on placements with nonprofit organizations that work on civil cases and issues, leaving criminal cases and issues for the section below on Criminal Law Externships. There are a number of texts on public interest law that explore a wide range of topics and could be useful in developing a syllabus in this area.[40] In addition, *Learning From Practice* devotes a chapter to this topic and contains sample class exercises. Some of the topics discussed in Chapter 9 of this book in the section on social justice would also be appropriate for a course focused on public interest lawyering. For example, teaching students about the justice gap in the United States helps them understand one reason that the work of public interest lawyers is so important. Faculty can take the discussion one step further by helping students explore, either in class or in a journal assignment, whether and how their externship site works to close the justice gap.

Another foundational topic that should be included in any public interest externship course is the role of race in the legal system. Racial disparities and systemic racism are at the heart of much public interest work. Chapter 9 of this book includes extensive information on teaching externship students about bias and anti-racism. An

36. Chapter 12 discusses the need for students to be familiar with the use of technology by lawyers and judges.

37. For a good discussion of the evolution of the term through an externship teaching lens, see Alexi Freeman & Katie Steefel, *Uniting the Head, Hands, and Heart: How Specialty Externships Can Combat Public Interest Drift*, 25 CLINICAL L. REV. 325, 337–40 (2018).

38. *See* Susan B. Schechter & Jeffrey R. Baker, *Public Interest Lawyering, in* LEARNING FROM PRACTICE, *supra* note 3, at 606. *But see* Freeman & Steefel, *supra* note 37 (describing public interest externship courses organized by a common theme or by a common worksite).

39. *See* Schecter & Baker, *in* LEARNING FROM PRACTICE, *supra* note 3, at 608–09; ALAN K. CHEN & SCOTT L. CUMMINGS, PUBLIC INTEREST LAWYERING 3–32 (2013) (hereinafter "PUBLIC INTEREST LAWYERING").

40. *See, e.g.*, PUBLIC INTEREST LAWYERING, *supra* note 39; MARTHA R. MAHONEY, JOHN O. CALMORE & STEPHANIE M. WILDMAN, SOCIAL JUSTICE: PROFESSIONALS, COMMUNITIES, AND LAW (2d ed. 2013); AUSTIN SARAT & STUART A. SCHEINGOLD, CAUSE LAWYERS AND SOCIAL MOVEMENTS (2006) (hereinafter "CAUSE LAWYERS").

externship course for students working in public interest agencies might dig deeper into historical (and often continuing) discrimination that affects current legal issues faced by clients at their agencies. For example, students could research the current consequences of discrimination in housing, lending, employment, and education for client populations served by their externship sites.[41] Faculty can also ask students to reflect on how their externship sites incorporate (or do not) an anti-racist approach in their representation of clients. There is a wide range of race-related topics that would be appropriate for a public interest externship course, and faculty may want to consider a number of factors in deciding which ones to cover, including the issues addressed and clients served by the externship sites and students' prior exposure to issues of racial discrimination and structural racism.

Pro bono is another topic discussed in Chapter 9 that is appropriate for a public interest externship course. An additional layer to add to the conversation in a public interest course is the view of public interest lawyers on the role of pro bono. While teaming up with law firm pro bono lawyers is a strategy used by many public interest agencies, it can create its own set of challenges for the lawyers at those agencies.[42] Some law firms are motivated to participate in pro bono in part to train young lawyers and/or to create positive publicity for the firm, goals that may not always align with the needs of the agency and its clients.[43] Other topics to explore could include what should count as pro bono, whether lawyers should be required to do pro bono, and whether law students should be required to do pro bono. Students may want to discuss the role of pro bono at their externship site with their supervisors, including the benefits and challenges of working with pro bono attorneys.

Another important topic in public interest lawyering is that of triage—faced with a large demand for free legal services, how do agencies determine which cases to accept? Students might start by discovering how their externship agencies approach these issues. What criteria do their agencies use in case selection? Faculty can help students understand and debate different approaches to case and client selection.[44] Related discussions might include what kinds of legal issues each agency works on and who should decide—the lawyers, the clients, the funders, the community, the government? A final element of case selection involves the difficult task of saying "no" to clients who are desperately in need of representation. Helping students iden-

---

41. For a good collection of essays on the importance of considering race in legal services work, see 47 Clearinghouse Rev. 135 (2013).

42. *See* Lenore Carpenter, *"We're Not Running a Charity Here": Rethinking Public Interest Lawyers' Relationships with Bottom-Line Driven Pro Bono Programs*, 29 Buff. Pub. Int. L.J. 37 (2011).

43. *See id.* at 38–39; Scott Cummings, *The Politics of Pro Bono*, 52 UCLA L. Rev. 1, 140–44 (2004).

44. For two different approaches to this topic, see Paul R. Tremblay, *Acting "A Very Moral Type of God": Triage Among Poor Clients*, 67 Fordham L. Rev. 2475 (1999), and Justine A. Dunlap, *I Don't Want to Play God—A Response to Professor Tremblay*, 67 Fordham L. Rev. 2601 (1999).

tify the importance of self-care and appropriate case loads so that they can represent their clients effectively is a critical topic for public interest externship seminars.

Cause lawyering is another topic that often leads to lively and interesting class discussions, small group work, or journal entries. While there is no one accepted definition of cause lawyering, in general it describes lawyers who seek to use the law to bring about social change and advance a particular cause.[45] In fact, many students are attracted to public interest law as a way of furthering a cause they care about—the environment, racial justice, voting rights, and more conservative causes like gun rights. Faculty may want to help students identify potential ethical issues involved in such work. How can one reconcile cause lawyering with client-centered representation? What happens when the interests of the cause and the client differ? Who decides who speaks for a cause and what is the best legal strategy to advance a cause? Students may also want to speak to lawyers at their externship sites about whether they consider themselves cause lawyers and why or why not. Students should also explore their own attitudes towards cause lawyering.

A related issue for a public interest externship course is movement lawyering, which one commentator has described as "a version of cause lawyering in which the cause is defined and advanced by social movement leaders and constituents in dynamic processes of grassroots organization building and community engagement."[46] Movement lawyering often involves work with community organizers and activists and a rejection of traditional approaches to social change, such as litigation, in favor of more grassroots efforts, including community organizing and protest.[47] It may be helpful to invite guest speakers on the topic, including a movement lawyer and a community activist who works with lawyers. Faculty can help students explore how this work differs from more traditional legal work and the approach each student prefers.

Another issue frequently faced by public interest lawyers and a good topic for a public interest externship seminar is representing groups. Impact litigation and community lawyering often involve representation of groups, both formally organized groups (like a nonprofit organization or a class action) and informal (like a group of tenants or a community facing a shared problem). Lawyers representing groups need to consider who speaks for the group and what to do when group members disagree about issues. The rules of professional responsibility offer guidance for representing an individual client or a corporation, but they do not always provide a clear answer on how best to represent informal groups that have no leadership structure. The ethical issues raised by representing groups and how to

---

45. For a good discussion of cause lawyering and lawyers, see STUART A. SCHEINGOLD & AUSTIN SARAT, SOMETHING TO BELIEVE IN: POLITICS, PROFESSIONALISM, AND CAUSE LAWYERING (2004).

46. Scott Cummings, *Movement Lawyering*, 2017 U. ILL. L. REV. 1645, 1690 (2017).

47. One of the first writers to propose this kind of client and community-driven approach was Gerald Lopez in his book *Rebellious Lawyering, One Chicano's Vision of Progressive Law Practice* (1992). *See also* Freeman & Steefel, *supra* note 37 at 339; CAUSE LAWYERS *supra* note 40, at 2; Cummings, *supra* note 46, at 1691.

resolve them[48] are excellent topics for class discussion, journal assignments, small group discussion, and final papers.

Another issue that helps students develop a more holistic understanding of issues facing public interest lawyers and organizations is how those lawyers and organizations fund their work. One way to start the discussion is to ask students to find out how their externship site funds its operations. Does it receive money from the government? Foundations? Individual donors? The class can then explore the benefits and drawbacks of different kinds of funding. Another approach to this topic is to ask students to put themselves in the shoes of a philanthropic foundation that wants to further social justice advocacy and ask them what kind of work they would fund and why.[49]

The Supreme Court considers cases that involve public interest issues every term. One way to highlight the breadth of public interest law as well as its importance is to assign each student to identify a pending or recently decided Supreme Court case that involves a public interest issue. Ask students to learn about the case and then teach the class about it, including its relevance to public interest law. This assignment also helps students develop their legal analysis and presentation skills.

A topic that might be especially helpful near the end of the semester is a discussion of how to close the justice gap. As described in Chapter 9 of this book, some commentators have suggested creating a right to counsel for low-income persons in certain civil cases where basic human needs are at stake, including housing, sustenance, safety, health, and child custody. This approach raises many interesting questions about the potential cost, types of cases, and efficacy of such an approach, especially given the continuing issues in the criminal justice system where defendants have a right to counsel. Other ideas for closing the justice gap include increased use of technology, unbundled legal services, relaxing rules on the unauthorized practice of law, increased or mandatory pro bono, increased funding for legal services organizations, and many others. Faculty may want to assign each student to identify and research the pros and cons of one approach and report back to the class.

---

48. *See* Stephen Ellmann, *Client-Centeredness Multiplied: Individual Autonomy and Collective Mobilization in Public Interest Lawyers' Representation of Groups*, 78 Va. L. Rev. 1103 (1992); William B. Rubenstein, *Divided We Litigate: Addressing Disputes Among Group Members and Lawyers in Civil Rights Campaigns*, 106 Yale L.J. 1623 (1997).

49. *See* Freeman & Steefel, *supra* note 37, at 349.

3. Civil Government Externships

Government lawyers face ethical and other issues that are unique to their practice. One such issue is who is the client of the government lawyer.[50] Is it the public? The agency for whom they work? Who speaks for that client? These are good questions for students to ask their supervisors and to discuss in class. Faculty may also want to identify cases in the news that raise these issues.

The issue of how the duty of confidentiality should apply to government lawyers is another topic that can lead to good class discussions and journal entries. The issue is often intertwined with the question of whether the government lawyer ultimately answers to the public or someone else. Is it ever appropriate for government lawyers to become whistleblowers and report on dangerous or illegal government activity?[51] The issue is more complicated for government lawyers than in the private sector, in part because there are certain laws that require government disclosure, including open meeting laws and freedom of information laws.[52]

A similar dilemma arises around the duty of loyalty for government lawyers. Should there be any limits on their duty of loyalty to the agency or government official they represent?[53] When, if ever, can or should government lawyers refuse to follow directions from their superiors?[54] Of course in all of these discussions, the externship teacher should remind students that they should be following the ethical rules and the guidance of their supervisor. Discussion of theoretical limits on government lawyers in class should not affect their approach to their work at the externship site.

The influence of politics is another important topic to consider for externships at government sites.[55] Many students will work at sites where the head of the office was elected or was appointed by an elected official. How does politics affect the work of government lawyers? What are the dangers of political influence in the work of their agency? How do lawyers respond to those political pressures? How

---

50. See Jeffrey R. Baker & Susan B. Schechter, *Public Service Lawyering, in* Learning From Practice, *supra* note 3, at 630; Steven K. Berenson, *Public Lawyers, Private Values: Can, Should, and Will Government Lawyers Serve the Public Interest?* 41 B.C. L. Rev. 789 (2000); Geoffrey P. Miller, *Government Lawyers' Ethics in a System of Checks and Balances*, 54 U. Chi. L. Rev. 1293 (1987).

51. See Mika C. Morse, *Honor or Betrayal? The Ethics of Government Lawyer-Whistleblowers*, 23 Geo. J. Legal Ethics 421 (Spring 2010).

52. *See* Kathleen Clark, *Government Lawyers and Confidentiality Norms*, 85 Wash. U. L. Rev. 1033, 1087–91 (2007).

53. *See* Baker et al., *in* Learning From Practice, *supra* note 3, at 634 (lawyer may feel dissonance between the action of the government and the effect of that action on the public).

54. *See* Michael Stokes Paulsen, *Government Lawyering: Hell, Handbaskets, and Government Lawyers: The Duty of Loyalty and Its Limits*, 61 Law & Contemp. Probs. 83 (Winter 1998).

55. *See* Baker et al. in Learning From Practice, *supra* note 3, at 635.

do students deal with their own political beliefs, especially when they differ from those of the agency head?

Many students may work on policy issues at their government externship sites, making it an excellent topic for class discussion. Policy work might involve drafting or commenting on legislation, drafting rules or regulations, researching and analyzing different strategies for addressing an issue, and performing many other lawyering tasks.[56] Policy work may also involve politics, and it is important for students to observe and reflect on the role of politics in legislative and policy work.

4. Criminal Law Externships

While many externs will have some background knowledge of criminal law from a 1L course on the topic, there are many issues to explore in more depth in a criminal law externship course. These topics could be used for a class with both prosecution and defense placements or for classes that are limited to one side or the other. Having a combined class can create additional challenges for the externship teacher because students are working at agencies that are on the opposite sides of cases. On the other hand, a combined class may lead to richer discussions and better understanding of both sides of the criminal justice system. Faculty for combined classes have to be especially vigilant about students revealing confidential information. The decision of whether to create separate classes or to combine prosecution and defense externships may depend on a number of factors, including ethical concerns, resources, faculty preference, and numbers of students at each kind of placement.

Regardless of whether the class combines kinds of externships, it may be helpful to discuss the roles of both prosecutors and defense lawyers in the criminal justice system[57] early in the semester. Externship teachers may want to ask students what preconceived notions they have of these lawyers and of the criminal justice system. Students can also reflect on how their perceptions might affect their work at the externship sites. It may also be helpful to return to this topic near the end of the semester, to see if students' perceptions have changed.

While most first year criminal law courses survey the leading Supreme Court cases, it is helpful early in the semester to review and teach some basics of criminal law procedure. Topics might include charging and indictments, the role of the grand jury, pre-trial motion practice, motions to suppress, disclosure obligations,

---

56. *See id.* at 642–43.

57. *See, e.g.*, American Bar Association Criminal Justice Standards, *The Prosecution Function* (2017), www.americanbar.org/groups/criminal_justice/publications/ criminal_justice_section_archive_crimjust_standards_pfunc_toc (last visited March 7, 2022); John B. Mitchell, *The Ethics of the Criminal Defense Attorney—New Answers to Old Questions*, 32 Stan. L. Rev. 293 (1980); Bruce A. Green, *Why Should Prosecutors "Seek Justice"*, 26 Fordham Urb. L.J. 607 (1999).

and other issues that may arise in the students' externships.[58] Faculty may also want to point out differences between federal and state law on these issues.

As students observe different proceedings, it is important that they understand the concept of prosecutorial discretion. Ask students with externships at prosecutors' offices to inquire about prosecution priorities in the office and factors that go into decisions to file criminal charges. Students at criminal defense sites could ask the same questions. The answers may lead to an interesting class discussion. The externship teacher may also want to lead students in a more theoretical discussion of factors that may influence prosecutorial discretion and when it should be exercised.[59]

Plea bargains and agreements are another area that is unique to criminal law and a good topic for a criminal law externship course. Faculty may want to start with a discussion of the topic by focusing on the role of plea bargains in the criminal justice system. Other issues to address might include the ethical duties of the lawyers, power dynamics, and why so many cases result in a plea.[60] Faculty can ask students to discover what percentage of cases in their offices are resolved by plea bargains and then discuss why.

Sentencing is another important topic in the criminal justice system, and it is a good topic to cover right before or after plea bargains. Externship faculty may want to ask students to review any sentencing guidelines that apply to the system where they are doing their externship and share their findings with the class. The externship teacher can then lead students in discussions about the constitutional limits on sentencing as well as policy issues.[61] Other possible topics include the role of judicial discretion in sentencing and mandatory minimums. Faculty may want to go beyond sentencing to look at the collateral consequences of criminal convictions, which include access to financial aid, certain types of employment, food and cash assistance, housing, voting rights, drivers' licenses, and custody of children, to name just a few.[62] The externship teacher may want to encourage students to use their experiences at

58. Russell Gabriel & Hans P. Sinha, *Criminal Justice Law Placements, in* LEARNING FROM PRACTICE, *supra* note 3, at 563–66 and 582–83.

59. *See, e.g.*, Stephanos Bibas, *The Need for Prosecutorial Discretion*, 19 TEMP. POL. & CIV. RTS. L. REV. 369 (2010).

60. *See* AMERICAN BAR ASSOCIATION CRIMINAL JUSTICE SECTION STANDARDS, Prosecution Function, Plea Discussions, www.americanbar.org/groups/criminal_justice/publications/ criminal_justice_section_archive_crimjust_standards_pfunc_toc (last visited March 7, 2022); FRONTLINE, *The Plea*, www.pbs.org/video/frontline_the_plea.

61. *See, e.g.*, *U.S. v. Booker*, 125 S. Ct. 738 (2005); Adelman, *supra* note 28.

62. For more resources, *see* The Prison Policy Initiative resources on Collateral Consequences at www.prisonpolicy.org/collateral.html#:~:text=who%20are%20incarcerated%2C%20tens%20of,they%20have%20a%20criminal%20record (last visited March 13, 2022).

their externship to look at these issues through the lens of their externship site but also from the other side.

Racial disparities are a continuing problem in the criminal justice system.[63] At every step of the process—police stops, arrests, convictions, and incarceration—people of color and particularly Black people are overrepresented compared to their presence in the national population.[64] Chapter 9 of this book includes exercises and approaches to teaching students about the role of race in the law. Students may recognize the disparities on their own through observations at their externships, when they often see that the majority of people facing criminal prosecution are BIPOC. Engaging in thoughtful conversations about these issues will be an important part of student learning.

Some courts are starting to consider the use of restorative justice techniques as an alternative to incarceration. Faculty can help students understand the theory and practice of restorative justice.[65] Topics for class discussion or journal entries could include how and when restorative justice could be used in the criminal justice system and what are its benefits and drawbacks. Another non-traditional solution students should be aware of is the increasing use of therapeutic or drug courts, particularly where the underlying cause of the criminal behavior is substance abuse or mental illness, including post-traumatic stress disorder.[66]

5. Corporate Counsel Externships

Externships with corporate legal departments have become a popular option with students, and many schools now offer these opportunities.[67] One good way to start a class on this topic is to discuss the ways the role and work of the corporate general counsel and legal department have changed over time. These changes include more work being done in-house, a more global practice, increased efforts to

---

63. For an excellent discussion of the long history of racism in the U.S. criminal justice system, see MICHELLE ALEXANDER, THE NEW JIM CROW: MASS INCARCERATION IN THE AGE OF COLORBLINDEDNESS (2010).

64. *See NAACP Criminal Justice Fact Sheet,* www.naacp.org/criminal-justice-fact-sheet (last visited March 7, 2022).

65. *See, e.g.*, Lynn S. Branham, *Plowing in Hope: A Three-Part Framework for Incorporating Restorative Justice into Sentencing and Correctional Systems*, 38 WM. MITCHELL L. REV. 1261 (2012); Annalise Buth & Lynn Cohn, *Looking at Justice Through a Lens of Healing and Reconnection*, 13 NW. J. L. & SOC. POL'Y 1 (2017).

66. For more on drug courts, see the National Institute of Justice resources on Drug Courts, https://nij.ojp.gov/topics/articles/overview-drug-courts (last visited on March 13, 2022). *See also* Courtney Black, *Mental-Health Courts: Expanding the Model in an Era of Criminal Justice Reform*, 63 WASH. U. J. L. & POL'Y 299 (2020).

67. *See* 2019–20 CSALE REPORT, *supra* note 2, at 43 (twelve percent of externship courses focus specifically on the work of in-house counsel; other schools include in-house counsel externships in general externship courses).

reduce costs, involvement in crisis management and corporate management, and many other issues.[68] Faculty may want to ask students to interview a senior member of the legal team at their externship site to gain insights on changes over time at that site.

One factor driving the increased amount of work being done in-house is the rising cost of hiring outside counsel. Faculty may want to assign readings examining the practice of hourly billing, fee negotiations, and alternative billing and ask students to consider those issues from the point of view of the client corporation.[69] These are also good topics for externs to discuss with their supervisors and other attorneys at their externship site and report back to the class or reflect on in their journal.

There is a wide range of ethical and regulatory issues facing in-house counsel that could be addressed in the externship seminar.[70] These include ethical rules about representing corporations, including how the attorney-client privilege applies to corporations.[71] Externship teachers may also want to raise potential exceptions to the privilege and to explain that corporate counsel are covered by the Sarbanes-Oxley rules requiring them to report corporate wrongdoing under certain circumstances.[72]

One topic students may not have considered elsewhere in law school is the role of in-house lawyers in crisis management.[73] In addition to reading scholarly or other legal articles, faculty can often draw from cases in the headlines. The externship teacher may want to create a role-play exercise based on a real or hypothetical case to help students explore these issues in more depth. Internal investigations are another important area of work for in-house counsel that often are not discussed in the law school curriculum[74] and that lend themselves well to role play or other interactive class exercises.

---

68. *See* Elaine McArdle, *In the Driver's Seat: The Changing Role of the General Counsel*, Harvard Law Today (Summer 2012), https://today.law.harvard.edu/feature/in-the-drivers-seat-the-changing-role-of-the-general-counsel/; David B. Wilkins, *The In-House Counsel Movement: Metrics of Change*, The Practice, Harvard Law School Center on the Legal Profession (May/June 2016), https://thepractice.law.harvard.edu/article/in-house-counsel-movement (last visited March 7, 2022).

69. *See* Paresh Khushal, *Legal Cost Control* (2016), https://mena.thomsonreuters.com/en/articles/legal-fee-fear-factors.html; Scott Turow, *The Billable Hour Must Die,* ABA Journal (August 2007), www.abajournal.com/magazine/ article/the_billable_hour_must_die.

70. See Ann Vessels, Stacey Bowers, & Mark Popielarski, *Transactional Lawyering, in* Learning From Practice, *supra* note 3, at 657–62.

71. *See* Model Rules of Prof'l Conduct R. 1.13 (1983).

72. *See* Peter C. Kostant, *From Lapdog to Watchdog: Sarbanes-Oxley Section 307 and a New Role for Corporate Lawyers*, 52 N.Y.L. Sch. L. Rev. 535 (2007–2008).

73. *See, e.g.*, Deborah DeMott, *The Stages of Scandal and the Roles of General Counsel*, 2012 Wis. L. Rev. 463 (2012).

74. *See* Association of Corporate Counsel, *Corporate Internal Investigations* (2012), www.acc.com/ sites/default/files/2019-02/ACC-CLE-2-Corporate-Internal-Investigations.pdf (last visited March 7, 2022).

Chapter 11

Teaching Techniques and Resources for Externship Teachers

1. Adult Learning Theory and General Principles

a. Adult Learning Theory

Faculty considering possible teaching techniques for their externship course[1] would be well-advised to review research about how adults learn. It is not surprising that adults learn differently than children do. One of the leading adult learning theorists in the United States, Malcolm Knowles, called the practice of helping adults learn "andragogy" and distinguished it from "pedagogy," which is helping children learn.[2]

Knowles identified four characteristics of adult learners that are different from those of child learners and that should lead to different educational methods. First, adults see themselves as self-directed, as opposed to children, who see themselves as depending on the will of the instructor. Second, adults have a wide range of experiences from which to draw in their learning. Third, adults are especially open to learning about topics concerning what are known as "developmental tasks," which are related to what is expected of adults in their social role. Fourth, adults seek to

1. This Chapter will focus on techniques for teaching externship courses. There are a range of resources that explore best practices and advice for teaching all law school classes, including externships. *See, e.g.*, Michael Hunter Schwartz, Gerald F. Hess & Sophie M. Sparrow, What the Best Law Teachers Do (2013) (hereinafter "What the Best Law Teachers Do"); Michael Hunter Schwartz, Sophie M. Sparrow & Gerald F. Hess, Teaching Law by Design: Engaging Students from the Syllabus to the Final Exam (2d ed. 2017) (hereinafter "Teaching Law by Design"); Roy Stuckey & Others, Best Practices for Legal Education: A Vision and a Road Map (2007) (hereinafter "Best Practices for Legal Education").

2. Malcolm S. Knowles, The Modern Practice of Adult Education 37–38 (1970). While "andragogy" is a more accurate description of the learning that happens in law school, "pedagogy" still remains the dominant term used in higher education, and it is the term used in the title and elsewhere in this book.

acquire knowledge that they can apply immediately to problems they face, while children are content with acquiring knowledge that has some future benefit.[3]

Law professor Frank Bloch has analyzed how clinical legal education incorporates each of these aspects of adult learning.[4] While his analysis focused on in-house clinical courses, much of it applies with equal force to externship teaching.[5] Clinical and externship teachers seek to participate in a shared learning experience with their students, appealing to the self-directed nature of adult learners.[6] Self-direction is an important part of externship education, where students navigate a legal workplace and take responsibility for their learning. In-house clinics and externship courses are experiential, both in terms of students drawing from prior learning about the law and work and in terms of the nature of the work students do.[7] Student work in externship courses and in-house clinics is related to the developmental task of becoming a lawyer, which makes externships a good instructional environment for adult learners.[8] Finally, students engage in problem solving throughout their externships and clinics, consistent with the andragogy of ideal adult instruction.[9]

Externship courses also follow adult learning theory by combining experiential learning with multiple opportunities for reflection. "A central tenet of adult learning theory is bolstering the learners' ability to be a self-directed learner in the future through opportunities for reflection on the lessons gained through experience."[10] As explained in Chapter 8, both meaningful learning experiences and opportunities to reflect on those experiences are integral components of every externship course.

b. Shared Teaching Methods with In-House Clinical Courses

In-house clinical courses and externship courses use many of the same teaching techniques that fit well with adult learning theory. In fact, a good source of ideas for externship teaching is the rich literature describing and analyzing in-house clinical teaching.[11] Many of the teaching techniques below, including rounds, small group

3. Malcolm S. Knowles, The Adult Learner: A Neglected Species 57–63 (1990).

4. Frank S. Bloch, *The Andragogical Basis of Clinical Legal Education*, 35 Vand. L. Rev. 321 (1982).

5. *See* Elizabeth Ford, *Toward a Clinical Pedagogy of Externships*, 22 Clinical L. Rev. 113, 131–32 (2015).

6. *See* Bloch, *supra* note 4, at 338.

7. *See id.* at 341.

8. *See id.* at 343.

9. *See id.*

10. Fran Quigley, *Seizing the Disorienting Moment: Adult Learning Theory and the Teaching of Social Justice in Law School Clinics*, 2 Clinical L. Rev. 37, 48–49 (1995–1996).

11. There are hundreds of books and articles on this topic. The Clinical Legal Education Association publishes a bibliography each year as part of its *Handbook for New Clinical Teachers*, https://www.cleaweb.org/resources/Documents/ CLEA%20NCC%20Handbook.2019.FINAL.pdf (last visited March 7, 2022). The Clinical Law Review is devoted to articles about clinical teaching and practice. There are a number of excellent books focused on designing and teaching clinical courses. *See,*

discussions, and role play exercises, are excellent methodologies for both in-house clinics and externship teaching.[12] Both externship and in-house clinic faculty rely heavily on teaching techniques that require active learning. According to leading experts on law course design, "[a]ctive learning occurs when students engage in more than listening."[13] Long lectures from a faculty member simply are not suited to the type of reflective and active learning that are inherent parts of all externship courses. Active involvement by students enhances their learning and is especially effective in achieving four core goals of legal education: critical thinking skills, deep understanding of concepts, lawyering skills, and professional values.[14] Excellent law school teachers "use active and varied teaching and learning methods...."[15]

An interactive classroom format helps to further one important goal of the externship seminar, which is to bring the students' externship experiences into the classroom for review and exploration.[16] Using a format where all students are expected to speak and participate facilitates the sharing of externship experiences, similar to in-house clinic seminars where students share their work on different cases. The interactive format also helps students learn from each other through discussion and class exercises. One important benefit of having a seminar class is that it allows students to learn about externship settings other than their own and to talk through issues with peers who are also participating in externships.[17]

c. Confidentiality

While active student participation is essential to the externship seminar, as has been discussed in previous chapters, students must take care not to reveal any confidential information in class or elsewhere. Students are at different externship sites, and they must not reveal any confidential information to anyone outside their site, including their teacher and classmates. While some externs have already taken a

---

e.g., SUSAN BRYANT, ELLIOTT S. MILSTEIN & ANN C. SHALLECK, TRANSFORMING THE EDUCATION OF LAWYERS: THE THEORY AND PRACTICE OF CLINICAL PEDAGOGY (2014) (hereinafter "TRANSFORMING THE EDUCATION OF LAWYERS"); DEBORAH EPSTEIN, JANE H. AIKEN & WALLACE J. MLYNIEC, THE CLINIC SEMINAR (2014) (hereinafter "THE CLINIC SEMINAR").

12. *See* BUILDING ON BEST PRACTICES: TRANSFORMING LEGAL EDUCATION IN A CHANGING WORLD (Deborah Maranville, Lisa Radtke Bliss, Carolyn Wilkes Kaas & Antoinette Sedillo Lopez eds., 2015) (hereinafter "BUILDING ON BEST PRACTICES") at 237–38 (recommending teaching the externship seminar using simulation exercises, reflective discussions, rounds, and small group discussion); TRANSFORMING THE EDUCATION OF LAWYERS, *supra* note 11, at 14 (recommending whole group and small group discussion, quick-writes, exercises and role play, and simulations for clinic seminar teaching).

13. TEACHING LAW BY DESIGN, *supra* note 1, at 17.

14. *Id.*

15. WHAT THE BEST LAW TEACHERS DO, *supra* note 1, at 20.

16. *See* BUILDING ON BEST PRACTICES, *supra* note 12, at 236–37 (benefits of having a seminar include providing students with opportunities to reflect on and critique their experiences).

17. *See id.*

class in Professional Responsibility, others have not.[18] As highlighted in Chapter 9, externship teachers should provide students with the rules on confidentiality in the jurisdiction[19] before class even starts and review the key concepts during the first class. Students should also discuss confidentiality responsibilities with their externship supervisor.

Students benefit from seeing the rules regarding confidentiality in context. The teacher might choose a typical placement for the course and walk through what would be confidential and what could be shared in class and in written assignments. For example, assume that a student is working on a case where the client is a woman who is seeking a divorce and custody of her children. The student sits in on an interview with the client, conducts legal research, and accompanies the supervisor to court. Confidential information would include the identity of the client, anything the client told the attorneys, any identifying information about the case, the results of the legal research as applied to the facts of the case, the legal strategy, conversations between the student and the attorney about the case, and drafts of any work for the case. Information the student could share in class or a written assignment without breaching the duty of confidentiality would include things the student observed in open court that were on the record; general reflections on the courtroom and courthouse; what the student is learning in general about family law or the lives of low-income clients; what the student thinks about that law; the social justice implications of the work; reflections on what the student has learned about research, writing, and interviewing; whether the student is drawn to this type of work and why or why not; and many other reflective topics.

Many externship faculty also ask students to keep classroom conversations confidential and not share them outside of class. This class confidentiality can help build an environment where students feel free to discuss difficult issues openly and honestly. Such an environment encourages the honest reflection that is at the heart of externship education.

d. Learning Goals

Just as course design should begin with learning outcomes, as detailed in Chapter 7, the design of each individual class session should start with one or more learning outcomes or goals for that session. It is helpful to share those goals with students at the start of each class, so they have an understanding of the lessons they should try to take away from that class. The teaching techniques are not goals, but rather means to achieve the learning goals. The interactive classroom teaching techniques

18. Some schools choose to make a Professional Responsibility class a pre-requisite for taking an externship course.

19. *See, e.g.*, Model Rules of Prof'l Conduct R. 1.6 (1983).

described below can be combined in any number of ways in a single class or over the course of the semester.

2. Teaching Techniques for the Classroom

The descriptions of the techniques explained below will include examples of how they could be used in an externship class. The descriptions will assume an in-person class, but they can be adopted for online video classes. In addition to the suggestions described below, there are many other places to get ideas for specific class exercises. Chapter 8 has ideas about how to teach the skills of reflection, self-evaluation, and goal-setting. Chapters 9 and 10 include some sample class exercises for teaching different topics. Each chapter of *Learning From Practice*[20] contains examples of class exercises and discussion questions for the topic being taught, and the Teacher's Manual contains even more. LexternWeb has a whole section on teaching that includes syllabi, teaching ideas, and other materials.[21] Presentations and materials from national or regional conferences on clinical and externship teaching are other great sources of ideas for interactive externship class exercises.

a. Rounds

Rounds are facilitated classroom conversations where one or more students present on some issue in their fieldwork and get feedback from their peers. Rounds serve a number of pedagogical purposes, including helping students work through challenging legal and ethical issues, highlighting the value of teamwork and learning from others, and improving students' communication skills.[22] Students learn the value of honest dialogue with peers and how it can help strengthen their professional reasoning and ethical decision-making skills.[23] Rounds incorporate reflection, which is an essential part of externship teaching. In addition to a student's own reflections, rounds include multiple viewpoints and insights from other students.

The authors of *Transforming the Education of Lawyers: The Theory and Practice of Clinical Pedagogy* describe rounds used in teaching in-house clinics as having five stages: (1) describing the event; (2) identifying and clarifying the problem; (3) identifying the presenter's goals; (4) identifying and developing responsive lawyering strategies; and (5) identifying lawyering lessons from the discussion.[24] This general

---

20. Learning From Practice: A Text for Experiential Education (Leah Wortham, Alexander Scherr, Nancy Mauer, Susan L. Brooks eds., 3d ed. 2016) (hereinafter "Learning From Practice").

21. LexternWeb, https://www.lexternweb.org/externship-teaching (last visited March 7, 2022).

22. *See* Transforming the Education of Lawyers, *supra* note 11, at 113.

23. Susan Bryant & Elliott S. Milstein, *Rounds: A "Signature Pedagogy" for Clinical Education?*, 14 Clinical L. Rev. 195 (2007).

24. Transforming the Education of Lawyers, *supra* note 11, at 133–35.

structure can be used in externship classes for a wide range of topic areas. Faculty should feel free to adapt the structure to fit their class size, externship site diversity, and course goals.

The teacher should establish some ground rules, either orally or in writing. One general guideline should be an expectation that students will be active participants in the conversation. The model is an exchange between peers rather than a conversation between a teacher and student.[25] In order to encourage reflection, including self-reflection, students should be open and honest with their feedback. Sometimes this means respectful disagreement, which students should be encouraged to see as part of a healthy and safe learning environment.[26] Finally, as explained above, students must take care not to reveal any confidential information. This restriction is one important way that rounds in an externship course, where students work in different offices, are different from rounds in an in-house clinic course, where students are in the same office. Externship students seeking input or advice about an issue they are facing in their fieldwork will have to phrase the inquiry in a way that does not reveal any confidential information. For example, a student could describe their client and legal issues in general terms, saying they represent a low-income single mother who is facing eviction. Those facts give the class a general sense of the case without revealing client confidences.

The role of the teacher in rounds should be less directive and controlling than it often is with some other teaching techniques. In rounds, the teacher serves more as a facilitator. The goal is for the class to have conversations between peers where they help each other problem solve and learn. The teacher may help by modeling effective questions and by clarifying points. Sometimes the teacher's help is needed to move the conversation along and progress through the stages of the round. However, if students miss major points, the teacher should avoid giving answers or solutions until later in the round. The teacher may also help summarize the lawyering strategies and lessons from the exchange.[27]

A typical rounds discussion would start with a student describing a challenge they are encountering or a difficult situation they have experienced. The student should be allowed initially to explain the situation without interruption. Then other students should ask clarifying questions, eliciting additional information about the facts and context. The professor's role here is to encourage questions and then summarize what is known so far and what else students would like to know in order to offer helpful advice. Students may be eager to jump to solutions, but it is important to first identify and clarify the problem and understand the presenter's goals. With those goals in mind, students can move on to identifying strategies to address

25. Bryant & Milstein, *supra* note 23, at 229.

26. *Id.* at 229–30.

27. For a more extensive discussion on leading class rounds, *see id.* at 239–49 and Transforming the Education of Lawyers, *supra* note 11, at 131–48.

the challenge, including advice for the student on next steps. Finally, the professor should ask first the presenter and then the other students if the rounds process was helpful and, if so, in what way, including specific lessons learned.[28]

In order to maximize the educational benefits of rounds, faculty should look for "generative" topics that encourage an energetic exchange between students, build community, support group learning, and demonstrate the value of a collaborative discussion.[29] These topics invite students to brainstorm and encourage multiple approaches and perspectives. It is helpful to identify topics that engage the experience of multiple students. Topics that explore ethical and professional issues often create excellent rounds discussions.[30] Teachers might also identify some common themes they are seeing in student journals and present those as rounds topics. Faculty may want to pick a particular topic some weeks and allow students to identify current issues or concerns other weeks. Some externship faculty allow students to vote on topics that they would like to see addressed in rounds.

Some externship seminars start every class with rounds.[31] Others use them periodically or in connection with specific class topics. Some faculty give students questions for rounds in advance; others tell students that they may be called on in any class to participate in a rounds discussion. The frequency and length of rounds differ widely between externship courses depending on class size, learning goals, and pedagogical approach.

One example of using rounds in an externship seminar is to ask students early in the semester to present on some project or aspect of their work.[32] It is a good way to get students used to discussing their work in a reflective way but without revealing confidential information. These more simplistic rounds may not have an identified "problem" and so may not progress through all five stages of a typical rounds discussion. However, they do start to build students' communication skills as well as allow them to learn from each other about the type of work done in different practice settings. In these initial discussions, the teacher may need to encourage students to

---

28. LexternWeb has some helpful resources on conducting rounds in an externship class. *See* LexternWeb at https://docs.google.com/document/d/1bmpDx4-jGJOfEwxbFfUW0tSuAyJzgeCl/edit.

29. Bryant & Milstein, *supra* note 23, at 231.

30. *Id.* at 234–35.

31. For a more thorough discussion of using rounds in an externship class, *see* Rebecca Rosenfeld, *The Examined Externship Is Worth Doing: Critical Self-Reflection and Externship Pedagogy*, 21 Clinical L. Rev. 127, 147–58 (2014).

32. *See* Building on Best Practices, *supra* note 12, at 237–38 (the classroom provides a site for enhanced reflection on the externship work and responses from peers, and faculty can use rounds to promote that reflection).

ask each other questions and model questions, including clarifying questions and questions designed to draw other students into the conversation.

A more specific use of rounds might be in a class where the topic is supervision and how to get effective supervision. One student would be asked to describe a challenge they are facing in getting appropriate supervision. Stage 1 of the rounds would include the student describing the work they had done and the supervisor's response or lack of response. Stage 2 would involve the class asking questions to better understand the issue, including whether the assignment included a written product, how long it had been since the assignment had been submitted, how long the submission was, whether the student and supervisor had regular meetings, etc. The discussion in Stage 3 would clarify what the student hoped would happen next (the student's goals). Stage 4 would be a brainstorming session where students could share ideas, identify what they had done under similar circumstances, and discuss the pros and cons of different approaches. Finally, in Stage 5, the students could discuss future situations where they might face a similar issue, how what they learned might change what they do when they receive an assignment, how to deal with different supervision styles, and a host of other lessons. The faculty member might tie that discussion back to the assigned reading on getting and using feedback.

Faculty may choose to assess students on their participation in rounds. Sometimes students are more willing to participate if they know that it "counts" for their grade or for whether they receive credit (in classes where students are not graded). Faculty could use rounds to assess a number of skills, including oral presentation skills, ability to ask probing questions, problem-solving skills, ability to respectfully debate issues with peers, and many others.[33] The Appendix materials for Chapter 7 contain a rubric for a rounds discussion on an issue involving professional values. Assessing rounds might also be part of a larger assessment of class participation. If rounds will be a basis for assessment, students should be given the criteria and rubric in advance.

b. Role Play

Role play in an externship course is when students (or faculty) act out a situation related to an externship. The teacher usually briefly explains the situation and assigns students to play different roles. Those roles might include a supervisor, an extern, a client, a judge, or anyone else a student may encounter in an externship. Role play is generally done without the use of a formal script. It allows students to practice a variety of skills and to try out different approaches to situations in the safety of the classroom.[34] Role play can be a relatively quick way to test different responses to issues students are facing in their externship or questions posed by class assignments

33. Chapter 7 explains how to develop assessment tools.

34. TEACHING LAW BY DESIGN, *supra* note 1, at 128.

or discussion. Role play also helps students to see a situation through someone else's eyes, which can be useful in deciding how to approach that situation.[35]

For example, the rounds discussion above about supervision could end in a role play exercise. The class could start with a rounds exercise where a student explains an issue they are having with a supervisor and the class gives a number of suggested approaches. The students could then role play an interaction between the supervisor and the affected student, trying out some of the suggested responses. Students can go through several iterations of role playing this interaction, including having students switch roles. The students can then discuss how playing different roles affected their views on the issue, which approach seemed to have the best results, and how they might adapt the approach depending on the supervisor's response. All the students in the class can learn from this exercise, not just the student who shared the original situation during rounds.

A class on cultural competence and implicit bias might include a role play involving difficult conversations on racial or other bias. Students could volunteer to share an externship situation where they experienced or observed bias or discrimination. Faculty might start with a class or small group discussion on how that incident might affect the people involved and the larger community, and what emotional, social, physical, and financial costs might result from similar incidents of bias. Students could then role play ways that they could point out or discuss the bias. Students might need examples of starting language. One way to start might be, "I don't know if you know how that sounded, but it could be interpreted that you think... (identify hurtful bias)." An alternative start might be to say "help me to understand what you meant by... (insert bias statement)." In addition, it might be helpful to employ the Giving Voice to Values (GVV) framework described in Chapter 9 to help students stay true to and voice their values in situations where they face a values conflict.

c. Simulations

Simulations are often more complex than role plays, and they may engage students in a variety of activities, including reading and drafting documents, solving problems, and presenting information.[36] Faculty design simulations in advance, which allows them to teach skills in an experiential manner with control over the specific facts or situations set up by the scenarios.[37] Simulations can range from a

35. *See* Transforming the Education of Lawyers, *supra* note 11, at 76 (playing different roles can help students develop empathy and better understanding of a situation and potentially new creative ideas about how to solve a problem).

36. Teaching Law by Design, *supra* note 1, at 129.

37. *See* Transforming the Education of Lawyers, *supra* note 11, at 77. For a good discussion on how to design simulations for an externship class, *see* Rosenfeld, *supra* note 31, at 140–47.

single exercise to weekly simulations using the same case scenario where students can practice a range of skills.[38]

Simulations may be conducted in class, with or without advance preparation by the students. One challenge of this approach is that it engages a limited number of students at a time, depending on the number of roles in the scenario. One solution to this challenge is to arrange the discussion as a "fishbowl conversation." This technique puts the participating students in the middle of the room (in the fishbowl), with the rest of the class in a circle around them. The students can engage in the simulation for a set amount of time, after which a new group of students moves to the fishbowl. Alternatively, students can choose when to step into one of the roles in the simulation and replace a participant.[39]

Teachers can also assign students to engage in a simulation exercise outside of class and then write a reflection on the experience. Faculty members could choose to have the simulations videotaped to allow review by both the students and the teacher. Teachers can use class time to compare experiences, draw out common mistakes, and summarize intended lessons.[40] Debriefing with students after a simulation is important for their learning, whether the simulation happens in class or elsewhere. The debrief should include a return to the goals of the exercise and allow students to reflect on and critique their own and others' choices in the exercise.[41]

For example, continuing with the issue of supervisor feedback, teachers could design a simulation for students to engage in outside of class. Students are assigned to work in pairs, with one playing the role of a student receiving feedback and the other playing the role of the site supervisor providing feedback. The teacher could draft a short memo that is the work of the "student" in the simulation. The person playing the role of the supervisor would review the memo and fill out an evaluation on a form provided by the teacher. Then the two actual students would meet in their roles for a feedback session. Once that session is completed, the students would switch roles and do the exercise again. Then all students could draft a short reflection paper about what they learned from the experience and submit it to the teacher. Class time would be spent discussing takeaways from the exercise, with the teacher pulling out important lessons from the written assignments and the discussion.

Another example of a simulation exercise that is well-suited to many externship courses involves an exploration of different issues and interests in creating pro bono policies in law firms. The teacher could design a hypothetical law firm and create specific roles for students to play. Those might include a managing partner, a corpo-

38. Teaching Law by Design, *supra* note 1, at 129.

39. *See* Facing History and Ourselves, *Teaching Strategy: Fishbowl*, at https://www.facinghistory.org/resource-library/teaching-strategies/fishbowl (last visited March 7, 2022); Wikipedia, *Fishbowl (conversation)*, https://en.m.wikipedia.org/wiki/ Fishbowl_(conversation) (last visited March 7, 2022).

40. *See* Transforming the Education of Lawyers, *supra* note 11, at 77–80.

41. Rosenfeld, *supra* note 31, at 145.

rate partner, a litigation partner, an associate, a pro bono partner, a summer associate, a pro bono client, and a lawyer at a pro bono agency. The teacher could create background information for each role that includes that person's view of pro bono. One exercise could include designing the firm's pro bono policy, with input from the different participants. The simulation could be extended over several weeks, starting with a discussion of the policy, moving to a drafting and editing exercise, and culminating in presentations of the final policy to different audiences. These simulation exercises could be coupled with assigned readings on pro bono programs.[42]

Simulations can also be a good way to teach certain lawyering skills that students may be using in their externships. For example, many students will help with client intake and interviewing, but they may have very little experience or training in this area. Starting with a simulated interview is a good way to build confidence and skills before working with an actual client in the externship.[43]

d. Quick Write

A quick write is when a teacher poses a question in class and asks each student to take a few minutes to write a response. These exercises give students a short time to reflect on an issue and clarify their thinking,[44] rather than simply answering aloud. All students participate at the same time and initially are guided only by their own experiences and thoughts and not by what they are hearing from other students.

Once students have completed their written responses, there are a number of ways to use the information. One approach is for each student to read their responses to the class. A benefit of this approach is that every student gets a chance to share, including students who are often quiet during class discussions. As students are reading their responses, the teacher can summarize and group the answers on the board or an electronic display. Students can quickly see where their responses align with or differ from those in the class. The next step for the exercise might be for students to brainstorm solutions to some of the issues. Another approach would be to put students into small groups of two or more to share and discuss their responses. Then each group can report back to the whole and share their reflections. Finally,

42. *See, e.g.*, Scott L. Cummings & Deborah L. Rhode, *Managing Pro Bono: Doing Well by Doing Better*, 78 FORDHAM L. REV. 2357 (2010); Lenore Carpenter, *"We're Not Running a Charity Here": Rethinking Public Interest Lawyers' Relationships with Bottom-Line Driven Pro Bono Programs*, 29 BUFF. PUB. INT. L.J. 37 (2011).

43. For a good discussion of how to teach interviewing skills, including using simulation techniques, *see* THE CLINIC SEMINAR, *supra* note 11, at 135–216. The book also contains helpful resources for teaching a variety of other lawyering skills, including conducting factual investigations and trial, negotiation, and presentation skills.

44. *See* TRANSFORMING THE EDUCATION OF LAWYERS, *supra* note 11, at 74.

students could further reflect on the prompt in their journal, including adding personal issues that they were not comfortable sharing with the group in class.

A quick write geared at the topic of supervision would be to ask students to take several minutes to write down two challenges they have encountered in getting effective supervision and feedback. A quick write is also a good way to start a discussion on students' goals and the ways they propose to measure their progress on those goals. There are many examples of topics for quick writes in externship courses in most chapters of *Learning From Practice.*

e. Small Group Work

Having students work in small groups can help them understand course content at a deeper level and learn how to collaborate as professionals.[45] Group work actively engages many students at once and is often less intimidating than speaking in front of the entire class. Students who are engaged in active learning deepen their understanding and retention of information being presented.[46] Students bring different skills, values, and experiences to a group, which often results in better discussion and problem solving. Hearing different perspectives can prevent students from rushing to one "right" answer without considering complications and nuances in an issue.[47] Group work also helps students get to know each other better and create a class community.[48]

There are a number of things faculty can do to maximize the effectiveness of group work. It may be helpful to start with sharing some of the points above on the demonstrated benefits of group work, as some students may be skeptical. Give the group clear instructions, preferably in a way that they can refer back to (on a projection or handout or in the chat for an online class). Specify a time for the group to complete its tasks. Small group discussions do not have to take long. In fact, giving students a limited time to discuss a topic can incentivize them to use the time productively. Be clear about what will happen at the end of the time and what students are expected to have prepared.[49] Also think about the makeup of each group. Avoid letting students simply join together with their friends. Teachers can select groups at

45. Gerald F. Hess, Steven I. Friedland, Michael Hunter Schwartz & Sophie Sparrow, Techniques for Teaching Law 2 at 127 (2011).

46. *Id.*

47. *Id.*

48. Small group discussions through breakout rooms or other techniques can also be used to help build community in online classes, as is discussed in more detail in Chapter 12.

49. For a longer discussion of techniques to improve group work, *see* Techniques for Teaching Law 2, *supra* note 45, at 128–30.

random or be more purposeful, for instance putting people with similar placements together for some group topics and apart for other topics.

It is often helpful to have each group report back to the whole class. The group can choose a spokesperson or the teacher can ask a particular student to report back, perhaps focusing on students who are typically quiet during class discussions. The reporting back allows all students to hear each of the ideas that were generated in the discussions. The teacher may want to record the main points of the reports from each group on a white board or other display.

Small groups are a great way to start a discussion on a written or oral hypothetical. They also can be used to have students share their experiences on a common topic (supervision, research challenges and solutions, goals, etc.). Small group discussion of questions about assigned reading can help deepen students' understanding and create a better all-class discussion. Small group discussion would be appropriate for any of the externship class topics discussed in Chapters 9 and 10, and each chapter of *Learning From Practice* has ideas for discussion topics.[50]

f. Hypotheticals

Hypotheticals posed by a teacher are a familiar teaching tool in law school. In doctrinal courses faculty often use hypotheticals to help students explore the boundaries of a particular holding in a case. In an externship course, faculty can design hypotheticals that help students explore issues they may face in their externship or future practice. Hypotheticals allow the faculty member to control the facts to be considered and to present specific scenarios. Faculty may draw on issues described by students in their written reflections or common themes students have identified in prior semesters. This technique allows discussion of common issues without singling out a single student or externship site.

Hypotheticals may be written or oral, depending on the complexity of the facts. Faculty could provide the hypothetical in advance of class to give students more time to reflect on it. The exercise can be used with the entire class or assigned to students working in small groups, who could then report back to the class to allow comparison of suggested approaches.

Using the topic of supervision, the teacher might offer a hypothetical where a supervisor had provided the following feedback on student work: "Thanks for the research memo. It was helpful." The hypothetical could provide a good basis for small group or whole class discussion in a class where one of the goals was to identify ways to elicit helpful and constructive feedback. For a class dealing with relationships with clients and professional boundaries, the teacher could ask the students to consider

50. For a creative approach to group work that includes a wide range of exercises and resources, *see Liberating Structures*, www.liberatingstructures.com (last visited March 7, 2022).

a hypothetical situation where a client asked an extern for their cell phone number, so they could contact them with questions.

g. Student-Led Class Discussions and Presentations

Another technique that can help encourage more class participation is to have students lead some class discussions. The assigned discussion leaders need to immerse themselves in the assigned reading and topic. This technique allows each student to develop some expertise in a topic at least once each semester. Having student leaders can also mean greater participation from other students because they want to help out their fellow students and because they know they will have their own turn being discussion leaders. It is helpful to ask the discussion leaders to prepare several questions in advance about the reading and the class topic. They also could prepare a PowerPoint or handout to help them teach the lessons from the readings. Teachers may want to review these materials prior to class and suggest additional issues to consider. The teacher might also ask the discussion leaders to identify and assign a short reading related to the topic or to select all the assigned reading on a topic. Researching a topic is a good way for students to deepen their understanding.

Teachers may also want to engage students by asking them to make a presentation to the class. Preparing and presenting information to others is a great skill for students to practice. Presentations also allow students to learn about areas of practice or externship sites other than their own. It is helpful to give students guidelines about how long the presentation should be, whether they should include a visual form of presentation, what research they are expected to do, and what their goals should be in the presentation.[51] Faculty may want to review and comment on the topic and an outline in advance, to make sure the student is on track. The form of presentation could range from a simple talk, to a talk with a PowerPoint, to a TEDTalk, to an interactive exercise.

Faculty can assign presentation topics or allow students to pick their own. The presentations might be about the externship site, a topic covered in class, an area of law the student is learning at the externship, the client population of the externship site, a social justice issue students have identified during the externship, or any other of a very wide range of topics.

Teachers need to decide whether to assess presentations, either as part of a class participation assessment or as a stand-alone assignment. Utilizing peer assessment for presentations is another way to engage all students and give the presenter a wide range of feedback. Self-assessment is a good tool to help students reflect on their performance and to compare with the teacher and peer assessments. Students should be provided with the criteria for any type of assessment in advance.

---

51. Chapter 18 of *Learning From Practice* is an excellent resource for students giving presentations. Leah Wortham, *Making Presentations, in* LEARNING FROM PRACTICE, *supra* note 20, at 469–88.

h. Guest Speakers

Using guest speakers is a common practice in many kinds of courses, both law school courses and others. Students appreciate learning from experts in different fields. Sometimes it is helpful as a change of pace to include guest speakers, even if it is a topic where the teacher has expertise. Using guest speakers is also a way to let students hear different points of view on class topics from lawyers or others who work in the "real world" outside the law school.

It is advisable to work in advance of the class to prepare a guest speaker. Teachers may want to share the learning goals for the individual class where the guest is speaking and any reading assigned for that class. Giving speakers a range of topics to address or a list of specific questions to answer can also be helpful. Spending a little time in advance of class working with the guest speaker can help ensure that it is a successful experience for them and for the class.

The range of possible guest speakers is as wide as the range of topics for externship classes. For example, judicial writing is often a topic discussed in judicial externship courses, and having a judge come to class to discuss the topic is a great way for students to learn. A psychologist who specializes in workplace issues might be a great guest speaker for a class on receiving and learning from feedback. Externship supervisors also make interesting guest speakers. Teachers can take advantage of video technology to bring in guest speakers remotely. Using technology expands the universe of potential speakers and makes it more convenient for busy speakers who may not have time to travel to physically attend a class session.

i. Using Visual and Audio Tools

Students learn in different ways, and the current generation of law students often responds positively to learning from videos and other visual means. There are a number of ways to incorporate this kind of technology into an in-person class.[52] As described above, video technology is a great way to bring diverse voices of guest speakers into the classroom. Similarly, there are thousands of free videos on topics relevant to externship courses on platforms like YouTube and others. TED Talks have become a popular classroom learning tool. This is another way of providing students with views from experts in different fields without physically bringing those experts into the classroom. Teachers may assign videos in advance, play them in class, or have students find their own video sources and report on them in class.

Many law school teachers include a PowerPoint or other visual outline for each class, and externship teachers are no exception. These notes can then be posted on the course site, so that students can refer back to them. That step also can encourage more in-class discussion, since it reduces the need for students to spend class time taking careful notes. As with any teaching technique, faculty should consider how

52. For information on using technology for remote and online teaching, *see* Chapter 12.

the visual tool will help achieve the learning goals for the class.[53] Beware of including too much text and of simply reading the slides. Remember that students may assume that what is included in the visual outline is the most important information, so think about including questions, problems, hypotheticals and other more open-ended inquiries.

3. Classroom Assessment Techniques

Whatever teaching techniques faculty choose for their externship courses, it is important to continue to assess teaching and adjust as needed to maximize student learning.[54] Classroom Assessment Techniques (CATs) are tools for teachers to assess how well students are learning so the teacher can adjust the instruction if needed. They are centered on improving student learning and are not evaluative.[55] Classroom Assessment is intended to be an ongoing process where teachers use CATs to gather feedback about their students' learning and the effectiveness of teaching methods and then use the results to modify teaching methods.[56] Before implementing CATs, the teacher should explain their purpose and use to the students. It is important that students understand it is not an assessment of their performance but instead is meant to improve teaching and learning.[57] After students respond to a CAT, the teacher should read and analyze the results, identifying any common themes of the feedback. The teacher should then consider adjustments to their teaching that might respond to the feedback. Finally, the teacher should report back to the students the results of the CAT and any responses the teacher may be making.[58]

One good CAT for examining learning in a single class session is the minute paper. "The purpose of a minute paper is for the teacher to gather quick, targeted feedback from students about their learning and then to use that feedback to make appropriate teaching choices."[59] The teacher develops question(s) based on the learning goals for a class and presents them to students near the end of class, either in writing on a screen or as a handout. The teacher might ask, "What are the three main points you learned today about how to elicit substantive and constructive feedback from a supervisor" or "What remaining questions do you have about how to develop attainable and measurable goals for the semester." Students take a couple of minutes to compose and submit written or electronic responses. The teacher reviews the responses after class, identifies common themes, and considers appropriate responses

53. For good discussions of how to use PowerPoint in class, *see* TEACHING LAW BY DESIGN, *supra* note 1, at 113–14; TECHNIQUES FOR TEACHING LAW 2, *supra* note 45, at 69–71.

54. For information on how to assess externship courses as a whole, *see* Chapter 7.

55. GERALD HESS & STEVEN FRIEDLAND, TECHNIQUES FOR TEACHING LAW 263 (1999).

56. *Id.*

57. *Id.* at 264.

58. *Id.* at 264–65.

59. Gerald Hess, Michael Hunter Schwartz & Nancy Levit, *Fifty Ways to Promote Teaching and Learning*, 67 J. LEGAL. EDUC. 696, 719 (2018).

to gaps in student learning. The teacher would later give brief feedback to the students about the responses and resulting teaching additions or adjustments.

A similar CAT that could be used to identify broader learning gaps and appropriate teaching adjustments is the teacher-designed questionnaire. The questionnaire could be presented as a handout or webpage in class. Allowing students to respond anonymously often improves the quality and candor of the responses.[60] The questionnaire could solicit additional class topics that students would like to discuss. It could ask about the teaching and learning methods that students have found most and least effective. The range of questions is as broad as the class topics and teaching techniques. As with the minute paper CAT, the teacher should review and analyze the responses and report back to the class on the results.

4. Out of Class Teaching Techniques

Externship faculty engage students in learning both inside and outside the classroom. While faculty often spend significant time creating a syllabus and planning class exercises and discussions, it is equally important to design and plan for teaching outside the classroom. Teaching outside of class time may include both written assignments and individual meetings and other communications with students.

a. Written Assignments

Writing is critical to the practice of law and is an excellent teaching tool in many law school classes, including externship courses. Most externships provide opportunities for students to draft a variety of legal documents for actual cases or projects at the externship site. Writing for the externship classroom is often more focused on examining what the student is learning by explaining it in writing.

Research on the connection between writing and developing complex thinking skills concludes that writing improves thinking.[61] Writing makes students explain what they are learning and can expose gaps in their understanding. Writing about an observation, assignment, or conversation in an externship necessarily involves some gap in time between the event and the written reflection. That time gap can give students room to pause, think, and reflect. As explained in Chapter 8, reflective writing helps students better understand and appreciate their own learning and examine their evolving understanding of the legal profession.

Externship faculty should have an identified pedagogical purpose for each writing assignment, just as they do for each class session. Faculty should also be conscious of the total amount of written work required for the externship course, especially because most students do a good deal of writing at their externship site. As explained above, writing for the class is a different kind of writing than that done at

60. *Id.* at 718.

61. Techniques for Teaching Law 2, *supra* note 45, at 179.

the externship site and serves a different educational purpose. Faculty attention to the total amount of writing of any kind is still warranted.

Students may be more motivated to put time and effort into written assignments for class if they are assessed by the faculty member and factored into the final grade. Faculty should provide students with assessment criteria in advance. It is advisable to provide students with some feedback on written assignments even if they are not formally assessed or graded.

1) Journals and Response Papers

Nearly all law school externship courses include written assignments in the form of student journals,[62] reflections, or response papers. Response papers are often stand-alone assignments involving a prompt and series of questions on a particular topic designed by the teacher. Journals also often include prompts on particular topics, but in addition may allow for more free-form reflection on the students' goals, work assignments, supervision, observations, thoughts on class readings, self-evaluation, and a wide variety of other topics. Given the concerns identified above about the amount of written work required for the course, faculty usually assign either journals or response papers, but not both.

While most externship students are familiar with writing a law school exam or research paper, they may not have experience with writing a reflective journal or response paper. Faculty should give students careful instructions on an optimal length for the written assignment, a reminder about confidentiality, and the date and time by which the assignment must be submitted. Some teachers assign journal entries or response papers that are due each week, while others have assignments due every other week or a set number of times during the semester. One factor in determining the frequency is when the teacher has time to review and provide feedback on the written assignments. Faculty should also consider the timing and sequencing of different assignments. For example, many externship teachers ask students to reflect on their goals and progress on those goals at the beginning, middle, and end of the semester. Including the assignments and instructions on the syllabus or other materials distributed on the first day of class can help students look ahead and plan for written work.

There are many topics for reflective journal entries and response papers that encourage and support student learning and growth. Chapter 8 details topics regarding student goals and self-evaluation, all of which would be appropriate for journal assignments or response papers. Each chapter of *Learning From Practice* has different exercises, any of which would be good topics for a journal entry or a short response paper. The chapter on reflection and journal writing in *Learning From Practice* has a

62. Some externship teachers prefer to call these written assignments something other than "journals" due to students not taking the assignment seriously. Alternatives might include "reflection assignments" or "written reflections."

long list of potential journal topics, all of which could also be topics for response papers.[63] They range from class readings and discussions to ethical issues to life balance and career satisfaction. Many of the syllabi posted on LexternWeb include journal or response paper topics. Faculty who teach a subject-specific externship course may want to consider topics related to that course. For example, students in a judicial externship course might be asked to reflect on the pros and cons of allowing judges to actively participate in social media. Students working for government agencies could be assigned to reflect on who their client is and what that means for their work.

2) Online Assignments

Using technology to engage student learning can be a successful technique in externship courses. Many students are accustomed to posting comments or other information on social media and other online platforms. Many students participated in online courses during the COVID-19 global pandemic. Chapter 12 provides ideas for maximizing the value of online teaching. This section will briefly discuss how to engage students in written online discussions outside of an in-person class. The lessons examined in Chapter 12 apply with equal force to these assignments.

Many courses use an online platform to host the syllabus, submission of student assignments, and other course necessities. Most of these platforms include a mechanism that allows the teacher and students to engage in an online dialogue. Teachers may want to post questions related to the reading for the week and ask for responses. This technique helps ensure that students are doing the reading and come to class prepared for an engaged discussion. Another way to use this online tool is to assign students to observe particular proceedings and post a reflection on what they saw and learned. These postings are visible to the entire class and encourage students to compare their views and observations to those of others in the class. Teachers might require that every student respond to every post by the teacher or require a minimum number of posts and responses over the course of the semester. If these posts will be evaluated and considered as part of the students' grades, the teacher should provide the criteria for such assessment in advance. Online discussions are often a way to be sure that all students share their thoughts on a variety of topics and may be an easier way for shyer students to engage in a discourse and reflect.

3) Final Papers

Some externship teachers require a final paper in addition to the journals or response papers and online responses. Final papers allow students to explore in more depth an aspect of the externship that particularly interested them in a way that weekly journal assignments or response papers on specific subjects do not always allow. Many externship teachers encourage student reflection in these final papers.

---

63. Alexander Scherr & Margaret Martin Barry, *Reflection and Writing Journals, in* LEARNING FROM PRACTICE, *supra* note 20, at 220–26.

The paper could include outside resources and research or be limited to the student's own experiences and reflections. Some teachers may prefer to assign a more traditional research paper on a topic related to the externship.

Teachers may want to review and approve final paper topics in advance, to help ensure that the topic is well-defined and appropriate for the length of the paper. As with other assignments, careful instructions on length, due dates, and other requirements will help ensure student success. Faculty should also design and share with students an assessment tool for the final paper.

b. Meetings with Students

In addition to the teaching techniques employed in the classroom, externship teachers use individual meetings with students to further student learning. Professor Harriet Katz asserts that "counseling—a teacher/student relationship encompassing empathy, perspective, and guidance—is critical to the best standards for externship.... A collaborative counseling relationship between student and faculty supervisor can provide a foundation for both problem-solving and encouragement and is a critical component of a successful externship experience."[64] Ideally, externship teachers should schedule individual student meetings, in addition to the group externship seminar class meetings, at multiple points during the semester.[65] The first meeting might be before the student begins an externship to determine what placements could help advance career and professional development goals. The second meeting might be at the beginning of the semester to review and discuss the student's articulated learning goals for the externship experience. The third meeting might be at mid-semester to review progress toward meeting the student's learning goals, to ensure that the student is receiving meaningful feedback from their externship supervisor, to review mid-semester assessments (self-assessment, preliminary performance assessment provided by the externship site, or both), and to address any concerns or perceived problems a student may be encountering at their placement. The final meeting is usually at the end of the semester to review the externship site's final evaluation of the student, to engage in a holistic reflection of the externship experience and progress toward professional development goals, and to discuss ideas for future externship or other professional experiences. In addition to scheduled meetings, externship teachers often hold unscheduled meetings throughout the semester to address unexpected student concerns such as a personal issue, an issue with the site supervisor, or a performance issue at the placement or

---

64. Harriet N. Katz, *Counseling Externship Students*, 15 CLINICAL L. REV. 239, 239–40 (2009).

65. In some instances, individual meetings might take the place of the externship seminar and serve as a means by which the faculty member is providing "faculty-guided reflection" as required by ABA Standard 304. *See* Chapter 2 for a full discussion of the ABA Standards.

in the externship course, and to answer questions about future externship or other professional experiences.

Professor Katz identifies three main challenges to counseling externship students: permission, competence, and time. "Care needs to be taken to develop the sense of permission necessary for a counseling relationship, to set the expectation that externship students will be asked to reflect on their own professional development and to be open to discussion with the faculty supervisor."[66] To secure permission, an externship teacher can define their role as an ally to the student's learning early in the semester. In addition, frequent counseling can demonstrate a commitment to the student's success and can create trust and rapport.

Competence is another challenge to effective student counseling. Often, externship teachers have not been trained in counseling and must fall back on their training as lawyers. In doing so, externship teachers must consider their own unique perspectives and "apply the lawyerly counseling skill of providing perspective as an informed, neutral, but empathetic professional while respecting [an individual's] autonomy."[67] That said, counseling students can be difficult. Externship teachers may receive pushback from their students, or they may inadvertently hurt feelings, overstep, or be wrong. For these reasons, it is important to prepare for every scheduled meeting with students. In addition, teachers need to be sure that they are not just hearing students, but that they are actively listening. The SOLER acronym facilitates self-awareness by reminding the listener of body language that can be employed to facilitate active listening. SOLER stands for: Sit straight; Open posture; Lean forward; Eye contact; and Relax.[68]

A general structure for a one-on-one externship meeting could include directed questions using an externship form such as a learning goals form, mid-semester self-evaluation, or a performance assessment to help guide the conversation; asking how things are going at the placement and what the student is working on; and making sure to ask the student if there is anything else they would like to discuss.[69] The content and tone of the student's response will help the externship teacher gather specific information about "the working relationship between the student and the field supervisor"[70] and the "student's engagement with and immersion in the legal work of the placement."[71]

At the end of any one-on-one student meeting, consider assigning "homework" that "stimulates learning and development" and ensures that the coaching relation-

66. Katz, *supra* note 64, at 241.

67. *Id.* at 242.

68. Gerard Egan, The Skilled Helper: A Systematic Approach to Effective Helping (4th ed. 1990).

69. Katz, *supra* note 64, at 242.

70. *Id.* at 247.

71. *Id.*

ship does not end with the meeting.[72] The homework can either be generated by the externship teacher or the student's own idea after brainstorming a particular issue and can take the form of something to think about, an action step to take, an article to read, or a TED Talk to watch. The key is that "devising appropriate homework involves talking with the [student] about what sorts of behaviors and experiences are likely to facilitate goal achievement, as well as what metrics can be used to measure progress toward that goal. These activities and metrics help build structure, accountability, and results into the process."[73] If a teacher has multiple scheduled meetings with students, the homework can be a connecting point and facilitate reflection between meetings.

When the meeting involves talking about student performance or behavior issues, having a script can be helpful. First, shift the tone of the conversation from personal to professional. Teachers should begin with a statement about what they want to talk about with the student, then describe what they have observed, the impact that it is having, and the request that they are making.[74] When providing constructive criticism, it is important that externship teachers stick to the facts and be specific: criticize the deed, not the doer; focus on the future, not the past; and be concrete regarding expectations.[75] Despite these efforts, students may have difficulty receiving feedback, which could prompt an emotional response. In that instance, externship teachers should not try to get the student to see things exactly their way. Rather, the externship teacher should try to help the student feel psychologically safe and identify points of agreement where there is a shared perspective.[76] Finally, teachers should consider looking to other professions for models. For example, the SPIKES protocol used by oncologists can be a helpful way to frame student performance discussions. SPIKES is an acronym that stands for: Setting up (allow for privacy, limit time constraints and interruptions, sit down, make eye contact); assess Perception (ask before you tell); obtain an Invitation (is the person ready to hear the information?); give Knowledge (relay the information); address emotion with Empathy (identify emotion); and Strategy and summary (what is the plan moving forward?).[77]

Finally, externship teachers need to be realistic about their time challenges. "In a larger program, with a leaner full-time teaching staff, counseling is likely to be lim-

72. Monique Valcour, *The Kind of Homework That Helps Coaching Stick*, Harv. Bus. Rev. (Mar. 3, 2015).

73. *Id.*

74. Bob Wall, Coaching for Emotional Intelligence: The Secret to Developing The Star Potential in your Employees (2007).

75. Randy Garner, Criticism Management: How to More Effectively Give, Receive and Seek Criticism in Our Lives (2006).

76. Amy Gallo, *Overcoming the Toughest Common Coaching Challenges*, Harv. Bus. Rev. (April 15, 2015).

77. W. F. Baile et al., *SPIKES—A Six Step Protocol for Delivering Bad News: Application to the Patient with Cancer*, The Oncologist 5:302-11 (2000). Using the SPIKES protocol was an idea inspired by a student in Georgia State University College of Law's Externship Program.

ited to students most in need, and therefore to focus mostly on negative situations requiring significant intervention...."[78] While it might be counter-intuitive, one of the ways externship teachers can increase the time they have to spend meeting with students is to plan them in advance. If a student has regular individual meetings with their faculty supervisor, they are more likely to take more ownership of their professional development and to communicate any perceived problems before they become larger issues.

5. Professional Development

It is important for externship faculty to continue to get new teaching ideas, improve their skills, and learn how externship programs operate at other schools. Fortunately, there are many opportunities for externship faculty to engage in this professional development. First, all externship teachers and program directors should subscribe to the law school externship community listserv, "LEXTERN."[79] On nearly a daily basis, externship teachers from around the country share information and pose questions on LEXTERN. The LexternWeb website,[80] which is referenced numerous times in this book, is a very helpful resource that contains syllabi, supervisor training materials, information for new teachers, scholarship on externship teaching, and other important information. Another helpful listserv to join is the Clinical Legal Education Listserv, "LAWCLINIC."[81] The listserv contains posts by clinical faculty, including externship faculty.

Two important professional organizations that externship faculty should consider joining are the Association of American Law Schools Section on Clinical Legal Education[82] ("AALS Clinical Section") and the Clinical Legal Education Association ("CLEA").[83] Both organizations support clinical legal education and faculty, including externship faculty. Each organization has an active externship committee, and the AALS Clinical Section Externship Committee has several subcommittees, including ones focusing on externship teaching, membership and outreach, and scholarship. Working on a committee is a good way to learn about externship programs at other schools, recent developments in legal education that affect externship teaching, and a host of other topics. CLEA publishes the CLEA New Clinician's

78. Katz, *supra* note 64, at 243–44.

79. Lextern@listserv.gsu.edu (last visited March 7, 2022). Requests to be added should be sent to Kendall Kerew at kkerew@gsu.edu.

80. https://www.lexternweb.org/ (last visited March 7, 2022).

81. http://lists.washlaw.edu/mailman/listinfo/lawclinic (last visited March 7, 2022).

82. https://www.aals.org/sections/list/clinical-legal-education/ (last visited March 7, 2022).

83. https://www.cleaweb.org/ (last visited March 7, 2022).

Handbook,[84] which contains helpful information on many topics, including seminar design, rounds, and assessment.

Conferences are another excellent place for professional development. There is a biannual Externship Conference. This conference focuses exclusively on law school externship teaching and is a great place to build knowledge and meet colleagues from around the country. LexternWeb has information on past conferences[85] and on the next planned Externship Conference. The annual AALS Conference on Clinical Legal Education[86] is intended for faculty who teach in-house clinics and externship courses and is another good place to gather ideas for teaching techniques. There is generally a one-day conference for new clinicians, including externship teachers, one day before the start of the AALS Conference, which is a great venue for new teachers to learn about the field.

Faculty also may want to participate in teaching rounds that are sponsored by the Teaching Methodologies Committee of the AALS Clinical Section. There are sessions exclusively for externship teachers. Participants present teaching challenges and discuss them in a rounds format with supportive colleagues from other schools.[87]

84. Clinical Legal Education Association, Handbook for New Clinical Teachers (2019), https://www.cleaweb.org/resources/Documents/CLEA%20NCC%20Handbook.2019.FINAL.pdf (last visited March 7, 2022).

85. https://www.lexternweb.org/clinical-conferences (last visited March 7, 2022).

86. https://www.aals.org/events/ (last visited March 7, 2022).

87. LexternWeb, *Teaching Rounds,* https://www.lexternweb.org/teaching-rounds (last visited March 7, 2022).

Chapter 12

Using Online Technology in Teaching Externships

The use of online technology in teaching externships is now a well-established practice, both for those who are new to the pedagogy and for those who have been teaching externships for a while. Before the curtailment of in-person interactions caused by the coronavirus pandemic, online education in the legal academy was not in widespread use. Two years of social distancing gave many a crash course in the use of online technology for the delivery of legal education. Law schools around the world experienced a dramatic increase in online education, and law offices experienced a similar surge in virtual practice. While in-person interactions resumed in both law practice and education, improvements in online technology, combined with benefits for the environment, flexibility for students and professionals, and increased collaboration at the national and international level, have resulted in permanent changes in online education.

Acceptance of these changes varies throughout educational institutions and among externship faculty as well. Views of technology are formed not just by individual experiences, but also by the setbacks experienced by educators, particularly those in higher education, who initially embraced online technology as an answer to many problems, only to find it created new ones. Broad sectors of society have experienced online education and online work, but many individuals participated in this new form of learning in an unplanned manner and within the context of fear, isolation, and economic upheaval brought on by a global pandemic. This legacy, combined with the required learning curve needed to adopt a new technology, has led some faculty to resist continued use of technology in teaching. Some of the assumed drawbacks have already been overcome by improved technology and continued use following the pandemic. Although other disadvantages to online education still exist, it is increasingly clear that all educators, including those in law schools, will need to use a substantial number of online tools in the foreseeable future.

This Chapter provides a rationale for the use of online technology in law school education and specifically in externships. It covers some design considerations and includes a guide to effective techniques. With these tools in hand, externship designers and faculty will be able to incorporate online technology into their programs to become more effective teachers, increase access to justice, and prepare their students for future practice. As many law schools will use a hybrid approach going forward, the suggestions in this Chapter can be used by those who want to incorporate some online technology (such as a Zoom class or a discussion board) into their in-person classes as well as those who wish to adopt or continue a completely online course that is taught asynchronously.[1]

1. Reasons to Use OnlineTechnology in Externships

First used in undergraduate and graduate education outside the law school, and initially developed to expand access to education through use of the internet, platforms such as the Massive Online Open Course (known as MOOC) promised a cheaper, more easily available alternative to expensive brick and mortar institutions. Most U.S. law schools were slower to take up the innovation,[2] but some embraced the new technology with bold promises.[3] Initial excitement was tempered with a more sober recognition of the time and effort required to produce truly effective online education; nonetheless, law schools such as Mitchell Hamline offer options that are completely online,[4] and law schools have continued to expand their offerings each passing year.[5]

Most law schools now use internet-based software platforms, such as TWEN, Blackboard, or Canvas, for many classes. Accessed by students through a personal computer, tablet, or smartphone, these programs allow professors to post and respond to assignments and share reading materials. These systems permit both synchronous communication—communication that takes place at the same time for all parties, including through videoconferencing or teleconferencing—and asynchronous interactions—in which students engage at different times during a set period of hours or days using either written comments or video, in a discussion forum.[6]

---

1. *See* Chapter 2 for a thorough discussion of how the ABA Standards on Distance Education affect online instruction where the professor is separated from the students and to determine how these requirements impact an externship seminar and field placement.

2. For a thoughtful essay on the impact of digital technologies on legal education, see Warren H. Binford, *Envisioning a Twenty-First Century Legal Education*, 43 Wash. U. J. L. & Pol'y 157 (2014).

3. Robert E. Oliphant, *Will Internet Driven Concord University Law School Revolutionize Traditional Law School Teaching*, 27 Wm. Mitchell L. Rev. 841, 880 (2000).

4. Mitchell Hamline, *Mitchell Hamline announces new blended-learning J.D. option* (Sept. 5, 2019), https://mitchellhamline.edu/news/2019/09/05/mitchell-hamline-announces-new-blended-learning-j-d-option/.

5. Trish Sammer, *8 ABA-Approved Online Law Schools*, Nitro (Sept. 10, 2021), https://www.nitrocollege.com/blog/online-degrees/aba-approved-online-law.

6. Such systems are known generally as learning management systems, which are software applications to administer, track and deliver educational programs. Iuliana Dobre, *Learning Management Systems for Higher Education—An Overview of Available Options for Higher Education Organizations*, Procedia—Social and Behavioral Sciences 180: 313-320 (2015).

Reasons for this expansion include the goal of increasing access to legal education across disciplines[7] and time zones, as well as providing it to specific groups such as disadvantaged or remote communities, students with disabilities,[8] international students,[9] and part-time students who are working. Other advantages include reducing an institution's environmental footprint, enlarging access to resources (posted online rather than produced as expensive, bulky handouts), avoiding traffic—increasingly a serious problem for urban law schools—and reducing the expense of maintaining buildings. These reasons are true world-wide and have led to the adoption of online methods in legal education outside the United States as well.[10]

One of the most compelling arguments for expanded use of technology inside an externship program classroom lies beyond it, in the law office itself. An article in the October 2016 issue of *The Atlantic* entitled "Do Lawyers Need Offices Anymore?"[11] described a law firm with fifty attorneys who represent Fortune 500 companies and never go to an office. As a result of changes caused by the coronavirus pandemic, the virtual office has been adopted not just by for-profits, but also by government offices and nonprofit agencies.[12] The pandemic lasted long enough to force most law offices, courts, and businesses to create relatively permanent alternatives to working on site; one of its long-term consequences was thus the rapid acceleration and widespread adoption of aspects of virtual practice.

While there are many reasons to adopt it, use of online technology in legal practice and legal education has costs as well as benefits. Law offices allow employees to use technology to work remotely because of the obvious advantages: no commute, reduced expenses for office space and travel, the global nature of practice with more geographically dispersed employees, and more time for employees with their families.[13] These firms also encounter challenges: it is harder to socialize with coworkers;

---

7. Paula E. Berg, *Using Distance Learning to Enhance Cross-Listed Interdisciplinary Law School Courses*, 29 Rutgers Computer & Tech. L.J. 33, 52 (2003).

8. Michael L. Perlin, *Distance Legal Education as an Agent of Social Change*, 24 Pac. McGeorge Global Bus. & Dev. L.J. 95, 98-100 (2011).

9. *Id.* at 101-06.

10. There were thirty-six law schools in Australia in 2015, and seven offered a fully online law degree. A fully online clinic is offered in at least one Australian law school. Les McCrimmon, Ros Vickers & Ken Parish, *Online Clinical Legal Education: Challenging the Traditional Model*, 23 Int'l J. Clinical Legal Educ. 33, 51 (2016); Sammer, *supra* note 5.

11. Leigh McMullan Abramson, *Do Lawyers Need Offices Anymore?*, Atlantic (Oct. 9, 2015) https://www.theatlantic.com/business/archive/2015/10/do-lawyers-need-offices-anymore/409417/.

12. Bob Ambrogi, *87% of Law Offices Working Remotely, Survey Finds, as They Struggle to Maintain Financial Stability, LawSites* (Apr. 30, 2020), https://www.lawsitesblog.com/2020/04/87-of-law-offices-working-remotely-survey-finds-as-they-struggle-to-maintain-financial-stability.html. For a discussion of remote work before the pandemic see David Dorion, *Working Remotely: How It's Impacting the Legal Industry and Your Firm*, LawCrossing, https://www.lawcrossing.com/employers/article/900048761/Working-Remotely-How-It-s-Impacting-the-Legal-Industry-and-Your-Firm/ (last accessed Sept. 25, 2022).

13. Ambrogi, *supra* note 12.

there can be some reduced productivity with multi-tasking at home; and work life boundaries are blurred further when a home is also an office.[14] The pandemic amplified many of the previously identified disadvantages to virtual work such as isolation and inadequate internet and technology.[15] Yet firms, like educational institutions,[16] are not turning away from online technology; they are simply refining it to meet their needs.[17] Educators planning for successful online externships will need to consider both the promise and the challenges to prepare students effectively.

Externship programs and law schools can play a role in helping students become familiar with online technology and its professional applications while in law school so they can enter the workplace practice ready. Future law graduates will conduct interviews and appear in some proceedings through videoconference, negotiate via email, and draft documents on the internet in virtual meetings. Using online technology in externships and clinics, which traditionally focus on skill development, is not a luxury to be delayed for the future, but a pedagogical approach to be incorporated into every program.

2. Considerations in Online Legal Education

The relative speed with which other disciplines have embraced online education, and the degree to which it has been studied[18] and improved, provide legal educators, particularly those in externships and clinics, with important lessons learned. These include the challenges of evolving technology, the need to tailor the technology to the student and technology-related learning outcomes, the ongoing importance of pedagogy as a guide, and the imperative of embracing online learning to thrive. A quick review of these considerations is useful in deciding which technology best fits a particular program.

---

14. Marnie Dobson Zimmerman & Pouran Faghri, *Blurred Boundaries: Work-Life Balance in the Time of COVID19*, Healthy Work Now (May 22, 2020), https://healthyworknow.medium.com/blurred-boundaries-work-life-balance-in-the-time-of-covid19-719e42e85cb5.

15. Simon Usborne, *End of the Office: The Quiet, Grinding Loneliness of Working From Home*, Guardian (July 14, 2020), https://www.theguardian.com/money/2020/jul/14/end-of-the-office-the-quiet-grinding-loneliness-of-working-from-home.

16. *See, e.g.*, Kristen E. Murray, *Take Note: Teaching Law Students to Be Responsible Stewards of Technology*, 70 Cath. U. L. Rev. 201 (2021).

17. For instance, there is growing awareness of the need to devote additional time to building relationships when colleagues are not working in the same space physically. Melanie Leonard, *How to Write a Law Firm Work from Home Policy, Clio*, https://www.clio.com/blog/law-firm-work-from-home-policy/ (last accessed Sept. 28, 2021).

18. *See* Berg, *supra* note 7, at 52; Ismail Sahin, *Predicting Student Satisfaction in Distance Education and Learning Environments*, 8 Turkish Online J. Distance Educ. 113 (2007); Michele T. Cole et al., *Online Instruction, E-Learning, and Student Satisfaction: A Three-Year Study*, 15(6) Int'l Rev. Res. in Open and Distance Learning 111 (2014); Sammer, *supra* note 5.

a. Rapid Evolution of Technology

The first consideration to keep in mind is that online technology is constantly evolving; keeping up with this evolution requires time and energy. Those who struggled through early videoconferencing programs, where the quality negatively impacted even the best class, are thrilled with the potential of new technologies.[19] However, learning to use the technology, for both educators and students, requires additional time and often outside technical expertise in both designing and running the course. Studies have provided useful information and led to new improvements, including a strong preference for hybrid learning environments with a mixture of remote work and face-to-face contact.[20] Studies and experience have also confirmed that some aspects of education transcend technology: relationships built with students, site supervisors, and teachers are crucial, and technology cannot take their place.[21] A second aspect of the rapid evolution of technology is the fact that regulations often lag behind in offering relevant guidance.[22]

b. Need to Address Challenges and Preserve Benefits

The second consideration for faculty is the need to be vigilant in identifying and addressing the disadvantages of online education while recognizing the benefits. Online education offers some clear advantages: the ability for students and professors to be in a different time zone and location and the opportunity for professors to engage students with written online communication to create interactions that are more individualized, include more feedback, and involve every student. These benefits are significant when compared to calling on one or two students using the Socratic[23] method in a large doctrinal class and are important even in a smaller externship or clinic class with students participating in a clinical rounds or class discussion. Having students reflect and address questions online, especially if feedback is given, can significantly increase their learning and engagement. That students find

---

19. One of these commonly used in law schools is Zoom, which provides a high-quality platform for classroom use. For updated lists of resources, see LexternWeb, *Teaching Methodologies Subcommittee*, https://www.lexternweb.org/aals-externship-committee.

20. Aaron S. Richmond & Jordan D. Troisi, *Technology in the Classroom: What the Research Tells Us*, Inside Higher Ed (Dec. 12, 2018), https://www.insidehighered.com/digital-learning/views /2018 /12/12/what-research-tells-us-about-using-technology-classroom-opinion.

21. Jeffery Martin, *Building Relationships and Increasing Engagement in the Virtual Classroom: Practical Tools for the Online Instructor*, J. of Educators Online, https://files.eric.ed.gov/fulltext/EJ1204379.pdf (last visited Oct. 1, 2021).

22. *See* Chapter 2 for a discussion of ABA Standard 306 on Distance Education and the ABA changes to this standard as a result of the coronavirus pandemic and increase in online work.

23. Paul L. Caron & Rafael Gely, *Taking Back the Law School Classroom: Using Technology to Foster Active Student Learning*, 54 J. Legal Educ. 551, 569 (2004).

online education effective for learning in other parts of their lives is evidenced by the volume of users on YouTube for everything from home repair to legal skills.[24]

On the other hand, these same advantages often include hidden challenges. Educators must invest significantly more time up front if written communication is used instead of oral presentation in a live class. If questions are not carefully planned, they can result in less engagement[25] for both educators and students. Unlike a live class setting, participants in an asynchronous learning experience have neither immediate visual cues (bored or confused looks) to help correct miscommunication, nor the sense of community (small talk before and after class, jokes, and sharing of personal information and passion for the work) that brings both teachers and students real time enjoyment in a shared learning process.

Students from marginalized communities or with less privilege may have limited access to adequate equipment and the internet, may feel more isolated when seen on screen with their privileged peers,[26] and may feel uncomfortable about having their cameras on and therefore not participate to the same degree as others.[27] Students with some disabilities, such as those who are deaf and hard of hearing,[28] or with mental illness, may also experience increased isolation in an online classroom.[29] Problems with disengagement and incivility, sometimes attributed to generational differences, may have more to do with the impact of technology and the internet.[30] Nonetheless, understanding these challenges allows educators to work to avoid

---

24. Matthew Lynch & Amy Antonio, *YouTube a Valuable Educational Tool, Not Just Cat Videos*, Tech Advocate (June 29, 2016), https://www.thetechedvocate.org/youtube-valuable-educational-tool-not-just-cat-videos/.

25. Līva Lurina, *12 Student Engagement Activities for Online Learning*, Infogram (April 8, 2021), https://infogram.com/blog/online-student-engagement-activities/.

26. Organizing students into smaller workgroups is particularly effective in online synchronous teaching, but teachers should be careful about breakout groups that are randomly assigned. Some students who are black, indigenous, or people of color may feel more comfortable in groups that have at least a few of their peers.

27. Natalie Spievack & Megan Gallagher, *For Students of Color, Remote Learning Environments Pose Multiple Challenges*, Urban Wire (June 23, 2020), https://www.urban.org/urban-wire/students-color-remote-learning-environments-pose-multiple-challenges.

28. Peter O'Dowd & Allison Hagan, *For Those with Hearing Loss, Zoom Has Closed Captioning—for $200 a Month*, Wbur (Nov. 23, 2020), https://www.wbur.org/hereandnow/ 2020/ 11/23/ zoom-closed-captioning-hearing.

29. Ben Aston, *When Zoom Is the Workplace: Facts About Remote Work & Mental Health, Stress* (Nov. 3, 2020), https://www.stress.org/when-zoom-is-the-workplace-facts-about-remote-work-mental-health.

30. *See* Susan K. McClellan, *Externships for Millennial Generation Law Students: Bridging the Generation Gap*, 15 Clinical L. Rev. 255, 282 (2009), for more on generational differences in externships.

them; surveys finding mixed responses to online education still come out with more positive than negative reviews.[31]

c. Importance of Pedagogy and Inevitability of Change

The third consideration for faculty to keep in mind is that online education relies on the same basic premises as all good pedagogies: clear learning outcomes, ongoing assessment, and engaged interaction between educator and student.[32] Online education is already a part of legal education and will continue to evolve. Current examples of use of online technology in law schools include classes posted on Canvas, Blackboard or TWEN; students doing research and participating in class with laptops that connect to the internet; and professors who are regularly employing videoconferencing, online responses to written work, and other online assessments. As a brief history of online education demonstrates, adoption of technology can happen in fits and starts, driven by external changes as well as individual educator preferences, but the need to adapt to some use of technology in law school education is inevitable.

3. Guide to Effective Use of Online Technology

The next part of this Chapter provides a guide for those who wish to incorporate online technology into their externship program, as well as for those who are interested in assessing and making improvements. The first three sections cover practicalities: technology, time, and communication. The last two sections focus on strategies to use online technology to achieve pedagogical goals and to create a learning community.

a. Technology (Assistance, Equipment/Technology, Training)

A first step in effectively using online technology is to ensure that the faculty member has technical assistance, the right equipment, and adequate training. Needs for technical assistance range from initial design to ongoing implementation. Most universities have specialized technical staff and faculty with expertise in designing online courses.[33] These departments are sources of knowledge about the

---

31. Univ. of Ill. Springfield, *Strengths and Weaknesses of Online Learning*, https://www.uis.edu/ion/resources/tutorials/online-education-overview/strengths-and-weaknesses/ (last visited Sept. 30, 2021).

32. For more on learning outcomes and assessment, see Chapters 5 and 7.

33. For example, Seattle University has a Center for Digital Learning and Innovation with resources to help faculty with course design and improvement. Seattle Univ., *Teaching Online*, https://www.seattleu.edu/cdli/teaching-online/ (last visited Oct. 1, 2021). For another example, ithe University of Louisiana at Lafayette Distance Learning Academic Affairs Division, https://distance-learning.louisiana.edu/teach-remotely/asynchronous-teaching-tips (last visited March 13, 2022).

best technology, equipment, and design; contacting them early in the process will save time and increase efficiency. They offer tutorials and one-on-one coaching, as well as group presentations and design workshops where externship faculty can design a seminar.

Having a technical assistant in the law school or even an assistant for the externship faculty once the course is established is also helpful for both synchronous videoconferencing and for asynchronous assignment posting and monitoring. Assistants can send out links for students, test student computer equipment ahead of time, and help troubleshoot for individual students having problems with logging in. This help, especially when setting up, allows the educator to remain focused on the teaching itself. Technical assistance for asynchronous course design can range from assistance in the creation of a template online (which can later be published so that students can see it and use it) to duplication of existing materials for future courses.

Investment in good equipment and technology is critical for success in courses using online technology. Equipment includes not just a computer with a good camera and microphone for conferencing, but also a second or third monitor if regularly teaching from either home or office, and a quiet keyboard if typing on a shared screen or using the chat function during class. Students also need laptops with cameras and microphones.[34] While most laptops do have these, it is important to check before class starts and to have some plan for providing equipment if the student does not have the means to procure it. While not equipment per se, adequate internet coverage is essential for teachers and students to participate with both video and audio communication. Consideration of equipment should also include what the externship site itself may provide, particularly as privacy concerns may mean that students are issued site owned laptops or cell phones to protect confidential communication and material.

Programs with remote students are advised to invest in technology[35] such as Zoom, WebEx, or Adobe Connect. Students must have good internet and a quiet place in order to participate, and faculty must engage remote students through direct questions if the class includes both remote and in-person students. In a mixed class with both in-person and remote students, having all students logged into Zoom on their laptops allows for better viewing of PowerPoint slides and easier participation by in-person students, since they can use the microphones in their laptops. It also permits the remote students to appear on a larger classroom screen and facilitates the use of breakout groups that combine in-person and remote students. Providing teachers in this type of class with a headset with a microphone allows them to move

34. Cell phones are too small to view documents such as PowerPoints and to see other class participants. Students also will benefit from having a second monitor in addition to their laptops.

35. For details about rates and options available, see the company websites available at Webex, https://www.webex.com/ (last visited Oct. 1, 2021); Skype, http://www.skype.com/en/ (last visited Oct. 1, 2021); Adobe, www.adobe.com (last visited Oct. 1, 2021); and Zoom, http://zoom.us (last visited Oct. 1, 2021).

about the room and still be heard. An alternative to having all students use their laptops is to use a room with speakers in the classroom ceiling or a long-range microphone placed in a central location. A best practice in a hybrid setting is to have remote students log in to class a few minutes before class starts so they can test that they can see and be heard; the classroom technology may have been adjusted by other faculty using the room beforehand.

Training on how to use videoconferencing for synchronous or live instruction through platforms like Zoom is necessary for effective education.[36] Knowing how to share one's screen, show videos on the internet with adequate sound, and employ polling and breakout rooms[37] will enhance techniques to keep students engaged. Using a white board to go through material sequentially, or incorporating options such as Google docs that allow participants to add input to documents during class, also allow students to participate more actively. PowerPoints provide helpful visuals but are not as dynamic as writing on a board or having students participate in exercises in breakout groups. When typing during class, teachers should make sure the microphone will not pick up the sound of the keyboard. If writing freehand, teachers should invest in a good stylus and check the lag time.

Using lots of technology can be challenging; if the lesson plan is complex, it is best to practice the technology ahead of time. Enabling the chat function allows students with bad connections to respond; they can simultaneously share thoughts and ask questions. When doing this, teachers should weigh the possibility of distractions and the need to monitor the chat for micro-aggressions and triggers. Teachers should keep in mind that a mixture of presentation styles is especially important in online synchronous and asynchronous education. These can be technically complex but simple approaches are also worthwhile. A conversation type presentation with questions from the class to a speaker is very effective with an engaging presenter whom students can get to know more easily without any breakouts or PowerPoints.

Another area of faculty training is in recording classes ahead of time for use in a flipped classroom.[38] A flipped classroom in which students view the recorded material before meeting for class is widely seen as offering positive benefits that can include the following: students arrive with a better understanding of the core material; the pedagogy engages with visual learners; it saves classroom time; it provides a flexible learning experience; and it makes optimal use of professional knowledge and

36. Helen Leskovac, *Distance Learning in Legal Education: Implications of Frame Relay Videoconferencing*, 8 ALB. L.J. SCI. & TECH. 305, 336 (1998); *see also* Joshua Aaron Jones, *Building a Community of Inquiry Through Interactive Materials: The Interactive Syllabus*, 45 NOVA L. REV. 353, 371 (2021).

37. Breakouts are when the class is subdivided into smaller groups that meet via videoconference. The smaller group allows for more effective group sharing and problem solving.

38. A flipped classroom refers to a classroom in which the students listen to a video of the instructional material before the class and use in-class time to work through problems that relate to the presented material. In contrast, the traditional classroom brings the students together for the lecture and has them work through problems after class on their own.

experience.[39] The idea behind the Socratic method is primarily that students come to class prepared; however, in a flipped classroom environment, more students can benefit, because they can learn at their own pace and then actively use the material they have absorbed.[40] Surveys of students and professors have shown this to be true.[41]

Training on flipped classrooms and the technology needed to accomplish a videotaped lecture is necessary when designing such classes. When videotaping a class, avoid lighting only from above. Turn off distractions and close all screens before starting to record to reduce the likelihood of not finding the right screen to share. Reduce ambient noise and avoid distractions in the background picture. Using virtual backgrounds can also be effective if supported by the technology. Additional considerations include the different energy levels of standing versus sitting and the use of some form of visual presentation to address different learning styles. Including a time marker in the videorecording makes it easier for students to go back and review certain portions of the class, especially if it is long. Where possible, teachers should break the videorecording into chunks that are followed by an assignment in which students apply the recorded material. Many new technologies allow for the recording of such educational material in a format that utilizes a voice recording and slides.[42]

Training on the use of technology is not just necessary for effective teaching, it should also be a learning goal for students. If possible, training on technology should be included as part of the syllabus; teachers must remember that students, even those who are digital natives, will need to learn these skills for professional use. Both the syllabus and the class introduction should set guidelines to facilitate student participation in this goal, reminding students they need good internet and a quiet place to participate in a videoconference class. Explaining that use of the computer for class increases the likelihood of distractions also helps students recognize that maintaining focus will similarly be a professional goal where work is either remote or mostly on a computer or other device. Training for students can be done during the class in several ways: by assigning them tasks to do in breakout groups, having

---

39. Peter Sankoff, *Taking the Instruction of Law Outside the Lecture Hall: How the Flipped Classroom Can Make Learning More Productive and Enjoyable (for Professors and Students)*, 51 ALBERTA L. REV. 891, 906 (2014); Alex Berrio Matamoros, *Answering the Call: Flipping the Classroom to Prepare Practice-Ready Attorneys*, 47 CAP. U. L. REV. 113, 130-31 (2015). For more on the use of technology by students working with supervisors at their sites, *see* Chapter 13.

40. *See* William R. Slomanson, *Blended Learning: A Flipped Classroom Experiment*, 64 J. LEGAL EDUC. 93 (2014), for more on this in other disciplines.

41. Cole et al., *supra* note 18.

42. One example of this is Canva.com that provides tutorials and templates for the creation of videos and other educational materials.

them present to the class, or having them perform work at their sites that includes the use of technology.

Learning management systems are constantly improving functionality and addressing glitches. Nonetheless, teaching students how to work with less sophisticated technology is also an important professional skill. Discussing what to do if students interrupt each other by mistake can help prepare students for online interviewing of a client, employer, or opposing party. Students will benefit from knowing about how different technologies address such issues, whether by allowing participants to raise a hand or highlighting the box of the speaking party. Training in technology can also extend beyond interviews to depositions, negotiations, and actual trials.

b. Time for Course Design and Asynchronous Response

As mentioned above, initial online course design and student training will take more time than a traditional course and should include consultation with the university or law school's online education technology and course design department or staff. Once created, however, an online course can save time. This is because the course can be created on a learning platform and then "published" when ready. Because the materials are saved electronically, they are easier to maintain and update from year to year. Course readings, syllabi, and exercises can be shared with colleagues and adjunct professors. Creating templates for certain materials such as assessments, mid-semester meetings, time sheets, and final evaluations can be simpler when all the information can be copied and shared instantaneously once it is updated. Likewise, asynchronous messages can be written ahead of time and then programmed to be released at set times.

Individualized student feedback, however, although more possible in an online setting because each student's engagement is available in written form, will still be time consuming and must be done each semester. Teachers should be realistic, use a calendar system, and space out assignments, keeping in mind that not all of them need feedback. Learning management systems can give data on which students have read assignments, and some systems can be programmed to alert students to missing work. Teachers also need to plan for students who have technical problems in posting on time by having the student send an email when the problem occurs, creating a record that can be retained. When posting to the whole class, faculty should be aware of privacy and confidentiality issues, particularly when discussions involve sensitive topics about race, gender, or trauma. Another choice for faculty is whether and how to use online grading systems. While these systems can be set to assign points for every aspect of an assignment, externship faculty may want to avoid some of these as part of a deliberate choice to emphasize that externships are an actual workplace where every student needs to perform at a high professional level, rather than an academic setting with a focus on gaining additional points for every assignment.

c. Communication Across Different Languages, Time Frames, and Cultures

Online asynchronous education requires careful attention to written communication. Compared to oral communication, written communication offers a greater possibility for misinterpretation, and there are no blank stares or raised hands if there is a misunderstanding. To address this concern, teachers should consider how students will communicate questions, and make sure communication is very clear. Successful teachers often use repetition and separate large chunks of information into more than one message.

When communicating asynchronously to generate discussion, teachers should remember that different techniques encourage different kinds of responses. Be intentional about civility, especially given the lack of body cues that indicate discomfort. Emotional questions can polarize discussion. Putting students in a role can generate empathy and reflection. Broad questions can spur creativity but may fail if they are too vague. On the other hand, if the required posts are too specific or narrow, they will be less spontaneous. Posting brief (less than 6 minutes) videos online for students to view is also an effective way to create an emotional response. Short videos such as TED Talks can be useful as discussion prompts since they are expertly produced, carefully edited, and different from a videotaped lecture.

Posting asynchronous prompts requires more attention than posing questions in a live room where an energetic discussion can spontaneously be created and lead to student engagement. For example, for a class discussion on interviewing, students can be encouraged to describe one take away they would share for preparing for a live client interview (leaving out confidential information), or to describe one piece of advice they wish they had been given before their first client interview.[43] Externship faculty should choose the topic so that students engage and immediately want to see where the discussion will go. When considering how to choose a topic, teachers should consider ideas that are compelling, recent, novel, multimedia, well written, multi-parted, long, complex, or about an area of tension or conflict. Other techniques include breaking topics into chunks of the discussion, sequencing them according to importance and complexity. Design questions that will introduce or motivate the discussions, using headings for each chunk so they can be reordered easily.

Online discussion can include single threads or multiple threads. Generally, it is best to limit response time to a week, or if each student responds only once, to a couple of days. Teachers can allow students to flag or "like" a post, summarize learning points, reflect, or share additional information. Requiring students to respond before they see others' replies ensures students provide their own reflections as part

43. A common approach to andragogy is to test the students live at the beginning of the class showing them that they don't know as much about a topic as they think they do. For more on teaching techniques, see Chapter 11. For an example of a syllabus for a completely asynchronous class, see https://www.lexternweb.org/course-syllabi.

of the process. Having students work together to respond to online posts builds connection and can be less stressful and less intimidating. Teachers should be thoughtful about response time frames when interacting with students across language and culture. For students who are not native English speakers, online communication has the advantage that it allows them more time to shape their answers. On the other hand, grammar and spelling errors are more apparent in written communication. Reminding all students how difficult it is to master another language fluently and what they gain from hearing perspectives of those raised in a different culture and country may encourage students to take risks in discussion. Part-time students will require longer time frames for responses than full-time students who can participate more fully. Faculty should also be alert to differences in writing abilities and to learning challenges.

For asynchronous communication, ensure that students have not screened out class assignment emails as spam. When communicating regarding the class or assignments, teachers should consider both the time and frequency of the communication. Several versions of the same message will increase its effectiveness, especially with respect to deadlines. For class discussion, reminders about when a discussion is open and when it will close are helpful for students. The need for training on such issues may depend on each educator's prior exposure to online learning, but for those with only in-person experience, they will need to plan carefully for events that they have previously done simultaneously in class.

d. Student-Centered and Active Learning Outcomes

When technology is an integral part of the course, at least one learning outcome should articulate the benefits to students of investing time in learning to use technology to facilitate discussion and communication. When defining the learning outcome, faculty should be explicit about engagement (*e.g.*, reading, preparing, interacting with each other, practicing a skill, thinking deeply, engaging in an active not passive mode). Articulate what students will demonstrate and how they will use the technology to demonstrate that they have learned it. For example, explain to students that much of their legal work will be in meetings and discussions with colleagues working remotely, analyzing legal issues, and formulating solutions together. Class discussions are thus an opportunity to build the necessary skills to excel, but doing so requires everyone to participate in depth and engage actively in the classroom. The acquisition of technology skills as a learning outcome must be student-centered.

The use of technology should also encourage active learning. If students lead the discussions, they can practice the skills discussed above. Faculty may consider allowing students to edit the syllabus, send out reminders and prompts to participants, and incorporate real world experience with technology. Including sufficient contextual information and supplemental reading at the design stage provides a foundation for planned discussion. If the topic is complex and the goal is for students to do research, choose asynchronous discussion as the learning environment. If the goal is for the student to actively guide the discussion, a synchronous class setting may be better. Helping students see the different uses for different types of communication will prepare them to be more effective lawyers.

e. Creation of a Learning Community

The final strategy is to focus on creating a learning community. Where possible, have students meet at least once in person, preferably at the beginning of the class, to forge a sense of community. Other approaches to creating community include doing ice breaker exercises at the beginning, and asking students to create individual profiles with photos, a favorite food, or an activity. Sharing cultural touchstones and creating a set of ground rules for engagement at the beginning of the class also encourage students to be vulnerable. All activities should be designed to encourage empathy, compassion, and kindness. As Professor Warren Binford eloquently explains, "Students who have 'a professor who care[s] about them as a person, ma[kes] them excited to learn, and encourage[s] them to pursue their dreams are more than twice as likely to be engaged at work after they graduate, and to be far more likely to thrive in all aspects of their well-being after graduation, than those who do not.'"[44]

Online education is often viewed as an intimidating challenge. This Chapter has provided some tools to embrace it as a continuum and opportunity for creative pedagogy, knowing that it can improve teaching. Today's students are "intent on using technology as part of the learning process; visual learners; multi-taskers; learners with shorter attention spans; and of the belief that learning should be both interactive and collaborative in nature."[45] When done well, online education can engage students more deeply and engage every student, even those too shy to participate in class. No matter which options are selected, keep in mind that a hybrid or blended combination is seen as best,[46] allowing students to get the benefits of online and in-person interaction.[47]

---

44. Warren Binford, *How to Be the World's Best Law Professor*, 64 J. Legal Educ. 542, 560-61 (2015) (citations omitted).

45. Sankoff, *supra* note 39, at 906.

46. Daniel C. Powell, *Five Recommendations to Law Schools Offering Legal Instruction Over the Internet*, 11 J. Tech. L. & Pol'y 285, 312 (2006); Caroline Spiezio, *For Most Law Students, Remote Classes Didn't Make the Grade—Report, Reuters* (June 16, 2021), https://www.reuters.com/legal/government/most-law-students-remote-classes-didnt-make-grade-report-2021-06-16/.

47. Gerald F. Hess, *Blended Courses in Law School: The Best of Online and Face-to-Face Learning*, 45 McGeorge L. Rev. 51, 84 (2013).

Effective blended learning courses require students to interact with each other, the content, and their own thoughts. Students need a way to not only take in information but also to process it: checking their understanding, organizing their knowledge, and making connections with what they already know. Blended learning that incorporates active online learning strategies provides students with vehicles to help them do just that.

Section IV

Guidance for Site Supervisors

Chapter 13

Guidance for Site Supervisors

1. The Basics of Hosting an Extern

An externship should be a rewarding experience for both the site supervisor and the student extern. For the site supervisor, an externship provides an opportunity to teach and mentor a law student and to give back to the profession. For the student, an externship provides an opportunity to learn from lawyers and judges in a real practice setting by performing substantive legal work and receiving meaningful feedback.

Unlike internships, which typically are not regulated by the law school in any way, an externship is offered for academic credit and overseen by a law school faculty member. Accordingly, externship faculty at ABA-accredited law schools must ensure that all externships comply with the accreditation standards set forth by the American Bar Association's Council of Legal Education and Admissions to the Bar, which is the nationally recognized accreditor for law schools. While externship faculty must be familiar with all the ABA Standards applicable to externships, site supervisors should be aware of those Standards that apply to their role in the teaching and supervision of students.

a. What the ABA Standards Require of Site Supervisors

Law students must complete at least six credit hours of experiential coursework as part of the required law school curriculum.[1] Externships are one of three types of experiential courses that can satisfy this requirement.[2] ABA Standard 304 states the requirements for experiential courses, identifies what qualifies as a "field placement course" (the ABA's term for an externship course), and outlines the specific requirements governing externships.[3] Standard 304, in pertinent part, is set forth

1. ABA Standards and Rules of Procedure for Approval of Law Schools 2022–2023, Standard 303(a)(3).

2. *Id.*

3. The ABA Standards use the term "field placement" rather than "externship," but these terms are used interchangeably in legal education.

below. Those provisions of particular importance to site supervisors are set forth in bold and italics.

Standard 304. EXPERIENTIAL COURSES: SIMULATION COURSES, LAW CLINICS, AND FIELD PLACEMENTS

(a) Experiential courses satisfying Standard 303(a) are simulation courses, law clinics, and ***field placements that must be primarily experiential in nature and must:***

(1) integrate doctrine, theory, skills, and legal ethics, and engage students in performance of one or more of the professional skills identified in Standard 302;

(2) develop the concepts underlying the professional skills being taught;

(3) provide multiple opportunities for performance;

(4) provide opportunities for student performance, self-evaluation, and feedback from a faculty member, or, for a field placement, a site supervisor;

(5) provide a classroom instructional component; or, ***for a field placement, a classroom instructional component, regularly scheduled tutorials, or other means of ongoing, contemporaneous, faculty-guided reflection;*** and

(6) provide direct supervision of the student's performance by the faculty member; or, ***for a field placement, provide direct supervision of the student's performance by a faculty member or a site supervisor.***

[Sections (b) and (c), which define simulation courses and law school clinics, have been omitted.]

(d) A field placement course provides ***substantial lawyering experience that*** (1) is reasonably similar to the experience of a lawyer advising or representing a client or engaging in other lawyering tasks in a setting outside a law clinic under the supervision of a licensed attorney or an individual otherwise qualified to supervise, and (2) includes the following:

(i) a written understanding among the student, faculty member, and a person in authority at the field placement that describes both (A) the substantial lawyering experience and opportunities for performance, feedback and self-evaluation; and (B) the respective roles of faculty and any site supervisor in supervising the student and in assuring the educational quality of the experience for the student, including a clearly articulated method of evaluating the student's academic performance;

(ii) a method for selecting, training, evaluating and communicating with site supervisors, including regular contact between the faculty and site supervisors through in-person visits or other methods of communication that will assure the quality of the student educational experience. When appropriate, a school may use faculty members from other law schools to supervise or assist in the supervision or review of a field placement program;

(iii) evaluation of each student's educational achievement by a faculty member; and

(iv) sufficient control of the student experience to ensure that the requirements of the Standard are met. The law school must maintain records to document the steps taken to ensure compliance with the Standard, which shall include, but is not necessarily limited to, the written understandings described in Standard 304(d)(i).

(e) Credit granted for such a simulation, law clinic, or field placement course shall be commensurate with the time and effort required and the anticipated quality of the educational experience of the student.

(f) Each student in such a simulation, law clinic, or field placement course shall have successfully completed sufficient prerequisites or shall receive sufficient contemporaneous training to assure the quality of the student educational experience.

b. Substantial Lawyering Experience

Standard 304(d) defines a field placement or "externship," the term used in the remainder of this Chapter, as a course that "provides a substantial lawyering experience that... is reasonably similar to the experience of a lawyer advising or representing a client or engaging in other lawyering tasks in a setting outside a law clinic under the supervision of a licensed attorney or an individual otherwise qualified to supervise...."[4] Accordingly, in coordination with externship faculty at the law school, site supervisors must ensure that they are giving student externs a substantial lawyering experience through the work they assign, the experiences they provide, and the feedback they give.[5] In delivering this substantial lawyering experience, site supervisors serve a crucial role; they act as teachers and mentors to student externs and as partners to externship faculty in providing an experiential opportunity that is only available in a real legal practice setting.

---

4. *Id.* Most law schools require an experienced licensed attorney to act as the supervising attorney except in unique circumstances as described in Chapter 4.

5. This substantial lawyering experience must be "primarily experiential in nature" and "provide opportunities for student performance, self-evaluation, and feedback from... a site supervisor." ABA Standards and Rules of Procedure for Approval of Law Schools 2022–2023, Standard 304(a)(4).

c. Three-Way Written Agreement

In externships, students learn from both the site supervisor and the law school faculty member. This three-way relationship has been illustrated as an inverted triangle[6] with the externship faculty member, the site supervisor, and the student each occupying one of the triangle's three points as illustrated below.

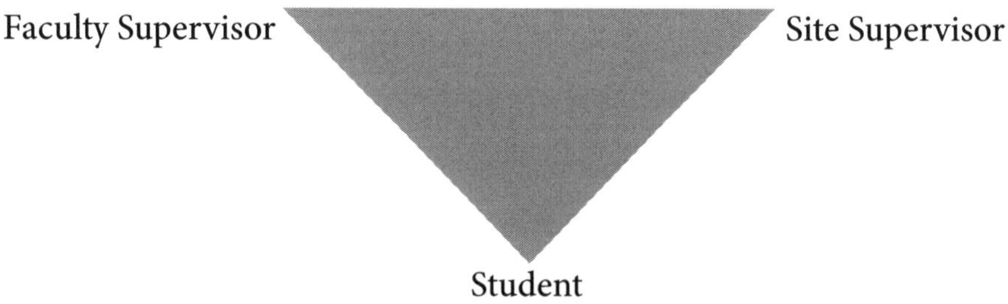

Each participant has slightly different roles with respect to one another. The site supervisor's role is to teach and mentor the student at the externship site by assigning the student legal work, supervising the student's work, providing meaningful feedback, and providing perspective regarding the practice of law.[7] The externship faculty member's role is to set criteria for selecting and evaluating supervisors, provide training to supervisors, teach the student, offer perspective, prompt reflection, assure the quality of the externship experience, evaluate the student's educational achievement, and solve any problems that might arise.[8] The student's role is to learn from the externship faculty member and the site supervisor by completing the work each assigns, incorporating feedback, and engaging in reflection.[9]

To confirm each participant's understanding of their respective role in the externship course, Standard 304 requires that the student, externship faculty member, and a person in authority at the externship site enter into a three-way written agreement. The written agreement must describe two things: "the substantial lawyering experience and opportunities for performance, feedback and self-evaluation" and "the respective roles of faculty and any site supervisor in supervising the student and in assuring the educational quality of the experience for the student, including a

---

6. *See, e.g.*, Cynthia Adams, Cynthia Baker, Shawn Boyne, Max Huffman, Andrew Klein, Margaret Ryznar, Mark Shope & Frank Sullivan, *Upward—Higher: How a Law Faculty Stays Ahead of the Curve*, 51 Ind. L. Rev. 413, 430–31 (2018) (explaining externship triangle and types of communications it represents in externship pedagogy).

7. Alexander Scherr & Susan L. Brooks, *Introduction*, *in* Learning From Practice: A Text for Experiential Education 4–5 (Leah Wortham, Alexander Scherr, Nancy Mauer, Susan L. Brooks eds., 3d ed. 2016) (hereinafter "Learning From Practice").

8. *Id.*

9. *Id.*

clearly articulated method of evaluating the student's academic performance."[10] The externship faculty member typically drafts the written agreement, and the faculty member or externship student then provides it to the site supervisor for signature. This written agreement may be one that a site supervisor signs every semester or one that is signed only periodically; the frequency is dictated by the law school program and should be managed by the law school faculty member. The remainder of this Chapter will address the supervisor's role in teaching, mentoring, and supervising the student to ensure the educational quality of the substantial lawyering experience, which are the remaining supervisor responsibilities set forth in Standard 304.

2. Working with Student Externs

Before agreeing to supervise student externs, site supervisors will want to consider the best way to integrate students into the externship placement while considering the organizational structure of the office, the number of supervising attorneys, and the nature and pace of the legal work. The fact that site supervisors work in real legal settings and have a primary responsibility to the clients and public they serve can present challenges to the amount of time and attention site supervisors can devote to teaching students in an externship. Because it takes more time to teach students than to do the legal work themselves, site supervisors must realistically assess the amount of time and attention they can spend working with students and make sure that they or the supervising attorneys they assign have the time and desire to do so.

As teachers and mentors, site supervisors will want to consider what a student can learn at the externship and identify the knowledge (how to think like a lawyer), skills (how to do like a lawyer), and values (how to be a lawyer)[11] that they want to impart to students through their teaching and mentorship. Supervisors also will want to ensure that students are equipped to successfully perform and complete the externship. To that end, site supervisors should provide a description of the type of work the student will perform and identify any prerequisites such as courses, background checks, work experience, etc. that might be necessary for a student to complete prior to starting an externship. This information can be gathered during or after an initial site approval meeting and included in a database or on a website accessible to students.[12] In addition, site supervisors should confirm that they understand the structure of the law school externship course and the course learning outcomes. This information should be provided by the law school faculty member

10. ABA Standards and Rules of Procedure for Approval of Law Schools 2022–2023, Standard 304(d)(i).

11. *See* Lou Bilionis, *Professional Formation and the Political Economy of the American Law School*, 83 Tenn. L. Rev. 895, 910–11 (2016).

12. Georgia State University College of Law's Externship Website at https://law.gsu.edu/student-experience/experiential-learning/externships/externship-opportunities/ (last visited March 20, 2022), provides just one example of how such information can be communicated to students.

as part of an externship supervisor manual or informational materials. If this information is not provided, site supervisors should ask the law school for a supervisor manual, informational materials, or a course syllabus to ensure that all expectations and objectives can be met.

In addition, it is important for site supervisors to understand the process by which the law school places students in externships. Some law schools post externship opportunities at pre-approved externship sites, collect student application materials, and leave it to the externship sites to interview and select students. Some law schools ask students to secure and propose their own externships for approval by the law school faculty. Still others determine which students to place at which externship site. It is also important for site supervisors to know whether externships are offered only during the regular academic year or whether they are offered in the summer, or both, and to determine the semesters the externship placement can incorporate students into its work.

a. Preparing for an Extern's Arrival

As part of the onboarding process, site supervisors should determine the information students will need before they begin their externship. Because students likely will be taking other classes in addition to their externship, supervisors should establish the extern's work schedule as soon as possible. In determining the schedule, site supervisors should consider their own work schedules, including the days they will be in the office, and the days where any regular meetings, court hearings, trials, or other work outside of the office typically happen, and should set a start date that coordinates with the beginning of the semester or quarter depending on how the law school structures its academic terms. Prior to the start of the academic term, supervisors should provide students with all the information they will need on the first day, including office location, where to park, expected work attire, whether to bring a laptop or phone, and security procedures for accessing the site. Some externship placements will conduct a formal orientation and provide training on the first day or within the first week. Others provide a written handbook and rely on individual discussions about expectations and office policies.

Regardless of the method used to handle the orientation process, students should end the first week understanding the mission of the externship placement, having made introductions to the lawyers and staff in the office, and having an idea of where to access case files, templates, sample documents, and any other resources they might need over the course of the semester. This information and the orientation process itself is of particular importance when a student is working remotely from the externship site and, therefore, is not physically present in the office to get acclimated.

b. Setting Learning Goals

At the beginning of an externship, most externship faculty require students to identify learning goals for their externship experience. Students should share those learning goals with the site supervisor. Site supervisors should consider the goals and assignments identified when reviewing the student's articulated learning goals both to ensure that the student's goals are realistic and to ensure that the student will receive the most out of the educational experience. In addition, both students and supervisors should consider whether they have identified goals relating to all three aspects of legal education—knowledge, skills, and values. Many externship programs will require students to reflect on how well they are working toward meeting their learning goals and whether they have identified any new ones as the semester progresses.

c. Giving Assignments

Because the purpose of an externship is educational, the assignments and observational opportunities given to students should be designed for learning and should help the student to achieve their learning goals. In addition, supervisors will want to ensure that assignments are appropriate to the student's skill and experience level and cover a variety of different types of work and experiences. It often can be helpful to have students begin with smaller, more discrete assignments that allow the supervisor to gauge their abilities, and then progress to more complex assignments.

Assignments should progress from student observation and review of lawyer work to student performance under supervision. To facilitate this progression, supervisors will want to model certain skills such as conducting a client interview, taking a deposition, doing a bond hearing, etc. After the supervisor has modeled the skill, the student should be given the opportunity to perform the skill with the supervisor present to provide guidance and feedback.

Students should be given prompt and constructive feedback (discussed in more detail below) and, ideally, additional opportunities to revise and resubmit work until it is of the quality that it can be used without further corrections. In their mentorship roles, site supervisors should expect to talk with students about their career paths, well-being challenges, and the values of the profession more generally, and provide students with networking opportunities.

When giving assignments, supervisors should consider that students likely are not going to have the full context of the case or legal problem to which the assignment is connected. Providing contextual facts and the case file, if appropriate, will help students better understand not only the question being asked or the assignment being given, but also how it fits into the broader context of the case or legal work of the externship site. In addition, supervisors should identify the best way for students to communicate with them when questions arise and provide a realistic deadline for the assignment to be completed. When trying to determine a realistic deadline, supervisors should consider the work schedule of the student. For example, if a student is scheduled to work approximately 10–12 hours per week and the project should take approximately 20 hours for the student to complete, the student will need at least two weeks to complete the assignment. Supervisors also should provide guidance to students on the best method for communicating about the completion of assignments and the need for additional work. This is of particular importance if a student is working remotely from the externship site.

d. Providing Feedback

As with providing meaningful assignments, the feedback supervisors give students is a critical and integral component of the students' learning experience.[13] In addition, supervisors can model how to give and receive feedback effectively. Without feedback, students do not know what they are doing well and what they need to improve. While giving feedback is often the most time-consuming part of supervising an extern, it is often the part of the externship that students most value because they see and appreciate the supervisor's investment in their professional growth. Students look to supervisors to tell them the "real deal" and to teach them the lessons about lawyering they can learn only from being immersed in law practice. This is evidenced by the following excerpt from a student's written reflection:

> *I am very thankful to that attorney for taking time to teach me how to think like a lawyer; especially since a staff attorney could have done the task I was given in probably half the time. Instead of taking the easy route, she not only gave me a practical skill, but also nurtured my confidence in my ability to think like an attorney. Looking back, what was most successful about her approach is that while she took the time to walk through a way to solve the proposed problem with me, she never solved it for me. In effect, she handed me tools to address this situation and similar circumstances that I can take with me the rest of my career in the law; whether I am an employee [at this placement] or not. This is an example of great mentorship and what I believe most of us looked to experience when signing up for externships. To feel yourself growing as an attorney is an exciting feeling.*[14]

---

13. *See* Liz Ryan Cole & Leah Wortham, *Learning from Supervision*, *in* LEARNING FROM PRACTICE, *supra note* 7, at 33–58 (providing tips for effective feedback and summarizing lessons from DOUGLAS STONE & SHEILA HEEN, THANKS FOR THE FEEDBACK: THE SCIENCE AND ART OF RECEIVING FEEDBACK WELL (2014)); *see also* THERESE HUSTON, LET'S TALK, MAKE EFFECTIVE FEEDBACK YOUR SUPERPOWER (2021).

14. This student reflection was part of the GALE supervisor training on Giving Feedback presented by Alex Scherr and Kendall Kerew. *See* https://law.gsu.edu/files/2019/07/GALE-Pathways-to-Profession-II-Giving-Feedback.pdf (last visited March 20, 2022).

Because supervisors are busy and have many different demands on their time, delay in giving feedback is the most common barrier to a student receiving meaningful feedback. This delay can be exacerbated when an extern is working remotely from the externship placement or even when a student is reporting in person but not working at the externship placement full-time. To help avoid delay, supervisors should consider how best to incorporate feedback into their workflow. By doing so, they can be proactive rather than reactive. To facilitate a proactive approach, it is helpful to plan regular, weekly meetings with the student. These regular meetings will make it more likely that feedback will be given in a timely manner and can provide an opportunity to answer questions, check on progress, and give the student a sense of the other work happening at the externship site.

To facilitate providing feedback, it can be helpful to think about giving feedback using the following steps. First, see the performance and determine what points of feedback to prioritize. While it may be tempting to provide feedback on every aspect of the performance, it is usually best to focus the feedback on a few specific points that will most improve the student's next performance. Providing feedback on every aspect of the performance may overwhelm the student, which can make feedback counterproductive. It is also helpful for a supervisor to set aside time each week both for planning feedback (if the feedback is not given directly after the performance) and for meeting with the student to discuss the feedback. Even if the supervisor provides the feedback orally immediately following the performance or chooses to send the feedback in an email, the student may have questions about the feedback, which can be asked during a weekly meeting. Supervisors also can ask externship faculty to provide rubrics for various types of externship work, which supervisors can use as a guide or checklist in evaluating student performance and providing feedback.

Providing feedback to students can be difficult for several reasons beyond the pressures of time. Supervisors want to encourage students and might avoid giving negative feedback so as not to discourage the student. When supervisors give constructive feedback, students may have a hard time receiving it because of generational differences in communication style, lack of confidence (or overconfidence), an intense desire to do well, a worry about a bad grade in the externship or a poor recommendation, and the potential impact it could have on the possibility of a future job if externs are routinely hired. These potential difficulties can be addressed by some preliminary preparation and attention to the way the feedback is framed. To begin with, it is important for a site supervisor to establish their role as a teacher and mentor and acknowledge that the student is there to learn. In addition, it is helpful to frame the feedback in a way that reminds the student that the primary purpose of the externship is to learn rather than to impress or to try to attain a job at the externship site. Another way to avoid students taking feedback in a negative way is to consider how to frame the conversation. It might be helpful to frame the feedback with "I" rather than "you" statements. "I" statements keep the message centered on the speaker. "You" statements tend to sound accusatory and may prompt a defensive response.

When giving feedback on research and writing specifically, supervisors might want to focus on the usefulness of the work product; whether it is in the expected format; the effectiveness of the organization; specifics such as length, grammar, syntax, and spelling; and accuracy, depth, and quality of the research and/or analysis. When giving feedback on oral presentations, supervisors might want to focus on the student's interaction with the audience, the effectiveness of the organization; word choice and clarity; and forensics such as volume and pace, verbal fillers, and eye contact. While prompt feedback is important to both written work and oral presentations, immediate feedback is even more important with oral presentations because, unless recorded, the performance is not preserved.

In addition to research, writing, and oral performance, supervisors may need to provide feedback to students on their office demeanor and professionalism. In doing so, supervisors should keep the feedback specific, explain the impact of the student's behavior, articulate the reasons why the conduct must change, and offer alternative approaches. They should also keep in mind that such feedback is more personal in nature and may be harder for the student to hear. In deciding whether to address a certain behavior, supervisors should consider cultural, racial, generational, and other differences that might account for the student behavior. In addition, supervisors should consider how their own implicit and cognitive biases inform their perceptions of student behavior and approach to student supervision. Professor Anne Gordon's article, *Better than our Biases: Using Psychological Research to Inform our Approach to Inclusive, Effective Feedback*,[15] provides a comprehensive discussion and concrete suggestions for how to combat implicit and cognitive biases when providing feedback to students. In addition, supervisors should consider talking with the externship faculty member about how best to deliver this type of feedback to a student.

e. Communication and Evaluation

In addition to the requirement that supervisors provide a substantial lawyering experience and opportunities for performance, feedback, and self-evaluation, Standard 304 requires "regular contact between the faculty and site supervisors through in-person visits or other methods of communication that will assure the quality of the student educational experience."[16] Externship faculty use a variety of methods to engage in this regular contact, including regular in-person visits, emails, videoconferences, and telephone calls. Because it is their responsibility, most of these communications are initiated by the externship faculty. That said, supervisors should always feel that they can reach out to externship faculty for support, guidance, and to ask

15. Anne D. Gordon, *Better than our Biases: Using Psychological Research to Inform our Approach to Inclusive, Effective Feedback*, 27 Clinical L. Rev. 195 (2021).

16. ABA Standards and Rules of Procedure for Approval of Law Schools 2022–2023, Standard 304.

questions about the externship program generally or regarding a particular student or situation. In addition to individual communication, some externship programs provide supervisor training sessions either in person or as a recorded webinar for continuing legal education credit. Often supervisor trainings focus on the logistics and mechanics of effective supervision.

Externship faculty also must evaluate the quality of the student educational experience at externship sites. Student evaluations may be used to assess the quality of the externship site. In addition, performance evaluations may be required of supervisors at both mid-semester and at the end of the semester. The performance evaluations may be used by externship faculty to assess the quality of the experience for the student and to evaluate the student's academic performance at the externship site.

3. Ethical Duties of Supervisors

Externship faculty typically provide their students with at least a general overview of the ethical issues that may arise in their externship work.[17] But, site supervisors must also be aware of these ethical issues and address them in their work with students. This responsibility is part of the three-way relationship between the faculty member, supervisor, and student that is described above. The site supervisor also has an ethical duty to ensure that the extern's conduct is compatible with the supervisor's own professional obligations, and the supervisor may be responsible for the extern's actions that violate the rules of professional conduct.[18]

It is helpful for site supervisors to start the conversation with students about the importance of ethical behavior at the beginning of the externship. Supervisors should review key ethical issues that often arise in their practice area and how they apply to the work students will be doing. Externs may not yet have taken a course in professional responsibility. Even if they have taken a course, students may not recognize issues of professional responsibility when they arise, so supervisors should be ready to raise these issues and help students learn to spot them. The student experience of learning about ethical issues in a practice context can be quite different from the experience of studying professional responsibility rules in a classroom. Supervisors are an important part of students' bridge in this area from classroom learning to ethical practice.

The rules of professional responsibility in each state cover a wide range of topics. Several basic ethical concepts arise in most externships, and supervisors should be prepared to help students with all of them. These include confidentiality; conflicts of interest; competence and diligence; candor to the tribunal and truthfulness with others; and the unauthorized practice of law.

17. *See* ABA Standards and Rules of Procedure for Approval of Law Schools 2022–2023, Standard 304(a)(1).

18. *See* ABA Model Rules of Prof'l Conduct R. 5.3.

a. Confidentiality

Externship faculty understand the importance of confidentiality and include it in their teaching. But supervisors must also explain to students why confidentiality is so important and what information is confidential. As detailed earlier in this Chapter, this dual teaching by both the faculty member and the site supervisor is one of the hallmarks of externship courses. It is helpful to start by reviewing the language of the applicable rule on confidentiality in the jurisdiction[19] and explain the basic concepts. If the externship site is bound by other rules or regulations that address confidentiality, such as a judicial code of ethics or office-specific protocols, the site should provide students with those rules and highlight key provisions.[20]

Students benefit from seeing the rules around confidentiality in context. Supervisors should have a discussion with the student about the work they will be doing and identify what is confidential and what is not. For example, assume that a student is working on a case where the client is a tenant who has been served with an eviction notice and plans to assert an affirmative defense. The student sits in on an interview with the client, conducts legal research, and accompanies the supervisor to court. Confidential information would include the identity of the client, anything the client told the attorneys, any identifying information about the case (such as the client's address), the results of the legal research as applied to the facts of the case, the legal strategy, conversations between the student and the attorney about the case, and drafts of any work for the case.

Student learning depends on reflection, including reflection on what they are doing and learning. Accordingly, externship courses require students to speak or write about the work they are doing at the externship site and what they are learning from it. Any discussion of work done by externs of course raises issues of confidentiality. Supervisors might be tempted to simply prohibit students from revealing anything about their work, but such an approach would not be consistent with the educational purpose of the externship. Information the student could share in class or a written assignment without breaching any duty of confidentiality could include anything the student observed in open court that was on the record, general reflections on the courtroom and courthouse, what the student is learning in general about landlord tenant law, what the student thinks about that law, reflections on what the student has learned about research and writing, whether the student is drawn to this type of work and why or why not, and many other reflective topics.

---

19. *See, e.g.*, ABA Model Rules of Prof'l Conduct R. 1.6.

20. For example, if the site requires all work to be saved on its computer network, and prohibits students from saving their work on their laptop computers or a thumb drive, it should inform students of this requirement.

b. Conflicts of Interest

All externship sites should be aware of potential conflicts of interest when agreeing to host law student externs. There are numerous sources of potential conflicts. "A potential or actual conflict of interest exists when a lawyer's ability to fulfill her professional responsibilities to one client may or will be impaired by the lawyer's responsibilities to another current or former client, the lawyer's duties to a third person, or the lawyer's own interests."[21] Even though students are not yet licensed lawyers, given their active involvement in cases and exposure to confidential information, supervisors should analyze potential extern conflicts the same way they would lawyer conflicts.

The rules governing lawyer conflicts of interest are complex and beyond the scope of this Chapter.[22] The rules also differ from jurisdiction to jurisdiction, and supervisors should use the rules that apply to lawyers at the externship site. Workplace policies involving conflicts checks for new lawyers at the site will be helpful in analyzing potential conflicts with a new extern.

It is best to identify any potential conflicts before the start of the externship. If the law school is involved in matching students and sites, it will often consider potential conflicts as part of that process.[23] Supervisors should still be alert for conflicts, even if the faculty member is attempting to identify them before the student applies. If students apply independently to sites, both the supervisor and the student share responsibility for identifying conflicts.[24]

Students' resumes will reveal some potential conflicts, but not all. Supervisors can start by asking students about past positions that involved legal work, including summer or full-time jobs, in-house clinic work, and prior externships. They should also inquire about any plans the student has to volunteer, serve on a board, or work on legal issues during the semester. Supervisors should find out about the students' future employment plans or current job searches. Finally, supervisors may want to ask students if they have any personal, financial, or family interests that might create conflicts with work at the site. It may be helpful to use an existing conflict identification form or create one for externs.[25]

When supervisors identify a potential conflict, they must determine whether it prevents the student from participating in the externship under the governing professional responsibility rules. Some conflicts involving externs may be resolved

---

21. Cindy B. Slane, *Ethical Issues in Externships: Conflicts of Interest*, *in* LEARNING FROM PRACTICE, *supra* note 7, at 299.

22. There are at least six Model Rules of Professional Responsibility that deal directly with conflicts of interest. ABA MODEL RULES OF PROF'L CONDUCT 1.7, 1.8, 1.9, 1.10, 1.11, 1.12.

23. *See* LEARNING FROM PRACTICE, *supra* note 7, at 314.

24. *Id.*

25. *See Externship Program Conflicts of Interests Inventory*, *in* LEARNING FROM PRACTICE, *supra* note 7, at 332–33.

through informed client consent[26] or by screening the student from the case that involves the conflict. In some cases, however, it may be best for the extern to find another placement, assuming that the conflict is identified before the semester starts or early enough to make such a change possible.[27] It is important to work closely with the externship faculty member in this process.

c. Competence and Diligence

While most students recognize that they should approach their externship work seriously and try to do a good job, they may not recognize that competence and diligence are part of a lawyer's ethical responsibilities.[28] Hearing supervisors speak about these responsibilities is a great way to help students understand their importance. Supervisors should also encourage students to ask questions to help them understand what competence and diligence look like in practice. Diligently representing clients often requires resilience and determination. Supervisors can encourage students in these efforts by explaining how the students' work fits into the client's case or into the larger project. Knowing that they are part of an effort to provide excellent representation to a client is a motivating factor for students.

Ensuring competent and diligent work by students can be time-consuming for a supervisor. Often work done by students could be done much more quickly by an experienced lawyer. Taking the time to help students through challenging situations and teach them how to work both efficiently and effectively is part of the work that comes with being an externship supervisor. Externship faculty are available to help brainstorm about how to teach and support students in these situations; site supervisors should not hesitate to seek their assistance.

d. Candor to the Tribunal and Truthfulness with Others

As externs start to assume the role of a client representative, they also need to understand the ethical rules regarding truthfulness.[29] In their eagerness to advocate for the agency's clients, they might be tempted to "bend" the truth or reach too far with an argument. Externship supervisors play an important role in helping students learn where to draw the line between vigorous advocacy and making false statements of fact or law. Talking through case strategy with externs and identifying arguments that are supported by the law and the facts is one way to help students understand the proper role of a legal advocate and the ethical boundaries within which lawyers must operate. It may be helpful to identify arguments that would not

---

26. *See* Model Rules of Prof'l Conduct R. 1.7, 1.8. 1.9.

27. *See* ABA Model Rules of Prof'l Conduct Rule 1.0(k), 1.10, 1.11.

28. *See* ABA Model Rules of Prof'l Conduct R. 1.1 and 1.3.

29. *See, e.g.*, ABA Model Rules of Prof'l Resp. R. 3.3, 3.4, and 4.1.

be allowed under the ethical rules, to help students see the difference. When reviewing students' written work, supervisors should highlight effective advocacy and edit out arguments that cross the line. Those edits are excellent points to discuss during weekly supervision meetings with students.

e. Unauthorized Practice of Law

Students are not yet licensed lawyers, and absent authorization under student practice rules, they may not give legal advice, appear in court, or otherwise engage in the practice of law. The unauthorized practice of law is generally regulated under state law, and externship supervisors should familiarize themselves with the relevant statutes and cases governing the work of non-lawyers. Externship faculty will also emphasize these issues to students, and supervisors should feel free to reach out to faculty for assistance and clarification. Supervisors should discuss these issues with students at the beginning of the externship and continue to identify what work is allowed and what is not throughout the externship. Supervisors should remind externs to always identify themselves as students to clients, judges, witnesses, and anyone else involved in their work.

f. Student Practice Rules

Some students may be able to take on more of the duties and responsibilities of a practicing lawyer through permission granted by state or federal courts.[30] The rules governing student practice differ by state, so supervisors should familiarize themselves with the procedure and what is allowed in their state;[31] externship faculty can usually help with this task.

Students must apply for permission to assume some of the duties of a practicing lawyer. Most states require students to have completed at least one year of law school and to obtain written permission from an official at their law school.[32] Applications also usually require agreement from a lawyer at a qualifying agency to serve as the student's supervisor. Supervisors should carefully review the rules and the application to ensure they understand their responsibilities.

Students authorized for limited practice may only perform lawyering duties under the close supervision of their supervising attorney. Duties may include appear-

---

30. *See, e.g.*, Ill. Sup. Ct. R. 711, http://www.illinoiscourts.gov/SupremeCourt/ Rules/ Art_VII/ artVII.htm#711; Cal. R. Ct. R. 9.42, https://www.courts.ca.gov/cms/rules/ index.cfm?title=nine &linkid=rule9_42; N.Y. State R. Sec. 805.5, http://www.courts.state.ny.us/ ad3/admissions/805.5_ ActivitiesOfEligibleLawSTudents.pdf.

31. The Georgetown Law Library has assembled links to student practice rules in each state found here: https://guides.ll.georgetown.edu/c.php?g=271042&p=1808947 (last visited March 7, 2022).

32. *See, e.g.*, Ill. Sup. Ct. R. 711(a) (student must have completed half the credits required for graduation, be in good academic standing, and have application certified by the dean of the law school); Cal. R. Ct. R. 9.42(c) (student must have completed one full year of studies, completed or be enrolled in evidence and civil procedure).

ing in court, preparing briefs and other court documents, counseling and advising clients, negotiating settlements, and other work that licensed attorneys do. Supervisors should carefully review and approve any document prepared by the student before it is filed with a court or sent to the client or opposing counsel. Supervisors have an important role in helping students carefully prepare for court appearances, client interviews, depositions, negotiations, and other lawyerly duties. While students may not perform these tasks with the same level of skill as experienced attorneys, supervisors need to ensure that the student's representation will meet the professional responsibility standards and serve the client's interests. Be sure to check local student practice rules for other requirements, such as whether supervisors need to sign any document prepared by a student, or appear in court with the student, or obtain written client approval for student representation.[33]

4. Applicable Laws

While externship sites are familiar with employment laws applicable to its employees, there are several laws specific to student externs of which supervisors should be aware. Because externs are students, the externship site is governed by all school policies in addition to the federal laws described below.

a. Title IX

Title IX of the Education Amendments of 1972 protects students from sex discrimination when participating in educational programs or activities that receive federal financial assistance. In other words, "[a] recipient institution that receives Department funds must operate its education program or activity in a nondiscriminatory manner free of discrimination based on sex, including sexual orientation and gender identity. Some key issue areas in which recipients have Title IX obligations are: recruitment, admissions, and counseling; financial assistance; athletics; sex-based harassment, which encompasses sexual assault and other forms of sexual violence; treatment of pregnant and parenting students; treatment of LGBTQ+ students; discipline; single-sex education; and employment."[34] In addition to Title IX, most law schools have policies prohibiting sexual harassment. Externship placements should be aware of all school policies and comply with them.

33. *See, e.g.*, Ill. Sup. Ct. R. 711(c); Cal. R. Ct. R. 9.42(c).

34. *Sex Discrimination Overview of the Law*, https://www2.ed.gov/policy/rights/guid/ocr/sexoverview.html (last visited March 20, 2022).

b. FERPA

The Family Educational Rights and Privacy Act (FERPA)[35] is a federal law that:

> applies to all educational agencies and institutions (e.g., schools) that receive funding under any program administered by the Department.... The term "education records" is defined as those records that contain information directly related to a student and which are maintained by an educational agency or institution *or by a party acting for the agency or institution*....FERPA generally prohibits the improper disclosure of personally identifiable information derived from education records.[36]

Therefore, if an externship site maintains its own student timesheets, onboarding documents, performance evaluations, or other materials as part of the externship, those documents are considered education records and should not be disclosed.

c. FLSA

Prior to 2016, students were prohibited from receiving both academic credit and compensation for the work performed during an externship. In 2016, however, the ABA Council removed that prohibition, and the ABA Standards now allow for students to receive both academic credit and compensation. This compensation can be from fellowships, third parties, or the externship site itself. Although compensation is allowed, many law school externship programs continue to prohibit payment for the work performed in an externship. One of the main reasons law schools continue to prohibit payment is the concern that the payment could shift the nature of the site supervisor-extern relationship from an academic focus of teacher-student to an employment focus of employer-employee. Because Standard 304 requires the law school to ensure the quality of the educational experience, compensated externship placements can present challenges to this requirement. Nevertheless, there are several externship programs that allow students to receive compensation at the same time they are earning academic credit for the work they are performing as part of the externship course.

If an externship site is not providing compensation, it must be mindful of the Fair Labor Standards Act of 1938, as amended. "The FLSA requires 'for-profit' employers to pay employees for their work. Interns and students, however, may not be 'employees' under the FLSA—in which case the FLSA does not require compensation for their work."[37] "But because the FLSA expressly applies to government offices

35. 20 U.S.C. § 1232g; 34 C.F.R. Part 99.

36. The Family Educational Rights and Privacy Act Guidance for Eligible Students (February 2011), https://www2.ed.gov/policy/gen/guid/fpco/ferpa/for-eligible-students.pdf (emphasis added).

37. https://www.dol.gov/agencies/whd/fact-sheets/71-flsa-internships (last visited March 20, 2022).

and may potentially apply to both private and for-profit firms and companies,"[38] all externship sites should be aware of the FLSA requirements. The central question under the FLSA is the extern's status; whether "the nature of the extern's responsibilities and the employer's role" would cause the extern to fall within the definition of "employee" and, thus, trigger the protections of the FLSA, or whether the extern will "qualify for one of the narrow exclusions or exemptions from the FLSA coverage under which a person may provide services to a covered employer without being deemed an 'employee' covered by law."[39]

Courts use a seven-factor test to determine whether a student is the "primary beneficiary" of the extern-employer relationship and, thus, whether the FLSA requires minimum wage and overtime pay. "[I]n the law school context, an externship program that is carefully designed to meet ABA standards is likely to satisfy the concerns of the Labor Department as well."[40] This is evidenced in the seven factors that emphasize the academic nature of the student's work and are as follows:

1. The extent to which the intern and the employer clearly understand that there is no expectation of compensation. Any promise of compensation, express or implied, suggests that the intern is an employee—and vice versa.
2. The extent to which the internship provides training that would be similar to that which would be given in an educational environment, including the clinical and other hands-on training provided by educational institutions.
3. The extent to which the internship is tied to the intern's formal education program by integrated coursework or the receipt of academic credit.
4. The extent to which the internship accommodates the intern's academic commitments by corresponding to the academic calendar.
5. The extent to which the internship's duration is limited to the period in which the internship provides the intern with beneficial learning.
6. The extent to which the intern's work complements, rather than displaces, the work of paid employees while providing significant educational benefits to the intern.
7. The extent to which the intern and the employer understand that the internship is conducted without entitlement to a paid job at the conclusion of the internship.[41]

---

38. Niki Kuckes, *Designing Law School Externships That Comply with the FLSA*, 21 Clinical L. Rev. 79, 82 (2014).

39. *Id.* at 87.

40. *Id.* at 82.

41. *See supra* note 35.

"If analysis of these circumstances reveals that an intern or student is actually an employee, then he or she is entitled to both minimum wage and overtime pay under the FLSA. On the other hand, if the analysis confirms that the intern or student is not an employee, then he or she is not entitled to either minimum wage or overtime pay under the FLSA."[42]

42. *Id.*

Appendix

Materials Referenced in Chapter 3: Designing and Executing Externship Programs

1. Law Student Clinic/Externship Planning Guide

Externship/Clinic Planning		
1L Summer		
2L Fall		
2L Spring		
2L Summer		
3L Fall		
3L Spring		
Total credits limited to 21 credits for students in top half of class and 15 credits for the lower half of the class. See below for exceptions.		21/90

What is a Clinic? A Clinic is a course for credit in which students represent clients in one of a variety of practice areas and are directly supervised by Seattle University Clinical Faculty. Seattle University School of Law's Ronald A. Peterson Law Clinic is a fully functioning law firm with faculty practicing in the areas listed below.

What is an Externship? An Externship is a course for credit in which students are placed with an external organization, are supervised by that outside legal organization, and participate in an associated seminar taught by Seattle University Clinical Faculty.

What is a Practicum? A practicum is a course for credit in which students learn about a substantive area of law in-depth in a classroom setting, then apply that learning to hands-on work in the Practicum's legal focus area. Practicums fulfill the professional skills requirement, but don't count toward clinic/externship credit limits.

There are two available:

Homeless Rights Advocacy Practicum (F, S, 3 cr.)

Moderate Means Practicum (F, S, 3 cr.)

In What Areas Can I Do an Externship?	In What Areas Can I Do a Clinic?
Prosecuting Attorney's Office and Public Defender (Crim. Seminar) Legal Services Organization and other Non-profit (Civil Seminar) Governmental Agency (IH/GOV Seminar)+ In-House Counsel (IH/GOV Seminar)+ Courts and Administrative Tribunal (Judicial Seminar) Legislative and Lobbying Organization (Legislative Seminar) International Organization or Tribunal. (International Seminar)	Arts Law (S, 1 cr.) Civil Rights (F. S, 6 cr.) The Defender Clinic (S, 6 cr., R9) Federal Tax (F, S, 3 cr./4 cr., UW Clinic) Housing Justice (F, 6 cr., R9) Immigration (S, 4 cr.) International Human Rights (F, S, 4 cr.) Estate and Disability Planning S, 4 cr.) Workers' Rights (S, 6 cr.) Not for Profit Org (S, 2 cr.) Trademark (F, S, 3 cr.) (Fall Semester=F; Spring Semester=S) (Rule 9= R9

How Many Clinics and Externships Can I Do?

You may not take an externship and a clinic simultaneously and you may not take the same externship seminar more than once. You can do several externships and clinics as long as you do not exceed the credit maximum for experiential learning.

Who is Eligible to do an Externship? Requirements vary based on number of prior SU law credits completed.

Legal experience	Possible sites/clinical courses (includes past, present and future experiences)
Client Interviewing and Counseling, Negotiation and Dispute Resolution, Transactional Work	
Pre-trial Practice and Trial Skills (Rule 9)	

Research and Writing (e.g. Judicial positions, Impact Litigation)	
Other Specialization (Policy, Business, In-House Counsel, Legislative, International etc.)	

Full-Time Externship (12–15 credits – Fall/Spring; 7–8 credits – Summer) Includes 2-credit Seminar		
Prior Credits Earned	Class Rank	Hours Worked Per Week
60	Top 50% (Bottom 50% need ARC Bar Success Plan and Dean of Student Affairs Approval)	7 Credits Summer 34 hours 8 credits Summer 37.5 hours 12 credits – 30 hours (Fall/Spring) 13 credits – 32.5 hours (Fall/Spring) 14 credits – 35 hours (Fall/Spring) 15 credits – 37.5 hours (Fall/Spring) (Some sites require 39 hours)
Part-Time Externship (Includes 1-credit Seminar)		
Prior Credits Earned	Class Rank	Hours Worked Per Week
Completion of 1st year	All students eligible	**2 credits** – 5 hours (Fall/Spring); 9 hours (Summer) **3 credits** – 7.5 hours (Fall/Spring); 14 hours (Summer) **4 credits** – 10 hours (Fall/Spring); 19 hours (Summer) **5 credits** – 12.5 hours (Fall/Spring); 24 hours (Summer) **6 credits** – 15 hours (Fall/Spring); 29 hours (Summer) **7 credits** – 17.5 hours (Fall/Spring) **8 credits** – 20 hours (Fall/Spring) **9 credits** – 22.5 hours (Fall/Spring) **10 credits** – 25 hours (Fall/Spring) **11 credits** – 27.5 hours (Fall/Spring)

Externship Application Process

Review information on the Externship Program website and browse through the Externship Database to review available opportunities.

Schedule an appointment on TWEN (Appointments with Externship Faculty) if you have not met with us before.

Fill out the Externship Application Form (on the Externship website) and submit it to externships@seattleu.edu.

Gather your application materials (cover letter, resume, etc.). Info on what is needed for each site is on the profile in the Externship Database.

Ask CPD to review your resume and cover letters. Incorporate CPD's feedback before submitting to the Externship Program Office.

Email your application materials to the Externship Program Office at externships@seattleu.edu. To secure a place in a given seminar you must submit the Externship Application Form and send cover letters for at least THREE sites within that area/seminar. Please indicate which site is your first choice. The Externship Program Office will proofread before submitting your applications to the externship placements.

IMPORTANT: For each semester, you should begin by submitting applications for sites that fall within ONE area/seminar. Externs are assigned to a seminar based on the following categories and can only enroll in each seminar once:

- Legal Services Organizations and other Non-profits (Civil Seminar);
- Government Agencies and In-house Counsel's Offices (IH/GOV Seminar); SUMMER ONLY – THIS SEMINAR IS SPLIT INTO TWO SEPARATE SEMINARS: In House Counsel Seminar and Government Attorney Seminar.
- Courts and Administrative Tribunals (Judicial Seminar);
- Legislative and Lobbying Organizations (Legislative Seminar- SPRING ONLY);
- International Organizations and Tribunals (International Seminar).

Can I Extern for a Site Not Already Listed in the Database?

If you hope to earn credit, be sure to contact the Externship Program before you apply! The site can be approved only if it offers experiential learning different from what is available in current sites. The Externship Faculty will speak with the site and notify you and the site supervisor if it can be approved.

Can I Extern for a Site Where I Have Worked, Volunteered or Externed Before?

No. The only exception is if you work on a different list of tasks and skills from what you did before and the Externship Faculty approve in advance.

What Should I Do Once I Have Applied for an Externship?

Sites typically take 2–4 weeks to contact you for an interview. If you have not heard back, please contact the Externship Program.

What Do I Do if I am Offered a Position?

We require that you accept the first offer you receive. This assures supervisors that all applicants are interested in their site and keeps opportunities open for future students. Therefore, apply only to sites you would accept.

Once you have accepted, contact the Externship Program Office to register you.

Discuss your schedule with your site supervisor. You and your supervisor will receive more detailed information from the Externship Program Office two weeks before the semester begins.

EXTERNSHIP SEMINAR DAYS/TIMES Part-time Externships include a 1-Credit Seminar.

Full-time Externs take the 1-Credit seminar AND do a 15–20 pages paper to earn a total of 2 graded credits.

Judicial Seminar	Spring Olympia Legislative and Judicial+ Seminars
One Day Intensive first Friday* of the Semester, then Mondays 6:00 – 7:15pm (Fall/Spring), 6:00 – 7:30pm (Summer)	Leg: 1 day Intensive before Semester, then TBD Jud: 1 day Intensive first Friday of Semester then TBD (+Seminar for students in judicial placements in OLY) SPRING ONLY All Classes Held in Olympia
Civil Seminar	**International Seminar**
One Day Intensive first Friday* of the Semester, then Thursdays 4:00 – 5:15pm (Fall/Spring), 4:00 – 5:30pm (Summer)	1 day Intensive before Semester, then biweekly on Wednesdays, 11:00 am to 12:30 pm PST (Fall /Spring) 1 day Intensive + 2 additional 2 hr. seminars (Summer)
Criminal Seminar	**In-House/Government Atty. Seminar +**
One Day Intensive first Friday* of the Semester, then Tuesdays 4:00 – 5:15pm (Fall/Spring), 4:00 – 5:30pm (Summer	One Day Intensive first Friday* of the Semester, then Thursdays 4:00 – 5:15pm (Fall/Spring), 4:00 – 5:30pm (Summer)

+NOTE: In-House Counsel and Gov't Attorney Seminars are only split in the summer. This allows you to extern at one in-house counsel and one government attorney site if at least one of the externships is in the summer. The summer Gov't Attorney Seminar is held on Tuesdays. The summer In-House Counsel Seminar is held on Thursdays.

*NOTE: Summer Intensives take place the first Monday of the Semester. For 2022 it is May 31, the Tuesday after Memorial Day.

Materials Referenced in Chapter 4: Selecting, Training, and Evaluating Site Supervisors

1. Questionnaire for Prospective Externship Placements[1]

Field Placement Questionnaire

Organization

Name:

Address:

Primary Field Supervisor[2]:

Contact email & telephone number:

Additional supervision may be provided by (list field supervisor names and titles):

Description of Organization's Practice and/or Mission: (Please use additional pages as needed; You may also provide a link to information found on your organization's website.)

Do you have any experience supervising law students? Yes / No.

If yes, please provide when and a brief explanation of your experience.

1. This questionnaire was shared with the authors by Cecily Becker, Director of the Externship Program at the Texas A & M University School of Law.

2. A field supervisor must have at least 3 years of experience and be a member in good standing with the appropriate jurisdictional bar. (If the opportunity is non-traditional, JD advantaged, the field supervisor must have a JD.) Additionally, the field supervisor should not have been subject to sanctions either by a court or state (jurisdictional) bar. If the field supervisor has been sanctioned, please attach a brief statement providing the date and nature of the sanction.

Students can work with more than one field supervisor, but there should be a primary field supervisor who will oversee and evaluate the student's experience and performance, and be available to communicate with the school as necessary.

Educational Goals and Description of Work:

Please identify the educational goals[3] that a student would work toward achieving while externing with you and describe the type of duties/assignments that you anticipate the student to perform to fulfill these goals. (Please use separate or additional pages if desired.)

Student Criteria:

Students can earn between 2 to 4 pass/fail credits, requiring for following, minimum fieldwork hours: 2 cr – 73 hours; 3 cr – 115; 4 cr – 158. The externship term starts and ends with the semester term, with a minimum 10-week commitment in spring or fall, and 5-week commitment in summer.

---

3. The Extern Program's educational objectives for students include:

Improve their lawyering skills such as research, writing, analysis, and oral advocacy;

Increase their understanding of the range of skills necessary to effectively perform legal or law-related work.

Develop a deeper understanding of substantive law and the legal or law-related issues facing the host organization and its mission;

Enhance their understanding of professionalism, professional responsibility, and other workplace issues that arise in a professional work environment;

Develop productive working relationships and explore career options; and

Engage in critical self-reflection to promote self-directed, lifelong learning.

Is there a minimum time commitment that you would like to see from an extern?

Is there a preferred schedule that would be most beneficial for a student's experience? For example, mornings/afternoons, Mondays vs. Fridays, etc.?

Do you have any preferred experience, courses taken, or other academic criteria that you would like a student to possess?

Evaluation of Student Performance: We/I understand that the Extern Program is an academic program and to this end:

Commit to the educational goals of the program and will ensure that the externship is of substantial educational value, assigning tasks that are representative of the field supervisor's typical day's work, including opportunities to observe that work

Will meet with the student at the beginning of the externship to discuss goals, and meet regularly thereafter to providing mentorship and feedback throughout the process;

Will sign and return to the school the Memorandum of Understanding once an externship is offered to a student; and

Commit to being available to discuss the student's performance both during and at the end of the semester with both the student and school.

Submitted by: ____

Field Supervisor

2. Externship Agreement for Student, Faculty, and Site Supervisor

Externship Educational Plan

Field Placement: ______________________________

Supervising Attorney: ______________________________

Law Student: ______________________________

The UALR William H. Bowen School of Law Public Service Externship Course ("Course") provides participating law students with substantial lawyering experience reasonably similar to the experience of a lawyer advising or representing a client or engaging in other lawyering tasks under direct attorney supervision at the field placement. The Course includes opportunities for performance, feedback, and self-evaluation to assist students in making progress toward individual and Course learning goals.

The Supervising Attorney, Law Student, and UALR Bowen School of Law Externship Director agree to the following responsibilities that constitute an educational plan for the Student's externship experience at the field placement:

Responsibilities of the Supervising Attorney at the Field Placement:

1. The Supervising Attorney understands that the Student is the primary beneficiary of the Course and that the purpose of the Course is to allow the student to learn from the experience of working as a lawyer.
2. The Supervising Attorney has read the Course's Guidelines for Field Supervisors and agrees to abide by them and other applicable Course rules and policies.
3. The Supervising Attorney accepts primary responsibility for overseeing the Student's experience at the field placement throughout the semester and monitoring the progress of the Student's work.
4. The Supervising Attorney agrees to assign tasks to the Student that are representative of the work of the Supervising Attorney and the placement. If appropriate to the work of the placement, a Student who meets the requirements of the Arkansas Student-Practice Rule may be certified to appear in court or personally represent a client under attorney supervision.
5. The Supervising Attorney agrees to work with the Student to establish a work schedule that will allow the Student to complete by the end of the semester the number of hours necessary to satisfy the Course requirements.

(100 hours of work for a first externship, and 115 hours of work for a second externship.)

6. The Supervising Attorney agrees that, as appropriate, the Student will be offered opportunities to participate in all aspects of placement work, cases, or projects, including, but not limited to, client interviewing, counseling, case planning, negotiation, fact investigation, trial preparation and trial, meetings, policy development, legal research, drafting, legal writing, and guided observation of these or other lawyering activities.
7. The Supervising Attorney will not assign the Student clerical tasks, such as filing, photocopying, library updating, indexing, etc., unless such tasks are specifically related to an educational activity.
8. The Supervising Attorney and/or other attorneys assigning work to the Student agree to provide timely feedback on assignments.
9. The Supervising Attorney agrees to meet with the Student at the start of the semester to review and discuss the Student's Learning Agenda and strategies for achieving learning goals.
10. The Supervising Attorney agrees to review the Student's timesheets on a weekly basis and sign the timesheets if the time recorded is accurate.
11. The Supervising Attorney agrees that, if a significant problem occurs regarding the Student or the ability of the field placement to continue the Student's externship, the Supervising Attorney will contact the Externship Director as soon as possible.
12. Once the Student completes the required number of work hours at the field placement, the Supervising Attorney agrees to complete and submit to the Externship Director a copy of the Field Supervisor Review Form. (The Student will provide this form to the Supervising Attorney.)

Responsibilities of the Law Student:

1. The Student agrees to perform work assigned by the Supervising Attorney in connection with the field placement and to complete the number of hours necessary to satisfy the Course requirements. (100 hours of work for a first externship, and 115 hours of work for a second externship.) The Student further agrees to complete weekly timesheets recording his or her work at the field placement and submit the timesheets to the Supervising Attorney and the Externship Director.
2. The Student agrees to set a regular work schedule with the Supervising Attorney and seek permission for any changes or modifications in the placement work schedule.
3. The Student agrees to comply with the Arkansas Rules of Professional

Conduct and other rules, guidelines, or policies applicable to the particular field placement.

4. The Student has read the Course Syllabus and agrees to abide by the policies and requirements stated therein.
5. The Student agrees to complete the Externship Learning Agenda, submit a copy of the Learning Agenda to the Externship Director, and review and discuss the completed Learning Agenda with the Supervising Attorney.
6. The Student agrees to complete a mid-semester self-evaluation and an end-of-semester Student Review Form.

Responsibilities of the UALR Bowen School of Law Externship Director:

1. The Externship Director oversees the Course to assure the educational quality of the Student's experience and to evaluate the Student's academic performance.
2. The Externship Director will review and evaluate the Student's timesheets, learning goals, weekly journal assignments, mid-semester self-evaluation, final essay, and Student Review Form.
3. The Externship Director will provide classroom instruction related to the field placement experience and will ensure on-going, contemporaneous, faculty-guided reflection.
4. The Externship Director will meet with the Student at mid-semester to review the Student's progress toward goals, and more often as needed to assist the Student and assure educational progress.
5. The Externship Director will provide training for the Supervising Attorney on the Course requirements and techniques for working with law students, provide other information or materials as necessary, and engage in regular communication with the Supervising Attorney.
6. The Externship Director agrees to be available to assist the Student and/or Supervising Attorney should any questions or concerns arise during the semester.
7. The Externship Director will evaluate the Student's academic performance at the end of the semester and determine the Student's final grade for the Course, based on the Field Supervisor Review Form, the Student's

completion of the requisite number of work hours, and the Student's performance in the seminar component of the Course.

Signatures:

1. The Student, Supervising Attorney, and Externship Director agree that this Educational Plan may be signed in any number of counterparts, each of which when signed shall constitute a duplicate original, but all counterparts together shall constitute a single Educational Plan.
2. By signing below, the Student, Supervising Attorney, and Externship Director certify that they agree with the terms of this Educational Plan.

Supervising Attorney: ______________________________

Law Student: ______________________________

Externship Director: ______________________________

3. Externship Program Acknowledgement of Program Requirements

Student Extern Name: ____________________ Semester/Year:____________________

Externship Site: ____

Externship Site Supervisor: ____

Name and Title

Supervising Attorney: ____

Name and Title (Please indicate if same as Externship Site Supervisor)

Faculty Supervisor: ____

Georgia State University College of Law Externship Program relies on an ongoing collaboration between the externship site supervisor, supervising attorney, student extern, and faculty supervisor. To maintain the integrity and ensure the standards of the externship program, all participants in the program shall adhere, at a minimum, to the standards as outlined below.

Externship Site Supervisor's Responsibilities:

As the externship site supervisor, I agree to the following:

The externship site description as posted on the Georgia State University College of Law website (https://insidelaw.gsu.edu/externships/sites/) along with the student extern's completed Goals Form describes the substantial lawyering experience and opportunities for performance available to the student extern.

I will ensure that each extern has a supervising attorney who will be primarily responsible for the supervision of the student extern at the externship site, as outlined below in Section B. If I am serving as the supervising attorney as well as the site supervisor, I agree to the responsibilities outlined below in Section B.

I will ensure that the externship site facilitates a method of orientation, which shall include a discussion of the rules, policies, procedures, methods, and operation of the externship site, confidentiality rules, and an overview of the work and expectations of the student extern.

I will secure a designated workspace for the student extern, and provide him/her access to system networks and any other resources necessary for the student extern to complete assignments.

I will maintain email and/or telephone communication with the faculty supervisor regarding any relevant issues related to the student extern, supervising attorney, and/or the externship site.

Supervising Attorney's Responsibilities

As a supervising attorney, I agree to the following:

I have authority or have been delegated authority to supervise the student extern and designate a portion of my work time to supervising the student extern.

I accept primary responsibility for supervision of the student extern at the externship site.

I will supervise and mentor the student extern throughout the semester.

I will meet with the student extern at the start of the semester to review and sign the Goals Form, which sets forth the student extern's goals/expectations for the externship, and will approve stated goals/expectations only if it appears that the student extern will have the opportunity to achieve them. I will also indicate any additional goals/expectations I have for the student extern.

I will have a discussion with the student extern about the externship site's confidentiality rules at the start of the semester, and will review and sign the Confidentiality Form completed by the student extern.

I will review and sign the Conflicts Form completed by the student extern at the start of the semester and will discuss and resolve any potential conflicts identified.

I will complete the Preliminary Performance Assessment at mid-semester and will meet with the student extern to review his/her performance and to discuss whether the student extern is meeting all identified goals/expectations.

I will complete the Student Evaluation Form at the end of the semester and will meet with the student to discuss his/her performance, and provide specific, individualized feedback regarding the student extern's overall performance.

In assigning work, I will clearly describe the task to be completed, set forth my objectives for the assignment, and discuss the relationship of the work to the larger substantive, procedural and/or practical issues pertaining to the matter assigned.

As appropriate, I will include the student extern in discussions of strategy and implementation that arise out of matters handled by the externship site.

In general, I will not assign the student extern clerical tasks (filing, library updating, photocopying, etc.).

In supervising the student extern, I will keep in mind the objectives of the externship course: to explore the student extern's developing professional identity as a lawyer; to develop practices necessary to self-directed professional learning, including goal-setting and reflective skills for future law practice; to develop strategies to help initiate and sustain professional relationships; to develop strategies to facilitate working with others toward a common goal; to develop a deeper understanding of key communication skills; to develop strategies to interact effectively with people across cultural differences; to develop a sense of professional responsibility; to develop time management techniques including timekeeping, meeting deadlines and managing multiple assignments; and to observe and critique a specific practice area and how the legal system works.

I will be available to meet with the student extern as needed to provide support and feedback on assignments.

I will consistently provide timely, specific feedback to the student extern on his/her work. The feedback will constructively assess his/her lawyering skills and advise the extern on his/her strengths and areas of improvement.

I will ensure compliance with O.C.G.A. §§ 15-19-50, 15-19-51 and 15-19-56 pertaining to the unauthorized practice of law and Georgia Supreme Court Rules 91–95.

Student Extern Responsibilities

As a student extern, I agree to the following:

I will perform the assigned work at my externship site for the total hours required based on the number of S/U externship credit hours I have registered for this semester in no less than 14 weeks without the express permission of my externship site and faculty supervisor.

I understand that the purpose of the externship program is to grant me the opportunity to receive hands-on lawyering experience and, in doing so, I must be familiar with and abide by the Georgia Rules of Professional Conduct and other rules, guidelines, or policies applicable to my externship site.

I will articulate specific, measurable goals and discuss both my goals and strategies for achieving them with my supervising attorney at the beginning of the semester. I will assess my progress in meeting my articulated goals throughout the semester.

I will meet separately with my supervising attorney and with my faculty supervisor at mid-semester and at the end of the semester.

I will complete the academic component of the externship program, which includes participating in the externship seminar (if applicable) and the timely submission of all evaluations, reflection papers, timesheets, and/or other assignments required by my faculty supervisor.

I will reflect on and self-assess my lawyering competencies throughout the externship experience.

Faculty Supervisor Responsibilities

As a faculty supervisor, I agree to the following:

I will review all forms submitted by the student extern to ensure that he/she is adhering to the requirements of the externship program and that the student extern is receiving substantial lawyering experience.

I will review the student extern's signed Goals Form at the beginning of the semester to ensure that the student extern has articulated specific goals that are in line with the purpose of the externship program.

I will review the student extern's signed Confidentiality Form to confirm that the student is abiding by the confidentiality rules of the externship site when engaged in class discussion, if applicable, and when completing class assignments.

I will meet with the student extern at the middle and end of the semester to discuss his/her progress on meeting his/her goals and to provide an opportunity for the student extern to express any questions or concerns regarding his/her externship experience. I will also be available throughout the semester should any concerns or issues arise.

I will evaluate the student extern's academic performance throughout the semester based upon performance in the externship seminar (if applicable), reflection papers, timesheets, evaluations completed by the student extern and/or supervising attorney, and any other relevant information.

I will regularly communicate with the site supervisor and/or supervising attorney about the student extern and the externship site.

By signature below, we acknowledge that we have reviewed this document and agree to act in accordance with the expectations outlined above:

______________________________ _______________

Externship Site Supervisor Signature Date

______________________________ _______________

Supervising Attorney Signature Date

______________________________ _______________

Student Extern Signature Date

______________________________ _______________

Faculty Supervisor Signature Date

4. Externship Student Evaluation Form

Student Review Form

Student Name: ______________________________

Supervisor Name: ______________________________

Externship Placement: ______________________________

Review Date: ______________________________

In completing this form, you should carefully evaluate your externship experience based on the course description and the goals you set during the externship. Please read the evaluating factors and definitions carefully, place a check mark next to the description (where applicable), and make the necessary comments that most accurately reflect and support your evaluation. Use an attachment if more space is needed.

1. DESCRIPTION OF PLACEMENT			
1.1	Substantive Areas.		
	Describe the substantive areas of law that you encountered during your externship:		
			_____ 1 pt.
1.2	Skills		
	Indicate with an "X" the skills that you encountered during the externship:		
	Legal Research		Client Interviews/Counseling
	Writing		Trial Advocacy/Litigation
	Negotiation		Legal Presentations/ Public Speaking
	Fact Investigation		Other – Please describe:
	Legal Analysis		
			_____ 1 pt.
1.3	Professional Values		

	a. Did your externship expose you to the professional values of the legal profession – such as honesty, integrity, competency, civility, and justice? If so, how? b. After your externship, do you feel that you have a better understanding of the values of the legal profession? Why or why not?
	_____ 2 pts.
1.4	Physical Set-up
	Please describe the physical area where you worked during the externship and the resources available (e.g., private office with a telephone, computer, and desk; access to support staff; etc.):
Comment:	
	_____ 1 pts.

2. EVALUATION OF FIELD PLACEMENT SUPERVISOR	
2.1	Orientation
	The field placement supervisor is required to provide an orientation to the organization's (1) work, history, structure or objectives, (2) office policies and procedures, (3) office resources, and (4) staff members.
	No orientation provided.
	Minimal orientation provided.
	Acceptable level of orientation provided.
Comment:	
	_____ 1 pt.
2.2	Setting of Goals
	The field placement supervisor is asked to meet with the student to discuss the specific goals of the externship and how the practical externship experience will meet and complement the student's learning goals and needs.
	No formal goal setting. Often confused about supervisor's goals for the externship.
	Minimal goal setting.

	Acceptable level of goal setting. Generally understood supervisor's goals for externship.
Comment:	
	______ 1 pt.
2.3	Caseload Management.
	The field placement supervisor is asked to provide the student with an overview of the matter(s) or case(s) in which the student will be involved and how the student's particular projects and assignments fit into the matter as a whole. The field placement supervisor is requested to explain clearly (1) the desired finished project; (2) the amount of time the student should spend on the project; (3) the due date; and (4) other conditions or requirements of the project.
	Assignments given with no explanation. Student often confused about desired work.
	Assignments given with minimal explanation. Student required to ask repeatedly for additional information.
	Acceptable level of explanation given. Student generally understood assignment.
	Superior level of explanation provided – in written form for complex matters.
Comment:	
	______ 1 pt.
2.4	Oversight Availability
	The field placement supervisor is directed to meet with the student at least once a week to review progress, answer questions, provide ongoing feedback on the student's performance, schedule assignments, and discuss any specific issues, including policy, professional, or ethical considerations raised by the assignments. Ideally, the field placement supervisor should be available for informal, brief conferences on individual issues in addition to the weekly meeting.
	No oversight provided.
	Minimal oversight provided.

	Acceptable level of oversight provided.
	Superior level of oversight provided.
Comment:	
	_____ 1 pt.

2.5	How would you describe the office environment of your placement? (i.e., formal, relaxed, hectic, organized, chaotic, friendly, etc.
Comment:	
	_____ 1 pt.

2.6	Future Placement with Organization.
	Would you recommend this organization to future externs?
Comment:	
	_____ 1 pt.
2.7	Future Participation by Field Placement Supervisor.
	Would you recommend that this supervisor be asked to participate as a field placement supervisor for the externship course in the future? Why or why not? Is there another attorney in the organization that you would recommend as a better supervisor?
Comment:	
	_____ 1 pt.

3. CLASSROOM EVALUATION		
	Class Presentations.	
	Please comment on the seminar component of the externship course. Were the presentations interesting and useful? Would you like to see other topics addressed? If so, what additional topics would you suggest?	
Comment:		
		_____ 1 pt.

4.	COURSE RECOMMENDATIONS
	Please indicate whether there are any ideas or changes that you believe the Law School should implement to make the externship course function better for Law School students:
Comment:	

5.	REQUIRED SIGNATURE		
Yes	No	May Prof. Terry provide your contact information to the next extern who will work at your placement office so that student may contact you if he or she has questions about the office?	
Date			Student Signature

*** Please sign and submit the form to Professor Terry by uploading it to the designated dropbox on TWEN.

Submitted on Time: _____ Yes (2 points) Total Points: _____ out of 15

Materials Referenced in Chapter 7: Designing Individual Externship Courses

1. Rubric for Externship Timesheet

Task Description: Students shall complete and submit a timesheet for each week of externship work.

	Needs Work	Competent
Professionalism: Compliance w/ Instructions ________6	Information is hand-written. (0 pts) Does not correctly state date of work week. (0 pts) Time not calculated in tenths of hour. (0 pts) Does not provide sufficient detail regarding work performed. (0 pts) Does not use time codes provided. (0 pts) Not signed by student. (0 pts) Not approved by supervisor. (0 pts)	Information is typed. (1 pt) Correctly states date of work week. (1 pt) Time calculated in tenths of hour. (1 pt) Provides sufficient detail regarding work performed. (1 pt) Uses time codes provided. (1 pt) Signed by student. (1 pt) Approved by supervisor. (2 pts)
Professionalism: Maintaining Workplace Confidentiality ________2	Includes confidential workplace information. (0 pts)	Does not include confidential workplace information. (2 pts)
Total: _______ out of 10		

2. Rubric for Externship Rounds Discussion

Task Description: During a seminar class, each student will present an externship experience during a rounds discussion. Students should be prepared to:

Briefly discuss a specific externship experience;

Identify the presence or absence of a professional value in conjunction with the externship experience presented; and

Explain the effect that the presence or absence of that professional value had on the externship experience and lesson(s) learned from the experience for the student's future practice of law.

<table>
<tr><th></th><th>Needs Work</th><th>Competent</th></tr>
<tr><td rowspan="3">Learning Profes-sional Values:</td><td>Unable to identify the presence or absence of a professional value in conjunction with an externship experience. (0 pts)</td><td>Able to identify the presence or absence of a professional value in conjunction with an externship experience. (1–5 pts)</td></tr>
<tr><td>Unable to explain the effect that the presence or absence of the professional value had on the externship experience being discussed. (0 pts)</td><td>Able to explain the effect that the presence or absence of the professional value had on the externship experience being discussed. (1–5 pts)</td></tr>
<tr><td>Unable to explain personal lesson(s) learned from this experience and impact on future practice. (0 pts)</td><td>Able to explain personal lesson(s) learned from this experience and impact on future practice. (1–5 pts)</td></tr>
<tr><td rowspan="2">Professionalism:
Preparation for Rounds Discussion</td><td>Not prepared to present externship experience during rounds. (0 pts)</td><td>Was prepared to present externship experience during rounds. (1–5 pts)</td></tr>
<tr><td>Did not present the externship experience in a logical and organized manner. (0 pts)</td><td>Presented the externship experience in a logical and organized manner. (1–5 pts)</td></tr>
</table>

Total: ________ of 25

3. Rubric for Class Participation

Criteria	Undeveloped: 1	Developing: 2	Competent: 3	Exemplary: 4
Attendance	N/A	N/A	N/A	Student attends all classes.
Punctuality	Student is late to five or more classes	Student is late to three or four classes	Student is late to one or two classes	Student is on time to every class.
Contribution to Discussion	Student does not contribute to class discussions.	Student occasionally contributes to class discussions and/ or contributions indicate that the student is minimally familiar with the assigned materials.	Student regularly contributes to class and/or contributions indicate that the student is somewhat familiar with assigned materials.	Student consistently and in a meaningful manner contributes to class discussions. Contributions consistently demonstrate that the student is familiar with assigned materials.
Listening	Student interrupts others in small and/or large group discussions and does not listen or respond to the comments and questions of others.	Student occasionally listens to and responds to the comments and questions of others in small and large group discussions.	Student regularly listens to and responds to the comments and questions of others in small and group discussions.	Student consistently and in a thoughtful manner listens and provides responses to the comments and questions of others in small and large group discussions.

4. Rubric for Reflective Journal

<table>
<tr><th>Criteria</th><th>Needs Work: 1</th><th>Developing: 2</th><th>Competent: 3</th><th>Exemplary: 4</th></tr>
<tr><td>Timeliness</td><td>N/A</td><td>N/A</td><td>N/A</td><td>Submitted on time.</td></tr>
<tr><td rowspan="4">Depth of Self-Reflection</td><td colspan="4">What? – Describe something you did or an event you observed at your externship.</td></tr>
<tr><td>Does not provide a narrative of externship experience.
Mentions a task performed or event observed.</td><td>Provides a cursory narrative of externship experience–Lists tasks performed or events observed at externship with minimal detail that provides little context.</td><td>Provides a general narrative of externship experience – describes task performed or events observed with some detail that provides some context.</td><td>Provides a thorough narrative of externship experience – describes task performed and/or events observed with detail sufficient to give full context.</td></tr>
<tr><td colspan="4">So What?–Personal Reaction–Describe your reaction to what you did or observed</td></tr>
<tr><td>Does not provide any personal reactions to experience or critical evaluation of the experience.</td><td>Provides minimal personal reactions to externship experience, with only a cursory evaluation of how the observation informed his or her values and beliefs or strengths and weaknesses.
Considers the experience from his or her own perspective.</td><td>Provides personal reactions to externship experience, providing some description of insights gained and developments or changes in his or her values and beliefs or strengths and weaknesses.
Considers the experience from the perspective of others but fails to identify and examine other perspectives in a meaningful way.</td><td>Provides meaningful personal reactions to externship experience, providing a full description of insights gained, and developments of changes in his or her values and beliefs and shows self-awareness as to strengths and weaknesses in contemplating what he or she still needs to learn.
Considers the experience from the perspective of others in a meaningful way.</td></tr>
</table>

Depth of Self-Reflection (continued)	So What?–Lesson about Lawyering–Describe the lesson you can take away from the experience.			
	Does not generalize personal reactions by connecting experience(s) to lessons learned and/or conclusions reached. Does not demonstrate a clarified meaning or broader perspective regarding prior lessons learned inside or outside the classroom.	Attempts to generalize personal reactions but does not effectively step back to see the big picture by including lessons learned and/or conclusions reached. Demonstrates only a slightly clarified meaning or a somewhat broader perspective regarding prior lessons learned inside and outside the classroom.	Generalizes personal reactions by stepping back to see the big picture, including lessons learned and/or conclusions reached. Demonstrates a fully clarified meaning or broader perspective regarding prior lessons learned inside and outside the classroom.	Critically assesses and thoroughly articulates the lessons learned and/or conclusions reached from the externship experience. Demonstrates significantly clarified meaning and changed perspective regarding prior lessons learned inside and outside the classroom that provides a foundation for expanded knowledge and growth.
	Now What?–What do you plan to do the same or differently in your professional future?			
	Does not include any future application of lessons learned. Only focuses on the past (backward looking) with no indication of how insights might be applied in the future.	Mentions that the lessons learned will apply to similar experience(s) in the future, but does not describe how they will apply. Provides minimal plans for further action that are incomplete and not concrete.	Provides some description of how the broader generalizations or lessons learned will apply to similar experience(s) in the future, with minimal detail. Provides solid plans for some future action.	Provides a full description of how the broader generalizations –lessons learned or conclusions reached –will apply to similar experience(s) in the future. Provides in-depth, concrete plans for further action or reflection for a specific purpose such as developing skills, improving self-understanding, or refining belief systems.

Quality of Writing and Attention to Detail	Writing is unclear and disorganized. Thoughts are not expressed in a coherent or logical manner; or Many (6 or more) spelling errors and/or typos.	Writing is not consistently clear, concise, and/or well-organized. Thoughts are not always expressed in a coherent and logical manner; or Several (3–5) spelling errors and/or typos.	Writing is not consistently clear, concise, and/or well-organized. Thoughts are not always expressed in a coherent and logical manner; or Few (1–2) spelling errors and/or typos.	Writing is clear, concise, and well-organized. Thoughts are expressed in a coherent and logical manner; and No spelling errors and/or typos.

5. Rubric for Oral Presentation

Criteria	Needs Work: 1	Developing: 2	Competent: 3	Exemplary: 4
Time	N/A	N/A	N/A	Presentation is long enough to effectively communicate the required content and research but does not exceed 6 minutes.
Forensics	**Eye Contact**			
	Does not make eye contact, relies heavily on notes, reading most of the presentation.	Inconsistent eye contact and reads directly from notes during some of the presentation.	Maintains generally consistent eye contact and reads from notes at several points during the presentation.	Maintains consistent and comfortable eye contact throughout the presentation and only occasionally references notes.
	Cadence and Verbal Fillers ("um," "like," "you know," etc.)			
	Speaks so fast or so slow and/or uses so many verbal fillers that it impedes the audience's ability to understand the presentation.	Speaks too fast or too slow and/or uses many verbal fillers.	Speaks with a steady pace that is at times too fast or too slow, and/or rarely uses verbal fillers.	Speaks with a varied, dynamic pace that is not too fast or too slow and avoids verbal fillers.
	Volume			
	Does not project voice.	Projects voice at a volume that varies and is not always appropriate for the size of the room/ audience.	Projects voice at a volume appropriate for the size of the room/audience throughout the presentation.	Projects voice at a volume appropriate for the size of the room/audience, and stylistically integrates varied intonation.

<table>
<tr><td rowspan="6">Structure and Content</td><td colspan="4">Organization</td></tr>
<tr><td>Information is not presented in a logical sequence.</td><td>Information is presented in a somewhat logical sequence that is often difficult to follow.</td><td>Information is presented in a generally logical sequence that is occasionally difficult to follow.</td><td>Information is presented in a logical sequence that is easy to follow.</td></tr>
<tr><td colspan="4">Required Content</td></tr>
<tr><td>Does not address one of the Shultz-Zedeck Lawyering Effectiveness Factors.</td><td>Addresses a Shultz-Zedeck Lawyering Effectiveness Factor, but does not connect it to his/her externship experience or does not provide a new perspective on its relevance to future practice.</td><td>Discusses a Shultz-Zedeck Lawyering Effectiveness Factor and its connection to his/her externship experience and provides some insight regarding its relevance to future practice.</td><td>Connects a Shultz-Zedeck Lawyering Effectiveness Factor to his/her externship experience and provides a new perspective regarding its relevance to future practice.</td></tr>
<tr><td colspan="4">Research</td></tr>
<tr><td>Does not provide research/data.</td><td>Provides research/data but does not reflect a clear understanding of the research/data and/or does not connect the research to the topic presented.</td><td>Provides relevant research/data, indicates a working understanding of the research/data, and establishes some connection of the research to the topic presented.</td><td>Provides relevant research/data, demonstrates a clear understanding of the research/data presented, and clearly connects the research/data to the topic presented.</td></tr>
</table>

6. Rubric for Final Essay

Task Description: Students shall write a final essay explaining their understanding of the concept of professional identity, including the elements and qualities they aspire to incorporate into their own professional identity, actions they will take to achieve those qualities, and steps they will take to overcome challenges that lawyers face in achieving the ideals of their professional identity.

	Needs Work	Competent	Excellent
Professionalism			
Compliance w/ Instructions ________/10	Submitted late. (0 pts) Less than 2,500 words in length. (0 pts)	Submitted by deadline or sought extension for good cause prior to deadline. (4 pts) Minimum of 2,500 words in length. (4 pts)	Submitted by deadline or sought extension for good cause prior to deadline. (4 pts) Minimum of 2,500 words in length. (4 pts) Includes a word count certification indicating compliance with required word count (2 pts)
Good Written Communication			
Organization and Structure ________/20	Lacks organized structure; "stream of consciousness" style; no flow between topics. (0–12 pts)	Organized and has some structure that reader can follow; some connection and flow between topics. (13–18 pts)	Well-organized; clear and logical structure; coherently connects sections; uses transitions to effect good flow between topics. (19–20 pts)
Punctuation, Grammar, Spelling ________/20	Many errors in grammar, spelling, or punctuation. (0–12 pts)	Some errors in grammar, spelling, or punctuation. (13–18 pts)	Few or no errors in grammar, spelling, or punctuation. (19–20 pts)

Professional Tone ________/5	Casual tone; uses lots of slang, idioms, colloquialisms. (0–2 pts)	Professional tone, but uses some slang, idioms, colloquialisms. (3–4 pts)	Professional tone; no use of slang, idioms, colloquialisms. (5 pts)
Quality of Reflection and Introspection			
Understanding of Concept of Professional Identity ________/25	Fails to demonstrate the student's own personal understanding of the concept of professional identity (for example, just repeats a scholar's definition of the concept); or, demonstrates a personal understanding but discusses it in terms that are vague or unclear. (0–14 pts)	Demonstrates the student's own personal understanding of the concept of professional identity, but at a basic level, without explaining the student's understanding of the concept in detail or with depth. (15–22 pts)	Demonstrates the student's own understanding of the concept of professional identity, showing a sophisticated and deep understanding of the concept, explaining in detail what the concept means, and synthesizing different ideas to explain the student's understanding. (23–25 pts)
Elements and Qualities to Incorporate into Professional Identity ________/25	Fails to identify specific elements/qualities that student aspires to incorporate into their professional identity; or, identifies specific elements / qualities but discusses them in terms that are vague or unclear. (0–14 pts)	Identifies specific elements/qualities that student aspires to incorporate into their professional identity, but discusses those elements/qualities in a superficial way without exploring the reasons and motivations for choosing those elements/qualities. (15–22 pts)	Identifies specific elements/qualities that student aspires to incorporate into their professional identity, and discusses those elements/qualities in a meaningful and thoughtful way, exploring the reasons and motivations for choosing those elements/qualities. (23–25 pts)

Actions to Achieve Desired Elements and Qualities of Professional Identity _________/25	Fails to identify concrete and specific actions that student will take to achieve the desired elements/qualities of their professional identity; or, identifies actions but discusses them in vague or unclear terms. (0–14 pts)	Identifies concrete and specific actions that student will take to achieve the desired elements/qualities of their professional identity, but discusses the actions at a superficial level, without explaining how the actions will enable the student to achieve the desired elements/qualities of professional identity. (15–22 pts)	Identifies concrete and specific actions that student will take to achieve the desired elements/qualities of their professional identity and explains clearly and with depth how the actions will enable the student to achieve the desired elements/qualities of professional identity. (23–25 pts)
Actions to Address Challenges to Professional Identity _________/25	Fails to identify challenges to professional identity that student anticipates will arise in practice; or, identifies anticipated challenges but fails to identify actions student will take to overcome the anticipated challenges. (0–14 pts)	Identifies challenges to professional identity that student anticipates will arise in practice and identifies actions that student will take to address the challenges, but does not explain with depth or in detail how the actions will address the challenges. (15–22 pts)	Identifies challenges to professional identity that student anticipates will arise in practice and identifies specific actions that student will take to address the challenges, comprehensively explaining with depth and clarity how the actions will effectively address the challenges. (23–25 pts)
		Total: _________ out of 155	

7. Rubric for Professional Development Plan

Criteria	Undeveloped: 1	Developing: 2	Competent: 3	Exemplary: 4
Timeliness	N/A	N/A	N/A	Submitted on time.
Depth of Response	Does not complete all questions in the relevant section of the Professional Development Plan. For the Final Professional Development Plan: Does not complete all sections.	Completes all questions in the relevant section of the Professional Development Plan, but the responses are surface-level or cursory with little to no detail or explanation. For the Final Professional Development Plan: All sections are complete, but the responses in some sections are surface-level or cursory with little to no detail or explanation.	Completes all questions in the relevant section of the Professional Development Plan, and the responses include some detail and explanation. For the Final Professional Development Plan: All sections are complete, and the responses include some detail and explanation.	Thoughtfully and thoroughly completes all questions in the relevant section of the Professional Development Plan. For the Final Professional Development Plan: All sections are complete with thoughtful, thorough responses to the questions asked.
Quality of Writing and Attention to Detail	Writing is unclear and disorganized. Thoughts are not expressed in a coherent or logical manner; or Many (5 or more) spelling errors and/or typos.	Writing is not consistently clear, concise, and/or well-organized. Thoughts are not always expressed in a coherent and logical manner; and Several (3–5) spelling errors and/or typos.	Writing is not consistently clear, concise, and/or well-organized. Thoughts are not always expressed in a coherent and logical manner; or Few (1–2) spelling errors and/or typos.	Writing is clear, concise, and well-organized. Thoughts are expressed in a coherent and logical manner; and No spelling errors and/or typos.

8. Externship Course Student Performance Evaluation Form

Name of Student: ______________________________

Name of Supervising Attorney: ______________________________

Signature of Supervising Attorney: ______________________________

Externship Site: ______________________________

Supervising Attorney Phone/Email: ______________________________

Semester and Calendar Year: ______________________________

Note to Supervising Attorney(s) Completing this Form: In this Student Performance Evaluation Form, we ask you to assess student performance as to the institutional learning outcomes Georgia State University College of Law has identified pursuant to ABA Standard 302. By way of information, Georgia State University College of Law has identified the following seven institutional learning outcomes:

Outcome 1: Graduates will demonstrate knowledge and comprehension of substantive and procedural laws generally, including rules of procedure, common law, statutory law, administrative law, and constitutional law.

Criterion 1: Identify, describe and apply sources or relevant law to solve client problems and/or address policy issues.

Criterion 2: Identify, describe, and apply appropriate procedural steps and factual development to solve client problems and/or address policy issues.

Outcome 2: Graduates will demonstrate effective legal analysis and reasoning skills to address client problems and/or policy issues and achieve client objectives.

Criterion 1: Identify legal issues when presented with client problems and/or policy questions using applicable legal theory, rules and facts.

Criterion 2: Critically evaluate the strengths and weaknesses of arguments.

Outcome 3:	Graduates will conduct legal research effectively and efficiently.
Criterion 1:	Find information through effective and efficient research strategies, including consideration of time and cost limitations.
Criterion 2:	Critically evaluate information and sources, including hierarchy and weight of authority.
Criterion 3:	Apply information effectively to a specific issue or need.
Outcome 4:	Graduates will communicate effectively and professionally in a variety of settings.
Criterion 1:	Compose well-written documents and memoranda.
Criterion 2:	Adapt speaking and writing to audience and circumstance.
Outcome 5:	Graduates will engage in active self-reflection and take ownership of their professional development.
Criterion 1:	Listen actively and respond appropriately during group and one-on-one exchanges.
Criterion 2:	Critically assess one's own contributions and take responsibility for individual work product and group outcomes.
Criterion 3:	Manage projects by implementing clear plans and efficient timelines.
Outcome 6:	Graduates will demonstrate effective and professional engagement with clients, colleagues, opposing counsel, judges, and others.
Criterion 1:	Demonstrate respect for clients, colleagues, opposing counsel, judges and others.
Criterion 2:	Demonstrate the ability to work effectively as a member of a team.
Criterion 3:	Display commitment to the profession through regular attendance, timely completion of tasks and respectful interactions.
Outcome 7:	Graduates will demonstrate professionalism through conduct consistent with their ethical obligations and professional responsibilities.
Criterion 1:	Explain and apply the rules and standards of professional conduct
Criterion 2:	Recognize the leadership role and responsibility that attorneys play in maintaining the rule of law and upholding justice.

GSU College of Law values your honest assessment of the student extern's performance pursuant to the level definitions outlined below:

Level 4: Student produces superior work-product demonstrating the student's likely success in performing independently in a professional setting with minimal supervision.

Level 3: Student produces competent work-product demonstrating the student's likely success in performing independently in a professional setting with some employer supervision and some additional training.

Level 2: Student produces satisfactory work-product demonstrating a student's progress toward developing the necessary skills to perform independently in a professional setting, but also demonstrating the need for additional skills development and substantial employer supervision.

Level 1: Student's work-product demonstrates that the student has not made sufficient progress toward developing the necessary skills to perform independently in a professional setting even with employer supervision.

N/A: Not a significant component of the experience.

Criterion Competence	Proficiency Level				
Legal Knowledge and Analysis	Level 1	Level 2	Level 3	Level 4	N/A
Knowledge of substantive law & procedural rules: Demonstrates an understanding of the legal and procedural rules; clearly explains the law applicable to the legal question, problem, or case	RARELY demonstrates knowledge and understanding of applicable legal and procedural rules	SOMETIMES demonstrates knowledge and understanding of applicable legal and procedural rules	OFTEN demonstrates knowledge and understanding of applicable legal and procedural rules	CONSISTENTLY demonstrates knowledge and understanding of applicable legal and procedural rules	N/A
Legal Analysis–Issue Spotting: Correctly identifies legal issues based upon relevant law and policy considerations	RARELY spots and analyzes relevant issues; and/or frequently analyzes irrelevant issues	SOMETIMES spots and analyzes issues; and/or sometimes analyzes irrelevant issues	OFTEN spots and analyzes issues; and/or occasionally analyzes irrelevant issues	CONSISTENTLY spots and analyzes relevant issues; rarely analyzes irrelevant issues	N/A

Legal Knowledge and Analysis	Level 1	Level 2	Level 3	Level 4	N/A
Legal Analysis –Use of Facts: Correctly identifies and uses applicable facts and reasonable inferences from facts, based upon relevant law and policy considerations	RARELY uses applicable facts; and/or often uses inapplicable facts	SOMETIMES uses some applicable facts; and/or sometimes uses inapplicable facts	OFTEN uses most applicable facts; and/or occasionally uses inapplicable facts	CONSISTENTLY uses all or almost all applicable facts; rarely uses inapplicable facts	N/A
Legal Analysis –Critical Reasoning: Makes appropriate arguments, comparisons, and distinctions to the legal question, problem, or case based upon applicable law; considers all sides of an argument and multiple perspectives when appropriate	RARELY engages in complete analysis	SOMETIMES engages in complete analysis	OFTEN engages in complete analysis	CONSISTENTLY engages in complete analysis	N/A
Legal Analysis –Policy: Raises applicable policy arguments when analyzing a legal question, policy, or case	RARELY engages in relevant and accurate policy analysis	SOMETIMES engages in relevant and accurate policy analysis	OFTEN engages in relevant and accurate policy analysis	CONSISTENTLY engages in relevant and accurate policy analysis	N/A

Legal Knowledge and Analysis	Level 1	Level 2	Level 3	Level 4	N/A
Legal Research –Strategy: Implements effective and efficient research plan that identifies appropriate primary and/or secondary sources, and uses search techniques and platforms that minimize the time and cost of the research project	RARELY employs a research strategy that identifies appropriate sources and/ or uses efficient search techniques for stage and type of research task	SOMETIMES employs a research strategy that identifies appropriate sources and/ or uses efficient search technique for stage and type of research task	OFTEN employs a research strategy that identifies appropriate sources and/ or uses efficient search techniques for stage and type of research task	CONSISTENTLY employs a research strategy that identifies appropriate sources and/or uses efficient search techniques for stage and type of research task	N/A
Legal Research –Methods: Identifies and critically evaluates relevant sources of law by considering the weight of authority, hierarchy, validity, and relationships between sources	RARELY finds applicable sources of law and considers the weight of authority, hierarchy, validity, and relationships between sources	SOMETIMES finds applicable sources of law and considers the weight of authority, hierarchy, validity, and relationships between sources	OFTEN finds applicable sources of law and considers the weight of authority, hierarchy, validity, and relationships between sources	CONSISTENTLY finds applicable sources of law and considers the weight of authority, hierarchy, validity, and relationships between sources	N/A
Legal Research –Application: Applies relevant law from appropriate sources to a legal problem	RARELY applies relevant law from appropriate sources to assess the scope of the legal problem	SOMETIMES applies relevant law from appropriate sources to assess the scope of the legal problem	OFTEN applies relevant law from appropriate sources to assess the scope of the legal problem	CONSISTENTLY applies relevant law from appropriate sources to assess the scope of the legal problem	N/A

Legal Writing	Level 1	Level 2	Level 3	Level 4	N/A
Legal Writing –Style: Uses clear language and format appropriate for audience and circumstance	RARELY employs appropriate communication tools, demonstrates attention to detail, and uses proper language and tone	SOMETIMES employs appropriate communication tools, demonstrates attention to detail, and uses proper language and tone	OFTEN employs appropriate communication tools, demonstrates attention to detail, and uses proper language and tone	CONSISTENTLY employs appropriate communication tools, demonstrates attention to detail, and uses proper language and tone	N/A
Legal Writing –Organization: Uses clear and logical organization that is easy to follow	RARELY presents ideas and supporting information in logical order, utilizing an appropriate paradigm and without unnecessary repetition	SOMETIMES presents ideas and supporting information in logical order, utilizing an appropriate paradigm and without unnecessary repetition	OFTEN presents ideas and supporting information in logical order, utilizing an appropriate paradigm and without unnecessary repetition	CONSISTENTLY presents ideas and supporting information in logical order, utilizing an appropriate paradigm and without unnecessary repetition	N/A
Legal Writing –Written Analysis: Engages in a complete analysis and uses authoritative sources	RARELY supports observations, conclusions, and/or arguments with authoritative sources and a meaningful, thorough, and focused discussion or analysis	SOMETIMES supports observations, conclusions, and/or arguments with authoritative sources and a meaningful, thorough, and focused discussion or analysis	OFTEN supports observations, conclusions, and/or arguments with authoritative sources and a meaningful, thorough, and focused discussion or analysis	CONSISTENTLY supports observations, conclusions, and/or arguments with authoritative sources and a meaningful, thorough, and focused discussion or analysis	N/A

Oral Communication	Level 1	Level 2	Level 3	Level 4	N/A
Oral Communication –Style: Uses clear language and format appropriate for audience and circumstance	RARELY employs appropriate communication tools, and uses proper language and tone	SOMETIMES employs appropriate communication tools, and uses proper language and tone	OFTEN employs appropriate communication tools, and uses proper language and tone	CONSISTENTLY employs appropriate communication tools, and uses proper language and tone	N/A
Oral Communication –Organization: Uses clear and logical organization that is easy to follow	RARELY presents ideas and supporting information in logical order, utilizing an appropriate paradigm and without unnecessary repetition	SOMETIMES presents ideas and supporting information in logical order, utilizing an appropriate paradigm and without unnecessary repetition	OFTEN presents ideas and supporting information in logical order, utilizing an appropriate paradigm and without unnecessary repetition	CONSISTENTLY presents ideas and supporting information in logical order, utilizing an appropriate paradigm and without unnecessary repetition	N/A
Oral Communication –Analysis: Engages in a complete analysis and uses authoritative sources	RARELY supports observations, conclusions, and/or arguments with authoritative sources and a meaningful, thorough, and focused discussion or analysis	SOMETIMES supports observations, conclusions, and/or arguments with authoritative sources and a meaningful, thorough, and focused discussion or analysis	OFTEN supports observations, conclusions, and/or arguments with authoritative sources and a meaningful, thorough, and focused discussion or analysis	CONSISTENTLY supports observations, conclusions, and/or arguments with authoritative sources and a meaningful, thorough, and focused discussion or analysis	N/A

Professionalism and Ethics	Level 1	Level 2	Level 3	Level 4	N/A
Ethical Knowledge –Lawyer-client relationship: Recognizes and understands the ethical duties owed to clients, including confidentiality, attorney-client privilege, conflicts of interest, diligence, and competence	RARELY demon-strates knowledge of duties owed to clients. Needs considerable development of this competency	SOMETIMES demonstrates knowledge of duties owed to clients. Needs substantial direction from faculty member or supervising attorney	OFTEN demonstrates knowledge of duties owed to clients. Needs some direction from faculty member or supervising attorney	CONSISTENTLY demonstrates knowledge of duties owed to clients. Needs minimal or no direction	N/A
Ethical Knowledge –Tribunals and Third Parties: Demonstrates knowledge of the ethical duties owed to tribunals and third parties, including diligence, competence, candor, fairness, and regard for the rule of law	RARELY demon-strates knowledge of duties owed to tribunals and third parties. Needs considerable development of this competency	SOMETIMES demonstrates knowledge of duties owed to tribunals and third parties. Needs substan-tial direction from faculty member or supervising attorney	OFTEN demonstrates knowledge of duties owed to tribunals and third parties. Needs some direction from faculty member or supervising attorney	CONSISTENTLY demonstrates knowledge of duties owed to tribunals and third parties. Needs minimal or no direction	N/A
Fiscal Responsibility: Demonstrates knowledge of lawyer's responsibilities in handling client funds and other property	RARELY demon-strates knowledge of a lawyer's fiscal responsibili-ties to clients. Needs considerable development of this competency	SOMETIMES demonstrates knowledge of a lawyer's fiscal responsibilities to clients. Needs substan-tial direction from faculty member or supervising attorney	OFTEN demonstrates knowledge of a lawyer's fiscal responsibilities to clients. Needs some direction from faculty member or supervising attorney	CONSISTENTLY demonstrates knowledge of a lawyer's fiscal responsibilities to clients. Needs minimal or no direction	N/A

Professionalism and Ethics	Level 1	Level 2	Level 3	Level 4	N/A
Time Management: Meets deadlines; keeps regular and dependable hours; is punctual; implements and communicates clear and efficient timelines	RARELY exhibits ability to manage time. Needs considerable development of this competency	SOMETIMES exhibits ability to manage time. Needs substantial direction from faculty member or supervising attorney	OFTEN exhibits ability to manage time. Needs some direction from faculty member or supervising attorney	CONSISTENTLY exhibits ability to manage time. Needs minimal or no direction	N/A
Professional Communication: Interacts effectively and respectfully when speaking, listening, and/or writing to lawyers, clients, staff, adversaries, judges, and others	RARELY interacts with others in a professional manner. Needs considerable development of this competency	SOMETIMES interacts with others in a professional manner. Needs substantial direction from faculty member or supervising attorney	OFTEN interacts with others in a professional manner. Needs some direction from faculty member or supervising attorney	CONSISTENTLY interacts with others in a professional manner. Needs minimal or no direction	N/A
Active Listening: Listens and responds appropriately during group and individual exchanges by articulating thoughtful responses to questions and discussions	RARELY employs active listening. Needs considerable development of this competency	SOMETIMES employs active listening. Needs substantial direction from faculty member or supervising attorney	OFTEN employs active listening. Needs some direction from faculty member or supervising attorney	CONSISTENTLY employs active listening. Needs minimal or no direction	N/A

Professionalism and Ethics	Level 1	Level 2	Level 3	Level 4	N/A
Learning from Experience: Learns from feedback, critique, observations, and experience; reflects critically and honestly about performance; identifies ways to improve future performance	RARELY learns from experience. Needs considerable development of this competency	SOMETIMES learns from experience. Needs substantial direction from faculty member or supervising attorney	OFTEN learns from experience. Needs some direction from faculty member or supervising attorney	CONSISTENTLY learns from experience. Needs minimal or no direction	N/A
Teamwork: Keeps team members informed; listens to others ideas; contributes ideas; accepts feedback; substantially contributes to the final work product	RARELY contributes to team. Needs considerable development of this competency	SOMETIMES contributes to team. Needs substantial direction from faculty member or supervising attorney	OFTEN contributes to team. Needs some direction from faculty member or supervising attorney	CONSISTENTLY contributes to team. Needs minimal or no direction	N/A

Narrative Comments:

For any area in which you marked "Level 1" as your assessment, please briefly explain your assessment.

Did the student produce any work that you felt was particularly superior or inferior? Please briefly explain.

What are this student's strengths?

What should this student work to improve?

Materials Referenced in Chapter 8: Essential Elements of Externship Teaching: Student Goal-Setting, Meaningful Learning Experiences, and Reflection

1. Seattle University School of Law Reflection Topics

Assignments should be two to three pages in length (double spaced). They are broken down into a series of questions. You do not need to copy the sub-questions onto your assignment, but you do need to answer all the questions separately. You will be graded on the completeness of the assignment and the quality of the written work (includes spelling, grammar, and organization).

Reflection I: Evaluation of Your Work Performance

Write and upload a two to three-page reflection on your work performance. Be sure to include detailed responses to all three questions below:

One key skill for lawyers is learning how to evaluate our own performance and how to enhance our ability to exercise independent professional judgment. Without revealing confidential information, describe a task you have completed at your site. How did you evaluate your own performance before you received feedback from your supervisor?

In answering this question, please discuss how the following three factors influenced your performance:

Internal factors include the preferences, experiences, biases, and characteristics owned by each of us that shape our performance, actions, and the decisions we make.

External factors include the preferences, experiences, biases, and characteristics of the other people involved in the lawyering performance. These other people include clients, supervisors, other lawyers, judges, and third-party neutrals.

Societal factors include systemic power dynamics, political and social realities, hierarchies, biases, and economic forces that affect decisions.

Now describe the feedback you received from your supervisor and any differences between your initial view of your performance and your supervisor's. Explain what you learned from your own and your supervisor's assessment and how you can use that in the future.

Considering the Washington Race Equity and Justice Initiative (REJI found at https://wareji.org/commitments/) Commitment #5 to "continually explore how race and poverty intersect to make worse the effects of racial discrimination," describe how the skill you performed contributes to the larger legal system. Are there aspects of this work that you see as needing change?

Finally, include how the process of reflecting on your performance in this way will influence your performance/preparation in the future. If you have done a previous externship, describe any differences in the way you have learned this current skill compared to your previous one.

Reflection II: Managing Stress and Self-Care

Assignments should be two to three pages in length (double-spaced). They are broken down into a series of questions. You do not need to copy the sub-questions onto your assignment, but you do need to answer all the questions separately. You will be graded on the completeness of the assignment and the quality of the written work (includes spelling, grammar, and organization).

Each of us, throughout our careers, must develop ways to manage stress and take care of ourselves so that we can sustain a commitment to our profession. This includes maintaining competent representation and upholding our values, while at the same time creating space for our personal lives.

What challenges and stressors have you had to tackle in the work at your placement?

What are the internal, external, and societal factors that may impact your ability to handle these work-related challenges and stressors?

Internal factors include the preferences, experiences, biases, and characteristics owned by each of us that shape our performance, actions, and the decisions we make.

External factors include the preferences, experiences, biases, and characteristics of the other people involved in the lawyering performance. These other people include clients, supervisors, other lawyers, judges, and third-party neutrals.

Societal factors include systemic power dynamics, political and social realities, hierarchies, biases, and economic forces that affect decisions.

What can you do to make sure that you are able to take care of yourself, no matter what kind of legal or non-legal career you choose to pursue? Be sure to include your use of compassion for yourself and others.

REJI Commitment #5 asks that we "Ensure our organizations invest in active, ongoing learning that will teach us to see, reveal, and transform structures that create racialized outcomes and push communities of color outside the Circle of Human Concern. This commitment requires that we help members of our organizations and communities to actively and expressly challenge the use of racist language and behaviors, openly listen when we ourselves are challenged, and learn techniques and tools for reducing and eliminating implicit and explicit bias." This process can be uncomfortable for those expressing the bias and traumatizing for those receiving it. Describe an example you have experienced or observed and your own response.

Include how the process of reflecting on this topic has influenced what actions you will take in the future. If you have done an externship before, do you notice any differences in your approach to work life balance or reflection this semester? Please describe and explain why or why not.

Reflection III: Professional Development.

Assignments should be two to three pages in length (double-spaced). They are broken down into a series of questions. You do not need to copy the sub-questions onto your assignment, but you do need to answer all the questions separately. You will be graded on the completeness of the assignment and the quality of the written work (includes spelling, grammar, and organization).

Each externship gives you a window into your future professional development. Discuss how your current externship has influenced the career (type of work) that you hope to pursue after law school and compare it with previous externships if you have done them. Specifically, how has your current and/or prior externship experience impacted your level of confidence? Describe the ways in which this potential career will be consistent, or will challenge, your personal values.

Discuss the internal, external, and societal factors that may be influencing you.

Internal factors include the preferences, experiences, biases, and characteristics owned by an individual that shape his/her performance, actions, and decisions.

External factors include the preferences, experiences, biases, and characteristics of the other people involved in the lawyering performance. These other people include clients, supervisors, other lawyers, judges, and third-party neutrals.

Societal factors include systemic power dynamics, political and social realities, hierarchies, biases, and economic forces that affect decisions.

Choose one of the following four REJI values/commitments and describe how you see yourself implementing this commitment in your future legal career.

1. Work together with, take guidance from, be part of, and hold ourselves accountable to community-based movements in communities most affected by structural racialization and structurally racialized systems.
2. Change structures, policies, processes, and practices in the law, legal profession, and justice system that allow harm and disparate outcomes for communities of color to continue unabated.
3. Promote and support legal and policy reforms to advance race equity and racial justice, recognizing that differently situated groups may require different strategies to achieve more equitable outcomes.
4. Continuously examine whether we and the organizations we work with operate in ways that align with the race equity and justice values and goals we support. This commitment includes ensuring that race equity is reflected in policies and practices for recruitment and hiring, work acceptance, priority-setting, governance, organizational culture, and community partnerships and accountability, particularly with low-income communities of color.

Finally, describe how the process of reflecting will influence your future work. Thank you!

2. Externship Course Student Performance Evaluation Form

Name of Student: ______________________________

Name of Supervising Attorney: ______________________________

Signature of Supervising Attorney: ______________________________

Externship Site: ______________________________

Supervising Attorney Phone/Email: ______________________________

Semester and Calendar Year : ______________________________

Note to Supervising Attorney(s) Completing this Form: In this Student Performance Evaluation Form, we ask you to assess student performance as to the institutional learning outcomes Georgia State University College of Law has identified pursuant to ABA Standard 302. By way of information, Georgia State University College of Law has identified the following seven institutional learning outcomes:

Outcome 1: Graduates will demonstrate knowledge and comprehension of substantive and procedural laws generally, including rules of procedure, common law, statutory law, administrative law, and constitutional law.

Criterion 1: Identify, describe and apply sources or relevant law to solve client problems and/or address policy issues.

Criterion 2: Identify, describe, and apply appropriate procedural steps and factual development to solve client problems and/or address policy issues.

Outcome 2: Graduates will demonstrate effective legal analysis and reasoning skills to address client problems and/or policy issues and achieve client objectives.

Criterion 1: Identify legal issues when presented with client problems and/or policy questions using applicable legal theory, rules and facts.

Criterion 2: Critically evaluate the strengths and weaknesses of arguments.

Outcome 3: Graduates will conduct legal research effectively and efficiently.

Criterion 1: Find information through effective and efficient research strategies, including consideration of time and cost limitations.

Criterion 2: Critically evaluate information and sources, including hierarchy and weight of authority.

Criterion 3: Apply information effectively to a specific issue or need.

Outcome 4: Graduates will communicate effectively and professionally in a variety of settings.

Criterion 1: Compose well-written documents and memoranda.

Criterion 2: Adapt speaking and writing to audience and circumstance.

Outcome 5: Graduates will engage in active self-reflection and take ownership of their professional development.

Criterion 1: Listen actively and respond appropriately during group and one-on-one exchanges.

Criterion 2: Critically assess one's own contributions and take responsibility for individual work product and group outcomes.

Criterion 3: Manage projects by implementing clear plans and efficient timelines.

Outcome 6: Graduates will demonstrate effective and professional engagement with clients, colleagues, opposing counsel, judges, and others.

Criterion 1: Demonstrate respect for clients, colleagues, opposing counsel, judges and others.

Criterion 2: Demonstrate the ability to work effectively as a member of a team.

Criterion 3: Display commitment to the profession through regular attendance, timely completion of tasks and respectful interactions.

Outcome 7: Graduates will demonstrate professionalism through conduct consistent with their ethical obligations and professional responsibilities.

Criterion 1: Explain and apply the rules and standards of professional conduct

Criterion 2: Recognize the leadership role and responsibility that attorneys play in maintaining the rule of law and upholding justice.

GSU College of Law values your honest assessment of the student extern's performance pursuant to the level definitions outlined below:

Level 4: Student produces superior work-product demonstrating the student's likely success in performing independently in a professional setting with minimal supervision.

Level 3: Student produces competent work-product demonstrating the student's likely success in performing independently in a professional setting with some employer supervision and some additional training.

Level 2: Student produces satisfactory work-product demonstrating a student's progress toward developing the necessary skills to perform independently in a professional setting, but also demonstrating the need for additional skills development and substantial employer supervision.

Level 1: Student's work-product demonstrates that the student has not made sufficient progress toward developing the necessary skills to perform independently in a professional setting even with employer supervision.

N/A: Not a significant component of the experience.

Criterion Competence	Proficiency Level				
Legal Knowledge and Analysis	Level 1	Level 2	Level 3	Level 4	N/A
Knowledge of substantive law & procedural rules: Demonstrates an understanding of the legal and procedural rules; clearly explains the law applicable to the legal question, problem, or case	RARELY demon-strates knowledge and understand-ing of applicable legal and procedural rules	SOMETIMES demonstrates knowledge and under-standing of applicable legal and procedural rules	OFTEN demonstrates knowledge and under-standing of applicable legal and procedural rules	CONSISTENTLY demonstrates knowledge and understanding of applicable legal and procedural rules	N/A
Legal Analysis –Issue Spotting: Correctly identifies legal issues based upon relevant law and policy considerations	RARELY spots and analyzes relevant issues; and/or frequently analyzes irrelevant issues	SOMETIMES spots and analyzes issues; and/or sometimes analyzes irrelevant issues	OFTEN spots and analyzes issues; and/or occasionally analyzes irrelevant issues	CONSISTENTLY spots and analyzes relevant issues; rarely analyzes irrelevant issues	N/A

Legal Knowledge and Analysis	Level 1	Level 2	Level 3	Level 4	N/A
Legal Analysis–Use of Facts: Correctly identifies and uses applicable facts and reasonable inferences from facts, based upon relevant law and policy considerations	RARELY uses applicable facts; and/or often uses inapplicable facts	SOMETIMES uses some applicable facts; and/or sometimes uses inapplicable facts	OFTEN uses most applicable facts; and/or occasionally uses inapplicable facts	CONSISTENTLY uses all or almost all applicable facts; rarely uses inapplicable facts	N/A
Legal Analysis –Critical Reasoning: Makes appropriate arguments, comparisons, and distinctions to the legal question, problem, or case based upon applicable law; considers all sides of an argument and multiple perspectives when appropriate	RARELY engages in complete analysis	SOMETIMES engages in complete analysis	OFTEN engages in complete analysis	CONSISTENTLY engages in complete analysis	N/A
Legal Analysis –Policy: Raises applicable policy arguments when analyzing a legal question, policy, or case	RARELY engages in relevant and accurate policy analysis	SOMETIMES engages in relevant and accurate policy analysis	OFTEN engages in relevant and accurate policy analysis	CONSISTENTLY engages in relevant and accurate policy analysis	N/A

Legal Research	Level 1	Level 2	Level 3	Level 4	N/A
Legal Research –Strategy: Implements effective and efficient research plan that identifies appropriate primary and/or secondary sources, and uses search techniques and platforms that minimize the time and cost of the research project	RARELY employs a research strategy that identifies appropriate sources and/ or uses efficient search techniques for stage and type of research task	SOMETIMES employs a research strategy that identifies appropriate sources and/or uses efficient search technique for stage and type of research task	OFTEN employs a research strategy that identifies appropriate sources and/or uses efficient search techniques for stage and type of research task	CONSISTENTLY employs a research strategy that identifies appropriate sources and/or uses efficient search techniques for stage and type of research task	N/A
Legal Research –Methods: Identifies and critically evaluates relevant sources of law by considering the weight of authority, hierarchy, validity, and relationships between sources	RARELY finds applicable sources of law and considers the weight of authority, hierarchy, validity, and relationships between sources	SOMETIMES finds applica-ble sources of law and considers the weight of authority, hierarchy, validity, and relationships between sources	OFTEN finds applicable sources of law and considers the weight of authority, hierarchy, validity, and relationships between sources	CONSISTENTLY finds applicable sources of law and considers the weight of authority, hierarchy, validity, and relationships between sources	N/A
Legal Research –Application: Applies relevant law from appro-priate sources to a legal problem	RARELY applies relevant law from appropriate sources to assess the scope of the legal problem	SOMETIMES applies relevant law from appro-priate sources to assess the scope of the legal problem	OFTEN applies relevant law from appro-priate sources to assess the scope of the legal problem	CONSISTENTLY applies relevant law from appropriate sources to assess the scope of the legal problem	N/A

Legal Writing	Level 1	Level 2	Level 3	Level 4	N/A
Legal Writing –Style: Uses clear language and format appropriate for audience and circumstance	RARELY employs appropriate communication tools, demonstrates attention to detail, and uses proper language and tone	SOMETIMES employs appropriate communication tools, demonstrates attention to detail, and uses proper language and tone	OFTEN employs appropriate communication tools, demonstrates attention to detail, and uses proper language and tone	CONSISTENTLY employs appropriate communication tools, demonstrates attention to detail, and uses proper language and tone	N/A
Legal Writing –Organization: Uses clear and logical organization that is easy to follow	RARELY presents ideas and supporting information in logical order, utilizing an appropriate paradigm and without unnecessary repetition	SOMETIMES presents ideas and supporting information in logical order, utilizing an appropriate paradigm and without unnecessary repetition	OFTEN presents ideas and supporting information in logical order, utilizing an appropriate paradigm and without unnecessary repetition	CONSISTENTLY presents ideas and supporting information in logical order, utilizing an appropriate paradigm and without unnecessary repetition	N/A
Legal Writing –Written Analysis: Engages in a complete analysis and uses authoritative sources	RARELY supports observations, conclusions, and/or arguments with authoritative sources and a meaningful, thorough, and focused discussion or analysis	SOMETIMES supports observations, conclusions, and/or arguments with authoritative sources and a meaningful, thorough, and focused discussion or analysis	OFTEN supports observations, conclusions, and/or arguments with authoritative sources and a meaningful, thorough, and focused discussion or analysis	CONSISTENTLY supports observations, conclusions, and/or arguments with authoritative sources and a meaningful, thorough, and focused discussion or analysis	N/A

Oral Communication	Level 1	Level 2	Level 3	Level 4	N/A
Oral Communication–Style: Uses clear language and format appropriate for audience and circumstance	RARELY employs appropriate communication tools, and uses proper language and tone	SOMETIMES employs appropriate communication tools, and uses proper language and tone	OFTEN employs appropriate communication tools, and uses proper language and tone	CONSISTENTLY employs appropriate communication tools, and uses proper language and tone	N/A
Oral Communication–Organization: Uses clear and logical organization that is easy to follow	RARELY presents ideas and supporting information in logical order, utilizing an appropriate paradigm and without unnecessary repetition	SOMETIMES presents ideas and supporting information in logical order, utilizing an appropriate paradigm and without unnecessary repetition	OFTEN presents ideas and supporting information in logical order, utilizing an appropriate paradigm and without unnecessary repetition	CONSISTENTLY presents ideas and supporting information in logical order, utilizing an appropriate paradigm and without unnecessary repetition	N/A
Oral Communication–Analysis: Engages in a complete analysis and uses authoritative sources	RARELY supports observations, conclusions, and/or arguments with authoritative sources and a meaningful, thorough, and focused discussion or analysis	SOMETIMES supports observations, conclusions, and/or arguments with authoritative sources and a meaningful, thorough, and focused discussion or analysis	OFTEN supports observations, conclusions, and/or arguments with authoritative sources and a meaningful, thorough, and focused discussion or analysis	CONSISTENTLY supports observations, conclusions, and/or arguments with authoritative sources and a meaningful, thorough, and focused discussion or analysis	N/A

Professionalism and Ethics	Level 1	Level 2	Level 3	Level 4	N/A
Ethical Knowledge–Lawyer-client relationship: Recognizes and understands the ethical duties owed to clients, including confidentiality, attorney-client privilege, conflicts of interest, diligence, and competence	RARELY demonstrates knowledge of duties owed to clients. Needs considerable development of this competency	SOMETIMES demonstrates knowledge of duties owed to clients. Needs substantial direction from faculty member or supervising attorney	OFTEN demonstrates knowledge of duties owed to clients. Needs some direction from faculty member or supervising attorney	CONSISTENTLY demonstrates knowledge of duties owed to clients. Needs minimal or no direction	N/A
Ethical Knowledge –Tribunals and Third Parties: Demonstrates knowledge of the ethical duties owed to tribunals and third parties, including diligence, competence, candor, fairness, and regard for the rule of law	RARELY demonstrates knowledge of duties owed to tribunals and third parties. Needs considerable development of this competency	SOMETIMES demonstrates knowledge of duties owed to tribunals and third parties. Needs substantial direction from faculty member or supervising attorney	OFTEN demonstrates knowledge of duties owed to tribunals and third parties. Needs some direction from faculty member or supervising attorney	CONSISTENTLY demonstrates knowledge of duties owed to tribunals and third parties. Needs minimal or no direction	N/A
Fiscal Responsibility: Demonstrates knowledge of lawyer's responsibilities in handling client funds and other property	RARELY demonstrates knowledge of a lawyer's fiscal responsibilities to clients. Needs considerable development of this competency	SOMETIMES demonstrates knowledge of a lawyer's fiscal responsibilities to clients. Needs substantial direction from faculty member or supervising attorney	OFTEN demonstrates knowledge of a lawyer's fiscal responsibilities to clients. Needs some direction from faculty member or supervising attorney	CONSISTENTLY demonstrates knowledge of a lawyer's fiscal responsibilities to clients. Needs minimal or no direction	N/A

Professionalism and Ethics	Level 1	Level 2	Level 3	Level 4	N/A
Time Management: Meets deadlines; keeps regular and dependable hours; is punctual; implements and communicates clear and efficient timelines	RARELY exhibits ability to manage time. Needs considerable development of this competency	SOMETIMES exhibits ability to manage time. Needs substantial direction from faculty member or supervising attorney	OFTEN exhibits ability to manage time. Needs some direction from faculty member or supervising attorney	CONSISTENTLY exhibits ability to manage time. Needs minimal or no direction	N/A
Professional Communication: Interacts effec-tively and respectfully when speaking, listening, and/or writing to lawyers, clients, staff, adversaries, judges, and others	RARELY interacts with others in a professional manner. Needs considerable development of this competency	SOMETIMES interacts with others in a professional manner. Needs substantial direction from faculty member or supervising attorney	OFTEN interacts with others in a professional manner. Needs some direction from faculty member or supervising attorney	CONSISTENTLY interacts with others in a professional manner. Needs minimal or no direction	N/A
Active Listening: Listens and responds appro-priately during group and individual exchanges by articulating thoughtful responses to questions and discussions	RARELY employs active listening. Needs considerable development of this competency	SOMETIMES employs active listening. Needs substantial direction from faculty member or supervising attorney	OFTEN employs active listening. Needs some direction from faculty member or supervising attorney	CONSISTENTLY employs active listening. Needs minimal or no direction	N/A

Professionalism and Ethics	Level 1	Level 2	Level 3	Level 4	N/A
Learning from Experience: Learns from feedback, critique, observations, and experience; reflects critically and honestly about performance; identifies ways to improve future performance	RARELY learns from experience. Needs considerable development of this competency	SOMETIMES learns from experience. Needs substantial direction from faculty member or supervising attorney	OFTEN learns from experience. Needs some direction from faculty member or supervising attorney	CONSISTENTLY learns from experience. Needs minimal or no direction	N/A
Teamwork: Keeps team members informed; listens to others ideas; contributes ideas; accepts feedback; substantially contributes to the final work product	RARELY contributes to team. Needs considerable development of this competency	SOMETIMES contributes to team. Needs substantial direction from faculty member or supervising attorney	OFTEN contributes to team. Needs some direction from faculty member or supervising attorney	CONSISTENTLY contributes to team. Needs minimal or no direction	N/A

Narrative Comments:

For any area in which you marked "Level 1" as your assessment, please briefly explain your assessment.

Did the student produce any work that you felt was particularly superior or inferior? Please briefly explain.

What are this student's strengths?

What should this student work to improve?

3. Extern Professional Development Plan

Final Professional Development Plan

Throughout the semester, both in your externship and the externship seminar, you have been prompted to explore your developing professional identity. The Final Professional Development Plan provides the opportunity to reflect on the progress you have made in forming your professional identity over the course of the semester. The Final Professional Development Plan includes questions from previous Professional Development Plan assignments, as well as new questions that allow you to think about your experiences collectively. All new questions or new parts of previous questions are italicized. Carefully consider and provide a thorough response to each question. For those questions that were posed on previous Professional Development Plan sections, your responses may be the same. However, do not simply copy and paste previous responses. Make sure to review your previous responses, and update your responses based upon the experiences you have had at your externship.

[Insert Your Name]

Section 1 – Lawyering Skills and Goal-Setting

Reason for Attending Law School

What prompted your decision to go to law school? Be specific in articulating your reason(s) and include any specific experiences that informed your decision.

Lawyering Effectiveness Competencies

Using the Shultz-Zedeck 26 Lawyering Effectiveness Factors, identify the three lawyering competencies you believe are your strongest and the three lawyering competencies you would like to develop. Include the reason(s) for listing each competency. In thinking about your reason(s), consider past experiences and any externship experiences in which you received recognition or constructive criticism. *Please update these lists if they have changed as a result of your externship experience.*

Strength Competencies

1.
2.
3.

Growth Competencies

1.
2.
3.

Assessment of Strength and Growth Competencies

Have your strength and/or growth competencies changed since the beginning of the semester? If so, why do you think they have changed? If not, why do you think they have stayed the same?

Proactive Development of Concrete Goals

Assess how proactive you were throughout the semester in developing the goals you identified at the beginning of your externship. In your response, address the following:

Have you been able to measure your progress toward meeting each goal you articulated at the beginning of your externship? If so, how have you measured your progress toward meeting each goal? If not, how would you change your stated goals to make them easier to measure?

Did you take any concrete steps to ensure that you received quality assignments in furtherance of your stated goals? If so, what steps did you take? If not, why not?

Did you take steps to ensure that you received meaningful feedback? If so, what steps did you take? If not, why not?

Short-Term Career Goals (1–3 years)

Thinking about your remaining time in law school, describe your short-term career goals. These goals should encompass something in addition to your assumed goals of performing well in class, graduating, and passing the bar exam. Be specific in stating your short-term career goals and explain why you selected them. *Have these goals changed since the beginning of the semester?*

Skills Needed to Achieve Short-Term Career Goals

Considering these goals, describe what skills are necessary to achieve them. In your response, discuss which of those skills you possess and which you seek to improve.

Proactive Development of Short-Term Career Goals

Describe how you are proactively approaching these goals, including what steps you are taking to achieve them, and what challenges, if any, you anticipate encountering as you seek to obtain these goals.

Long-Term Career Goals (5–10 years post-graduation)

Thinking about your career five to ten years after graduation, describe how you envision your career as a lawyer and member of the profession and community. Examine your career goals from a variety of perspectives (ex. type of work environment and community in which you would like to live and work, type of professional service you would provide, etc.), not just based narrowly on the type of law you think you might like to practice. Be specific in stating your long-term career goals and explain why you selected them. *Have these goals changed since the beginning of the semester?*

Skills Needed to Achieve Long-Term Career Goals

Identify additional skills, that were not identified in discussing your short-term career goals, which are necessary to achieve your long-term goals. In your response, discuss which of those skills you possess and which you seek to improve.

Proactive Development of Long-Term Career Goals

Describe how you are proactively approaching these goals, including what steps you are taking to achieve them, and what challenges, if any, you anticipate encountering as you seek to obtain these goals.

Statement of Purpose

Now that you have reflected on the reason(s) you attended law school, your future goals, and the reasons for selecting those goals, consider your purpose as a lawyer. Provide one sentence that reflects this purpose.

Reflection on Statement of Purpose

How did your externship experience impact your statement of purpose? Did it change or remain the same?

Section 2: Core Values, Life Priorities and Work-Life Balance

Personal Core Values

Following the example below, list each of your top five core values, how you define it and the behaviors you believe demonstrate that you are living in alignment with that particular core value.

Core Value	Definition	Indicative Behaviors
Example: Relationships	Demonstrate the awesome value of others	Engage with those around me to develop and cultivate strong bonds Whenever possible, share my resources to equip others to succeed Expand my circle of influence Resolve conflicts in a meaningful way Recognize and reward the success of others

Focus on Personal Core Values

How do your core values align with the Statement of Purpose that you set forth in Section 1 of this Professional Development Plan?

Challenges to Personal Core Values

What, if any, challenges do you see with aligning your core values with your career goals?

Plan to Practice Balance This Semester

Spend one hour a week this semester doing something to maintain or realign the balance in your life. Report on your plan to do this (describing the activity, time of day, etc.).

Impact of Plan to Practice Balance This Semester

Assess the effectiveness of your plan to practice balance this semester. In your response, include answers to the following:

Did you follow through with your plan to practice balance? If so, what changes, if any, did you notice as a result of your practice at balance? What did you learn about your work-life balance from integrating this practice into your schedule? If not, what hampered your ability to follow through? What did you learn about your work-life balance from your inability to integrate this practice into your schedule?

Did you do anything else to maintain or realign balance?

Plan for Work-Life Integration in the Future

Identify at least one way to integrate your work and life after you graduate from law school and begin your legal career.

Lessons Learned about Work-Life Integration

Were the attorneys you worked with able to achieve a work-life integration? If so, what did they do to ensure this? If not, what seemed to be the biggest barrier?

Section 3: Networking and Business Development

Personal Board of Directors

List up to 10 people to consult when making major personal or professional decisions. Consider including people on your board of directors who offer different points of view, experience, expertise, or knowledge.

1.
2.
3.
4.
5.
6.
7.
8.
9.
10.

Professional Network Assessment

Using the network assessment exercise you completed in class, identify the strengths of your existing network and areas where you would like to see your network grow.

Current Strengths:

Areas for Growth:

Personal Networking Strategy

List three ways you plan to develop your professional network (ex. networking events, organization memberships, participation in seminars and workshops, writing and speaking opportunities, pro bono work, social functions, etc.). Be sure to consider the type of networking that is best for you based upon your personality, career goals, and core values.

1.

2.

3.

Networking at your Externship

What did you learn about your networking style from your externship? Identify and describe your strengths. Identify and describe your areas of improvement, and how you plan to improve them.

Current Networking Opportunities

Describe how you might use your externship to develop your network. Consider both your short-term and long-term career goals when answering this question.

Externship Contacts

Identify the people at your externship with whom you wish to develop an ongoing relationship. How do you plan to maintain and further develop those relationships? Be specific in your response and articulate your networking plan for each identified individual.

Section 4: Teamwork and Problem Solving

DISC Profile

List the results (percentages) of the online DISC assessment and discuss whether the DISC assessment results align with your perception of who you are.

Teamwork Benefits and Challenges

Considering your DISC assessment and the role you typically play, describe potential benefits and challenges that you may face when you engage in collaborative work.

Benefits to Approach:

Challenges to Approach:

Proactive Development

Identify and describe at least one strategy to combat potential challenges resulting from your approach to teamwork.

Teamwork at your Externship

Reflecting on your externship experience, discuss any lessons learned about effective or ineffective approaches to teamwork. In addition, discuss any opportunities you had to develop your teamwork and problem-solving skills.

Section 5: Cultural Awareness

Implicit Association Test

Did the IAT results align with what you expected your implicit preferences to be? Explain.

Cultural Identity

How do you define culture?

Cultural Competence

Identify your strengths and weaknesses in dealing with cultural differences (when a person is of a different culture, race, ethnicity, generation, etc. from your own).

Strengths:

Weaknesses:

Cultural Differences at your Externship

Reflecting on your externship experience, discuss any lessons learned about effective or ineffective approaches to cultural differences. In addition, discuss any opportunities you had to develop your cultural competence.

4. Extern Learning Goals Form

Student Name: ______________________________ Semester: ________________

Supervising Attorney Name: ___________ Externship Site: __________________

Supervising Attorney's Email Address and Telephone Number: _______________

____

Externship Faculty Supervisor Name: _____________________________________

Student: Use this form to list your educational goals for the externship and a plan for how to achieve them. Then, meet with your Supervising Attorney to review and, as necessary, revise your goals and/or plan for achieving them.

Supervising Attorney: Please discuss with the student both the learning goals and desired assignments and experiences. In addition, please add any additional learning goals and/or expectations you have for the student.

Category	Student Learning Goals	Helpful Assignments & Experiences for Goal Attainment
KNOWLEDGE Describe the substantive, procedural, practical, environmental, or other types of knowledge you seek to gain.		
SKILLS Describe one or more lawyering skills (cognitive, practical, technical, etc.) you seek to develop.		
VALUES Describe ethical, behavioral, cultural, or other professional values and habits you seek to understand and cultivate.		
OTHER Describe any other goal you have for this externship.		

By signature below, I confirm that I have reviewed my goals and expectations for this externship with my supervising attorney.

Student Extern Signature: ______________________ Date: ___________________

By signature below, I confirm that I have reviewed the student extern's goals and expectations and have added any additional goals I have for the student extern.

Supervising Attorney Signature: ___________________ Date: _________________

By signature below, I confirm that I have reviewed this form for completion and receipt of necessary signatures.

Externship Faculty Supervisor Signature: ______________ Date: ___________

5. Mid-Semester Self-Assessment Form

Please complete this form before you meet with your supervising attorney regarding the Preliminary Performance Assessment.

Name: ______________________________ Date: ________________

E-Mail Address: ____

Agency: ____

Direct Supervisor: ____

Please list your goals and evaluate your progress in meeting each goal. Please include any written or oral work you have completed when evaluating your progress.

Is there something you want to get out of the experience that you are not getting? Do you have any new goals? If so, what are they?

Using the scale below, please rate your skills in the following areas (only if applicable):

1 = Needs Significant Improvement; 2 = On Track; 3 = Very Strong

_______ Legal Knowledge and Analysis

_______ Legal Research

_______ Legal Writing

_______ Oral Communication

_______ Ethical Knowledge

_______ Time Management

_______ Professional Communication

_______ Active Listening

_______ Learning from Experience

_______ Teamwork

What kind of feedback have you received on your written or oral work from your supervising attorney or judge?

Do you know what your supervising attorney or judge thinks of your work? If so, what? If not, why not?

On a weekly basis, how much time do you get with your supervising attorney and/or judge?

At this point, what has been the most challenging for you or has caused you the greatest discomfort?

Do you have anything you specifically want to discuss during your mid-semester meeting with your assigned Professor?

Materials Referenced in Chapter 9: Topic Ideas for the General Seminar Course

1. Rubric for Assessing Learning Outcomes Relating to Well-Being

	Novice Learner	Intermediate Learner	Competent Learner	Exceptional Learner
Defining the Concept of Well-Being	Student cannot define the concept of well-being or explain how well-being relates to a lawyer's duty of competence.	Student can articulate a basic definition of well-being but cannot demonstrate understanding of the relationship between well-being and a lawyer's duty of competence.	Student can articulate a complete definition of well-being and demonstrate a basic understanding of the relationship between well-being and a lawyer's duty of competence.	Student can articulate a sophisticated definition of well-being and demonstrate an in-depth understanding of the relationship between well-being and a lawyer's duty of competence.
Identifying and Explaining the Multiple Dimensions of Well-Being	Student can identify few or none of the dimensions of well-being.	Student can identify some of the dimensions of well-being, but cannot explain what those dimensions mean or how they contribute to an individual's well-being.	Student can identify most or all dimensions of well-being and can explain in basic terms what the identified dimensions mean and how they contribute to an individual's well-being.	Student can identify all of the dimensions of well-being and can provide an in-depth explanation of what each dimension means and how it contributes to an individual's well-being.
Self-Awareness of One's Own Well-Being	Student cannot self-assess individual level of development in any of the dimensions of well-being and cannot identify resources or strategies for enhancing well-being.	Student can self-assess individual level of development in some dimensions of well-being but cannot identify resources or strategies for enhancing well-being.	Student can self-assess level of development in most of the dimensions of well-being, can identify some areas for improvement, and can identify some resources and strategies for enhancing well-being.	Student can self-assess level of development in all dimensions of well-being, can accurately identify areas for improvement, and can identify and implement resources and strategies for enhancing well-being.
Implementing Well-Being Practices in One's Life	Student rarely or never uses a practice that fosters well-being.	Student occasionally uses at least one practice that fosters well-being.	Student regularly and consistently uses at least one practice that fosters well-being.	Student creates and consistently follows a comprehensive plan for achieving personal well-being goals.

2. Advanced Cross-Cultural Communication Assessment

Advanced Cross-Cultural Communication Assessment: developed by Gillian Dutton based on materials from *A Survey Instrument to Develop, Tailor, and Help Measure Law Student Cultural Diversity Education Learning Outcomes*, Andrea A. Curcio, Teresa E. Ward, and Nisha Dogra.

Name ____

This scale asks you to assess your comfort level in the knowledge, attitudes/values and skills of cultural competence. Go through the assessment and using a scale of 1 to 6 rate your comfort level in each area.

Scale: 1=Not at all comfortable to 6=Very Comfortable

Knowledge

I can identify examples of culturally and racially biased assumptions that lawyers and clients may bring into the lawyer-client relationship;

1__ 2__ 3__ 4__ 5__ 6__

I can explain my own cultural and racial biases and how those may impact legal representation generally as well as in the context of a particular case or factual scenario;

1__ 2__ 3__ 4__ 5__ 6__

I can explain how subconscious schemas and categories make it difficult to identify when my reactions to other people are based upon culturally and racially biased assumptions or stereotypes;

1__ 2__ 3__ 4__ 5__ 6__

I can describe how stereotyping and biases may affect a lawyer's interpretation of the facts and application of a legal rule to the facts;

1__ 2__ 3__ 4__ 5__ 6__

In a particular case or factual scenario, I can identify cultural experiences of the parties and the lawyers that may affect the legal and factual analysis;

1__ 2__ 3__ 4__ 5__ 6__

I can describe challenges in cross-cultural communication.

1__ 2__ 3__ 4__ 5__ 6__

Attitudes/Values

I can reflect on how different values systems and communications styles may affect lawyers' interpretations of client and litigant reactions and behaviors;

1__ 2__ 3__ 4__ 5__ 6__

I can reflect upon how my own varied cultural and racial experiences affect my perceptions and interactions with clients, colleagues, and staff;

1__ 2__ 3__ 4__ 5__ 6__

I can evaluate why people are resistant to admitting that they make judgments based upon cultural and racial biases and stereotypes;

1__ 2__ 3__ 4__ 5__ 6__

I can evaluate the role my own cultural and racial experiences have had in shaping my views about the law and legal systems;

1__ 2__ 3__ 4__ 5__ 6__

I can recognize the need to suspend judgment when encountering unfamiliar conduct or views;

1__ 2__ 3__ 4__ 5__ 6__

I can demonstrate curiosity about the ways in which my cultural beliefs and practices influence my perceptions and interactions;

1__ 2__ 3__ 4__ 5__ 6__

I can demonstrate curiosity about clients', witnesses, and parties' cultural beliefs and practices.

1__ 2__ 3__ 4__ 5__ 6__

Skills Learning Outcomes

I can incorporate cultural and racial considerations into my discussion of a hypothetical legal problem and the appropriate solution;

1__ 2__ 3__ 4__ 5__ 6__

I can provide examples of how my own cultural and racial assumptions and biases affected my understanding of the factual and legal issues in a given case or transaction;

1__ 2__ 3__ 4__ 5__ 6__

I can identify situations in which my cultural and racial biases or stereotypes impeded successful legal representation;

1__ 2__ 3__ 4__ 5__ 6__

I can ask appropriate questions to elicit client, witness or party information about cultural beliefs or practices that may affect representation;

1__ 2__ 3__ 4__ 5__ 6__

I can communicate effectively using a wide range of strategies to engage with clients, witnesses and parties;

1__ 2__ 3__ 4__ 5__ 6__

I can respond appropriately to feedback about key cross-cultural and racial justice issues;

1__ 2__ 3__ 4__ 5__ 6__

I can demonstrate strategies to assess, manage, and reduce bias in encounters with clients, witnesses, and parties;

1__ 2__ 3__ 4__ 5__ 6__

I can explain techniques and tools that can help identify red flags that there has been a cross-cultural miscommunication;

1__ 2__ 3__ 4__ 5__ 6__

I can use reflective practices that bring in a consideration of internal and external factors, racial and cultural biases, and systemic injustice, when working on legal cases or transactions;

1__ 2__ 3__ 4__ 5__ 6__

I can use reflective practices when considering cultural contexts and cultural norms and whether particular cultural norms and practices create injustices which should be challenged.

1__ 2__ 3__ 4__ 5__ 6__

3. ABA Values & Skills Initial Student Survey

Student Name__________________________

Placement ____________________________

Seminar _____________________________________

Each value or skill contains a list of subcategories that help define it. These definitions are taken from the ABA MacCrate Report and the Washington Racial Equity Justice Initiative commitments https://wareji.org/commitments/ with additions to incorporate cultural humility and awareness of implicit bias. Think about any work (in a class or elsewhere) in each of the subareas listed, then assess your general experience as a whole and write in a number from 1 to 5 (values) or 1 to 6 (skills) based on the different scales below. The values section contains a description of the values we will be working on during the seminars. We have also given you space for an additional skill.

As you go through the survey, assess yourself in each area and choose at least one value and two skills that you hope to work on. You will complete the whole survey and then list these in the space directly below. Take this completed survey with you to your meeting with your supervisor and fill out your Goals Chart & Supervision Agreement due at the end of week 2. After they are completed, give a copy of both documents to your supervisor and post them to Canvas. The goal of this form is for you to think carefully about your plan for the semester in light of your past experiences and current level of skills and values. If you prefer, you can share that information with your supervisor and post a description of the conversation on Canvas instead of using this form.

ONCE YOU HAVE COMPLETED THE SURVEY YOU SHOULD HAVE AT LEAST 1 VALUE AND 2 SKILLS (you can pick an additional value or skill to work on) TO DISCUSS WITH YOUR SUPERVISOR AND INCLUDE ON YOUR GOALS CHART & SUPERVISION AGREEMENT

Value

Skill

Skill

Value

Skill

Skill

VALUES PROFICIENCY SCALE (to be used when assessing ABA Values 1–4 below)

1	2	3	4	5
Receiving:	Responding:	Valuing:	Organizing:	Internalizing:
Being aware of the existence of certain ideas/values	Being committed to the ideas/values in some small measure by actively responding to them	Being willing to be perceived by others as valuing the ideas	Relating the new value to those one already holds/harmonizing it with existing philosophy	Acting consistently, pervasively, and predictably in accordance with the values that control one's behavior

Value 1: Competent Representation

As a member of a profession dedicated to the service of clients, a lawyer should be committed to the values of:

Attaining a Level of Competence in One's Own Field of Practice

Maintaining a Level of Competence in One's Own Field of Practice

Representing Clients with Cultural Humility and Attention to Implicit and Explicit Bias (Underlined language in Value 1.3 has been added to the original ABA language by the SU Law Externship Program.)

Relevant REJI Values/Commitments

1. Work together with, take guidance from, be part of, and hold ourselves accountable to community-based movements in communities most affected by structural racialization and structurally racialized systems.

5. Continually explore how race and poverty intersect to make worse the effects of racial discrimination.

Your Overall Experience Level (1–5) ________________

What work experience do you have with this value? ______________________

____

____

What additional work could you do in this area during your externship? _____

____

____

If this is a value you hope to work on during this semester's externship, list at the top of this document.

Value 2: Justice and Fairness

As a member of a profession that bears special responsibilities for the quality of justice, a lawyer should be committed to the values of:

2.1 Promoting Justice Fairness and Morality in One's Own Daily Practice

2.2 Contributing to the Profession's Fulfillment of its Responsibility to Ensure that Adequate Legal Services Are Provided to Those Who Cannot Afford to Pay for Them

2.3 Contributing to the Profession's Fulfillment of its Responsibility to Enhance the Capacity of Law and Legal Institutions to Do Justice Taking into Account Cultural Humility and the Impact of Implicit and Explicit Bias. (Underlined language in Value 2.3 has been added to the original ABA language by the SU Law Externship Program.)

Relevant REJI Values/Commitments

2. Change structures, policies, processes, and practices in the law, legal profession, and justice system that allow harm and disparate outcomes for communities of color to continue unabated.

3. Promote and support legal and policy reforms to advance race equity and racial justice, recognizing that differently situated groups may require different strategies to achieve more equitable outcomes

Your Overall Experience Level (1–5) ________________

What work experience do you have with this value? ________________________

____

____

What additional work could you do in this area during your externship? ______

____

____

If this is a value you hope to work on during this semester's externship, list at the top of this document.

Value 3: Improving the Profession

As a member of a self-governing profession, a lawyer should be committed to the values of:

3.1 Participating in Activities Designed to Improve the Profession

3.2 Assisting in the Training and Preparation of New Lawyers

3.3 Striving to Rid the Profession of Bias Based on Race, Religion, Ethnic Origin, Gender, Age, Sexual Orientation, or Disability, and to Rectify the Effects of These Biases

Relevant REJI Values/Commitments

7. Ensure our organizations invest in active, ongoing learning that will teach us to see, reveal, and transform structures that create racialized outcomes and push communities of color outside the Circle of Human Concern. This commitment requires that we help members of our organizations and communities to actively and expressly challenge the use of racist language and behaviors, openly listen when we ourselves are challenged, and learn techniques and tools for reducing and eliminating implicit and explicit bias.

Your Overall Experience Level (1–5) ________________

What work experience do you have with this value? ______________________

____

____

What additional work could you do in this area during your externship? _____

____

____

If this is a value you hope to work on during this semester's externship, list at the top of this document.

Value 4: Professional Self-Development

As a member of a learned profession, a lawyer should be committed to the values of:

4.1 Seeking Out and Taking Advantage of Opportunities to Increase Knowledge and Improve Skills including those in Cultural Competence, Anti and Awareness of Implicit and Explicit Bias. (Underlined language in Value 4.1 has been added to the original ABA language by the SU Law Externship Program.)

4.2 Selecting and Maintaining Employment That Will Allow the Lawyer to Develop as a Professional and to Pursue Professional and Personal Goals

Relevant REJI Values/Commitments

4. Continuously examine whether we and the organizations we work with operate in ways that align with the race equity and justice values and goals we support. This commitment includes ensuring that race equity is reflected in policies and practices for recruitment and hiring, work acceptance, priority-setting, governance, organizational culture, and community partnerships and accountability, particularly with low-income communities of color.

6. Expand and strengthen the REJI alliance to include diverse partnerships and thesharing of our resources with anyone who is committed to dismantling structurallyracialized systems.

Your Overall Experience Level (1–5) ________________

What work experience do you have with this value? ________________________

____

What additional work could you do in this area during your externship? ______

____

____

If this is a value you hope to work on during this semester's externship, list at the top of this document.

SKILLS PROFICIENCY SCALE (to be used when assessing ABA Skills 1–10 below)

1	2	3	4	5	6
Able to describe the skill but not to perform it	Able to perform the skill in a simulated environment	Able to perform the skill in a live environment but only with assistance	Able to perform the skill with minimal assistance	Able to perform the skill independently	Able to perform the skill independently in any new situation

Skill 1: Problem Solving

In order to develop and evaluate strategies for solving a problem or accomplishing an objective, a lawyer should be familiar with the skills and concepts involved in:

Identifying and Diagnosing the Problem

Generating Alternative Solutions and Strategies

Developing a Plan of Action

Implementing the Plan

Keeping the Planning Process Open to New Information and New Ideas

Your Overall Experience Level (1–6) ________

What work experience do you have with this skill? ______________________

____

____

What additional work could you do in this area during your externship? _____

____

____

If this is a skill you hope to work on during this semester's externship, list at the top of this document.

Skill 2: Legal Analysis and Reasoning

In order to analyze and apply legal rules and principles, a lawyer should be familiar with the skills and concepts involved in:

2.1 Identifying and Formulating Legal Issues

2.2 Formulating Relevant Legal Theories

2.3 Elaborating Legal Theories

2.4 Evaluating Legal Theories

2.5 Criticizing and Synthesizing Legal Argumentation

Your Overall Experience Level (1–6) ________

What work experience do you have with this skill? ______________________

____

____

What additional work could you do in this area during your externship? ______

____

____

If this is a skill you hope to work on during this semester's externship, list at the top of this document.

Skill 3: Legal Research

In order to identify legal issues and to research them thoroughly and efficiently, a lawyer should have:

3.1 Knowledge of the Nature of Legal Rules and Institutions

3.2 Knowledge of and Ability to Use the Most Fundamental Tools of Legal Research

3.3 Understanding of the Process of Devising and Implementing a Coherent and Effective Research Design

Your Overall Experience Level (1–6) ________

What work experience do you have with this skill? ______________________

____

What additional work could you do in this area during your externship? ______

____

____

If this is a skill you hope to work on during this semester's externship, list at the top of this document.

Skill 4: Factual Investigation

In order to plan, direct, and (where applicable) participate in factual investigation, a lawyer should be familiar with the skills and concepts involved in:

4.1 Determining the Need for Factual Investigation

4.2 Planning a Factual Investigation

4.3 Implementing the Investigative Strategy

4.4 Memorializing and Organizing Information in an Accessible Form

4.5 Deciding Whether to Conclude the Process of Fact-Gathering

4.6 Evaluating the Information that has Been Gathered

Your Overall Experience Level (1–6) ________

What work experience do you have with this skill? ______________________

____

____

What additional work could you do in this area during your externship? ______

____

____

If this is a skill you hope to work on during this semester's externship, list at the top of this document.

Skill 5: Communication

In order to communicate effectively, whether orally or in writing, a lawyer should be familiar with the skills and concepts involved in:

5.1 Assessing the Perspective of the Recipient of the Communication

5.2 Using Effective Methods of Communication

Your Overall Experience Level (1–6) ________

What work experience do you have with this skill? ______________________

____

____

What additional work could you do in this area during your externship? _____

____

____

If this is a skill you hope to work on during this semester's externship, list at the top of this document.

Skill 6: Counseling

In order to counsel clients about decisions or courses of action, a lawyer should be familiar with the skills and concepts involved in:

6.1 Establishing a Counseling Relationship that Respects the Nature and Bounds of a Lawyer's Role

6.2 Gathering Information Relevant to the Decision to be Made

6.3 Analyzing the Decision to be Made

6.4 Counseling the Client about the Decision to be Made

6.5 Ascertaining and Implementing the Client's Decision

Your Overall Experience Level (1–6) ________

What work experience do you have with this skill? ______________________

____

____

What additional work could you do in this area during your externship? ______

____

____

If this is a skill you hope to work on during this semester's externship, list at the top of this document.

Skill 7: Negotiation

In order to negotiate in either a dispute-resolution or transactional context, a lawyer should be familiar with the skills and concepts involved in:

7.1 Preparing for Negotiation

7.2 Conducting a Negotiation Session

7.3 Counseling the Client about the Terms Obtained from the Other Side in the Negotiation and Implementing the Client's Decision

Your Overall Experience Level (1–6) ________

What work experience do you have with this skill? ______________________

____

What additional work could you do in this area during your externship? _____

____

____

If this is a skill you hope to work on during this semester's externship, list at the top of this document.

Skill 8: Litigation and Alternative Dispute-Resolution Procedures

In order to advise a client about the options of litigation and alternative dispute resolution, a lawyer should understand the potential functions and consequences of these processes and should have a working knowledge of the fundamentals of:

8.1 Litigation at the Trial-Court Level

8.2 Litigation at the Appellate Level

8.3 Advocacy in Administrative and Executive Forums

Your Overall Experience Level (1–6) ________

What work experience do you have with this skill? ______________________

____

____

What additional work could you do in this area during your externship? _____

____

____

If this is a skill you hope to work on during this semester's externship, list at the top of this document.

Skill 9: Organization and Management of Legal Work

In order to practice effectively, a lawyer should be familiar with the skills and concepts required for efficient management, including:

9.1 Formulating Goals and Principles for Effective Practice Management

9.2 Developing Systems and Procedures to Ensure that Time, Effort, and Resources Are Allocated Efficiently

9.3 Developing Systems and Procedures to Ensure that Work is Performed and Completed at the Appropriate Time

9.4 Developing Systems and Procedures for Effectively Working with Other People

9.5 Developing Systems and Procedures for Efficiently Administering a Law Office

Your Overall Experience Level (1–6) ________

What work experience do you have with this skill? ________________________

____

____

What additional work could you do in this area during your externship? _____

____

____

If this is a skill you hope to work on during this semester's externship, list at the top of this document.

Skill 10: Recognizing and Resolving Ethical Dilemmas

In order to represent a client consistently with applicable ethical standards, a lawyer should be familiar with:

10.1 The Nature and Sources of Ethical Standards

10.2 The Means by Which Ethical Standards are Enforced

10.3 The Processes for Recognizing and Resolving Ethical Dilemmas

Your Overall Experience Level (1–6) ________

What work experience do you have with this skill? ________________________

____

What additional work could you do in this area during your externship? ______

____

____

If this is a skill you hope to work on during this semester's externship, list at the top of this document.

Additional skill that is not listed in the ABA MacCrate Report

You may choose to articulate a skill that is not listed above (e.g., policy advocacy, community education) ____

____

Your Overall Experience Level (1–6) ________

What work experience do you have with this skill? ____________________

____

____

What additional work could you do in this area during your externship? _____

____

____

If this is a skill you hope to work on during this semester's externship, list at the top of this document.

4. Goals Chart and Supervision Agreement

Take your completed ABA Values and Skills Initial Student Survey with the list of values and skills you hope to work on to your meeting with your supervisor. There, review your survey and discuss a plan for working on your goals in the areas you have identified. You may need to choose different areas to work on after discussing the kind of work done at your site with your supervisor. Now, complete the Goals Chart on the next page as thoroughly and completely as you can.

Value/Skill Area: These should correspond only to the broad categories of the Initial Student Survey that apply to this externship. For example, if you decide to set a goal in the area of legal research you should simply say, "Legal Research" here.

Goals: Use this to set out the specific, measurable goals you want to achieve in each value/skill area by the end of the semester. Using the proficiency scales below, enter the number you have assessed as your starting point, as well as the number you and your supervisor agree you should try to reach by the end of the semester.

VALUES PROFICIENCY SCALE

1	2	3	4	5
Receiving:	Responding:	Valuing:	Organizing:	Internalizing:
Being aware of the existence of certain ideas/ values	Being committed to the ideas/ values in some small measure by actively responding to them	Being willing to be perceived by others as valuing the ideas	Relating the new value to those one already holds/ harmonizing it with existing philosophy	Acting consistently, pervasively and predictably in accordance with the values that control one's behavior

SKILLS PROFICIENCY SCALE

1	2	3	4	5	6
Able to describe the skill but not to perform it	Able to perform the skill in a simulated environment	Able to perform the skill in a live environment but only with assistance	Able to perform the skill with minimal assistance	Able to perform the skill independently	Able to perform the skill independently in any new situation

Progression of Tasks: In this section, work with your supervisor to identify the kinds of tasks that will help you to achieve your goals. Ideally, this will include a progression of tasks, moving from less to more complex as you proceed through the semester.

Feedback Plan: This is a description of your plan for getting feedback from your supervisor. In addition to weekly meetings, feedback can include written comments and oral debriefing, using a rubric or checklist if helpful. Whatever you choose, it is important to make it concrete.

Below is a sample to give you an idea of what a plan could look like. It need not be complex; the idea is to create a tangible expression of your intentions.

Value/Skill Area	Description of Goals	Progression of Tasks	Feedback Plan
Legal Analysis	By the end of the semester, I will be able to identify independently all legal issues raised by a set of facts. Starting # 4 Ending # 5	–Research and prepare a memo on a single issue identified by the supervisor –Research and prepare a memo on all issues raised by the case, with assistance identifying issues –Research and prepare a memo on all issues independently	–Develop a checklist for effective memos based on sample from supervisor –Receive supervisor edits in track changes –Check in for help where assistance is needed

Complete the chart below, picking at least one value and two skills and including a final number for your ending goal. You may do so electronically or by hand. After the assessment is completed and signed, give a copy to your supervisor and post to Canvas. The Externship Faculty will print it and sign it. you would like a final copy.

Value/Skill Area	Description of Goals Starting Number & Ending Number	Progression of Tasks (Opportunities for Multiple Performance)	Feedback Plan
1.	Goal: Starting #__, Ending #__		
2.	Goal: Starting #__, Ending #__		
3.	Goal: Starting #__, Ending # __		
4.	Goal: Starting #__, Ending #__		

To signify commitment to this plan, the student and supervisor should each sign below. Electronic signatures are acceptable. The student will give a copy of the Goals Chart and Supervision Agreement to the supervisor and also post it on Canvas.

Student: ______________________________ Site: ______________________

Supervisor: ___________________________ Date: ______________________

______________________________ ______________________________

Extern Name Site Name

______________________________ ______________________________

Extern Signature Date

______________________________ ______________________________

Supervisor Signature Date

______________________________ ______________________________

Faculty (SU Externship Program) Signature Date

Field Supervisor Agreement

I agree to act as Field Supervisor for the Extern during the externship. I have the authority, ability, and resources to ensure the Extern is adequately supervised. I have read the GUIDELINES FOR EXTERNSHIP SPONSORS and FREQUENTLY ASKED QUESTIONS provided by the Seattle University School of Law Externship Program Office (SU) and agree to conduct the supervision in accordance with the requirements described in those documents.

I agree to incorporate the following goals into the supervision, feedback, and task assignment for the Extern:

To integrate doctrine, theory, skills, and legal ethics, and engage students in the

performance of the professional values and skills identified in the Goals Chart & Supervision Agreement,

To develop the concepts underlying the professional skills and values being taught,

To provide multiple opportunities for performance, and

To provide opportunities for self-evaluation.

REQUIREMENTS DUE TO COVID-19. I understand that in light of the coronavirus (COVID-19) pandemic, all externs will be expected to perform their work remotely except in the following situation: 1) the supervisor indicates they would like the student to work on site, 2) the student agrees, and 3) the student has emailed the Externship Program Director and copied their supervisor, to confirm their intent. In addition, in the event the externship will involve on site work, I represent and agree that the site and the student will comply with all applicable guidelines and directives from federal, state and local government and public health officials, including but not limited to, social distancing, vaccination, and face covering requirements.

COMMITMENT TO ADDRESSING RACISM IN LEGAL INSTITUTIONS. I understand that Seattle University Law School's goal is to educate students in accordance with the Washington Race Equity and Justice Initiative https://wareji.org/commitments/

WORKLOAD AND RESOURCES. I understand a central goal of SU is to enable students to gain useful and challenging legal training in a realistic setting. I will give the Extern responsibility for the agreed-to workload and will ensure the Extern is directly and substantively involved in all matters relating to this workload. I will keep to a minimum the time spent on matters with which the Extern is not fully involved and will avoid assigning the Extern non-substantive or menial tasks. I will verify that the Extern has a workspace along with access to the necessary tools and support to complete the work assigned. I will also ensure the Extern has opportunities to observe proceedings and other professional activities related to work assigned.

TRAINING, MEETINGS AND FEEDBACK. I further understand that an additional goal of SU is to provide the Extern with adequate supervision and feedback. As part of this supervision, I will provide training (including initial orientation, weekly meetings to discuss the purpose and theory of the work assigned and how to approach the work); critical review and feedback (quality of the work performed, discussion of whether work goals were achieved); and perspective (legal and other implications of the work; connection between the work being done and the case to which it relates, connection to analogous/similar cases and to the sponsor's overall workload; and the ethical/moral considerations raised by the issues). If we are working in a remote capacity because of public health concerns, I also understand that it is preferable to meet weekly via videoconference and I will make every effort to conduct a weekly video supervision meeting.

FORMS. In addition to my regular weekly supervisory meetings with the Extern, I agree to sit down with the student during the first week of the externship, review the Extern's ABA Values and Skills Initial Student Survey, discuss goals and expectations for the externship, and fill out the Goals Chart & Supervision Agreement. Halfway through the semester, I will meet with the Extern to evaluate how the externship is going, in light of these original goals and expectations and complete the Mid-Semester Values and Skills Assessment. At the end of the semester, I will meet with the Extern to discuss performance and to help fill out the Final Values and Skills Assessment. I will also provide the Externship Coordinator with a separate Final Written Evaluation of the Extern's work.

LEGAL COMPLIANCE. I will make myself available throughout the semester to discuss with the Externship Faculty Supervisor and/or with the Externship Director the Extern's progress and/or other matters relating to the externship when needed. My organization is responsible for ensuring that our labor and employment practices are in compliance with state, local, and federal laws as related to the externship. In accepting SU Law School students for placement, the placement organization hereby agrees to abide by the Seattle University Law School Externship Program policies described below.

As a site supervisor, or field placement/agency representative, I agree to the following (initial each standard):

Provide: the student with copies of harassment (including sexual harassment) and protected racial discrimination policies and reporting procedures that the field placement site/agency has in place. ____ (Supervisor initials)

Provide: the student and SU School of Law the date (month and year) of the most recent trainings on sexual harassment, discrimination, and bias, within the last three years. ____ (Supervisor initials)

Provide: students with the name and contact information of personnel that the field placement site/agency has designated for reporting harassment and protected-class discrimination in the workplace. ___ (Supervisor initials)

Extern's Agreement

PROFESSIONALISM: I agree to follow directions, seek clarification and advice in a timely fashion, and comport myself with professionalism and integrity. I will also review the "Tips for Working Remotely" document if we are in a remote working situation.

DEVELOPMENT GOALS: With my supervisor, I will create goals for the semester of how I plan to develop professionally and will work to complete the tasks set out as steps to achieve my goals.

SEMINAR: I agree to complete all required readings, assessments, and/or other assignments requested by the Externship Faculty and to participate in exercises/classroom activities during the seminar.

REFLECTION: I will reflect on the observations, experiences, ethical considerations, and other issues that arise during my externship. As directed by the Externship Faculty, I will submit reflection papers analyzing my experiences. In so doing, I will be mindful of my confidentiality obligations.

EVALUATION: I will strive to self-assess on each assignment I complete. I will consider what I did effectively and areas for improvement. Where appropriate, I will discuss my self-assessment with my faculty and site supervisors. I will be open to feedback from my supervisors and will consider how it can be applied specifically and globally to my future work.

ACKNOWLEDGMENT OF RESTRICTIONS DUE TO COVID 19

In the event my externship site will involve in-person work, I acknowledge and agree to the following:

There are potential increased risks in contracting the coronavirus (COVID-19) associated with participating in an in-person externship experience. I can earn credit for my externship remotely if I am not comfortable performing work on site due to the increased health risk. I have reviewed the following CDC guidance titled How to Protect Yourself & Others | CDC

I will comply with all applicable guidelines and directives from federal, state, and local government and public health officials, including but not limited to, social distancing and face covering requirements.

This externship is voluntary, and it is not required to progress in my program or obtain my degree. Seattle University School of Law has alternative opportunities for law students to engage in fully virtual practical and experiential learning experiences.

Seattle University highly recommends that all law students maintain health insurance and get vaccinated.

Faculty Member's Agreement

ACADEMIC REQUIREMENTS: I will establish requirements (including readings, reflective papers, and/or other assignments) designed to develop the extern's experience, including encouraging self-assessment and reflection.

SITE EVALUATION: I will remain in regular contact, including possible visits, with the externship site and the extern to ensure the quality of the educational experience.

AVAILABILITY: I will be available as a resource should any concerns or issues arise.

EVALUATION: I will evaluate the extern's academic performance during the externship. The assessment will be based on the extern and supervisor evaluations, timely compliance with requirements and assignments, quality of the self-reflections (and other written assignments), and professionalism. I will determine the grade and credit to be granted.

SEATTLE UNIVERSITY LAW SCHOOL EXTERNSHIP POLICIES

Non-Discrimination: The Seattle University Law School (SU) is committed to providing equal opportunity for all persons in admission to, participation in, or employment in, the programs and activities which the Law School conducts without regard to race, creed, color, marital status, sexual orientation, religion, sex, national origin, age, mental or physical disability or veteran's status. Seattle University Law School's goal is committed to educating students in accordance with the Washington Race Equity and Justice Initiative https://wareji.org/commitments/, a network of people, communities and organizations working together for racial fairness and justice in the law, legal profession, and justice systems.

Non-Harassment: SU in accordance with applicable Federal and State law and University policy, does not discriminate on the basis of race, creed, color, marital status, sexual orientation, religion, sex, national origin, age, mental or physical disability or veteran's status. SU also prohibits sexual harassment. This nondiscrimination policy covers admission, access, and treatment in SU programs and activities. Harassment is defined as unwelcome conduct, including verbal, nonverbal, or physical conduct that explicitly or implicitly affects a person's employment or education or interferes with a person's work or educational performance or creates an environment such that a reasonable person would find the conduct intimidating, hostile, or offensive. Harassment as used in these guidelines can include Sexual Harassment. Sexual Harassment is unwelcome sexual advances, unwelcome requests for sexual favors, and other unwelcome verbal, nonverbal or physical conduct of a sexual nature when:

A person's submission to such conduct is implicitly or explicitly made the basis for employment decisions, academic evaluation, grades or advancement, or other decisions affecting participation in a University program (Quid Pro Quo); or

Such conduct is sufficiently severe or pervasive that it unreasonably denies, adversely limits, or interferes with a person's participation in or benefit from the education, employment or other programs and services of the University and creates an environment a reasonable person would find to be intimidating or offensive (Hostile Environment); or

Includes threats, intimidation, reprisals, and/or adverse employment or educational actions against a person based on their report of Prohibited Conduct or participation in the investigation, report, remedial, or disciplinary processes provided for in these guidelines (Retaliation). SU will respond promptly and effectively to reports of any prohibited conduct and will take appropriate action to prevent, to correct, and when necessary, to remedy behavior that violates SU's policy.

5. Exercise Reflecting on Impact of Bias

Name ____

Describe an experience with bias (that you experienced or observed) __________

____

____

____

How might the incident affect people involved? (target, perpetrator, witnesses)

Target____

Perpetrator____

Witness____

How might the incident affect the community?

____

____

____

What are the emotional, social, physical and financial costs?

Emotional____

Social____

Financial____

We all face difficulty responding to bias. Why do we often not respond?

____

____

____

NOW. Imagine you are witnessing that incident again, think about how you would respond. Goal is to move away from "Message to deliver" toward "Some information to share and some questions to ask." Explain your point of view, share and understand feelings.

Examples of how to start: Check which one you would use.

I don't know if you know how that sounded, but it could be interpreted that you think...(identify hurtful bias) ____

____

____

I used to think I was able to put biases aside, but then I realized that many of these behaviors are unconscious...(describe your own experience similar to the behavior witnessed) ____

____

____

Help me to understand what you meant by...(insert statement) ______________

____

____

____

6. Sample Script for Addressing a Microagression

Conversation Responding to Bias –

(Sample Conversation to be acted out in class between professor and a student volunteer).

You can do this with any example that comes up in one of the student responses to the exercises. I contact the student ahead of time to ask permission and to ask which role they would like to read. I draft the example and then ask them to edit. We then act it out in the class session.

Student has emailed her Professor asking if she can meet with her. She took the class during a previous semester.

Prof.: Hi Ms. ______ how can I help you?

Student: Hi Prof. ______, I wanted to speak with you about something that bothered me in class last semester that really affected my ability to participate. I worry that it was distracting to other students too. And I know that some of them became misinformed because of it. I wanted to bring it to your attention because you have always stressed the importance to all of us of modeling professional behavior in class. You have also told us that you really value an inclusive classroom. I really appreciate that and know you take it seriously.

Prof.: Oh Ms. ______, thank you for coming to my office to speak with me. Can you tell me what it is?

Student: Yes, on the first day of class you asked us to identify our pronouns and you also called each of us by name. When you mispronounced my name, I corrected it and you seemed to hear me, but in the next class you did it again. Despite the fact that I corrected you for about three weeks, you continued to mispronounce my name for the whole 15 weeks of the semester. Other students then started saying it wrong. I stopped trying to correct you and I felt discouraged.

Prof.: Oh my gosh, I am so sorry. Your name is so hard to pronounce, I thought I had it right.

Student: I did keep correcting you class after class for three weeks in a row, and I kept wondering why you didn't try to say it correctly. The feeling that I got was that you didn't hear me. And then I felt as if you must not really care. I know that probably was not your intent at all, but that was the impact: that you didn't hear me or value what I had to say. Taking time to say it correctly seems a gesture of respect to me. I began to think that maybe you didn't hear or listen to other things I said in class. It felt awkward in front of the class to correct my name again and again. And then it got worse as other students started to mispronounce it. When I heard my name mispronounced it made me feel othered, as if I was unwelcome, as if you were telling me that based on my name, I don't belong

Prof.: Thank you so much for telling me. I had never thought of it before, I just always thought I am terrible with pronunciations, you know I am not good at other languages. Now I understand, that by mispronouncing your name after you tried to correct me, I have made you feel unwelcome and uncomfortable in class. I am realizing that I have done this many times before, and with other students. You are the first person who has raised this to me, and I want to thank you for the courage and energy it took for you to do that. You have explained how frustrating it felt. I am guessing you may have wondered if it was worth it to bring it up now, when you have told me before so many times. I am so truly sorry for that and grateful for you raising it. I will write down the phonetic form so that I can be sure to get it right. Would it be ok with you if I explain to the rest of last semester's class, so they know I have made this mistake? I think your point about professionalism is exactly right. What if an attorney doesn't pronounce their client's, or the opposing party's, or the judge's name, correctly? What does that signal? By these seemingly small actions we are communicating either respect or lack of respect for others. It doesn't matter if we don't intend to do that, our actions have consequences. As an attorney I carefully proofread my brief before I file it, why would I not then pronounce names correctly when I am speaking them? As lawyers we should all care deeply about that and I thank you again for raising it. I feel that there are other faculty who probably make this mistake and I'd like to try and stop that if I can. Do you feel comfortable with me sharing this story, perhaps anonymously?

Student: Thank you for understanding and for your apology. I don't want you to share it with students in last semester's class. The semester is already over and they are all in different classes. I have already explained it to them. But I would like you to make an effort to always pronounce names correctly, and to raise it whenever you hear someone not doing so. I would also like you to share it with other professors. I have a few more years of law school here and it would be nice to know that my other professors will make me feel like they are listening to me. I would also like to know that the students graduating from this law school will understand that while the work that needs to be done to build racial justice is pervasive and long term, each of them can engage in both small and large actions as part of that effort.

7. Oral Presentation Rubric

Criteria	Needs Work: 1	Developing: 2	Competent: 3	Exemplary: 4
Time	N/A	N/A	N/A	Presentation is long enough to effectively communicate the required content and research but does not exceed 6 minutes.
Forensics	**Eye Contact**			
	Does not make eye contact, relies heavily on notes, reading most of the presentation.	Inconsistent eye contact and reads directly from notes during some of the presentation.	Maintains generally consistent eye contact and reads from notes at several points during the presentation.	Maintains consistent and comfortable eye contact throughout the presentation and only occasionally references notes.
	Cadence and Verbal Fillers ("um," "like," "you know," etc.)			
	Speaks so fast or so slow and/or uses so many verbal fillers that it impedes the audience's ability to understand the presentation.	Speaks too fast or too slow and/or uses many verbal fillers.	Speaks with a steady pace that is at times too fast or too slow, and/or rarely uses verbal fillers.	Speaks with a varied, dynamic pace that is not too fast or too slow and avoids verbal fillers.
	Volume			
	Does not project voice.	Projects voice at a volume that varies and is not always appropri-ate for the size of the room/audience.	Projects voice at a volume appropriate for the size of the room/audience throughout the presentation.	Projects voice at a volume appropriate for the size of the room/audience, and stylistically integrates varied intonation.

Structure and Content	Organization			
	Information is not presented in a logical sequence.	Information is presented in a somewhat logical sequence that is often difficult to follow.	Information is presented in a generally logical sequence that is occasionally difficult to follow.	Information is presented in a logical sequence that is easy to follow.
	Required Content			
	Does not address one of the Shultz-Zedeck Lawyering Effectiveness Factors.	Addresses a Shultz-Zedeck Lawyering Effectiveness Factor, but does not connect it to his/her extern-ship experience or does not provide a new perspective on its relevance to future practice.	Discusses a Shultz-Zedeck Lawyering Effectiveness Factor and its connection to his/her extern-ship experience and provides some insight regarding its relevance to future practice.	Connects a Shultz-Zedeck Lawyering Effectiveness Factor to his/her externship experience and provides a new perspective regarding its relevance to future practice.
	Research			
	Does not provide research/data.	Provides research/data but does not reflect a clear understanding of the research/data and/or does not connect the research to the topic presented.	Provides relevant research/data, indicates a working understanding of the research/data, and establishes some connection of the research to the topic presented.	Provides relevant research/data, demonstrates a clear understanding of the research/data presented, and clearly connects the research/data to the topic presented.

List of Selected Resources Related to Externship Teaching and Experiential Education[1]

2022

Carolyn Young Larmore, *Just Compensation: An Empirical Examination of the Success of Legal Externships for Pay and Credit*, 70 Drake L. Rev. 145 (2022)

Carolyn Young Larmore, *Second Time's the Charm: An Empirical Examination of the Benefits and Potential Drawbacks of Repeat Legal Externships*, Wash. J. L. & Pol'y, forthcoming (2022)

2021

Megan Bess, *Grit, Growth Mindset, and the Path to Successful Lawyering*, 89 UMKC L. Rev. 493 (2021)

Anahid Gharakhanian, Carolyn Young Larmore, & Chelsea Parlett-Pelleriti, *Achieving Externship Success: An Empirical Study of the All-Important Law School Externship Experience*, 45 S. Ill. U. L. J. 165, 200 (2021)

Anne D. Gordon, *Better Than Our Biases: Using Psychological Research to Inform Our Approach to Inclusive, Effective Feedback*, 27 Clinical L. Rev. 195 (2021)

Kristen Uhl Hulse, *The Foundations for (Private) Practice: Building Professional Identity Through Law Firm Externships*, 89 UMKC L. Rev. 583 (2021)

Janet Thompson Jackson, *Wellness and Law: Reforming Legal Education to Support Student Wellness*, 65 How. L. J. 45 (2021)

Denise Platfoot Lacey, *Do All Roads Lead to Rome: Effectively Using Asynchronous Online Reflective Practice in an Externship Course*, 89 UMKC L. Rev. 609 (2021)

Spring Miller, *The Generalist Externship Seminar: A Unique Curricular Opportunity to Teach About the Legal Profession*, 27 Clinical L. Rev. 279, 281 (2021)

Thiadora A. Pina, Laura E. Jacobus, and Rupa Bhandari, Essential Lawyering Skills: A Companion Guide for Neil W. Hamilton's ROADMAP (2021)

1. This list of selected resources is based on a bibliography originally compiled and maintained by Harriet N. Katz, Professor Emerita, Rutgers University School of Law, Camden.

2020

Gillian Dutton, *International Experiences: A Path to Critical Legal Skills, Values, and Innovation for American Law Students*, 27 CLINICAL L. REV. 1 (2020)

Alexi Freeman, *Don't Hire Me as a Token: Best Practices for Recruiting and Supporting Externs From Historically Marginalized Backgrounds*, 72 S.C. L. REV. 357 (2020)

Allison Korn & Laila L. Hlass, *Assessing the Experiential (R̦)Evolution*, 65 VILL. L. REV. 713 (2020)

Roxanne Mykitiuk & C. Tess Sheldon, *Confronting Accessibility in Clinical Legal Education: Human Rights Law and the Accommodation of Law Students With Disabilities in External Placements*, 32 J.L. & SOC POL'Y 67 (2020)

2019

Alison Lintal, *Using Mindfulness Meditation to Foster Reflection in Externships*, 48 SW. L. REV. 329 (2019)

Debra Pogrund Stark & Christine Hunt, *Re-Imagining Law School Clinics: Leveraging Resources to Do More, for More, Under A Hybrid Model*, 43 OKLA. CITY U. L. REV. 129 (2019)

CARWINA WENG, DANIELLE R. COVER, MARGARET E. REUTER, AND CHRIS ROBERTS, LEARNING LAW THROUGH EXPERIENCE AND BY DESIGN (2019)

2018

Cynthia Anne Baker, *Externships: Teaching, Practice, and the Buildable Hour*, 51 IND. L. REV. 428 (2018)

Jodi S. Balsam, Susan L. Brooks, & Margaret Reuter, *Assessing Law Students As Reflective Practitioners*, 62 N.Y.L. SCH. L. REV. 49 (2018)

Jodi S. Balsam & Margaret Reuter, *Externship Assessment Project: An Empirical Study of Supervisor Evaluations of Extern Work Performance*, 25 CLINICAL L. REV. 1 (2018)

Jeff Cardella, *Reaction to Baker, Externships: Teaching, Practice, and the Buildable Hour*, 51 IND. L. REV. 438 (2018)

Alexi Nunn Freeman & Lindsey Webb, *Positive Disruption: Addressing Race in A Time of Social Change Through A Team-Taught, Reflection-Based, Outward-Looking Law School Seminar*, 21 U. PA. J.L. & SOC. CHANGE 121 (2018)

Alexi Freeman & Katie Steefel, *Uniting the Head, Hands, and Heart: How Specialty Externships Can Combat Public Interest Drift*, 25 CLINICAL L. REV. 325 (2018)

2017

Martina Cartwright & Thelma Harmon, *#blacklawyersmatter: The Importance of Pro Bono Initiatives and Experiential Opportunities at Historically Black College and University Law Schools in Preparing A New Generation of Social Engineers*, 18 FLA. COASTAL L. REV. 315 (2017)

EXPERIENTIAL EDUCATION IN THE LAW SCHOOL CURRICULUM (Emily Grant, Sandra Simpson, & Kelly Terry eds., 2017)

Scott Johns, *A Statistical Exploration: Analyzing the Relationship (If Any) Between Externship Participation and Bar Exam Scores*, 42 OKLA. CITY U. L. REV. 281 (2017)

Peter A. Joy, *The Uneasy History of Experiential Education in U.S. Law Schools*, 122 DICK. L. REV. 551 (2017)

Robert R. Kuehn, *Universal Clinic Legal Education: Necessary and Feasible*, 53 WASH. U. J.L. & POL'Y 89 (2017)

Linda F. Smith, Jeff Giddings & Leah Wortham, *Risks and Rewards of Externships: Exploring Goals and Methods*, 24 INT'L J. CLINICAL LEGAL EDUC. 30 (2017)

Linda F. Smith, *Community Based Research: Introducing Students to the Lawyer's Public Citizen Role*, 9 ELON L. REV. 67 (2017)

2016

REBECCA A. COCHRAN, JUDICIAL EXTERNSHIPS: THE CLINIC INSIDE THE COURTHOUSE (4th ed. 2016)

Melissa Deehring, *The Push for Practical Legal Skills Education in Qatar: Results From an Externship Program*, 2016 INT'L REV. L. 10 (2016)

Timothy W. Floyd & Kendall L. Kerew, *Marking the Path From Law Student to Lawyer: Using Field Placement Courses to Facilitate the Deliberate Exploration of Professional Identity and Purpose*, 68 MERCER L. REV. 767 (2016)

Karen A. Jordan, *Enhancing Externships to Meet Expectations for Experiential Education*, 23 CLINICAL L. REV. 339 (2016)

Harriet N. Katz, *The Past and Future of Externship Scholarship*, 23 CLINICAL L. REV. 397 (2016)

LEARNING FROM PRACTICE: A TEXT FOR EXPERIENTIAL LEGAL EDUCATION (Leah Wortham et al. eds., 3rd. ed. 2016)

Roy Stuckey, *The American Bar Association's New Mandates for Teaching Professional Skills and Values: Impact, Human Resources, New Roles for Clinical Teachers, and Virtual Worlds*, 51 WAKE FOREST L. REV. 259 (2016)

Steven M. Virgil, *The Role of Experiential Learning on A Law Student's Sense of Professional Identity*, 51 WAKE FOREST L. REV. 325 (2016)

2015

Cynthia Batt, *A Practice Continuum: Integrating Experiential Education Into the Curriculum*, 7 ELON L. REV. 119 (2015)

Susan L. Brooks, Cynthia Adcock, Stephen Ellmann, Robert L. Jones, Jr., Christine Cimini, & Margaret Berry, *Experience the Future: Papers From the Second National Symposium on Experiential Education in Law*, 7 ELON L. REV. 1 (2015)

Christine Cerniglia Brown, *The Integrated Curriculum of the Future: Eliminating a*

Hidden Curriculum to Unveil a New Era of Collaboration, Practical Training, and Interdisciplinary Learning, 7 ELON L. REV. 167 (2015)

BUILDING ON BEST PRACTICES: TRANSFORMING LEGAL EDUCATION IN A CHANGING WORLD (Deborah Maranville et al. eds., 2015)

Robert J. Condlin, *Assessing Experiential Learning, Jobs and All: A Response to the Three Professors*, 2015 WIS. L. REV. Forward 65 (2015)

Elizabeth G. Ford, *Toward a Clinical Pedagogy of Externship*, 22 CLINICAL L. REV. 113 (2015)

Alexi Freeman, *Teaching for Change: How the Legal Academy Can Prepare the Next Generation of Social Justice Movement Lawyers*, 59 HOW. L. J. 99 (2015)

Robert R. Kuehn, *Measuring Clinical Legal Education's Employment Outcomes*, 2015 WIS. L. REV. 645 (2015)

Stephanie A. Pisko, *Comment, Great Expectations, Grim Reality: Unpaid Interns and the Dubious Benefits of the DOL Pro Bono Exception*, 45 SETON HALL L. REV. 613 (2015)

Margaret E. Reuter & Joanne Ingham, *The Practice Value of Experiential Legal Education: An Examination of Enrollment Patterns, Course Intensity, and Career Relevance*, 22 CLINICAL L. REV. 181 (2015)

Daniel M. Schaffzin, *So Why Not an Experiential Law School... Starting With Reflection in the First Year?*, 7 ELON L. REV. 383 (2015)

Robert J. Tepper & Matthew P. Holt, *Unpaid Internships: Free Labor or Valuable Learning Experience?*, 2015 B.Y.U. EDUC. & L.J. 323 (2015)

2014

William L. Berman, *Why Not an International Clinical Legal Exchange Program? It Is Worth the Schlep*, 21 CLINICAL L. REV. 171 (2014)

Emma Lloyd Best, *Satisfying Experiential Education Requirements Through Expanding Externships in For-Profit Placements*, 21 CLINICAL L. REV. 1 (2014)

Jeffrey Blumberg, *Sitting by the Well: The Case for Intercultural Competency Training in International Experiential Learning*, 43 U. BALT. L. REV. 395 (2014)

SUSAN BRYANT, ELLIOTT S. MILSTEIN & ANN C. SHALLECK, TRANSFORMING THE EDUCATION OF LAWYERS: THE THEORY AND PRACTICE OF CLINICAL PEDAGOGY (2014)

Martina E. Cartwright & Thelma Harmon, *Fifty Plus Years and Counting: A History of Experiential Learning and Clinical Opportunities at Thurgood Marshall School of Law*, 39 T. MARSHALL L. REV. 187 (2014)

Timothy Casey, *Reflective Practice in Legal Education: The Stages of Reflection*, 20 CLINICAL L. REV. 317 (2014)

DEBORAH EPSTEIN, JANE H. AIKEN & WALLACE J. MLYNIEC, THE CLINIC SEMINAR (2014)

Amany Ragab Hacking, *Jumpstarting the Judicial Externship Experience: Building Upon Common Themes for Student Success in the Classroom and in the Judge's Chambers*, 21 Clinical L. Rev. 29 (2014)

Harriet N. Katz, *Fulfilling Skills and Writing Requirements in Externships*, 21 Clinical L. Rev. 53 (2014)

Martin J. Katz, *Understanding the Costs of Experiential Legal Education*, 1 J. Experiential Learning 28 (2014)

Lauren K. Knight, *The Free Labor Standards Act? A Look at the Ongoing Discussion Regarding Unpaid Legal Internships and Externships*, 44 U. Balt. L. Rev. 21 (2014)

Niki Kuckes, *Designing Law School Externships That Comply With the FLSA*, 21 Clinical L. Rev. 79 (2014)

Robert R. Kuehn, *Pricing Clinical Legal Education*, 92 Denv. U. L. Rev. 1 (2014)

Mary A. Lynch, *The Importance of Experiential Learning for Development of Essential Skills in Cross-Cultural and Intercultural Effectiveness*, 1 Touro J. Experiential Learning 129 (2014–15)

Benjamin V. Madison, III & Larry O. Natt Gantt, II, *The Emperor Has No Clothes, but Does Anyone Really Care? How Law Schools Are Failing to Develop Students' Professional Identity and Practical Judgment*, 27 Regent U. L. Rev. 339 (2015)

Wes Porter, *When Experiential Learning Takes Center Stage—Not Yet*, 1 J. Experiential Learning 79 (2014)

Rebecca B. Rosenfeld, *The Examined Externship is Worth Doing: Critical Self-Reflection and Externship Pedagogy*, 21 Clinical L. Rev. 127 (2014)

SpearIt & Stephanie Smith Ledesma, *Experiential Education as Critical Pedagogy: Enhancing the Law School Experience*, 38 Nova L. Rev. 249 (2014)

David I.C. Thomson, *Defining Experiential Legal Education*, 1 J. Experiential Learning 1 (2014)

2013

Cynthia F. Adcock, *Beyond Externships and Clinics: Integrating Access to Justice Education Into the Curriculum*, 62 J. Legal Educ. 566 (2013)

Deborah N. Archer, *There is No Santa Claus: The Challenge of Teaching the Next Generation of Civil Rights Lawyers in a "Post-Racial" Society*, 4 Colum. J. Race & L. 55 (2013)

James H. Backman & Cory S. Clements, *Significant but Unheralded Growth of Large Externship Programs*, 28 Byu J. Pub. L. 145 (2013)

Anna E. Carpenter, *The Project Model of Clinical Education: Eight Principles to Maximize Student Learning and Social Justice Impact*, 20 Clinical L. Rev. 39 (2013)

Steven I. Friedland, *The Rhetoric of Experiential Legal Education: Within the Context of Big Context*, 6 Ne. U. L.J. 253 (2013)

Susan Harthill, *Shining the Spotlight on Unpaid Law-Student Workers*, 38 Vt. L. Rev. 555 (2013)

J. P. Ogilvy, *Guidelines for the Self Evaluation of Legal Education Clinics and Clinical Programs*, 15 T.M. Cooley J. Prac. & Clinical L. 1 (2013)

Solomon Oliver, Jr., *Educating Law Students for the Practice: If I Had My Druthers…*, 2013 J. Disp. Resol. 85 (2013)

Sara K. Rankin, *The Fully Formed Lawyer: Why Law Schools Should Require Public Service to Better Prepare Students for Private Practice*, 17 Chap. L. Rev. 17 (2013)

Kelly S. Terry, *Embedding Assessment Principles in Externships*, 20 Clinical L. Rev. 467 (2013)

Karen Tokarz et al., *Legal Education at a Crossroads: Innovation, Integration, and Pluralism Required!*, 43 Wash. U. J. L. & Pol'y 11 (2013)

2012

Margaret Martin Barry, *Practice Ready: Are We There Yet?*, 32 B.C.J.L. & Soc. Just. 247 (2012)

James H. Backman & Jana B. Eliason, *The Student-Friendly Model: Creating Cost-Effective Externship Programs*, 28 Touro L. Rev. 1339 (2012)

Sudeb Basu & J.P. Ogilvy, *Externship Demographics Across Two Decades With Lessons for Future Surveys*, 19 Clinical L. Rev. 1 (2012)

Suzanne Darrow-Kleinhaus, *Developing Professional Identity Through Reflective Practice*, 28 Touro L. Rev. 1443 (2012)

Bernadette T. Feeley, *Guiding Law Students Through For-Profit Field Placements*, 19 Clinical L. Rev. 57 (2012)

Eric M. Fink, *No Money, Mo' Problems: Why Unpaid Law Firm Internships Are Illegal and Unethical*, 47 U.S.F. L. Rev. 435 (2012)

Daisy Hurst Floyd, Timothy W. Floyd & Sarah Gerwig-Moore, *Learning From Clergy Education: Externships Through the Lens of Formation*, 19 Clinical L. Rev. 83 (2012)

Robert L. Jones, Jr. et al., *When Things Go Wrong in the Clinic: How to Prevent and Respond to Serious Student Misconduct*, 41 U. Balt. L. Rev. 441 (2012)

Peter A. Joy, *The Cost of Clinical Legal Education*, 32 B.C.J.L. & Soc. Just. 309 (2012)

Nancy M. Maurer & Liz Ryan Cole, *Design, Teach and Manage: Ensuring Educational Integrity in Field Placement Courses*, 19 Clinical L. Rev. 115 (2012)

Michele Mekel, *Putting Theory Into Practice: Thoughts From the Trenches on Developing a Doctrinally Integrated Semester-in-Practice Program in Health Law and Policy*, 9 Ind. Health L. Rev. 503 (2012)

Laurie Morin & Susan Waysdorf, *The Service-Learning Model in the Law School Curriculum*, 56 N.Y.L. Sch. L. Rev. 561 (2012)

Wendy E. Parmet, *Beyond Externships: Health Law Co-Ops*, 9 Ind. Health L. Rev. 399 (2012)

2011

Charlotte S. Alexander, *Learning to Be Lawyers: Professional Identity and the Law School Curriculum*, 70 Md. L. Rev. 465 (2011)

Brook K. Baker, *Practice-Based Learning: Emphasizing Practice and Offering Critical Perspectives on the Dangers of "Co-Op"tation*, 56 N.Y. L. Sch. L. Rev. 619 (2011)

Laurie Barron, *Learning How to Learn: Carnegie's Third Apprenticeship*, 18 Clinical L. Rev. 101 (2011)

Susan L. Brooks, *Meeting the Professional Identity Challenge in Legal Education Through a Relationship-Centered Experiential Curriculum*, 41 U. Balt. L. Rev. 395 (2011)

Carrie Hempel, *Writing on a Blank Slate: Creating a Blueprint for Experiential Learning at the University of California, Irvine School of Law*, 1 UC Irvine L. Rev. 147 (2011)

Harriet N. Katz, *Stories and Students: Mentoring Professional Development*, 60 J. Legal Educ. 675 (2011)

Deborah Maranville et al., *Re-vision Quest: A Law School Guide to Designing Experimental Courses Involving Real Lawyering*, 56 N.Y. L. Sch. L. Rev. 517 (2011)

Carole Silver, Amy Garver, Lindsay Watkins, *Unpacking the Apprenticeship of Professional Identity and Purpose: Insights From the Law School Survey of Student Engagement*, 17 J. Legal Writing Inst. 373 (2011)

2010

James H. Backman, *Law School Externships: Reevaluating Compensation Policies to Permit Paid Externships*, 17 Clinical L. Rev. 21 (2010)

Cynthia Baker & Robert Lancaster, *Under Pressure: Rethinking Externships in a Bleak Economy*, 17 Clinical L. Rev. 71 (2010)

Ann Marie Cavazos, *The Journey Toward Excellence in Clinical Legal Education: Developing, Utilizing and Evaluating Methodologies for Determining and Assessing the Effectiveness of Student Learning Outcomes*, 40 SW. L. Rev. 1 (2010)

Carl J. Circo, *An Educational Partnership Model for Establishing, Structuring, and Implementing a Successful Corporate Counsel Externship*, 17 Clinical L. Rev. 99 (2010)

Nancy M. Maurer & Robert F. Seibel, *Addressing Problems of Power and Supervision in Field Placements*,17 Clinical L. Rev. 145 (2010)

Michael A. Yarnell, *An Externship Program: Start It, Grow It, Improve It*, 3 Phoenix L. Rev. 473 (2010)

2009

James Backman, *Externships and New Lawyer Mentoring: The Practicing Lawyer's Role in Educating New Lawyers*, 24 Byu J. Pub. L. 65 (2009)

Kathleen M. Burch, *Going Global: Managing Liability in International Externship Programs—A Case Study*, 36 J.C. & U.L. 455 (2009)

Jessica L. Curiale, *America's New Glass Ceiling: Unpaid Internships, the Fair Labor Standards Act, and the Urgent Need for Change*, Note, 61 HASTINGS L.J. 1531 (2009)

Lisa K. Halushka, *The Prosecution Externship From the Classroom to the Courtroom*, 11 T.M. COOLEY J. PRAC. & CLINICAL L. 323 (2009)

Diane E. Hoffmann, *Teaching Health Law: A Health Law Practice Workshop: Bridging Externship Placements and the Classroom*, 37 J.L. MED. & ETHICS 513 (2009)

Harriet N. Katz, *Counseling Externship Students*, 15 CLINICAL L. REV. 239 (2009)

Nancy Levit, *The Theory and the Practice—Reflective Writing Across the Curriculum*, 15 LEGAL WRITING: J. LEGAL WRITING INST. 253 (2009)

Susan K. McClellan, *Externships for Millennial Generation Law Students: Bridging the Generation Gap*, 15 CLINICAL L. REV. 255 (2009)

Kelly S. Terry, *Externships: A Signature Pedagogy for the Apprenticeship of Professional Identity and Purpose*, 59 J. LEGAL EDUC. 240 (2009)

2008

Bernadette T. Feeley, *Training Field Supervisors to Be Efficient and Effective Critics of Student Writing*, 15 CLINICAL L. REV. 211 (2008)

Becky L. Jacobs, *A Lexical Examination and (Unscientific) Survey of Expanded Clinical Experiences in U.S. Law Schools*, 75 TENN. L. REV. 343 (2008)

2007

James H. Backman, *Practical Examples for Establishing an Externship Program Available to Every Student*, 14 CLINICAL L. REV. 1 (2007)

Susan Bryant & Elliott S. Milstein, *Rounds: A "Signature Pedagogy" for Clinical Education?*, 14 CLINICAL L. REV. 195 (2007)

Bernadette T. Feeley, *Examining the Use of For-Profit Placements in Law School Externship Programs*, 14 CLINICAL L. REV. 37 (2007)

Anahid Gharakhanian, *ABA Standard 305's "Guided Reflections": A Perfect Fit for Guided Fieldwork*, 14 CLINICAL L. REV. 61 (2007)

Neil Hamilton & Lisa Montpetit Brabbit, *Fostering Professionalism Through Mentoring*, 57 J. LEGAL EDUC. 102 (2007)

J. P OGILVY ET AL., LEARNING FROM PRACTICE: A PROFESSIONAL DEVELOPMENT TEXT FOR LEGAL EXTERNS (2d ed. 2007)

Sarah E. Ricks & Susan C. Wawrose, *Comment, Survey of Cooperation Among Clinical, Pro Bono, Externship, and Legal Writing Faculty*, 4 J. ASS'N. LEGAL WRITING DIRECTORS 56 (2007)

ROY STUCKEY & OTHERS, BEST PRACTICES FOR LEGAL EDUCATION (2007)

Roy Stuckey, *Teaching With Purpose: Defining and Achieving Desired Outcomes in Clinical Law Courses*, 13 CLINICAL L. REV. 807 (2007)

WILLIAM M. SULLIVAN, ANNE COLBY, JUDITH WELCH WEGNER, LLOYD BOND & LEE S. SHULMAN, EDUCATING LAWYERS: PREPARATION FOR THE PROFESSION OF LAW (2007)

Carolyn R. Young & Barbara A. Blanco, *What Students Don't Know Will Hurt Them: A Frank View From the Field on How to Better Prepare Our Clinic and Externship Students*, 14 CLINICAL L. REV. 105 (2007)

2006

James H. Backman, *Where Do Externships Fit?—A New Paradigm Is Needed: Marshaling Law School Resources to Provide an Externship for Every Student*, 56 J. LEGAL EDUC. 615 (2006)

Harriet N. Katz, *Reconsidering Collaboration and Modeling: Enriching Clinical Pedagogy*, 41 GONZ. L. REV. 315 (2005–2006)

2005

Gregory Baker & Jennifer Zawid, *The Birth of a Therapeutic Courts Externship Program: Hard Labor but Worth the Effort*, 17 ST. THOMAS L. REV. 711 (2005)

Stacy Caplow, *"Tacking Too Close to the Wind": The Challenge to Prosecution Clinics to Set Our Students on A Straight Course*, 74 MISS. L.J. 919 (2005)

Leslie Larkin Cooney, *Heart and Soul: A New Rhythm for Clinical Externships*, 17 ST. THOMAS L. REV. 407 (2005)

Larry Cunningham, *The Use of "Boot Camps" and Orientation Periods in Externships and Clinics: Lessons Learned From a Prosecution Clinic*, 74 MISS. L.J. 983 (2005)

Peter A. Joy, *Prosecution Clinics: Dealing With Professional Role*, 74 MISS. L.J. 955 (2005)

Jean Montoya, *The University of San Diego Criminal Clinic: It's All in the Mix*, 74 MISS. L.J. 1021 (2005)

William P. Quigley, *Reflections From the Journals of Prosecution Clinic Students*, 74 MISS. L.J. 1147 (2005)

Hans P. Sinha, *Prosecutorial Externship Programs: Past, Present and Future*, 74 MISS. L.J. 1297 (2005)

Linda F. Smith, *Benefits of an Integrated (Prosecution & Defense) Criminal Law Clinic*, 74 MISS. L.J. 1239 (2005)

Margaret A. (Peggy) Tonon, *Beauty and the Beast? Hybrid Prosecution Externships in a Non-Urban Setting*, 74 MISS. L.J. 1043 (2005)

Nancy Ver Steegh, *Using Externships to Introduce Family Law Students to New Professional Roles*, 43 FAM. CT. REV. 137 (2005)

2004

Alexis Anderson, Arlene Kanter, & Cindy Slane, *Ethics in Externships: Confidentiality, Conflicts, and Competence Issues in the Field and in the Classroom*, 10 Clinical L. Rev. 473 (2004)

Cynthia Batt & Harriet N. Katz, *Confronting Students: Evaluation in the Process of Mentoring Student Professional Development*, 10 Clinical L. Rev. 581 (2004)

Barbara A. Blanco & Sande L. Buhai, *Externship Field Supervision: Effective Techniques for Training Supervisors and Students*, 10 Clinical L. Rev. 611 (2004)

Justine A. Dunlap & Peter A. Joy, *Reflection-in-Action: Designing New Clinical Teacher Training by Using Lessons Learned From New Clinicians*, 11 Clinical L. Rev 49 (2004)

Erica M. Eisinger, *The Externship Class Requirement: An Idea Whose Time Has Passed*, 10 Clinical L. Rev. 659 (2004)

Peter A. Joy, *Evolution of ABA Standards Relating to Externships: Steps in the Right Direction?*, 10 Clinical L. Rev. 681 (2004)

Mary A. Lynch, *Designing a Hybrid Domestic Violence Prosecution Clinic: Making Bedfellows of Academics, Activists and Prosecutors to Teach Students According to Clinical Theory and Best Practices*, 74 Miss. L.J. 1177 (2004)

Linda F. Smith, *Why Clinical Programs Should Embrace Civic Engagement, Service Learning and Community Based Research*, 10 Clinical L. Rev. 723 (2004)

2003

Kathleen Connolly Butler, *Shared Responsibility: The Duty to Legal Externs*, 106 W. Va. L. Rev. 51 (2003)

Gerard J. Clark, *Supervising Judicial Interns: A Primer*, 36 Suffolk U. L. Rev. 681 (2003)

J.P. Ogilvy, *Guidelines With Commentary for the Evaluation of Legal Externship Programs*, 38 Gonz. L. Rev. 155 (2003)

Louis J. Sirico, Jr., Judging: A Book For Student Clerks (2003)

Mary Pat Treuthart, *Weaving A Tapestry: Providing Context Through Service-Learning*, 38 Gonz. L. Rev. 215 (2003)

2002

Marty Geer, *Law School Externships: Building Another Bridge Over Troubled Waters*, 10 Nev. L. R. 15 (2002)

Peter Joy & Robert R. Kuehn, *Conflict of Interest and Competency Issues in Law Clinic Practice*, 9 Clinical L. Rev. 493 (2002)

2001

Susan Bryant, *The Five Habits: Building Cross-Cultural Competence in Lawyers*, 8 Clinical L. Rev. 33 (2001)

Elliott S. Milstein, *Clinical Legal Education in the United States: In-House Clinics, Externships, and Simulations*, 51 J. LEGAL EDUC. 375 (2001)

William Wesley Patton, *Creating an Externship Consortium: The Glace Experience*, 4 T.M. COOLEY J. PRAC. & CLINICAL L. 233 (2001)

2000

Margaret Martin Barry, Jon C. Dubin & Peter A. Joy, *Clinical Education for This Millennium: The Third Wave*, 7 CLINICAL L. REV. 1 (2000)

Deborah Maranville, *Passion, Context, and Lawyering Skills: Choosing Among Simulated and Real Clinical Experiences*, 7 CLINICAL L. REV. 123 (2000)

1999

Brook K. Baker, *Learning to Fish, Fishing to Learn: Guided Participation in the Interpersonal Ecology of Practice*, 6 CLINICAL L. REV. 1 (1999)

Sande L. Buhai, *Practice Makes Perfect: Reasonable Accommodation of Law Students With Disabilities in Clinical Placements*, 36 SAN DIEGO L. REV. 137 (1999)

Mary Jo Eyster, *Designing and Teaching the Large Externship Clinic*, 5 CLINICAL L. REV. 347 (1999)

Peter Jaszi, Ann Shalleck, Marlana Valdez & Susan Carle, *Experience as Text: The History of Externship Pedagogy at the Washington College of Law, American University*, 5 CLINICAL L. REV. 403 (1999)

Harriet N. Katz, *Using Faculty Tutorials to Foster Externship Students' Critical Reflection*, 5 CLINICAL L. REV. 437 (1998)

Lisa G. Lerman, *Professional and Ethical Issues in Legal Externships: Fostering Commitment to Public Service*, 67 FORDHAM L. REV. 2295 (1999)

Linda Morton, Janet Weinstein & Mark Weinstein, *Not Quite Grown Up: The Difficulty of Applying an Adult Education Model to Legal Externs*, 5 CLINICAL L. REV. 469 (1999)

Linda F. Smith, *Designing an Extern Clinical Program: Or As You Sow, So Shall You Reap*, 5 CLINICAL L. REV. 527 (1999)

1998

Joanne Carter, *Mixed Emotions: A Law Student's Perceptions While Working at a Public Defender's Office*, 2 T.M. COOLEY J. PRAC. & CLINICAL L. 329 (1998)

Meryl Markowitz, *My Experience at the Eaton County Prosecution Office*, 2 T.M. COOLEY J. PRAC. & CLINICAL L. 343 (1998)

1997

Kate E. Bloch, *Subjunctive Lawyering and Other Clinical Extern Paradigms*, 3 CLINICAL L. REV. 259 (1997)

Harriet N. Katz, *Personal Journals in Law School Externship Programs: Improving Pedagogy*, 1 T.M. COOLEY J. PRAC. & CLINICAL L. 7 (1997)

Robert MacCrate, *Educating A Changing Profession: From Clinic to Continuum*, 64 TENN. L. REV. 1099 (1997)

William Wesley Patton, *Externship Site Inspections: Fitting Well-Rounded Programs Into the Four Corners of the ABA Guidelines*, 3 CLINICAL L. REV. 471 (1997)

1996

Stacy Caplow, *From Courtroom to Classroom: Creating an Academic Component to Enhance the Skills and Values Learned in a Student Judicial Clerkship Clinic*, 75 NEB. L. REV. 872 (1996)

Robert J. Condlin, *Learning From Colleagues: A Case Study in the Relationship Between Academic and Ecological Clinical Legal Education*, 3 CLINICAL L. REV. 337 (1996)

Norman Fell, *Development of a Criminal Law Clinic: A Blended Approach*, 44 Clev. ST. L. REV. 275 (1996)

James E. Moliterno, *Legal Education, Experiential Education, and Professional Responsibility Teaching of Legal Ethics*, 38 WM. & MARY L. REV. 71 (1996)

J.P. Ogilvy, *The Use of Journals in Legal Education: A Tool for Reflection*, 3 CLINICAL L. REV. 55 (1996)

1995

Stephen R. Alton, *Mandatory Prelicensure Legal Internship: A Renewed Plea for Its Implementation in Light of the MacCrate Report*, 2 TEX. WESLEYAN L. REV. 115 (1995)

Daniel J. Givelber et al., *Learning Through Work: An Empirical Study of Legal Internship*, 45 J. Legal Educ. 1 (1995)

Robert F. Seibel & Linda H. Morton, *Field Placement Programs: Practices, Problems and Possibilities*, 2 CLINICAL L. REV. 413 (1995)

1994

Liz Ryan Cole, *Lessons From a Semester in Practice*, 1 CLINICAL L. REV. 173 (1994)

William W. Patton, *Law Schools' Duty to Train Children's Advocates: Blueprint for an Inexpensive Experientially Based Juvenile Justice Course*, 45 JUV. & FAM. CT. J. 3 (1994)

1993

Linda Morton, *Creating a Classroom Component for Field Placement Programs: Enhancing Clinical Goals With Feminist Pedagogy*, 45 ME. L. REV. 19 (1993)

Linda F. Smith, *The Judicial Clinic: Theory and Method in a Live Laboratory of Law*, 1993 UTAH L. REV. 429 (1993)

1992

Robert MacCrate, American Bar Association, Legal Education and Professional Development—An Educational Continuum (1992)

1991

Lawrence K. Hellman, *The Effects of Law Office Work on the Formation of Law Students' Professional Values: Observation, Explanation, Optimization*, 4 Geo. J. Legal Ethics 537 (1991)

1990

Frank G. Avellone, *The State of State Student Practice: Proposals for Reforming Ohio's Legal Internship Rule*, 17 Ohio N.U. L. Rev. 13 (1990)

Stephen T. Maher, *The Praise of Folly: A Defense of Practice Supervision in Clinical Legal Education*, 69 Neb. L. Rev. 537 (1990)

1989

Liz Ryan Cole, *Training the Mentor: Improving the Ability of Legal Experts to Teach Students and New Lawyers*, 19 N.M. L. Rev. 163 (1989)

Janet Motley, *Self-Directed Learning and the Out-of-House Placement*, 19 N.M. L. Rev. 211 (1989)

Marc Stickgold, *Exploring the Invisible Curriculum: Clinical Field Work in American Law Schools*, 19 N.M. L. Rev. 287 (1989)

1987

Henry Rose, *Legal Externships: Can They Be Valuable Clinical Experiences for Law Students?*, 12 Nova. L. Rev. 95 (1987)

Donald A. Schön, Eucating the Reflective Practitioner: Toward A New Design For Teaching and Learning in the Professions (1987)

1986

Robert J. Condlin, *"Tastes Great, Less Filling": The Law School Clinic and Political Critique*, 35 J. Legal Educ. 45 (1986)

Kenny Hegland, *Condlin's Critique of Conventional Clinics: The Case of the Missing Case*, 36 J. Legal Educ. 427 (1986)

1968

Howard R. Sacks, *Student Fieldwork as a Technique in Educating Students in Professional Responsibility*, 20 J. Legal Educ. 291 (1968)

Marshall S. Shapo, *An Internship Seminar for Law Students: A Test of Theory, A Critique of Practice*, 46 TEX. L. REV. 479 (1967–68)

1965

Robinson O. Everett, *The Duke Law School Legal Internship Project*, 18 J. LEGAL EDUC. 185 (1965)

1954

William Kelly Joyce, Mark E. Lefever, Lawrence N. Park & E. Blythe Stason, *Legal Internships*, 6 J. LEGAL EDUC. 504 (1954)

Index

T

U